Personal Psychology

For Life And Work

Psychology

Four

D1409307

About the Author

Rita K. Baltus has taught speech and psychology classes at the Northcentral Technical College for over twenty-five years. Early in those years, she developed a practical psychology course for vocational students. The objectives of this course were to help students gain an understanding of themselves and others and apply psychology to their lives and the world of work. The materials she developed for this course over a number of years evolved into *Personal Psychology for Life and Work.*

Dr. Baltus received her B.A. from the University of Michigan and her M.A. and Ph.D. from the University of Wisconsin. During her career, she has been involved in numerous aspects of vocational, technical, and adult education on local, state, and national levels. She has been an active member in numerous educational associations, including the American Vocational Association, American Association of Community and Junior Colleges, National Council for Occupational Education, American Society for Training and Development, American Association for Adult and Continuing Education, and Phi Delta Kappa, an honorary education society. Her experience also includes conducting workshops for business and industry and making presentations at conventions and conferences.

Personal Psychology

For Life And Work

Psychology

Fourth Edition

Rita K. Baltus, Ph.D.
Northcentral Technical College
Wausau, Wisconsin

McGraw-Hill

New York, New York
Columbus, Ohio
Mission Hills, California
Peoria, Illinois

Photo Credits List

Page 1: © Michael Goldman; Page 7: Courtesy of Ford Motor Company; Page 12: © Bob Daemmrich/The Image Works, Woodstock, NY. All Rights Reserved; Page 16: © Gale Zucker/Stock, Boston; Page 26: © Nita Winter/The Image Works, Woodstock, NY. All Rights Reserved; Page 28: © Elizabeth Crews/Stock, Boston; Page 37: © Judy S. Gelles/Stock, Boston; Page 43: © Bohdan Hrynewych/Stock, Boston; Page 48: © 1993 Comstock, Inc.; Page 54: © H. Schafer/Peter Arnold, Inc.; Page 57: © David M. Grossman; Page 62: AP/Wide World Photos; Page 68; Brian Masck/The Muskegon Chronicle; Page 71: Will & Deni McIntyre/Science Source, Photo Researchers; Page 77: © Robert Eckert/Stock, Boston; Page 81: © Peter Menzel/Stock, Boston; Page 92: © Abraham Menashe; Page 97: © Paul Dance: Tony Stone Images; Page 100: © Alberto Garcia/Saba; Page 105: © Spencer Grant/Stock, Boston; Page 112: © Michael Dwyer/Stock, Boston; Page 122: © Cameramann/The Image Works, Woodstock, NY. All Rights Reserved; Page 125: © Spencer Grant III/Stock, Boston; Page 130: © Harriet Gans/The Image Works, Woodstock, NY. All Rights Reserved; Page 136: © Franz Edson: Tony Stone Images; Page 142: © Elizabeth Crews/The Image Works, Woodstock, NY. All Rights Reserved; Page 143: © Karen R. Preuss/The Image Works, Woodstock, NY. All Rights Reserved; Page 156: © David Powers/Stock, Boston; Page 161: © Dion Ogust/The Image Works, Woodstock, NY. All Rights Reserved; Page 169: © Joel Gordon 1991; Page 172: © Spencer Grant/Stock, Boston; Page 183: © Ogust/The Image Works, Woodstock, NY. All Rights Reserved; Page 189: © Larry Dunmire/SuperStock; Page 195: © Harriet Gans/The Image Works, Woodstock, NY. All Rights Reserved; Page 205: © Dion Ogust/The Image Works, Woodstock, NY. All Rights Reserved; Page 213: © Bob Daemmrich/The Image Works, Woodstock, NY. All Rights Reserved; Page 222: © Alan Carey/The Image Works, Woodstock, NY. All Rights Reserved; Page 227: © Michael Greenlar, Woodstock, NY. All Rights Reserved; Page 237: © C. Boretz/The Image Works, Woodstock, NY. All Rights Reserved; Page 241: © Rob Crandall/Stock, Boston; Page 250: © Ed Honowitz; Tony Stone Images; Page 255: © Judy Gelles/Stock, Boston; Page 270: © Cary Wolinski/Stock, Boston; Page 275: © John Maher/Stock, Boston; Page 281: © David M. Grossman; Page 284: © Jim Whitmer/Stock, Boston; Page 297: © K. Preuss/The Image Works, Woodstock, NY. All Rights Reserved; Page 305: © D. LaBelle/The Image Works, Woodstock, NY. All Rights Reserved; Page 309: © 1992 Bruce Ayres: Tony Stone Images; Page 315: © Laimute Druskis/Stock, Boston; Page 320: © Rhoda Sidney/The Image Works, Woodstock, NY. All Rights Reserved; Page 326: Ken Kerbs/Dot Pictures; Page 336: © M. Douglas/The Image Works, Woodstock, NY. All Rights Reserved; Page 338: © C. Boretz/The Image Works, Woodstock, NY. All Rights Reserved; Page 340: © Rhoda Sidney/The Image Works, Woodstock, NY. All Rights Reserved; Page 357: © David J. Sams/Stock, Boston.

Library of Congress Cataloging-in-Publication Data
Baltus, Rita K.
    Personal psychology for life and work/Rita K. Baltus.—4th ed.
      p.   cm.
    Includes bibliographical references and index.
    ISBN 0-02-801096-5
    1. Self-actualization (Psychology)   2. Success. I. Title.
    BF637.S4B35   1994
    158—dc20   93–41127
                                         CIP

Personal Psychology for Life and Work, Fourth Edition
Imprint 1996

ISBN 0-02-801096-5

5 6 7 8 9 10 11 12 13 14 15   POH   02 01 00 99 98 97 96

Contents

7   Thinking and Problem Solving   136

8   Coping with Stress   161

9   Wellness   189

Preface

The fourth edition of Personal Psychology for Life and Work is meant to prepare students to successfully handle the many challenges they will face in their personal and professional lives. Success is determined partly by how well we understand ourselves and others. This text helps students comprehend human nature by exploring basic psychological principles within the context of everyday situations. Thus, students are provided a framework for exploring many issues related to human development—issues such as self-esteem, emotions and attitudes, and interpersonal relationships.

Society in general and the workplace in particular are experiencing changes at a rapid rate—politically, economically, and technically. Change in itself, whether good or bad, creates stress as individuals strive first to understand and then to respond and assimilate the impact it makes on their lives. There is no doubt we are living in a global society, where we need to cooperate with persons whose backgrounds, beliefs, and customs may be different from our own. We must learn to understand and accept others' viewpoints. Maturity, flexibility, open-mindedness, and tolerance are increasingly important. By gaining knowledge about the causes of our own behavior, we become more comfortable and less threatened by differences in other people.

Technology is at the forefront of our lives. We are surrounded by computers, cellular telephones, VCRs, and CD-ROMs. In five years, we will see other advances we can't begin to imagine. Though technology may grow in leaps, we must not lose sight of the importance of the basic pleasures of satisfactory interpersonal relationships and personal goal achievement. This textbook emphasizes the need for excellent communication skills, managing emotions, thinking and problem-solving skills, and maintaining and improving overall health.

Today's employers now place "people skills" on an equal footing with technical proficiency. Human relations skills are required for success, especially as our country moves into a service-oriented economy. We've added Chapter 13, "Human Relations at Work," to raise students' awareness of the growing need to interrelate successfully with others—whether they be peers, supervisors, subordinates, or customers.

Much of the content has been expanded and updated, but we've kept the text-workbook format that has proved so effective in past editions. In-text questions and quizzes provide a way for students to self-check understanding and apply concepts immediately to their own lives. Each chapter begins with a listing of Learning Objectives, followed by the text. Psychology in Practice activities, found at the end of the chapters, offer students ways to apply chapter concepts to their lives through further research, conducting interviews, and keeping journals. An icon distinguishes activities specifically intended for small-group projects and discussions. Learning Activities, which are correlated to the Learning Objectives, are then provided in a tearout section at the end of the book. These activities further show the relevance of the text topics to common situations. Enrichment Activities are included here for out-of-class work and may be used at the instructor's discretion. A comprehensive glossary provides definitions for all bold-faced terms.

The Instructor's Manual and Key contains comprehensive teaching suggestions, answers to the activities, selected resources, and transparency masters. A new microcomputer test bank (IBM) makes testing more convenient for the instructor.

Acknowledgments

My sincere appreciation is extended to the following people for their contributions to and assistance with *Personal Psychology for Life and Work,* Fourth Edition: MaryAnn Van Slyke, Linda Layton, Dan Dougherty, and Marilyn Siebert, coeducators; Mary Susa, Lee Susa, Therese Wilder, and Linda Baltus for their assistance with various aspects of manuscript development; Allen Henricks and Jean Tewksbury, of the Northcentral Technical College Library staff; Charles Henrichs for making it possible for me to keep working by solving my computer and printer problems; and especially Maggie McKay for her invaluable assistance with library research.

We would like to thank the following reviewers whose comments and suggestions helped to shape the final content of this fourth edition.

Judy Austin
Shelton State Community College
Dot Butler
State Area Vocational-Technical School
Jayne Crolley
Horry-Georgetown Technical College
Stacey Eggleston
Ridley Lowell Business Institute
Ellen Sheppard
American Business and Fashion Institute
Joan Smith
Kilgore College

Rita K. Baltus

Personal Psychology
For Life And Work

Psychology
Fourth Edition

1 Psychology in Our Changing World

Learning Objectives

After completing this chapter you will be able to do the following:

1. Explain how the purpose of psychology—to predict—might be useful to you in the area of work for which you are preparing.
2. Identify reasons for your interest in, or concern about, the future.
3. Examine the effects as nontraditional careers become more common for both males and females.
4. Recognize the nature and scope of problems caused by human behavior and suggest possible solutions.
5. Examine the possible advantages and disadvantages of working in one's home.
6. Anticipate the possible impacts of the increased use of robots in homes and at work in the future.
7. Identify ways in which cultural diversity can be beneficial to today's society.

> 66 *It is not the strongest species that survives nor the most intelligent but rather the one that is most adaptable to change.* 99
>
> CHARLES DARWIN,
> *naturalist*

1

The world in which we live influences who we are and what we do probably more than we realize. It is also important for us to remember that we, individually and collectively, can influence our world and the conditions of our lives.

You are one of over five billion people in the world.
You are a unique individual in a changing world.
You, an individual, can affect tomorrow's world.

The world in which you live is different from what it was in your grandparents' youth, in your parents' youth, and even from the world in which you were a child. It is even different in some ways from what it was a year ago—or perhaps yesterday.

The rate of change has increased so much that today's young people are involved in more radical discoveries and changes than have ever before occurred in one generation. It is an exciting, historical time to live, but change also requires the ability to make choices and adapt.

In 1970 Alvin Toffler, a futurist, wrote a book entitled *Future Shock*. His basic definition of future shock was "too much change in too short a time." He urged us to be aware of the accelerative or "snowballing" effect of change, the social and psychological effects of change, the effects on our values, and the side effects of solutions to problems.[1] An example of such side effects is the development of detergents for home use in 1933. They were more effective than soap for washing and cleaning, especially in hard water. The use of detergents for a multitude of applications grew rapidly. In the 1970s, however, it became apparent that the phosphates used in detergents were creating serious water pollution problems. We don't always know what the long-term side effects of new products will be, but we should at least be alert to possibilities.

We can see other effects of Toffler's concerns in our world today. To some extent they are effects that accompany change regardless of our awareness or concern. Individually and together, however, we must realize that we can have a positive effect on change in our world. Further, we can learn to anticipate and welcome change to keep our lives stimulating and challenging.

WHY STUDY PSYCHOLOGY?

Would you like to lead a more satisfying, productive life, with less conflict and hassle? Responses might range from, "I seem to be doing all right so far," to "There is no way to remove problems, frustration, and disappointment from life." Regardless of what your particular response would be, there are few people who could not improve the quality of their lives if they are willing to gain a better understanding of themselves and others and put related, proven principles into practice.

Psychology is defined as the scientific study of human behavior. Although you already know a great deal about human behavior simply from having lived and associated with others for quite a few years, you may not have studied behavior from a scientific perspective before. As with most things that we have learned from casual observation and experience in life, some of what we think we know is probably incomplete, or even inaccurate. And even if you have had a previous psychology course, your current learning can give you opportunities for personal, practical application to your activities at this time as well as achievement of goals in the future.

Interest in the functioning of the mind and causes of behavior can be traced back at least to Aristotle, who lived from 384–323 B. C. However, the first psychological laboratory was established by Wilhelm Wundt at Leipzig, Germany, in 1879. Since that time a more orderly, objective study of human behavior has developed. Since psychology is a social science, pertaining to human beings, it cannot be expected to be as exact as other sciences, such as physics, for example. Although psychologists have not yet reached complete agreement on theories of behavior, it can be a challenge to each of us to examine their work and develop our positions on how we believe our own lives and the world in which we live can be improved.

The purposes of psychology are usually identified as: to *describe,* to *understand,* to *predict,* and to *control or influence* behavior. There are a number of different methods of studying human behavior in attempts to achieve these purposes. Several of the more common ones are: *Comparative,* which compares observations and identifies similarities and differences; *Correlational,* which looks for relationships in existing factors; *Survey,* which seeks information and opinions through interviews or written questionnaires; *Case Study,* which follows the behavior of an individual over a period of time; and *Experimental,* which involves two groups of individuals, an *experimental* group and a *control* group. The experimental group receives an *independent variable,* or change in what they are experiencing to determine possible effects. The control group does not experience this change and is used for comparison to determine the effects of the independent variable. The original condition in both groups is called the *dependent variable.* All of these methods of studying psychology have contributed to a better understanding of human beings.

It might also be helpful to distinguish between the terms *theory* and *principle* as they pertain to the science of psychology. A *theory* is a belief based on present knowledge and thinking of an individual or group; a *principle* incorporates a generally accepted theory into a statement that applies to most cases and situations. We must remember, however, that social sciences are not exact and that there can be exceptions.

The entire spectrum of psychology has many specialized areas. Some of these are *clinical* and *counseling, industrial, business, education,* and *sports.* In this course we are primarily interested in understanding principles of human behavior and their applications to our lives and work.

WHY LOOK TO THE FUTURE?

What will your future world be like? One of the reasons for an interest in the answer to this question may be simple curiosity. We are usually curious about where we are going and what is going to happen when we get there. There are additional reasons why we should be interested in the future. If we have some idea what to expect, we can better prepare ourselves. This is particularly important as it pertains to preparing for work, updating job skills, and retraining for new jobs. It can be to our benefit also to be aware of what will be available in health care, housing, educational opportunities, and other important aspects of our lives.

A further reason for "future awareness" is to use our best efforts to control or influence what is happening to us and our environment. Although we may feel somewhat ineffective as individuals in many situations, we can make a difference. When we join forces with others who have similar concerns, we can have an even greater impact. We can influence the outcome of what is happening in our schools, neighborhoods, community; in our state or nation; and thus even in the world. Our right to vote is one way we can do this, but there are also numerous other ways. You can control, to a degree, what your future will be like. Take the responsibility to understand yourself, the world, and those around you.

In other instances we may foresee a change that we, individually or as a society, may want to prevent from happening. There are orderly, constructive ways to do this, especially if we are sure of what we want and know what our options are. It is easier to identify and oppose undesired changes in the planning stage than to try to counteract them after they are realities.

A still further reason for interest in the future is to promote desired change or make things happen. We can bring about some changes that would not occur without our efforts. If we want to live in a safer world with more advantages and opportunities, we cannot simply rely on luck, the natural course of events, or the efforts of others.

Since everyone in a society does not have the same needs or values, others do not always want what you want. In fact, some may want the opposite. This complicates the process of change and reaction to it. All persons cannot have what they want, but in a democracy voices are heard and everyone has responsibilities. Change affects everyone and everyone can effect change.

LIFE IN A GLOBAL COMMUNITY

We live in a global community—a term that appears almost to be a contradiction. We often think of a community as a relatively small town or city. Global, on the other hand, refers to encompassing the whole earth or globe. Yet the term global community is appropriate because our lives have become interrelated in a number of ways with people in all parts of the world. Advances in technology, particularly in communications systems, have brought this about. Even local television news programs often cover events in other countries because what is local and what is global are becoming almost inseparable.

Transnationality, another term referring to our global community, has brought about changes in business and the economy, religion, agriculture, politics, and values and human relationships. In fact, all major divisions and institutions of society are involved and have been affected.

Cultural diversity is an outstanding characteristic of today's society. Culture refers to values, beliefs, customs, and lifestyles learned as a member of a group of people with a common ancestry or background. The mix of people from different cultures in America in earlier generations was referred to a "melting pot." This suggested that, gradually, national and cultural differences would disappear or melt into a homogeneous society. There is more emphasis today on what has been called a "salad bowl" society in which individuality and identity are retained but will also represent contributions to the whole society. Life in such a global community is discussed by John Naisbett and Patricia Aburdene in their book *Megatrends 2000.* They describe life in the 90s and as it is expected to be in the future. They state, "The more homogeneous our lifestyles become, the more steadfastly we shall cling to deeper values—religion, language, art, literature. As our outer worlds grow more similar, we will increasingly treasure the traditions that spring from within."[2]

How are goals met and problems solved in a global community? The answer is complex, but there must be unified efforts and cooperation among countries. The United Nations and numerous international organizations, for example, are recognizing both responsibilities and opportunities in the global community. The United Nations, organized in 1945 after World War II, states in the Preamble of its Charter:

We the peoples of the United Nations determined

to save succeeding generations from the scourge of war which twice in our lifetime has brought untold sorrow to mankind, and

to reaffirm faith in fundamental human rights, in the dignity and worth of the human person, in the equal rights of men and women and of nations large and small, and

to establish conditions under which justice and respect for the obligations arising from treaties and other sources of international law can be maintained, and

to promote social progress and better standards of life in larger freedom,

and for these ends

to practice tolerance and live together in peace with one another as good neighbors, and

to unite our strength to maintain international peace and security, and

to ensure, by the acceptance of principles and the institution of methods, that armed force shall not be used, save in the common interest, and

to employ international machinery for the promotion of the economic and social advancement of all peoples,

have resolved to combine our efforts to accomplish these aims.

Although there has been criticism of the United Nations for not being more active in accomplishing these aims, in its almost 50 years, the very existence of the organization sends a message to the world. Also, the UN has done more than the average person probably realizes. In recent years there has been still more evidence of the force and effectiveness this organization can have.

It is no longer a matter of deciding whether we want to be involved. Our decisions pertain to the responsibilities we want to take in that involvement—and they are important decisions. One of the most important issues for the United States as a country is how to provide for our own national security and still be a positive force in promoting peace in the world. Another important decision pertains to the extent to which we can reasonably ease the suffering or protect the rights and freedom of human beings around the world.

 What do you THINK?   How does the Preamble of the UN Charter emphasize the need for practicing psychology?

HIGH TECH/ HIGH TOUCH   In *Megatrends,* an earlier book by John Naisbitt, major trends of the 1980s are identified. One of these is movement from forced technology to high-tech/high-touch. He explains, "High-tech/high-touch is a formula I use to describe the way we have responded to technology. What happens is that whenever new technology is introduced into society, there must be a counterbalancing human response—that is, high touch—or the technology is rejected. The more high tech, the more high touch."[3]

Naisbitt explains high touch further in saying, "But something else was growing alongside the technological invasion. Our response to the high tech all around us was the evolution of a highly personal value system to compensate for the impersonal nature of technology. The result was the new self-help or personal growth movement, which eventually became the human potential movement."[4]

An example of high tech/high touch that Naisbitt gives is that the high technology of transplants and brain scanners has led to a new interest in the family doctor and neighborhood clinic. Another example is that word processors have led to a revival of handwritten notes.

High tech, balanced by high touch, can improve the quality of our lives and of the community. This is expressed by Auzille Jackson, Jr. in "High Tech's Influence on our Lives": "High tech has the potential, if properly used, of giving us a more full, more useful, longer, dynamic, and exciting life, and to free many of us from dull and repetitive jobs. It will permit us to spend more time in cultural and learning activities, recreation, and helping others in the community."[5]

Human beings must decide on the technologies they want, learn to use them to their advantage, and still retain their humanness in the world of work as well as in their personal lives.

THE WORLD OF TELECOMMUNICATIONS

Fast, accurate communication is necessary in today's high-tech business. Telecommunications is an area of high technology that affects us all and will continue to open lines of communication. Human beings can now talk to one another from practically anywhere in the world and even from space. Computers talk to us and even to other computers.

Telecommunication, or the transfer of messages by electrical or electronic means, has an impressive role in the changing world in which we live. Consider this message heard by David on his arrival at work: "Good morning, David. You have a safety committee meeting this morning at 10:00. Bring this month's accident reports. Thank you. Take care."

David was listening to a "disembodied voice" known as a speech synthesizer. Such talking computers, and other communications technology, are products of the technology and information age in which you, David, and the rest of us live and work. Not long ago, futurists were referring to the "coming of the technological age." We are now living in that age—also referred to as the communications revolution, computer era, and information age and by other variations of these terms.

Other ages have preceded the technology and information age. Alvin Toffler in a later book, *The Third Wave,* refers to the agricultural age as the first wave, to the industrial age as the second wave, and to our current technological age as the third wave.[6]

What do you THINK?

What do you think the fourth wave will be? Some say space; others say genetics. There are any number of possibilities. We do know that change will continue and there will be other "waves" in the future of this planet.

Modern communications technology enables engineers to increase their technical knowledge at their workstations through closed-circuit university courses.

Modern telecommunications systems were preceded by the invention of the telegraph in 1844 and the telephone in 1896. A major development in telecommunications was *Telstar*, a satellite that first linked Europe and North America via television in 1962. Other technological developments of this age are citizens band (CB) radios, cordless telephones, microcomputers, fax machines, and picture phones.

By the twenty-first century, computers within the home are expected to be as common as television sets are today. These computers will be used to conduct business and to achieve numerous other purposes. There has been continuing progress with communications satellites, including the use of laser beams in place of radio waves. By the year 2000 it is expected that communications satellites could make it possible to contact another person anywhere by three-dimensional holography, whereby the image of the person is produced by means of laser light.

Innovations in technological communications are developing at an astounding rate. "Now what's new?" can be asked on a regular basis. It will be possible before too many years to give vocal commands to your electrical appliances—not only to start and stop but to inform a toaster, for example, how dark you would like your toast. Your TV will be in 3-D and interactive so that you will have the opportunity to request certain program features or express your opinion on issues. Kalman A. Toth, in an article in *Futurist,* describes another technological possibility: "If your car broke down or you were involved in an accident, you could just walk to the nearest SMI (serico magnetic intelligence) traffic light and yell up your wishes. The light would summon the police, an ambulance, or a tow truck for you."[7]

Also, photonics is a term you will be seeing and hearing more often. "Just as microelectronics propelled communications for the last 20 years, the technology of photonics, or lightwaves, will spur the telecommunications revolution of the 1990s," according to John S. Mayo of AT&T Bell Laboratories.[8]

And, by the way, have you had any messages from life on other planets? Perhaps not, but considering the possibility isn't "out of this world." National Aeronautics and Space Administration (NASA) since October 1992 has used the largest telescope on Earth to attempt to contact extraterrestrial life in the Milky Way galaxy.

Change can cause uneasiness and even resistance. This has been true to some extent with communications developments. We may hesitate to use or respond to a talking machine because of inexperience or "technological shyness." There are still those who hang up on a telephone recorder for this reason. (There is also growing concern over invasion of privacy.) Many people feel somewhat unnatural the first time they use a microphone or record their own voices with a tape recorder. We must recognize, however, that telecommunications is part of our world and will continue to advance. Knowledge and experience will also make us more comfortable with their functions and more competent in their use.

The program in which you are now enrolled, whether for job entry, career updating, or personal improvement, is affected by advances in telecommunications. We must be telecommunications literate to be a part of this nation's work force today. We must also, however, retain, or improve, our ability to communicate on a person-to-person basis. Technology may replace some functions formerly performed by humans, but it will never replace human beings. Ways to improve our communication with one another will be discussed in Chapter 12, Interpersonal Relationships.

What would you SAY? Suppose you own a small business and use an answering machine. You are discussing an order with a potential customer, whom you tell to call you with additional information and to leave a message on your answering machine if you are not able to answer the phone at that time. The customer tells you, "I don't like leaving messages on those machines." What would you say in response?

LIFELONG EDUCATION

The expression "getting an education" no longer applies. You can attend a school or college for a certain length of time, and even get a diploma, but your education must be a lifelong experience. The primary mission of most technical and community colleges today is to prepare individuals for entry or reentry into the world of work. The job market is rapidly and continuously changing, however. The job you are prepared to do tomorrow will not be the same even a few years from now. Not only will jobs change, but the average person will change jobs at least a half dozen times in his or her working lifetime.

Computers, robots, and other technology will continue to perform work done by humans in the past. This needn't be a threat to those who are willing to learn and possibly retrain. The best approach is to *continue* to learn on the job or in any way you can that is related to the service, business, or industry in which you are employed. Many companies provide for the continuing education of their employees. Motorola, for example, trains or retrains a large proportion of its employees each year. DuPont is another example of a company that has an extensive employee training program.

Learning occurs in many places other than school classrooms, and it takes many forms. Distance-learning by means of interactive television is available to many who could not otherwise attend classes, for example. Businesses and institutions conduct many of their own training sessions or take advantage of customized training and educational offerings of colleges. Such training includes courses in communications and the use of computers. Almost everyone now needs to master some level of computer knowledge or skill. This is emphasized in the book, *Succeeding in the World of Work:* "Certainly everyone needs to understand what computers can do, how they are used, and how they will continue to change our lives. This understanding is called computer literacy."[9]

Among other important objectives in any type of education today is the ability to solve problems, think creatively, and work effectively as a member of a team and adapt to change. That's why communications and human relations skills are included in the education of students preparing for vocational or technical careers.

You, as a citizen of today's world, must learn more than was required of your parents or grandparents. We have much better opportunities to learn, but our intellectual capacities aren't that much better.

One of the most valuable skills a person can have today is knowing how to learn. Sophfronia Scott Gregory discusses this challenge in a 1992 issue of *Time* magazine:

> The greatest mystery for the next century is whether scientists will discover fundamental ways to affect how the mind learns. The human brain has evolved over millions of years to process information in a certain way—the very act of perceiving the world is an integral part of the way it is understood. Can learning speed and capacity be "souped up"? While scientists have found ways to improve the learning ability of people with damaged and dysfunctional brains, nothing has yet emerged that could radically improve a normal brain's ability. No secret pill or process is on the horizon, just a steady enhancement of abilities people already have. And the most powerful ingredient will be motivation, since the working world will become ever more knowledge driven and information intensive. In the 21st century, nothing will be more fashionable—and essential—than doing one's homework.[10]

DOLLARS AND SENSE

Economic conditions affect our lives in many ways. For some, they determine whether work is available or whether earnings can satisfy their needs. Economic conditions can also affect to what extent we can provide for our wants beyond what we actually need, even though everything that is of value to us is not directly related to money. It is beneficial to each of us to have as thorough an understanding and as much control as possible over our own economic situation.

It is almost impossible to forecast economic conditions accurately today. Part of the forecasting problem is due to trying to make predictions about a $5.5 trillion economy. This figure represents the approximate annual value of goods and services produced in the United States in a recent year. Other factors have continued to complicate the American economy despite efforts to maintain a healthy free-enterprise system.

Numerous challenges facing us as consumers are expressed in the following quote from *Consumer Challenges and Issues:*

> The consumer faces a continually evolving marketplace. In the early 1980s, major industries were deregulated. Recessions had a dramatic effect upon consumers, business, and government. Technological advances are producing highly complex problems. New goods and services are continually appearing in the marketplace. World economic conditions are being felt in every phase of the nation's economy, and competition from foreign imports has been and will continue to be evident. The consumer has a broader range of goods and services from which to choose. Being a consumer has always been challenging, but as the world moves deeper into the "high-tech" society, consumer challenges will continually increase. If deregulation of major industries continues, other challenges will accrue.[11]

One of the more obvious changes in our economy over the years has been rising prices. A comparison of prices of a few common food items over a forty-year period is shown in the following table. Fill in the last section to represent current prices.

The Increase in Prices 1945–

	1945	1965	1985	Current Year
1 lb hamburger	$.27	$.51	$1.26	
1 lb pork chops	.37	.97	2.32	
1 dozen eggs	.58	.53	.76	
½ gallon milk	.29	.47	1.14	
1 loaf white bread	.09	.21	.55	
1 lb coffee	.31	.83	2.60	

Source: U.S. Department of Agriculture.[12]

According to the 1991 Economic Report of the President, an individual who earned $25,000 in taxable income in 1970 would have needed $59,300 in 1980 and $79,500 in 1990 just to stay even. Most people were not earning $25,000 in 1970, however.

Your standard of living is measured by how much your earnings exceed inflation, or raises in the cost of living. If income rose 7 percent and prices rose only 5 percent, your real standard of living would have risen 2 percent, for example.

The "good old days" cannot be judged by prices in earlier times alone. One has to consider how many hours one has to work to buy a particular item today in relation to past wages and prices. Wages or income increases generally match or exceed price rises. Most people have a higher standard of living today than people in general had when hamburger was $.27 a pound.

The standard of living does not automatically continue to rise, however. According to *New Age Journal,* Americans in the early 1990s were working one month longer than they did in 1970 and two months longer than most Europeans. The reason for this was that Americans had to work approximately 200 extra hours a year to maintain a standard of living equal to that of 1973. This has also led to more two wage-earner families, overtime, and moonlighting, or holding a second, part-time job.[13] This is in contrast to predictions just a few years ago that most Americans were headed toward a shorter work week.

One of the major factors affecting both labor and the economy in recent years has been that work traditionally done in the United States has been shifted to other countries, where labor is cheaper. This has caused concerns about job security and has necessitated difficult adjustments by those who have lost their jobs due to related plant closings. Trade agreements with other countries are intended to lessen or offset this practice.

Worries over the impact of inflation and a changing employment picture within the country are also concerns of our national government. These problems are met partially through taxation and spending decisions. All actions are further complicated by a national debt of trillions of dollars. Both the government and individuals, however, are more openly recognizing economic problems and are attempting to correct mistakes of the past. It is important to avoid developing an attitude of hopelessness, which can only paralyze efforts to improve both the national economy and individual efforts to become and remain healthy. The American people, since the beginning of their history, have earned a reputation for accomplishing whatever they consider a worthy cause. There is now evidence that the American spirit will prevail and that the economy will see the results of united effort.

It is extremely difficult for the average person to understand factors affecting the economy and what they can do individually, or encourage others to do, to improve it. This area—perhaps more than any other—is one in which even the experts disagree. Even so, we should attempt to be knowledgeable, as we are all directly affected by the economy as a whole.

An "Information Age Consumer Bill of Rights," developed by James H. Snider, enumerates:

1. The right to be educated about product strengths and weaknesses.
2. The right to trust sources of product information.
3. The right to state-of-the-art information infrastructures that empower consumers to efficiently use their time, money, and energy.
4. The right of all Americans, whether urban or rural, rich or poor, to access the information infrastructure.
5. The right to privacy, preventing sellers and others from abusing personal information gained in product transactions.[14]

THREATS TO OUR ENVIRONMENT

Past attitudes toward the environment included the ideas that it surrounds us and affects us and that we can use its resources and advantages. People also recognized its disastrous effects—earthquakes, tornadoes, hurricanes, landslides, for example. It is only in recent years, however, that we have begun to pay attention to what we are doing to the environment. Now we realize that our natural resources are limited and in many cases running low. We have also become aware that abuse of the environment leads to multiple forms of pollution and threats to our well-being.

Serious problems of waste disposal have arisen in recent years. More effective ways of disposing of wastes are being developed, and some progress has been made. Recycling is becoming more common, due to both mandatory regulation and voluntary efforts.

Less dramatic but continuing threats include pesticides in water supplies, solid waste disposal, noise, and air pollution. Every year each person in the United States generates over a ton of solid waste. In addition, our society produces millions of tons of smoke and fumes and trillions of gallons of industrial waste. Management of such waste—including recycling and conversion to energy—must be a major concern. Moreover, damage to the ozone layer is believed to have been caused by chemicals called fluorocarbons used in spray cans and as refrigerants. In addition to skin cancer, threats include damage to animals and plants as well as creating irregular climactic conditions.

Recycling efforts are both well organized and widely supported.

The Environmental Protection Agency, created in 1970, has reduced pollution and other abuses, but it has also been criticized for having too many regulations that can cause other problems. In balance, our waters are running clearer, and air pollution has been reduced in some areas. There are also state and local agencies and concerned citizens groups that are involved in bringing about these and other improvements. Global Response, for example, is a nonprofit environmental organization that provides information and education and encourages citizens to contact legislators.

In June of 1992, The United Nations Conference on Environment and Development, or Earth Summit, was held in Rio de Janeiro, Brazil. Three years of planning went into this historic 12-day conference, attended by over 100 world leaders. Even though there was considerable disappointment in the results, an appraisal of the conference in *The Environment,* states that it "should not be evaluated only by the number of signed treaties it produces. The conference spawned many new organizations and alliances the could have even greater impact than those of the treaties."

In his opening address to the Earth Summit, Secretary-General Maurice F. Strong said,

> The Earth Summit is not an end in itself, but a new beginning. The measures you agree on here will be first steps on a new pathway to our common future. Thus, the results of this conference will ultimately depend on the credibility and effectiveness of its follow-up. . . . The road beyond Rio will be a long and difficult one; but it will also be a journey of renewed hope, of excitement, challenge and opportunity, leading as we move into the 21st century to the dawning of a new world in which the hopes and aspirations of all the world's children for a more secure and hospitable future can be fulfilled.[15]

One thing is certain: The environment has been neglected and even abused in the past. If further measures are not taken to protect it and repair the damage that has been done, we will all be losers. There are very few people who would want their children or grandchildren to inherit a depleted or unnecessarily hazardous environment, but our responses may not be consistent and our behavior may not be in agreement. We have it within our power to improve the environment that we inherited and have affected, for better or worse. What every person does makes a difference.

WHAT ABOUT ENERGY?

For many years our citizens lived, worked, played, traveled, and relaxed without giving much thought to energy. People used energy and paid for it, but they were relatively unconcerned about where it was coming from or how much more was available.

The major sources of energy in the past have been wood, coal, crude oil, and natural gas. However, it is generally agreed upon that there are not unlimited supplies of these for the future.

There is a wide variety of possibilities for the future, most of which have both advantages and disadvantages. Realistic persons know that there is no ideal solution and no easy solution. Some of the energy in the future will be derived from solar, nuclear, hydroelectric, geothermal, and synthetic sources. Garbage, landfill, methane gas, and other forms of waste may be converted to usable energy. Natural forces such as ocean currents and the wind will serve some purposes. Research, experimentation, and ingenuity will be critical in the discovery of additional sources of energy.

Nuclear power, despite the controversy surrounding disposal of radioactive waste, is expected to be an increasingly significant energy source. Those who support further development of nuclear energy claim that safe disposal is possible and that many more Americans are threatened by such "controllable" hazards as automobile accidents, smoking, and drug abuse. Some of those opposed to nuclear energy maintain that it can never be used with complete safety.

Although coal is not a new discovery or the cleanest fuel available, it is still an abundant source of energy in the United States. It continues to offer a wide range of possibilities to meet industrial and residential needs. Estimates are that the available supply of coal could last into the middle of the next century, and scientific efforts are directed toward finding ways to burn coal with less pollution.

One of the most challenging areas of energy development is solar energy. Its growing use can be observed in industry, public housing, and private residences. Other new sources of energy are also being developed.

Efforts toward energy conservation include employing daylight saving time, using mass transit systems, increasing the efficiency of cars, including insulation materials in all buildings, making use of more efficient energy systems in industry, and increasing individual awareness of the avoidable waste in everyday living. Our objectives are not only to conserve energy, but also to become more independent in supplying our own sources, and to use energy in ways that are less hazardous to human beings and the environment. It is to everyone's benefit—and therefore it is everyone's responsibility—to become informed about and involved with future energy sources and uses.

PROTECTION OF HUMAN RIGHTS

Rights—civil, constitutional, human, and moral—are frequently the subject of news broadcasts and court cases. Every human being is entitled to certain rights. Minority groups, children, exceptional persons, women, and the elderly are among those seeking protection of their rights. No one wants to be discriminated against because of some characteristic over which he or she has no control. Some, such as the disabled and the elderly, claim to have special rights because of special circumstances. Thus senior citizens seek rights pertaining to property, income tax benefits, protection against age discrimination, and the right to receive—and also the right to refuse—medical treatment.

Many believe women and minorities have equal rights under the Constitution. Others believe that equal rights must be based on practice rather than on additional laws or constitutional amendments. Affirmative action policies protect some rights. Affirmative action requires that businesses and organizations hire, or at least attempt to hire, a representative number of women and minorities.

This is another area, however, where many believe that the government's attempt to correct problems of the past has led to a new set of problems. Rights of women have also centered in recent years on sex equity and protection from sexual harassment on the job. Individuals and groups have been in bitter conflict over a woman's right to an abortion as opposed to right-to-life issues.

The Americans with Disabilities Act of 1990 went into effect in 1992 and broadened the opportunities for those with disabilities to become independent and lead meaningful lives. The rights of the elderly have also received greater attention in recent years. Among the concerns of the elderly have been protection from age discrimination and the right to either receive or refuse medical treatment.

The 1990s have witnessed heightened insistence by homosexuals that they be given equal status in society and in the military. This is not a new human rights issue, but tensions escalated when President Clinton made a campaign promise that he would, if elected, lift the ban on gays in the military. Reactions included some approval, but also widespread objections and some violence. What some consider the moral element of the issue complicates the situation. The gays of America are largely "out of the closet," however, as evidenced by the largest march for rights ever in Washington, D.C., in April 1993. This quest for rights will not fade away, but neither will it be resolved quickly or easily.

The 200th anniversary of the Bill of Rights of the United States Constitution was observed in 1991. Additional amendments have included the 13th Amendment, which abolished slavery; the 14th Amendment, which prohibited the states from denying to citizens the right to life, liberty, and property without due process and equal protection; the 15th amendment, which gave voting rights regardless of race; and the 19th Amendment, which gave women the right to vote. In spite of these guaranteed rights, however, there are still many individuals who are denied basic rights for one reason or another.

It has been over 30 years since Dr. Martin Luther King's "I Have a Dream" speech. Although much progress has been made, many would claim there is still a long way to go. Prejudice and discrimination related to human rights will be discussed in Chapter 6, Attitudes.

THE WORLD OF WORK

The number of people employed is growing faster in some types of work than in others. For example, the number of employees in goods-producing industries has been declining in recent years, whereas the number working in services has been increasing steadily. Services related to electronics, health care, food, computers, and business will continue to create most new jobs. The demand for clerical workers will remain great, but they will be expected to be competent with word processors and other business machines. Technicians in every area of business and industry will also have favorable job opportunities.

Despite educational and occupational opportunities, young people can be under numerous pressures. As one young man said to his father, "It's not easy to cope with all the advantages you had to get along without." Opportunities are accompanied by the responsibility for making decisions and fulfilling requirements, and one must be willing to change and continue to learn. These are also characteristics of a stimulating, challenging life. Work today need not be boring. Moreover, it is likely that you will not be doing the same thing all of your working life. In fact, you may change jobs six or seven times in your lifetime. This will not mean that you "can't keep a job" or that you "won't stay put." It is representative of the changing world of work.

Unless both companies and individuals can actually foresee changes in the world of work, they will experience unfavorable consequences. These changes are brought about by the economy, competition and trade, wages, profit margins, new technology, and variations in the demand for products and services, as well as other factors.

An article entitled "Future Work" states, "What an individual worker can bring to the workplace—in terms of education, skills, self-reliance, and attitude—is becoming ever more important in reaching an organization's business goals. Businesses are recognizing that a worker is a resource and an asset, rather than merely a fixed cost."[16]

Nontraditional careers are chosen by a number of both males and females today, but this has come about slowly, due partially to attitudes of society toward what male and female roles should be. It is not uncommon today for females to choose a career in law enforcement and for males to choose nursing. Who does what should be determined by the characteristics of the work and the abilities and preferences of the individual regardless of sex.

Changes in where and when people work will also increase in years ahead. Over six million people are now working at least part-time in their homes. Some of these are self-employed, but growing numbers contract their work for businesses.

There are a number of advantages to working in one's home. These include avoiding travel time, traffic jams, and parking expenses and problems; being able to care for one's children and work at the same time; having flexible hours to attend outside activities of interest; and having less expense for lunches and clothing. Increased neighborhood contact and fewer burglaries of empty houses have also been noted as plus factors. There are also disadvantages, however, which include less accessibility to co-workers for consultation about problems. One can also miss the social interaction of the workplace.

Through the utilization of the computer, more and more individuals are able to work at home, at both their own businesses as well at interactively with other firms.

There have been a number of changes in work schedules and hours spent on the job. One of these is **flextime,** which allows flexibility in one's workday schedule. Some people, because of either other responsibilities or personal preferences, want to start work later in the morning but are willing to work later in the day. Others prefer to start earlier and finish earlier. Still others may need a longer lunch hour but can start earlier or work longer. Although an employee usually has a fixed schedule, he or she has some say in what that schedule will be. This has worked well for both companies and employees in most cases.

Another change in the world of work pertains to a type of part-time work known as **job sharing.** As the term suggests, this involves sharing a full-time job with another person. Some people do not want to work full-time or may not want to work during the summer. The sharing can be done in a variety of ways. Naturally, any arrangement must have the approval of the employer. Many employers like the idea, however.

Robots will be increasingly used for routine tasks or in situations that would be hazardous to the safety or health of human beings. They will become more human-like in a number of ways. The following excerpt give us an example: "An artificial muscle made from a gelatin-like substance has been developed at the Massachusetts Institute of Technology's Artificial Intelligence Lab. This invention may lead to smaller, stronger, and more flexible robots."[17]

Human factor engineering, or ergonomics, refers to the design of machines and the working environment to the capabilities of the worker. Although first practiced in aerospace, it is now evident in most businesses and industries. Business equipment and work environment are designed, for example, to avoid eye strain, back fatigue, and general stress. As manufacturers of industrial equipment apply principles of ergonomics to their designs, the employee is no longer expected to do all of the adjusting.

The difference between the work of management and workers is lessening. All typing used to be done by secretaries, for example; now many managers use word processors to produce some of their own messages and records. On the other hand, secretaries and other personnel are likely to be part of the team and may make contributions to management decisions. The same type of team functioning is becoming a major characteristic of numerous businesses and industries. Therefore, those doing the hiring will be attempting to identify candidates who can function effectively as a member of a team in addition to possessing other job requirements.

A growing respect for the abilities of workers is an outstanding characteristic of work in the 90s and this is expected to increase into the next century. Stephanie Overman, in an article entitled "Moving Labor into the 21st Century," writes, "When management, when ownership, when entrepreneurship, talk about capital assets, they must remember that the most valuable assets that any company has are the people who work there. That's not a cost; that's a capital asset, and it must be maintained. It must be improved."[18]

HOW WE ARE CHANGING

We have discussed some of the ways the world in which we live is continuously changing. We have also considered reasons why we should be paying attention to those changes and ways we can constructively react to them.

Let's give a little attention now to how we are changing. Essentially this book is intended to help you understand yourself and others so that you are better able to achieve your goals in life and work. We are each unique, but we are not entirely different from one another. In many ways we are the same person from one day to the next; yet, we are also in a constant state of change. This condition is not only physical, but involves other types of psychological, social, and emotional development discussed in later chapters.

Human Nature and Behavior

Does human nature change? You may have heard the expression, "You can't change human nature." The truth of this statement depends on the definition of human nature. If you define human nature as basic human needs and wants, then it does not change. However, if you define human nature as the way people act in satisfying these needs and wants, then human nature does change. Some of these changes result from changes in society or in how people influence one another. Some of this behavior change is based on alterations in custom or even standards of morality. For example, what may have seemed shocking fifty years ago may be acceptable behavior today.

People are more than muscle and bone and organic substance and functioning. They can reason and solve problems and are superior to other organisms in a number of ways. They also have emotions which affect practically all their behavior. "What is a human being?" is a philosophical question; therefore, a complete answer that is acceptable to everyone is impossible. However, it is easier to understand what a human being is by studying human nature and behavior.

Physical Changes

Even the physical appearance of the human has changed to a degree over the ages. Since prehistoric times, when humans discovered fire and made the first crude tools, their brains have grown larger and their faces smaller. Other physical changes also have occurred in the human population over thousands of years. Racial differences among people originating in various parts of the world have always been recognizable. These differences in appearance have sometimes led to false beliefs that the races were different in abilities. Differences in abilities and behavior among individuals exist, of course, but they aren't due to race or nationality. However, even differences in appearance among the races are becoming less noticeable in the offspring of interracial marriages.

Another relatively recent change in physical appearance that you may have noticed is size. Today's young adults are taller and generally bigger than their parents were at the same age. Your father probably couldn't get his wedding suit coat on and buttoned today. If you are a young man, it isn't likely that it would fit you either. His problem would probably be weight; yours would more likely be the length of your arms. If you are a young woman, you may want to wear your grandmother's wedding dress, but it would very likely be too small, also.

In addition to such changes, people have discovered ways of deliberately altering their physical appearance. The use of cosmetics is centuries old, and we can have our teeth capped or get dentures. Different hairstyles and weight control can also change physical appearance. Even hair transplants have been successful. Face-lifts and plastic surgery are not uncommon. It is even possible, now, to change the color of your skin. Modern men and women have new choices of how they wish to appear in their own mirrors and to the rest of the world.

CHANGES IN THE FAMILY

All of the other changes in society have had an impact on the family and how we live. In discussing some of these changes in the American family, David Hamburg has written,

> The dramatic changes in the American family can be highlighted by comparing its structure and function as it was in 1960 with what it has become in 1990. Until 1960 most Americans shared a common set of beliefs about family life. Family should consist of a husband and wife living together with their children. The father should be head of the family, earn the family's income, and give his name to his wife and children. The mother's main tasks were to support and facilitate her husband's, guide her children's development, look after the home, and set a moral tone for the family.
>
> Over the last three decades these ideals, although they are still recognizable, have been drastically modified across all social classes. Women have joined the paid work force in great numbers stimulated both by economic need and a new belief in their capabilities and right to pursue opportunities.[19]

The number of married persons among adults declined between 1970 and 1990, according to the U.S. Census Bureau. The nation's never-marrieds represent one of the fastest growing segments of the adult population, nearly doubling in the last generation. There are also many more single parents. Nearly one quarter of all children live in a single-parent family. Divorce and separation have led to increased joint custody of children. Stepfamilies are common, often including children from both previous marriages. Even with two parents living in the home, many children are latchkey, with no one home when they return from school each day. There are numerous other variations in what is now the family unit of society.

The importance of family relationships is evident through the development of **network families.** This is a support group for people with a special need. Such networks have become especially active in larger communities, where people with problems can feel isolated and helpless.

An article in *The Futurist* explains network families:

> Old-fashioned networking (turning to the neighbors for help) often breaks down in urban society. Many people thus begin to create networks among people with common interest and needs (like Alcoholics Anonymous), even though they live far apart. An interest group does not necessarily replace an extended family, however.
>
> A network family involves a certain amount of commitment—as any family does—and means choosing members of one's larger family, just as one chooses a spouse. There is much more variety in types of network families than in types of traditional families. Members of such networks come and go in a mobile society, so much more deliberate attention must be given, and expertise is needed, in the forming and maintaining of tomorrow's form of extended family.[20]

Those of us living today have many more material things and more advantages and opportunities than did our great grandparents, but we are not necessarily that much happier. Michael Argyle in his book *The Psychology of Happiness* recommends good relationships, satisfying work, and some leisure time as conditions for happiness.[21] For those who would agree with him, these are all reasonably attainable.

What would you DO?

What is one thing you could do to improve the quality of your life? What has been keeping you from doing this?

THE QUALITY OF LIFE

Quantity, or the number of years one lives, does not guarantee quality, or the degree to which one's life is satisfying and meaningful. Life expectancy is increasing, however, and most people consider a longer life desirable. A person born in 1800 could expect to live only thirty-five years. Life expectancy is now more than double that figure. Life expectancy is defined as the average number of years a person of a given population can expect to live beyond his or her present age. Life expectancy is also related to cultural and socioeconomic background. Control of disease and the aging process, organ transplants, synthetic organs, new surgical techniques, and improved environmental conditions contribute to longer life.

Concern for the quality of life is a characteristic of today's world. Everyone wants to be comfortable and to be happy and wants life to be satisfying and meaningful. The characteristics of quality living are largely a matter of personal values, of course. A better life is not guaranteed by more conveniences, more material possessions, or more free time. To a great extent it is the responsibility of the individual to make life meaningful and satisfying, but the society in which we live can make it easier. Many severely disabled individuals would tell you that the quality of their lives is high. We will have a better world if we can agree to some extent on the kind of world we want and are willing to work together to attain it. This need not interfere with individual rights and values.

THREATS, PROMISES, AND CHALLENGES

A look to the future reveals threats but also exciting promises and challenges. The future of the human race will be decided largely by its members, individually and collectively.

Some fear that science and technology will become the masters of the human race. Will the machines we have created ultimately make us their servants? How will the "robot revolution" affect the world of work and our personal lives? Will control of the human reproductive process, including production of test-tube babies and manipulation of genetics, cause undesirable results that we have failed to foresee? We are already aware of the legal problems and custody conflicts involving surrogate mothers.

Reformers in all areas of living have pointed out that one weakness of people who have many advantages and blessings is that they fail to see (or shut their eyes to) pending threats—until it is too late. The future also holds promises. Besides the future advances discussed earlier in this chapter, we can expect to find both education and work becoming more meaningful. Schools and universities will schedule more classes at times more convenient for part-time students and working adults who realize that education must be a lifelong experience. Open classrooms and laboratories and community-based learning will provide realistic opportunities.

Developments in our changing world that present threats also offer promises. Human insulin has been developed through genetic research. It is expected that ways to prevent hereditary diseases and genetic defects will be found. Other genetic research has led to advances in agriculture.

Further breakthroughs concerning cancer detection and cure are promised in the near future. Recent developments in the use of laser technology to close off arteries and capillaries and to pinpoint surgical incisions to within a millionth of an inch are among the lifesaving possibilities being discovered.

Projections and predictions are not promises, however. Although there seems to be little the mind can conceive that science and technology cannot make possible, the fulfillment of a promise demands human receptiveness and cooperation.

We also face challenges. Questions pertaining to some of them are: What will be the effects of the predicted cashless society on the spending habits of Americans? Will democratic government survive? Will a world government become a reality? Will education become more relevant to life and work? With faster transportation, will people know where they want to go or what to do when they get there? Will new energy supplies be developed? Will the federal budget become balanced? Can crime and drug abuse be reduced? Will genetic experimentation get out of hand? Will a cure for AIDS be found?

Maintaining peace in the world is one of the greatest challenges of governments and human beings. It requires more than maintaining defense missiles, recruiting armed forces, forming agreements, and training diplomats—even though all these may be necessary. It also takes an understanding of the problems and political intentions of other countries. It requires measures of reasonable trust. Further, clear policies and strong leadership backed by the support of an entire nation are needed in striving for a peaceful world. Internal problems can also be disruptive. People must have peace within themselves before they can live harmoniously with others. This is also true of nations.

Human beings, individually and as groups, have always had problems. But sociologists say that our ability to avoid or solve problems has not kept pace with other aspects of human progress. Through neglect—or lack of foresight in solving problems—we have often created new problems.

PEANUTS reprinted by permission of UFS, Inc.

News media bring the problems of society to everyone's attention. Crime and violence are daily occurrences. There is concern over the growing number of cases of acquired immune deficiency syndrome (AIDS) caused by the HIV virus. Economic conditions and unemployment have caused serious financial problems for many people. Threats of war, taking of hostages, and armed uprisings have brought uneasiness and tragedy. Additional problems pertain to human rights, energy shortages, waste disposal, and other environmental concerns. Not only must we recognize these and other problems, but we must take effective action to lessen their undesirable effects or solve them.

A great number of problems are **behavioral,** or caused by human beings themselves. The use of dangerous drugs is increasing even though knowledge of their harmfulness is growing. Almost all statistics concerning drug use and abuse are inaccurate, but even the lowest estimates are alarming. There are millions of alcoholics in the United States today. The number of young people among the mentally ill has been increasing in recent years. Suicide and homicide are major causes of death among young people. Child abuse and spouse abuse are also major concerns.

Another challenge relates to citizen involvement and capable, responsible leadership. Those in leadership positions must both deserve and receive respect if democracy is going to work. Those with leadership potential should have the opportunity to develop and use their potential both for their own satisfaction and for the benefit of all. Leaders and members of groups must recognize that leadership involves promoting active participation by everyone in achieving a common goal.

With tolerance, restraint, and united effort we can meet the challenges of today and prepare for the twenty-first century.

All of the threats, promises, or predictions discussed in this chapter will not become reality. Many unforeseen factors change the course of events. Steven A. Schnaars, in his book *Megamistakes,* discusses a number of past promises that did not materialize:

> Many technological forecasts are far too optimistic. . . . Only a few technological innovations have warranted the extreme optimism held for them. Only a few innovations have changed our lives as the forecasters believed they could. VCRs and microwave ovens, for example, and in a general sense, computers and information, have lived up to the high hopes forecasters had for them. More typically technological forecasters have seen greater visions than they should have.[22]

Barbara Burke, in an article entitled "Future Schlock," comments, "The future, a destination so close that it is arriving every second, is somehow always too distant to be clearly seen."[23]

A realistic evaluation of the past helps us to prevent some mistakes and to correct some errors. Placing the blame is not as important as finding solutions. Eliminating or reducing problems will assure even greater progress and achievement. We have already explored the moon, transplanted hearts, developed the laser, and unraveled some mysteries of life. Those with a positive approach believe that there are no problems to which there are no answers. There are only problems for which solutions have not as yet been found.

MAINTAINING BALANCES

The world in which we live will continue to change. Although this process of change is inevitable, it can be either disturbing or desirable. Any kind of change, momentarily at least, disturbs the status quo. Even with change that is welcome, adjustments are required.

We need balances to avoid extremes. We need balances between:

High tech and high touch
Old and new in social institutions
Work and recreation
Rest and exercise
Nourishment and overeating
Dependence and independence
Individuality and conformity
Rights and responsibilities
Care for others and care of ourselves

We also need balance between what we would like to do and what we can do as individuals and as a nation. We must constantly seek a balance in all of these respects.

SUMMARY

Psychology, the scientific study of human behavior, can improve our lives and the world in which we live. The purposes of psychology are to describe, to understand, to predict, and to control or influence.

Not only is the world in which we live constantly changing, but the rate of change is constantly increasing. We cannot help but be affected, but we can also affect the change that is taking place. If we can foresee some change, we can decide whether or not we want it to happen. Depending on our evaluations and decisions, we then can either support or attempt to counteract the trend. Even a small group or an individual can influence change in society. If we cannot immediately affect a condition to the degree we would like, we can prepare to cope with it while we initiate further action. We can also promote change we desire.

High tech/high touch emphasizes the need for the human element in our technology and information age. Some of the most dramatic changes have occurred in telecommunications. In the complex, tension-filled world of today, effective communication is more important than ever.

Changes can be seen in every aspect of our lives, including education, the economy, work, life-styles, and energy sources. Change can provide better living conditions and opportunities, but it can also cause frustration and necessitate difficult decisions and responsibilities.

Today's society has many problems in the areas of drug abuse, conflicts, rights, the environment, and health issues. The future holds many threats, promises, and challenges. How we react to these will affect our future world and our sense of purpose and achievement. With confidence and cooperation, we can change the world for the better.

Reaction to change is closely related to the way we see that change as affecting our immediate needs and wants or long-range goals. We want to improve the quality of our lives as well as live longer. We also need balance in society and in our individual lives.

What we want for ourselves and others can begin with a better understanding of self-concept and personality, the subject of Chapter 2.

Psychology In Practice

1. According to John Naisbitt in *Megatrends,* business and industry must balance high tech with high touch. Describe a specific high-tech industry or business and investigate to what extent they have achieved this balance. If you conclude that a balance has not been achieved, identify what you believe is lacking in high touch.

2. We are continuously seeking—and often finding—solutions to problems in today's world. Unfortunately, such solutions often have undesirable side effects or aftereffects. The development of detergent discussed in the chapter is an example. Identify another resulting problem that has been developed in this way. Discuss with two other students how the side effects or aftereffects might have been prevented.

3. Investigate how a company in your area provides for training and retraining of their employees. Find out who provides the training, where it takes place, and the joint commitment between the employer and employees. Report your findings to the class.

Learning Activities

Turn to page 379 to complete the Learning Activities and Enrichment Activities for this chapter.

Notes

1. Alvin Toffler, *Future Shock,* Bantam Books, Inc., New York, 1970, pp. 375–378.
2. John Naisbitt and Patricia Aburdene, *Megatrends 2000,* William Morrow & Company, Inc., New York, 1990, p. 120.
3. John Naisbitt, *Megatrends,* Warner Books, New York, 1982, p. 39.
4. Ibid., p. 40.
5. Auzille Jackson, Jr., "High Tech's Influence on Our Lives," *Vital Speeches,* January 1, 1985, pp. 164–166.
6. Alvin Toffler, *The Third Wave,* William Morrow & Company, Inc., New York, 1980, p. 4.
7. Kalman A. Toth, "Workless Society," *The Futurist,* May/June 1990, p. 36.
8. John S. Mayo, "The Telecommunications Revolution of the 1990s," *Vital Speeches,* December 15, 1990, p. 151.
9. Grady Kimbrell and Ben S. Vineyard, *Succeeding in the World of Work,* Bennett and McKnight Publishers, a Division of Glencoe (CA), 1986, p. 183.
10. Sophfronia Scott Gregory, "The Future Is Here," *Time,* Fall 1992, p. 60.
11. Bettye Swanson, *Consumer Challenges and Issues,* South-Western Publishing Company, Cincinnati, 1987, p. 419.
12. Roger L. Miller, *Economic Issues for Consumers,* 5th ed., West Publishing Company, St. Paul, MN, 1987, p. 372.
13. Eden Stone and Peggy Taylor, "The Overworked American," *New Age Journal,* November/December 1991, p. 34.

14. James H. Snider, "Consumers in the Information Age," *The Futurist*, January/February 1993, p. 18.

15. Peter M. Haas, Marc A. Levy, and Edward A. Parson, "Earth Summit," *Environment*, October 1992, p. 7.

16. Joseph F. Coates, Jennifer Jarratt, and John B. Mahaffie, "Future Work," *The Futurist*, May/June, 1991, p. 10.

17. "Future Scope," *The Futurist*, November/December, 1992, p. 8.

18. Stephanie Overman, "Moving Labor Into the 21st Century," *HRMagazine*, December 1991, p. 39.

19. David A. Hamburg, "The American Family Transformed," *Society*, January/February 1993, p. 60.

20. Parker Rossman, "The Network Family," *The Futurist*, December 1985, p. 2.

21. Michael Argyle, *The Psychology of Happiness*, Methuen & Company, New York, 1987, p. 21.

22. Steven P. Schnaars, *Megamistakes*, The Free Press, Division of Macmillan, Inc., New York, 1989, p. 47.

23. Barbara Burke, "Future Schlock," *Time*, Fall 1992, p. 90.

2 Self-Concept and Personality

Learning Objectives

After completing this chapter, you will be able to do the following:

1. Compare self-concept and personality in respect to both similarity and difference.
2. Determine whether a person is primarily an introvert, an extrovert, or an ambivert from a description of personality characteristics.
3. Explain why a particular belief is considered a pseudoscience and give another example of a pseudoscience.
4. Distinguish between nature and nurture by giving a definition of each and explain what you believe to be the influence of each in personality development.
5. Show the relationship between the *id* and the *superego* and explain the effect they have on the *ego,* or your self.
6. Match each ego state of transactional analysis with characteristic behavior and give a specific example of each type of behavior.
7. Develop a self-portrait by describing yourself in a number of categories and determine ways in which you might want to change.

> **❝** *We are human becomings rather than human beings.* **❞**
>
> AARON J. UNGERSMA,
> *author*

You are a unique individual. There is nobody, anywhere, exactly like you. But are you entirely and absolutely different from every other person? You have only to look at the person beside you or the next person you see to verify that you have much in common with others. To understand yourself and others you must understand both similarities and differences. You should remember that not only are you unique, but every other human being is also unique. We are who we are, and we act toward others as we do because of numerous factors. This chapter will give you a better understanding of yourself and others in terms of what are known as self-concept and personality.

How you perceive yourself and how you feel toward yourself is your self-concept. How you interact with others and adjust to your environment, including all the different characteristics that influence your behavior, determines your personality. Self-concept and personality are interrelated. Your actions toward others are greatly influenced by the way you feel about yourself. Your feelings about yourself are also determined to a great extent by how others act toward you and by what you believe their opinion of you is.

mask

SELF-CONCEPT

Everyone has a self-concept. You, personally, may find it difficult to exactly describe your self-concept. It would be reasonable to ask, then, How accurate is my present self-concept? It may be difficult to answer this question realistically because many characteristics and factors are involved. Nevertheless it can be of value to attempt to gain a better understanding of your self-concept because it can help you become the kind of person you want to be and can be an important factor in your success.

If you were given a list of all possible human characteristics and were asked to check the ones you think describe you, this would help you to better understand your self-concept. Another way to gain insight into your self-concept is to complete such sentences as the following. You will likely conclude, however, that in most cases the way you feel or react would depend on who the others are that are involved and on particular situations. Thinking about such variations of your responses is also helpful.

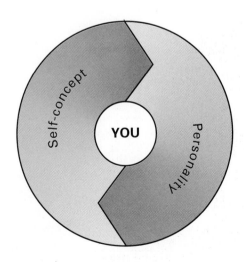

When I ask for advice or assistance, I feel ___*Allright*___

When I lose in a game or a contest, I feel ___*burnt*___

When I win in a game or a contest, I feel ___*Good*___

I am usually embarrassed when ___*Someone repeats what I say*___

I feel good about myself when I ___

I am uncomfortable when someone asks me ___

I usually react to criticism by ___*Giving stink looks*___

I usually react to a compliment by ___*Smiling*___

When I am asked for my opinion on a controversial issue I ___*answer to the best of my ability*___

Have your answers to these questions changed your self-concept?

Some people, of course, really do not want to understand themselves better. It's like not wanting to look in the mirror because they think they will not be satisfied with what they see. Others adopt a false identity as a substitute for self-understanding. These people may feel more comfortable temporarily but

A six-month-old considers her image reflected in a mirror.

PEANUTS reprinted by permission of UFS, Inc.

are not doing themselves any good in the long run. Still others are satisfied to identify with someone they admire. Thus a 15-year-old music student may identify with her instructor and may try to *be* just like her instead of seeing her teacher as a role model and developing her own individuality as a person and as a musician. Others may identify more with a uniform or with a particular type of career, rather than with their own potential as individuals.

How does self-concept develop? An infant does not have a sense of self. Our self-concepts begin to develop in early childhood, however, and continue to change somewhat throughout life. Our self-concepts are also influenced greatly by the ways others act toward us and by the experiences we have. If young people constantly get the message through words or actions that they do not have much worth, this will affect their opinion of themselves. With such poor self-concepts, they lower their expectations of themselves and, in a sense, fulfill their image of themselves as failures. They tend to blame disappointing experiences on themselves; on the other hand, they are likely to attribute successful experiences to luck. They have a tendency to take general criticisms personally with an "I think he is referring to me" attitude. This is how some people develop feelings of inferiority. On the other hand, if people are treated with respect for their personal worth, even though others may disapprove of some of the things they do, they will develop more positive self-concepts.

We also have a tendency to become the kind of person other people expect us to be. This pertains primarily to those with whom we have ongoing contact in our education, work, or personal lives. Living up to other people's expectations of us in this way is commonly called the "self-fulfilling prophecy."

It is equally possible for people to perceive themselves as having more favorable qualities than they actually have. In fact, an article in *Psychology Today* raises the question, Can we all be better than average? The authors discuss a tendency to see oneself more favorably than most others. Compared with ourselves, they say, "Most of us see our friends, neighbors, coworkers, and classmates as a sorry lot."[1] If this is true, it indicates that most of us have a favorable, but inaccurate, opinion of ourselves.

It should be the goal of all people to perceive and understand themselves as they *are*. Your self-concept should be realistic, but it should also be favorable. The following ideas can help a person maintain a positive self-concept:

- Everyone has worth as a human being.
- You are unique. There is no one exactly like you.

- You don't have to be perfect; no one is.
- You have more potential than you will ever develop or use.
- You are capable of loving and being loved.

SELF-ESTEEM

Your self-concept is thus related to your sense of self-esteem. Unless you develop a sense of self-esteem or self-worth, you will be unable to progress toward what Maslow calls self-actualization, a concept that will be discussed in Chapter 3, "Motives and Values."

Realistic, positive self-esteem should begin at an early age. T. Berry Brazelton, M.D., states:

> If I could give one gift to every child in America, it would be self-esteem, for this is surely a key to happiness. But what exactly is it?
>
> This is how I would depict a child who has high self-esteem: * He feels lovable, so he is open to loving and being loved. * He feels valued for his competence and secure about doing things for himself and others. * He has learned to value praise only when it reflects a genuine accomplishment or learning experience. * He feels worthy enough not to consider doing things that are too far-out or that devalue him. * Being sure of himself, he is not at the mercy of peer pressure; he knows and accepts his limits.
>
> This last quality is referred to by psychologists as a firm "locus of control." A child who has it as he enters adolescence will be able to experiment, but he will also understand the cost of going too far.[2]

Even though an early start at self-esteem is critical, self-esteem can also change during the course of one's life, depending on one's experiences. Actually, it is one's evaluations of those experiences that affect his or her sense of self-worth.

Self-esteem also has a direct relationship to one's work. In a survey conducted by *Newsweek,* the following was reported to the question:

> How important are the following in motivating a person to work hard and succeed? (Percent saying "very important")
> - 89% Self-esteem/the way people feel about themselves
> - 77% Family duty or honor
> - 49% Responsibility to community
> - 44% Fear of failure
> - 35% Status in the eyes of others[3]

 What would you SAY? If you were asked in an employment interview: "How would you describe yourself as a person?" What would you say?

PERSONALITY

We considered earlier that how we *think* others see us affects our self-concept. This may be quite different from their real opinion of us. People sometimes think of themselves as failures because they mistakenly believe that others look upon them as failures—even though in reality they may be quite capable and are favorably regarded and respected. There are also people who believe that they are regarded more favorably than they actually are. A superiority complex is often accompained by such a distorted estimation of oneself.

Personality consists of a relatively consistent combination of characteristics that affect how we react to others and our environment. Personality is often thought of as how others would see us and describe us.

The Scottish poet Robert Burns wrote a dialect poem that has a universal message about the self-concept and personality. The dialect of his lines can be restated as, "Oh, if only some Power would give us the gift to see ourselves as others see us. It would from many a blunder free us and foolish notion."

What do you THINK?

Is it always desirable to see ourselves as others see us? Why or why not?

As Others See You

You can expect that each of the people who see you under different circumstances will describe you somewhat differently. Parents, friends, teachers, and an employer certainly see an individual differently. Take the case of Yvonne, 19 years old, who has six older brothers. She has been pampered and protected by her family, who see her as a delicate child. Yet friends in Yvonne's interior decorating class see her as an equal and as having similar abilities and interests. Mr. Narlock, one of her instructors, sees her as a rather immature young woman, but he recognizes that she has talent for color and design. Mrs. Zelinski, the manager of the drapery department where Yvonne works part-time, describes her as knowing about fabrics and decorating but impatient with customers. These people describe Yvonne differently because she reacts to them differently. The various facets of one's personality that are evident at any given time are influenced both by circumstances and by interactions with others.

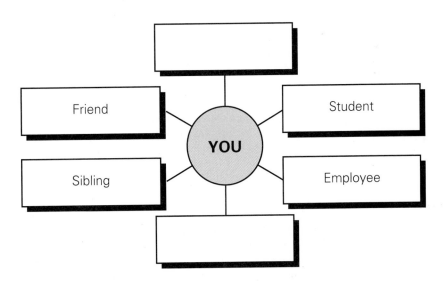

Different roles in an individual's relationship with others. Can you add any? If so, write them in.

It is natural and appropriate to act differently in different situations, or to assume the **role,** or type of behavior that is called for in particular circumstances. This does not mean that you are phoney or insincere. Everyone has many roles to play. For example, you may be a student, a brother or sister, a son or daughter, a parent, an employee, a tenant, a club member, a classmate, and a team member. In all these roles you may act somewhat differently, depending not only on your immediate needs and wants and feelings but also on the total situation. This may cause an onlooker to say, "Susan is not herself tonight." Susan *is* being herself, but she is not acting the way this person expects her to act on the basis of observations of past behavior. It is an indication of a well-adjusted individual to be able to accept the fact that one can act in different ways at different times.

Personality Traits

An article entitled "The Question of Personality" by Stanton Peele in *Psychology Today* is introduced by the question, "Is it a sometime thing, changing to meet different situations, or a solid, consistent core of character and temperament?"[4] There have been different theories developed in attempting to explain personality, and we continue to learn more about human behavior. Certainly the personality of a particular individual is difficult to define. If someone were asked to describe the kind of person you are, however, he or she probably would describe you in terms of characteristics, or **traits**—a relatively consistent style of reacting to others and to the environment.

Gordon Allport and Raymond Cattell are the psychologists primarily credited with developing the trait theory of personality. Thus an individual might be described as outgoing, sincere, considerate, boastful, selfish, suspicious, trusting, or in terms of whatever unique combination of traits others believe that person to have. Other characterizations might be clever, sarcastic, stubborn, apathetic, shy, or humane. There are hundreds of additional traits and a number of variations for each one. The uniqueness of an individual lies in the combination and the degree of behavioral traits characteristic of that person and in the way these traits are expressed in particular situations. In answer to the question that introduces his article in *Psychology Today,* Peele writes:

> Everyday experience tells us that people have fairly stable personalities. We all know friendly people, overbearing people, competitive people, easygoing people. But are these perceptions of consistency real, or are they simply a fantasy we have concocted?
>
> Recent psychological wisdom stands firm against consistency; it holds that personality isn't a stable, basic core of self but rather a flexible entity that reshapes to meet each situation. Psychologists who believe this point to experiments that demonstrate how dramatically people vary under different circumstances in traits such as sociability, honesty, assertiveness, and the ability to delay gratification. Some individuals would never lie to a friend, for example, but readily cheat on their tax or take office supplies home. Others are street angels and house devils; they go along uncomplainingly at work, but at home act like dictators with their spouses and children.

Personality Types

People who have particular combinations of personality traits can be referred to as **personality types.** It is always important, however, to keep in mind the uniqueness of the individual.

There are a number of ways to describe personality types. One method is to refer to individuals as introverts or extroverts. These terms resulted from personality analysis by Carl G. Jung, a noted twentieth-century psychologist.[5] The **extrovert** is described as a person who enjoys being with other people, is interested in the material world, and likes to be where the action is. In contrast, the **introvert** is a quieter person who enjoys being and working alone. The introvert is often more imaginative than the extrovert and is likely to be more sensitive to nature and art. The well-adjusted introvert often has a greater degree of self-awareness and self-understanding than the person who is primarily outgoing.

Some extroverts believe that an introvert is just a person who can't adjust to other people and the world. Some introverts think that in order to be happy and well adjusted everyone should really be an introvert. These are examples of misunderstandings or personal prejudices. It is not necessarily better to be one or the other, but understanding yourself and others will help you feel more comfortable about your work and other activities and will help you to avoid situations that could be frustrating.

Many other specific characteristics are associated with both introverted and extroverted personalities. It is seldom that a person is completely one or the other, however. A person who has a combination of extrovert and introvert characteristics, as most people do, is an **ambivert.** An ambivert will have a wider range of characteristics and therefore will have more options in selecting a career.

Some other methods of determining personality types identify individuals as having one or the other of opposing characteristics. These characteristics might be:

flexible	vs	rigid
dominant	vs	submissive
independent	vs	passive
composed	vs	anxious
emotionally	vs	emotionally
stable	vs	unstable

Another popular personality evaluation is the Myers-Briggs test. It is based on an individual's determining his or her preferences in self-description. Results identify a person as having a combination of four basic preferences. These relate to:

extraversion	or	introversion
sensing	or	intuition
thinking	or	feeling
judgment	or	perception

The Myers-Briggs test is intended primarily to help individuals better understand themselves and use their preferences in leading productive, rewarding lives.[6]

Business and Industry use psychological tests for another reason: to make better decisions regarding who should be hired and who should be promoted into supervisory or management positions. However, there are certain types of questions that cannot be asked in interviews and in job-related psychological testing. These pertain to personal or family status or disabilities, for example.

Many other types of psychological tests have been developed and their use has become more common in recent years. It should be remembered by those designing and interpreting such tests that people should be viewed as unique individuals rather than being quickly classified as a particular personality type.

 What would you SUGGEST? A friend is looking for someone with whom to share an apartment. She wants to be sure that she and the person are enough alike to avoid major conflicts. She has asked for your advice. What would you suggest?

DIFFICULT OR DIFFERENT?

It is often difficult for people who are very different in some ways to work together or to live together. They may look upon themselves as *incompatible*— as having personalities that are so much in contrast that they cannot get along with each other. It is questionable, however, whether most problems involving personality clashes arise because of incompatible traits, or because people are unwilling to accept one another as *different,* rather than *difficult.* Bruce and Gary entered a business partnership together but soon found that it was difficult to work with each other. Bruce was a perfectionist, but Gary was more concerned with quantity than quality and didn't give much attention to details. Neither may be the type of person who would be successful in the business; on the other hand, perhaps either of them could be successful alone or with another person with whom he had more in common. As business partners, however, they found that they were incompatible. Perhaps you know of examples of persons who were good friends but found that sharing an apartment or entering a business together did not work.

Other people, however, may only be different; this is not a problem in itself. Association with many different kinds of people makes life interesting and meaningful. Understanding the motives, values, and habits of others leads to tolerance, and tolerance leads to harmony and mutually satisfying relationships. This subject is discussed further in Chapter 6, "Attitudes," and Chapter 12, "Interpersonal Relationships."

HOW DID YOU GET TO BE YOU?

What you are is more important than how you became what you are, but efforts at self-understanding and personality improvement usually include a question such as, How did I become what I am?

Pseudosciences

Self-identity and personality are important subject areas in the social sciences today. Personality has not always been studied scientifically, however. Many **pseudosciences** that claim to explain much about human characteristics have developed over the centuries. The term "pseudo" means "false" or "erroneous." This term is applied to studies related to character and personality analysis that today's scientists do not accept as accurate.

One of these "sciences" that have been disproved is **phrenology,** the belief that a person's skills and personality characteristics could be identified by the analysis of the bumps on his or her head. The number, location, and shape of the bumps were believed to determine intelligence, musical talent, generosity, and other characteristics.

Another pseudoscience, which nevertheless still has many believers, is **astrology.** Astrologers say that each person is born under one of the twelve signs of the zodiac, an imaginary belt of the heavens. The sign is determined by the position of the heavenly constellations at the time of the person's birth. A daily horoscope reading based on the position of the constellations is meant to guide a person's activities.

Still another questionable type of personality study is **graphology,** the study of one's handwriting. Since handwriting is something the person does, graphology has a closer relationship to what a person is than some of the other pseudosciences, but it is not accepted as reliable in personality analysis.

In the Beginning

Your understanding of how you got to be what you are is related to your belief in your origin. Do you believe that you are solely a creature of evolution, or that you are a creature of a Supreme Being? Charles Darwin's theory of evolution was considered extremely radical in the midnineteenth century, when he concluded that higher forms of life evolved from lower forms. However, more and more religions have come to accept the theory of evolution as being compatible with a belief in a Divine Creator of human beings. Many people rely on their religion to help them better understand themselves as human beings and as individuals.

Heredity or Environment?

Some physicians who have studied early human traits and behavior have written in *Scientific American* that children differ in temperament from birth. **Temperament** involves one's natural sensitivies, likes or dislikes, and predetermined ways of reacting to environment.

The authors say that they cannot accept either the *nature* (heredity) or *nurture* (environment) theory of personality origin by itself. "Either by itself is too simplistic to account for the intricate play of forces that form the human character. It is our hypothesis that the personality is shaped by the constant interplay of temperament and environment."[7] The authors point out, however, that temperament is subject to change and can be affected by environmental circumstances. If the heredity factors and environment are in harmony, the child develops normally into a healthy individual. If there is too much friction between temperament and environment, a problem child may develop. These authors suggest that rearing, education, and other environmental influences should suit a particular child's temperament as much as possible.

More recent studies have put greater emphasis on the heredity theory of personality development. Results of a study of twins at the University of Minnesota, directed by Thomas J. Bouchard, Jr., support the theory that at least some personality traits are determined by heredity.

Behavioral genetics is the science of separating the contributions of genetics and environment in the determination of personality and behavior. A variety of psychological tests are used to determine similarities between twins who have been reared apart. Although there are differences, amazing personality similarities have been revealed. Some genetic influence was believed to be present no matter what trait was examined. It is still unknown, however, exactly how genetics determines or influences traits. No "personality" gene has been identified. It is still recognized, of course, that both nurture and environment have an important influence in personality development. It is the interaction of nature and nurture that makes us who we are. David Lykken, also involved with the twin studies, states that children who are naturally aggressive, for example, should be influenced to use their aggression in constructive ways.

This interaction is referred to by Maureen O'Hara, of the Association for Humanistic Psychology, as the development of a relational self. She says:

> Of course we do not start with a blank sheet and we do not work in an empty void. We craft ourselves drawing from the experience we have, the views others have, the symbols, values, stories and patterns of life of our community. Who we become emerges in a conversation between our biological limits and our interactional experiences in specific relationships.
>
> The human self is, then, properly understood as a relational self. We come to frame and to know who we are—what matters to us, what brings us a sense of significance and fulfillment, what we need, what we believe, who we belong to, what we will commit to—in other words where we will draw the boundaries of our identity, within relationships with other people trying to do the same thing.[8]

Stages in Self-Development

The individuality of every human being begins at conception and continues throughout life. There would not be much to study on the subject of personality, however, if human beings didn't have similarities as well as differences. Some similarities are basic needs and wants. Others are behavior similarities called stages. A **stage** is a recognizable type of behavior that is typical of a person over a limited period of time. Two-year-olds, for example, are likely to experience a negative stage. If Andy's father tells him to drink his milk, he may push it aside; if his mother tells him to come to her, he may run off in the opposite direction. This is an indication that Andy is developing a mind of his own, a step in the process of becoming an independent person, even though it may be disturbing to his parents.

When children begin to use the words "I" and "me," self-identity becomes evident. But by the time they start school, they have a distinct image of themselves as individuals. Later, when they experience the physical and emotional changes of puberty during adolescence, they have a stronger need to identify themselves as distinct persons. Rebelliousness in teenagers is not so much psychological warfare with their parents and the world as it is the result of an internal struggle to become independent individuals.

Sally, a high school sophomore, insists on choosing her own friends because she knows whom she likes and she has her own ideas about who is acceptable company. This can be disturbing to parents, who as a result are experiencing lessening influence, but it is a natural step in self-development. More will be said on this subject in Chapter 11, "Life-Span Development."

SEXUALITY

What does it mean to be male or female? How does **sexuality** affect your self-concept? How does it affect your personality and your relationships with others? How does it affect your roles in society and even your opportunities? It is essential to one's identity to consider these questions even though there may be wide differences in answers to them. Dennis Coon in *Essentials of Psychology: Exploration and Application* states, "You are by nature a sexual creature. This inescapable reality springs from the basic biology of reproduction and the division of people into male and female gender. So far-reaching are the effects of this division that personal identity and personal adjustment cannot be adequately understood without some reference to sexuality."[9] We can gain further understanding of what is involved from Letha Scanzoni in her book *Sexuality*. She says, "Sexuality encompasses so much more than sexual anatomy or

Unisex fashions are often worn by teenagers.

sex-role attitudes. It has to do with our entire *being* as body-spirit creatures. It involves our self-image, our body image, our self-esteem."[10]

The term **unisex,** meaning appropriate for either sex, is used to describe hair fashions, clothing, and numerous other articles and services. However, this classification is limited. Society must still recognize certain male and female differences. At the same time, changing societal attitudes and changing roles have lessened the differences.

Most human beings are **heterosexual,** or interested in the opposite sex. Part of the initial attraction is curiosity. Part of this attraction may be the result of hormone reaction; part of it may be perceptual, or what appeals to one's eye. However it is explained, it is unlikely that sexual attraction between opposites will ever be understood completely or will ever disappear from human experience.

A person who is sexually attracted to members of his or her own sex rather than to the opposite sex is **homosexual.** Why are some human beings homosexual? In spite of relatively new scientific evidence, there are still numerous and conflicting reasons given. The recent research shows that there is an actual difference in the brain structure of homosexuals, which appears in the hypothalamus, the part of the brain that regulates heart rate, hunger, sex drive, and sleep. The first evidence of this difference was revealed in studies of the brains of homosexual males. This difference in the hypothalamus, however, isn't necessarily the sole cause of homosexuality—still regarded as a very complex human characteristic. Many believe that it is determined by a combination of factors: biological, psychological, and social. It is believed, by most homosexuals as well as many others, that they did not choose their sexual preference. Apart from how they developed the preference, that is their orientation and they want to be accepted for what they are.

Homosexuality has received much attention in recent years. Some of this has resulted from protests both by and against homosexuals. People who are attracted to members of their own sex are beginning to be treated with more acceptance, however. In 1973 the American Psychiatric Association decided to stop classifying homosexuals as sexual deviants in need of treatment. The Association now considers homosexuality to be a "sexual orientation disturbance" which should be treated only if the person desires to change. Most homosexuals concede that they are not average, but they also maintain that they are not abnormal.

It is important that an individual receive some sexuality education in preparation for associations and relationships with others. One major objection to such education in public schools, however, has been that there might be too much emphasis on the biology of sex without enough emphasis on sexuality or the total experience of sexually related behavior.

INTEGRATE: SELF AND PERSONALITY

People play numerous roles in a lifetime, react to other individuals differently, and have conflicting forces within themselves and toward others. Yet they are striving to establish and maintain an integrated self-identity and personality. Although a type of behavior appropriate at a picnic would be different from that appropriate at a formal wedding, a person can act appropriately at each and yet remain unified and stable. A person is an integrated individual if there isn't too much difference between how he perceives himself and how others see him and between both of these and his ideal self, or the kind of person he would like to be.

Watch That Id!

Sigmund Freud, one of the most influential scientists to study human behavior, believed that there are three forces within you that determine what you do. He called these forces the *id, ego,* and *superego.* An interaction of these forces results in what a particular person does or does not do.[11]

Freud explained the **id** as an unconscious force that includes your most basic urges. There are many things you want to have or do. Some of these are things to eat or wear or use or experience. If you were an animal, whose rule of life is survival of the fittest, you would just take what you wanted without regard to moral standards, laws of society, or consideration for other people. What you want might be fruit in the supermarket, a neighbor's new car, or sex experience. The id wants immediate satisfaction.

So what *do* you do? Our crime rates indicate that many people attempt to take what they want regardless of laws, behavior standards, or others' rights. Most people, however, have better self-control. The force that keeps you from having your id rule your behavior is your **superego.** This force can be compared to what is called a *personal code of behavior or conscience.* Your id wants something, and your superego may determine that it isn't acceptable—resulting in a conflict. Without ever having studied human behavior, you would be familiar with this type of conflict. You were born with the basic urges that are related to the physiological needs discussed in Chapter 3, "Motives and Values." An individual develops a conscience or control over behavior, however. It is important to recall that people do control their own behavior and are, therefore, responsible for what they do.

What happens when the id signals "do" and the superego signals "don't?" Some people do; others don't. It depends on the interaction of these

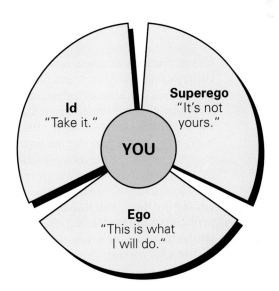

personality forces and the degree to which one has developed self-control. What kind of person you are or what you do is what Freud called the **ego.** The interaction of the id and superego results in the development of the ego, or your *self.* This is *you.* As an example, a friend buys camping equipment. Even though it is just what you've been wanting, you neither walk into a store and help yourself to similar equipment nor take away your friend's. Your id wants the equipment, but your superego determines that certain means of acquiring it are not acceptable. Your ego determines to go without the equipment another year until you can afford it.

Ego States

A modern approach to understanding ourselves and how we relate to others is *transactional analysis.* According to Eric Berne, author of *Games People Play,* every person has three ego states: *Parent, Adult,* and *Child.* Berne's simplified definition of **ego state** is "a system of feeling accompanied by a related set of behavior patterns."[12]

Each ego state has a basic function. Critical behavior often comes from the Parent ego state. Nurturing is also associated with this state. Problem solving and responsibility arise from the Adult ego state. And joy and laughter are based on the Child ego state. Wanting to have one's own way would also be associated with the Child ego state. You may be able to see that the Child compares to Freud's id, the Parent is like the superego, and the Adult is like the ego. Both theories point out that we have different and sometimes conflicting forces governing our total behavior. These theories help us to understand the variations in our reactions to situations, events, and other people.

When we are interacting with another person who is functioning from the same ego state as we are, we are not in conflict. Cross-transactions, or interacting with one another from different ego states, produce frustration and conflict. We should keep in mind, however, that functioning with another person from the same particular ego state may not be appropriate for a situation. For example, if you are having a test next hour, and a classmate says, "Let's cut class," and you agree, you are both functioning from your Child ego state. The two of you are not in conflict, but you are not being responsible as you would be if you were functioning from your Adult ego state.

ONE IS THREE?

Oliver Wendell Holmes, an early American doctor and writer, expressed the theory that whenever two people are engaged in a conversation, there are actually six different individuals involved.[13] For example, when John and Thomas have a conversation, it really involves John's John (his self-concept); the real John (known only to his Creator); Thomas's John (Thomas's perception of John as a person); as well as the corresponding three Thomases. This makes even a simple conversation a complicated activity. But it also sheds light on why we often misunderstand one another.

In actuality there are as many Johns and Thomases as there are people who know them. But if these images are more or less consistent, the person is probably quite stable. If there is not too much difference between how you see yourself, how you would like to be, and how others see you, you have it together as a person.

Functioning from the same ego state does not produce conflict.

Cross–transaction produces conflict. What are other possible transactions?

All these different approaches to self-understanding and behavior can be interesting and helpful. But they also can seem confusing or disturbing. It is not intended that you should become preoccupied with analyzing yourself or others. This discussion is intended to give you a better understanding of the individual you already are—and to provide insight into how to become the person you would like to be.

What would you DO?

What would you do if you are attempting to communicate with another person from your Adult ego state and you believe the person is responding from the Parent ego state?

PERSONALITY CHANGE

"I knew who I was when I got up this morning but I must have changed several times since then." This quotation from *Alice in Wonderland* has an element of truth to it. We all change—not only from year to year but even from day to day. Indeed, to develop in any way is to change, and that is a continuous process. Knowing oneself, then, is an ongoing challenge.

Personality change over a period of time can take two courses. Change can just happen as a result of many influences without one's being aware of what is happening. A second way is that changes can be caused, or at least directed, by an evaluation of what one is and through decisions about what one wants to be. Our main concern is with this second type of change.

Resistance to Change

There is a normal resistance to change that is in conflict with a normal desire for variety, new experience, and personal growth. This resistance is part of psychological self-preservation, similar to physical preservation. A person may not want to make the adjustment to a changed personality characteristic even if the change is perceived as an improvement. It is often more comfortable in psychological as well as physical respects to stay as one is.

"I've Got to Be Me" is the title of a song that was popular a number of years ago. There is some truth in that statement; yet it is not entirely accurate. Most hereditary physical characteristics are fixed. Attitudes, values, and personality traits, on the other hand, don't have to be or don't have to remain the way they are. The comment "Well, that's the way I am" is a statement that one does not intend to change, but it is not proof that one could not change.

Self-Concept and Personality **41**

Even I Have Faults?

The maxim "be yourself" doesn't mean that you should remain as you are; that is an impossibility. It means that you should develop according to your own potential and interests.

Some people resist even attempting to see themselves as they really are because they are afraid they will not like what they see. It is more comfortable not to recognize a personal weakness or fault if there is no intention of doing something about it.

The first step in purposeful personality improvement is to analyze your characteristics or traits. You will want to identify what you would consider strengths, but you will also recognize weaknesses, which are the specific targets for change. There are numerous personality self-analysis quizzes that can be interesting and somewhat helpful, but most of them should not be considered complete or entirely accurate.

Phoniness, bluffing, and showing off are often caused by feelings of inferiority. A person who puts on an act to impress people in most cases really feels like a nobody. Trying too hard to be somebody can hinder personality development. One *becomes* a unique personality; one does not acquire a personality.

Just becoming more aware of yourself and your behavior toward others will reveal some weaknesses. Being more observant of other people's reactions

Attitude
Gulible
Stop Showing off

to you will also give you clues about whether you are irritating or offending them in some way. However, if you pay too much attention to how other people are reacting to you, rather than paying attention to the other people themselves, you are only adding the fault of excessive self-centeredness. There is no magic formula or instant recipe for personality improvement. Personality growing pains include some frustrations and failings.

May I Know You?

Getting to know and understand others can be even more difficult than understanding yourself. A person who does not open up to other people may be considered unfriendly. Yet the real reason for the person's behavior may be quite different. The word "personality" comes from the Latin word *persona,* meaning "mask." The person who has a sense of personal worth is not fearful of criticism or rejection from others and does not try to hide from others or pretend to be something he or she is not. In his book *Why Am I Afraid to Tell You Who I Am?* John Powell explains that people hesitate to reveal themselves completely to others because they fear they won't be accepted, fearing that "If I tell you

The role of the social worker is a vital one not only in comforting but also in promoting the rehabilitation of patients.

who I am, you may not like who I am, and it is all I have."[14] Such hesitancy to remove one's mask, to reveal one's ideas and feeling—both good and bad—keeps people from attaining self-identity and from having meaningful relationships with others. This idea is discussed further in Chapter 12, "Interpersonal Relationships."

There are also variations in the way we perceive the personalities of others. We may think that a person is consistently in a good mood and that another person is very moody, with considerable variation in the way he or she feels and acts from one time to another. We may even be disappointed in ourselves at times, thinking, "Why did I do that? It wasn't like me." We can learn to understand ourselves and others better, and we can sometimes predict what another person will do or say in a given situation. Importantly, however, we should also expect occasional surprises.

PERSONALITY AND JOB SUCCESS

Various levels of rank and authority exist among employees in job situations. Workers find that some other employees are less experienced than they are and others are old-timers with more experience. Still others have more seniority. And some may not have been with the company as long as they but, at the same time, have more authority and higher pay.

There are many causes of layoffs and unemployment, but more people who are fired or terminated from jobs and will be replaced lose their jobs because of personality characteristics than because of inability to do the work. Walter Neff in *Work and Human Behavior* speaks of a "work personality" and describes it as "personal characteristics that the individual brings with him into the work situation—his motives, feelings, attitudes, emotions, preconceptions, and values."[15] Some people refuse to follow instructions or take orders. Others are frequently absent from the job or are continually negligent about safety. Still others may be jealous about any advancement another employee may achieve. The real reasons for losing a job or losing out on a raise or promotion are not always specifically stated, but undesirable personality traits are common causes.

Those who understand themselves and their position at work in relation to others are of value to both themselves and employers. Among the people who are capable at their work, those who can work harmoniously with others and the public come out ahead. Modern career education and job training programs recognize the need for the development of the total person in addition to the acquisition of knowledge and skills.

Some of the personality characteristics generally considered important in job success are the following:

- *Responsibility:* Employers seek and value employees who follow through with what they are expected to do and take proper care of equipment and supplies.
- *Ambition:* Employees not only should be willing to earn their pay, but should also be willing to do whatever is necessary to get a particular job done.
- *Ability to relate well to others on the job:* This includes both co-workers and those in management. It involves interest in others and good communication skills.

- *Presenting a favorable image to the public:* Not all jobs require direct contact with customers, but all employees in some way represent the business or organization to the public.
- *Honesty and loyalty:* These characteristics require an interest in the company and respect for others' rights and their property.
- *Emotional stability:* Employees should be able to accept constructive criticism without getting too upset and should be able to handle frustration without losing their tempers.

The preceding characteristics are important in the job market today, both in getting a job in the first place and in advancing within a business or organization. Job recruiters and personnel directors may have their own ways of evaluating the personality of a job applicant or an employee, but we may be certain that they are concerned with personality as well as career-related qualifications. It may surprise you that some employers not only want qualified, mature, conscientious employees, but they also are interested in whether candidates have a sense of humor. This is often associated with a sense of flexibility and the ability to adjust, which is important in today's world of work. A sense of humor is not the same as goofing off or horsing around, but rather the ability to recognize human weakness in oneself, an occasional harmless error, and the unexpected in situations. The importance of personality characteristics will again be emphasized in Chapter 13 "Human Relations at Work" and Chapter 14 "Goal Achievement."

 What do you THINK? So, just how important is personality to your job success? Might an employer at some time describe you as a person who has work skills for the job but, potentially, too many problems involving other people?

SUMMARY

Your individuality is a combination of self-concept and personality. Individuals can be classified as introverts, extroverts, or ambiverts, depending on their primary interests, personality characteristics, and behavior patterns. A variety of psychological tests can be used to determine other personality types.

Numerous explanations, some of them erroneous, have developed in the attempt to understand people and to interpret their behavior. Many social scientists believe that personality is determined primarily by environment and experience. On the other hand, there is increasing evidence that heredity also plays an important role. Numerous factors, and sometimes conflicting forces, influence what you are and what you do.

Many theories about personality have been developed. Sigmund Freud's theory is based on the id, ego, and superego—three forces within the individual. The interaction of these forces results in what you do. Eric Berne offers the transactional analysis theory, involving the Parent, Adult, and Child ego states. Oliver Wendell Holmes reminded us that there are three different concepts of the same individual: the person you think you are, the person someone else thinks you are, and the person you really are. All three concepts attempt to understand the complexities of self-concept and personality.

Personality characteristics are also important in job success. Employers are looking for more than specific job-related skills in evaluating potential employees and promoting desirable ones.

One's uniqueness as a person is based on one's particular combination of personality traits. Some of these involve feelings such as fear or love, which are emotions that will be discussed in Chapter 5.

Psychology In Practice

1. You surely are aware that friends and aquaintances who know and see you in different situations would describe you somewhat differently. Ask four of these people to write a description of you. Ask those who will, you believe, be honest. Remember that you have both personality strengths and weaknesses. Compare the descriptions and try to explain the differences. (If you cannot accept what they may say, do not accept this challenge.)

2. We know that people who are different are not necessarily being difficult. Nevertheless, we can sometimes be annoyed by different behaviors. For a week, keep track of things that other people do that annoy you. Determine what you believe to be the reason for your annoyance in each case. Share your findings with a group of two or three students. Discuss reasons for your annoyance, and how you and the others have handled similar situations in the past. Will you do anything differently in the future?

3. Look up additional information on the Myers-Briggs personality test, referred to in the chapter, and find out how a person could take this test to determine his or her combination of preferences. Or, if you prefer, find similar information on some other personality test.

Learning Activities

Turn to page 383 to complete the Learning Activities and Enrichment Activities for this chapter.

Notes

1. David C. Meyers and Jack Ridl, "Can We All Be Better Than Average?" *Psychology Today,* August 1979, p. 96.
2. T. Berry Brazelton, M.D., "Five Secrets for Self-Esteem," *Family Circle,* February 23, 1993, p. 48.
3. "America Seems to Feel Good About Self-Esteem," *Newsweek,* February 17, 1992, p. 50.
4. Stanton Peele, "The Question of Personality," *Psychology Today,* December 1984, p. 54. Reprinted with permission.
5. Violet S. DeLaszlio, ed., *The Basic Writings of Carl G. Jung,* Modern Library, Inc., New York, 1959, p. 248.
6. Sandra Hirsh and Jean Kummerow, *Lifestyles,* Warner Books, Inc., New York, 1989.
7. Alexander Thomas, Stella Chess, and Herbert G. Birch, "The Origin of Personality," *Scientific American,* August 1970, p. 102.
8. Maureen O'Hara, "If Not Now, When?" *Vital Speeches,* November 1, 1992, p. 43.
9. Dennis Coon, *Essentials of Psychology: Exploration and Application,* West Publishing Company, St. Paul, MN, 1979, p. 455. All rights reserved. Printed with permission.
10. Letha D. Scanzoni, *Sexuality,* The Westminster Press, Philadelphia, 1984, p. 13.

11. Sigmund Freud, *New Introductory Lectures on Psychoanalysis,* James Strackey (ed. and trans.), W. W. Norton & Company, Inc., New York, 1964.

12. Eric Berne, *Games People Play,* Grove Press, Inc., New York, 1964, p. 23.

13. Oliver W. Holmes, *The Autocrat of the Breakfast Table,* Henry Altemus, Philadelphia, 1899, p. 52.

14. John Powell, *Why Am I Afraid to Tell You Who I Am?* Argus Communications Company, Chicago, 1969, p. 20.

15. Walter S. Neff, *Work and Human Behavior,* Aldine Publishing Company, New York, 1985, p. 154.

3 Motives and Values

Learning Objectives

After completing this chapter, you will be able to do the following:

1. Identify the type of motivational conflict involved in four different situational examples.
2. Describe and differentiate among three major motivational theories.
3. Evaluate yourself as a self-actualizer in terms of common characteristics.
4. Suggest ways you might be motivated to do your best work as a full-time employee in the career for which you are preparing.
5. Suggest how a graduating student might increase his or her motivation in seeking a job.
6. Determine whether you believe control or influence is used in situational examples, and justify your decision.
7. Demonstrate your understanding of terms from the chapter by writing sentences using synonyms for the terms.
8. Analyze whether particular values are tangible or intangible and identify tangible and intangible values of your own.

> *When you believe in yourself, the power behind you is greater than any task in front of you.*
>
> RICHARD L. WEAVER II, *educator*

A basic principle of psychology is that behavior is caused—a statement that may raise more questions than it answers. For example, why does one parent desert the family while another works extra hours in order to provide for the family's needs? Do we personally have different reasons for similar behavior? Is there more than one reason for some particular action? Are you always aware of the reasons for what you do?

BEHAVIOR IS COMPLEX

Understanding what motivates people to behave as they do is obviously not simple. Nor are motivations always known or understood even by the persons involved. **Motivation** is a combination of ideas, needs, wants, feelings, or conditions that cause us to act in a certain way. This combination also keeps changing. Is it any wonder that we sometimes think, "Now, why did I do that?"

Each person shares basic needs and many wants with other human beings. If this were not true, we could study human behavior only by examining one individual at a time. We could not set up principles, or general laws, about human behavior. Fortunately, though, we do share common needs and wants. This not only makes it possible for us to study human behavior as a whole, but also makes it easier to satisfy our needs and wants, to understand others, and to share experiences.

Human beings sleep, read, work, and mate, as well as engage in many other activities. In fact, **behavior** is anything and everything a person does. Your behavior at any given time may be physical, mental, or emotional, although most actions are a combination of all three.

We must be careful not to assume that **overt** behavior, or what can be observed, is the total response. If you were to ask, "What was Roberta's reaction to hearing the news?" and were told, "She got up and walked out of the room," you would have a description of overt behavior. It would be more difficult, but probably more important, to know what Roberta thought and felt. Did she get up and leave because she was offended? Or did she want to use a telephone in the next room? Was she frightened or upset? Or did she leave for some other reason? **Covert behavior** is not apparent to the observer but must be considered in trying to understand the behavior of others.

Cause and Effect

The scientific principle of cause and effect applies to human activities. Many misunderstandings about the causes and effects of behavior result from trying to simplify the complex behavior of the highest form of life—the human being. People are naturally curious. We want answers to our questions. We feel more secure when we understand why things happen. We should remember, however, that human behavior is not easily understood.

In earlier times people often accepted false or simple answers to their questions rather than having no answers at all. But as the study of human behavior has become scientific, many false ideas and explanations have been discarded. For example, except in isolated, technologically undeveloped parts of the world, people no longer believe that thunder and lightning are caused by angry spirits.

Many early attempts to explain life's occurrences resulted in superstitions. A **superstition** is an illogical belief based on ignorance, sometimes related to good or bad luck. Many superstitions—such as knocking on wood, avoiding black cats that may cross your path, and not opening umbrellas inside a house to prevent bad luck—are recognized as meaningless. Even so, people sometimes still carry them out in a lighthearted way.

Early psychologists explained much of human behavior in terms of instincts. The most famous psychologist to take this view was William James, who is often considered the father of American psychology. An **instinct** is an unlearned or inborn type of behavior shared by all members of a species. The term is applied more accurately to animals than to human beings. For example, animals instinctively prepare for the birth of their young. Some animals instinctively know how to swim. Today the word instinct is seldom used to refer to human behavior; and when used, its meaning is usually not literal. For example, one might say that a successful salesperson "instinctively" recognizes a potential buyer. But this ability is not really an instinct, for the salesperson has had to learn to develop the skill.

Conflicts

Since many forces act on us at one time, we often have **conflicts,** or motives that are opposed to one another. You will readily agree that you want some things but do not want others. A conflict arises when things we want and things we don't want come together. You likely also have had the experience of wanting to do two different things, but realizing you could do only one of them.

Such conflicts make it necessary to make choices. This can often be difficult. You have to decide not only what your needs and wants are but also how important they are. You must be willing to pay the price for what you want; this may include time, effort, and money, as well as going without something else. Sometimes you must accept the undesirable along with the desirable. Although it may help in making your decisions to get information and opinions of others, you must remember that what might be an advantage for one person could be a disadvantage for you or vice versa.

The four basic types of conflicts—approach-approach, approach-avoidance, double approach-avoidance, and avoidance-avoidance—are discussed in more detail on the following pages.

Approach-Approach   The term "approach" means that a person desires an available object or goal. The availability of two desirable goals or courses of action presents an approach-approach conflict. Although either goal is attainable, you cannot have both. A choice must be made between the two. This type of conflict is sometimes referred to as a "can't lose" situation: Whichever choice is made in this type of conflict, the individual gets something that he or she wants. For example, Charles has to decide what to do during his vacation. He has been invited to visit friends in Ohio, where he used to live. He would also like to go camping and sightseeing with a co-worker who will be on vacation at the same time. He must choose between the two attractive vacation plans. Betty also has an approach-approach conflict, pertaining to her work. She has been offered a job working as a sales representative in an insurance

Conflicts

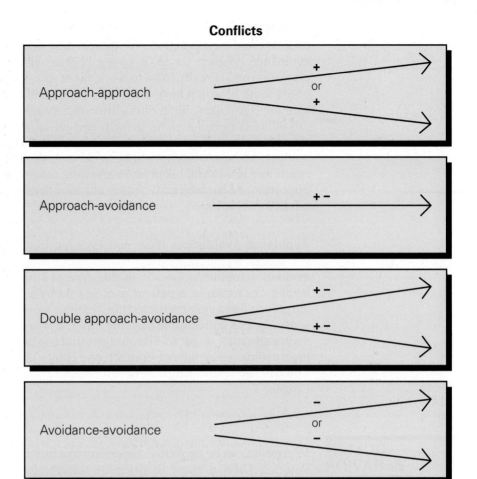

office and also one as an assistant buyer in the housewares department of a large department store. She must decide which of the two available, desirable jobs she would prefer.

Approach-Avoidance   In an approach-avoidance conflict a person tries to obtain something desirable while avoiding something undesirable that goes with it. It is a case of "take it or leave it," or accepting the undesirable with the desirable, or going without something you want. For example, Randy has been offered a grant to continue his education. He naturally would like to have part of his educational expenses paid, but he doesn't like the condition that, to receive the grant, he must live in a specified housing unit. Becky wants to spend her vacation in a distant state visiting her sister, but she doesn't want to spend the day alone while her sister works. You might be able to suggest some activities for Becky even in a city with which she is unfamiliar. It is well for us to keep in mind that the undesirable characteristics of conflicts can sometimes be changed. Also, something that might be a major avoidance factor for one person might be considered a minor factor by someone else.

Double Approach-Avoidance Another type of conflict presents two approach-avoidance situations, of the sort described previously in the approach-avoidance conflict. David, a young person who has completed specialized education and is ready to go to work, faces this type of conflict. He has two job offers, both of which have desirable and undesirable features. One job is in a location David likes, but it offers little opportunity for advancement. The other job offers opportunities for growth and advancement, but living expenses in the area are very high. In this type of conflict there are often a number of advantages and disadvantages to both choices. David must carefully consider his needs and wants and his present and long-range goals. He must evaluate both opportunities to determine which choice offers greater advantages than disadvantages for him.

Avoidance-Avoidance Have you ever felt that you had to choose between two things, neither of which you wanted or wanted to do? This is an avoidance-avoidance conflict. A person in this type of situation may have a "can't win" feeling. For example, a patient may be told by a physician that she must have surgery or live a very restricted life. Neither choice is attractive. Yet one choice is usually less undesirable than the other. It is important not to give up hope in such a situation or get so discouraged that the best decision is not made. Even in an avoidance-avoidance conflict, one choice is usually better than the other. You will see relationships between conflict situations and problem solving in Chapter 7.

HUMAN BEHAVIOR THEORIES

Motivation can be explained according to a number of different basic beliefs or theories. Three of these theories are referred to as psychoanalytic, behavioristic, and humanistic. They are sometimes referred to as the "three forces" of psychology, with humanism, the most recent theory, referred to as the third force. A complementary approach is Douglas McGregor's theory X and theory Y. Each of these theories will be explained further.

✳ Psychoanalytic Theory

The **psychoanalytic** theory is associated primarily with Sigmund Freud and emphasizes unconscious motivation in behavior. You will recall that Freud's ideas on personality based on the id, ego, and superego also involved the unconscious. Freud and others who followed his thinking and work believed that much of human behavior is caused or affected by earlier experiences that were so frightening or otherwise disturbing to individuals that they were unconsciously pushed back into the mind and "forgotten." They still continued to affect a person's dreams and behavior, however. Although there is less emphasis on the unconscious in explaining motivation and behavior today, the theory has not been discarded entirely. When you dream, as we all do, you have evidence that you have an active unconscious mind. Experiences of which you are no longer consciously aware affect not only your dreams but probably also your motivations and behavior in some ways today.

⚔ Behavioristic Theory

The person primarily associated with the **behavioristic** theory today is B. F. Skinner. This noted psychologist believed that our behavior is determined by our experiences and is controlled by our environment. He referred to this type of cause and effect as the stimulus-response chain.[1] A **stimulus** is anything that excites a need or want within a person and therefore causes a reaction, or **response.** The chain is made up of a sequence of stimuli and responses. Each response produces a change in the environment, which then becomes the stimulus for a new response. The continuation of this process results in the chain. When you are introduced to someone by a friend, for example, you say hello or some other appropriate greeting. That person responds to you. This becomes a stimulus to you for further conversation or activity.

You may be familiar with the term **behavior modification.** In very simple terms, the behaviorists say that people do what they do because of what happens to them when they do it. This includes the idea that an individual will continue behavior that provides a favorable response or **positive reinforcement.** We often think of positive reinforcement in terms of reward or satisfaction. Since behavior that is repeated over a period of time becomes a habit, we can in time influence the development of a favorable trait in an individual.

We should be familiar with several other terms associated with the behavioristic theory. Negative reinforcement is often assumed to mean the opposite of positive reinforcement, or punishment. This is not so, however. **Negative reinforcement** is an action that causes an undesirable experience to stop. If you find that a certain type of situation gives you a headache, and you discover there is something you can do to avoid or change that situation, this is what you will do.

We are no doubt all familiar with the idea of **punishment** as something happening to us that we do not want; therefore, we are likely to avoid the behavior that causes the undesirable reaction. A further type of stimulus-response basic to behaviorism is **extinction.** This means that a certain type of behavior will cease if there is no favorable response to it. That is why we are sometimes advised to ignore undesirable behavior of others rather than to try to change it.

Humanistic Theory

It is generally accepted that we have unconscious influences on our behavior and that we are also affected by our environments and others' reactions to us. Many who study human behavior, however, have found neither the psychoanalytic theory nor the behavioristic theory of motivation to be satisfactory in itself. Even if these two theories were combined, many felt that something essential was missing. Because of this, the **humanistic** theory developed. This theory not only recognizes unconscious and environmental influence, but also emphasizes conscious, personal control over one's own behavior. Abraham Maslow is one of the principal psychologists associated with the humanistic theory. You will learn more about him later in this chapter.

Humanism includes belief in both intrinsic and extrinsic motivation. **Intrinsic** motivation causes a person to do something solely because it is a good

This sculptor probably derives satisfaction from both the act of creation of the object as well as the end result.

experience and gives an individual satisfaction just in the doing of it rather than for some other reason. **Extrinsic** motivation is based on rewards or incentives that are not directly related to the activity itself.

Let's consider examples of these two types of motivation. Barry is a mechanic because he finds personal satisfaction in that kind of work and often works on cars for his friends in his spare time, simply because he enjoys doing it. In addition to her job as a middle manager, Brenda reads historical novels because she is interested in changing lifestyles and challenges. Both of these people have intrinsic motivation. On the other hand, Fritz isn't particularly interested in his work as an electrician and therefore works primarily for external rewards, or his paycheck and benefits. All three may do good work and be valued employees, but enjoying one's work is obviously an extra benefit.

Since most of us will have to earn a living, we must be practical and concerned about rewards and benefits for our work and other efforts. The best type of job or other activity, of course, includes both internal and external motivation. The more reasons we have for doing something, the more motivated we are.

Theory X and Theory Y

There are variations of these three motivational theories as well as additional ones. Douglas McGregor, who was a professor of industrial management, developed Theory X and Theory Y, for example. This approach to understanding motivation was primarily work related. Theory X was based on the traditional belief that human beings don't like to work and would only do so if they were

Intrinsic/Extrinsic Motivation

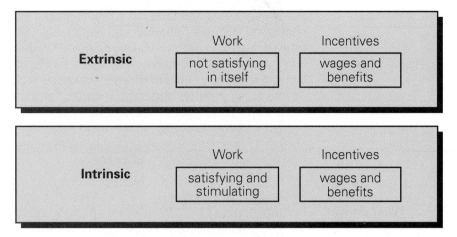

threatened in some way. Management assumed employees would avoid work if possible and therefore they attempted to control workers and "make them work."[2]

Theory Y is a more humanistic approach. B. L. Rosenbaum, in *How to Motivate Today's Workers,* explains, "According to Theory Y, the expenditure of both physical and mental effort in work is as natural as play or rest. The average person has an inherent need to be self-motivated and self-controlled. . . ."[3] *But,* someone may ask, "What about employees on the job today who do not seem to be threatened but who still are not doing their best work?" The explanation, according to humanistic psychology and Theory Y, is that these people have lost natural interest in developing and using their potential because of frustrating experiences. It is possible, but more difficult, for these people to regain a sense of self-worth and to look upon work as a challenge that can give them great personal satisfaction. Leadership styles related to employee motivation will be discussed in Chapter 14, "Goal Achievement."

TYPES OF MOTIVES

Many terms are used to refer to the factors that lead people to action. In reading and speaking, we often find the terms "needs," "wants," and "motives" used interchangeably. It is more accurate, however, to say that motives consist of needs and wants.

There are many ways to classify motives, or needs and wants. Basic motives, such as needs, can be grouped into just a few broad categories. But lists of a particular person's wants could be very long.

Physiological Needs and Drives

Physiological refers to the functioning of the human biological system. The human body must have basic human needs satisfied in order to function. A **drive** is the urge resulting from a physiological need that causes the individual to seek satisfaction. Human beings have a hunger drive, for example, that is activated when the body needs food. Other human drives involve thirst, sex, and the need for oxygen, sleep, and pain reduction.

Psychological Wants

Strictly speaking, a person has physiological needs for survival as well as **psychological wants** for comfort and happiness. But it isn't always easy to separate a need from a want. Children need love in order to grow into well-adjusted adults, for example. Studies show that a lack of love and attention can also affect physical development. People also need recognition to motivate them to develop their abilities and to do their best work. Certain things are needed in order to be comfortable or happy or to achieve another goal. In this respect, today's wants have a way of becoming tomorrow's needs. For example, when electricity first came into use in the home it was considered a luxury. Now most families think of electricity as a necessity.

 What do you THINK? Can you make a clear distinction between what you need and want? Is it possible for something to be a "need" to one person but to be only a "want" to someone else?

Maslow's Hierarchy of Motives

Abraham Maslow, a pioneer of humanistic psychology, developed a theory concerning a **hierarchy** of basic motives or needs.[4] This theory states that human beings have motives which have priority, or an order of importance in satisfaction.

According to Maslow, the first human concern is for survival, or satisfaction of *physiological needs.* If necessary, human beings devote all their time and energy to maintaining their very existence. Since it is possible for most of us in today's society to maintain life, or to satisfy physiological needs, without too much difficulty, we soon become concerned with many forms of *security* or *safety* needs. These concerns involve such considerations as national defense, insurance policies, spare tires, and vitamins. Indeed, there is an almost endless list of things that can be acquired and used to protect ourselves and increase our sense of security.

According to Maslow's theory, *belongingness* and *love* needs concern an individual only after physiological needs and safety needs are satisfied. However, some of the concern for security also involves our desire to protect our loved ones as well as ourselves. Many heroic persons have risked their lives to save others in a fire or some other emergency.

Esteem is listed fourth in Maslow's hierarchy of needs. This could explain why some people have much more self-esteem, or a feeling of personal worth, and why some people are more concerned about what others think of them. Maslow says that if people have met their physiological, safety, and belongingness needs, they show concern for esteem. Otherwise they do not. There may be exceptions to this, but it could explain much human behavior. Nearly every large city has a homeless population of unfortunate people who barely satisfy their needs for existence, have no sense of belonging, and neither give nor receive love. Thus they care little about esteem. They do not appreciate themselves as persons, and they are unconcerned about the disapproval of others.

Our concern for security involves a desire to protect our loved ones as well as ourselves.

Self-actualization, or the fullest development of one's potential, is not achieved by many people because it is difficult to satisfy the first four levels of needs. It takes both time and effort to satisfy physiological, safety, belongingness, and esteem needs. However, there can be degrees of achievement in self-actualization. A person may develop skill in aviation, electronics, cooking, farming, or whatever, while still not reaching his or her full potential. Self-actualization is achieved only when a person has both the opportunity and desire to develop to the fullest extent possible. Whether or not all other needs must be satisfied before we can achieve self-actualization, it is believed that only a small number of people actually become what they might be. This raises questions, of course, about just what a person's potentials are. You can gain some understanding of your potential through trial and error, through aptitude and interest tests, and through increased self-knowledge. It is likely that we all have some potential that we will never realize we have or will never develop.

Self-Actualizing People

Maslow and other psychologists have found that certain characteristics are common among people who make the most progress in developing their

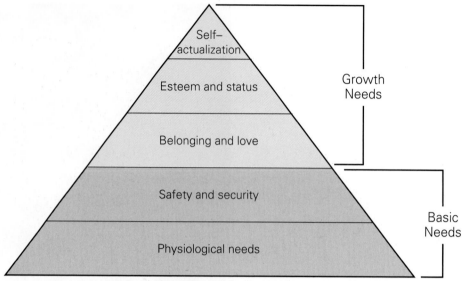

"Hierarchy of Needs" from MOTIVATION AND PERSONALITY, 3rd Edition, by Abraham H. Maslow, revised by Robert Frager, James Fadiman, Cynthia McReynolds, and Ruth Cox. Copyright, 1954, © 1987 by Harper & Row, Publishers, Inc. Copyright © 1970 by Abraham H. Maslow. Reprinted by permission of HarperCollins Publishers, Inc.

Maslow's Hierarchy of Needs

potential abilities. Such people, for example, are realistic. They are aware of their own abilities, strengths, and weaknesses. Indeed, a person cannot develop an ability until he or she is aware of having that potential.

Self-actualizers also seem to respond quickly and positively to inspiration. They recognize opportunities and make good use of them. They are sensitive to their surroundings and have a sense of urgency in responding. People who are not self-actualizers do not experience life in this way.

Another characteristic of self-actualizing people is their concern for problems outside themselves. They are basically unselfish people. Many scientists who have developed cures for diseases have devoted their lives to the service of humanity. Other high achievers can be found in government, education, and other areas of service to society.

Self-actualizers also enjoy a certain amount of privacy, which allows them to pursue their special interests. The development of one's abilities usually involves long hours of hard work or practice. People must usually narrow their interests in order to develop greater understanding or skill in one area.

These achievers have the further characteristic of appreciating the common, ordinary things of life. This frees them to a large extent from concern with the materialistic world, which could make great demands on their time, energy, and financial resources.

MOTIVATING OTHERS AND YOURSELF

It is difficult to motivate others. How successful has someone else been, for example, in trying to persuade you to do something that you didn't see any reason for doing? Motivating others begins with understanding their needs and wants.

"OH, I'M JUST KILLING TIME TILL THE TV IS REPAIRED."

Reprinted from *The Saturday Evening Post*.

Self-motivation is related to personal enjoyment and satisfaction or specific goals that a person believes are attainable. Self-motivation begins with knowing what you want.

Motivating Others

The idea of motivating others is often misunderstood. There are those who believe that if you try to get other people to do what you want them to do or think they should do for their own benefit, you are manipulating them. J. C. Williams and G. P. Huber in *Human Behavior in Organizations* explain:

> Some persons are uncomfortable learning techniques of motivating others. These people think that learning to motivate is synonymous with learning to *manipulate* others by controlling their thoughts and behavior for selfish ends through crafty, illusive methods. Manipulation is, of course, generally considered to be immoral. In addition to this it has other major drawbacks. Manipulators are usually found out, and the resulting distrust undermines their efforts. Employees can sometimes be deceived for a short time, but most employees are too insightful for manipulation to be effective in the long run. Managers who manipulate are not likely to be effective motivators. Effective motivators are usually characterized by integrity and straightforward behavior. They are sometimes tough, but they are seldom crafty . . . [5]

It is difficult to know what another person's motives are. It can be even more difficult to understand why someone might want something that you do not want or that you even consider harmful. But motivating other people must take into account their perception of needs and wants, which can change. Since behavior is caused, people will need some reason to change their behavior. They must perceive that it would be of value to them to make a change—a reason that is not necessarily entirely self-centered or selfish. A reason for changing behavior could pertain to one's family or to society as a whole, for example.

"Communication, understanding and empathy constitute the basic ingredients of motivation. The 'Empathetic Relationship' is, in essence, the key to motivation," according to Jud Morris, in *The Art of Motivating*.[6] Some people—including some teachers, parents, and employers—try to motivate others only by inducing them to want what they themselves want. This can be frustrating and fruitless for everyone. The first step toward motivating others is to understand *their* needs and wants. Then you must show them that the particular behavior you desire will help them get what they want. In helping others toward a common goal, you can also achieve what you want.

Since work takes up much of our lives, it is of value to understand motivation as it pertains to work. Ranking the following list of work-related factors can help you determine your priorities in a job. There is no correct way to rank the items, as the values of individuals will differ.

✎ Rank Your Work Priorities

	Rank
Good pay	II 2
Good fringe benefits	IV 4
Job security	III 3
Interesting work	I 1
Opportunity to use abilities	IX 9
Opportunity to develop new abilities	X 10
Up-to-date, adequate equipment and materials	V 5
Recognition for work well done	VII 7
Opportunity for advancement	VI 6
Effective communication with management	VIII 8

Priorities may change from one time to another. It is unlikely that job security would be rated No. 1 by everyone in your group or class. However, during periods of heavy unemployment or serious problems within a particular business or industry, job security may become the primary concern of all employees.

Self-Motivation

Whose responsibility is it to motivate you? Is it enough for you to go to class or to your job and to look for someone there to motivate you? Obviously, if you understand what must to be done to satisfy your needs and wants, you soon realize that it is your responsibility to motivate yourself. And this can be done even when external conditions are less than favorable.

If you don't think you have made enough progress toward your goals at this time, it might be a good idea to examine the reasons. Do you know what you really want? This does not mean that you will never change your mind, but it does mean that you have a realistic understanding of yourself, your potential, and your opportunities and that you do have some goals. What factors have stood in your way thus far? What are you willing to do or give up to obtain what you want? We must keep in mind the choices to be made because of the type of conflicts discussed earlier. To become more self-motivated, follow this basic formula:

1. Decide what you want to do or achieve.
2. Find out what you have to do (with respect to education, experience, financial planning, or whatever).
3. Determine what you have to do without, or give up, in order to accomplish your goal.
4. Begin, or take the first step toward achieving your goal.

Deciding on a goal may take a great deal of thought and investigation. There may be many steps along the way. These steps become subgoals that have their own order of priority. But once you are self-motivated—once you have decided that what you want is worth the cost in terms of time, money, and effort—you will have little difficulty in taking those first steps.

Many people think of their own motivation in terms of **willpower.** Have you ever really thought about what willpower is? Do you have willpower to do one thing but not to do something else? Do you have more willpower than you used to have? Does someone else have more willpower than you do? You can probably understand why willpower has also been referred to by some as "won't" power.

The best way to increase your willpower is to decide what you really want. It is less humiliating to admit, "I just don't have any willpower," than it is to say, "I wish I could make up my mind about which of these conflicting things I really want." But both statements have almost the same meaning. What you want must also be a realistic goal. The goal need not be easy, but you must believe that it is possible for you to attain it.

We must also have the physical energy to work toward achieving a goal, but many individuals have shown that people can accomplish more when they are enthusiastic and confident about the success of a project.

What would you DO? What would you do if you wanted to maintain a productive working relationship with a co-worker, but you felt that the person was trying to manipulate you?

Control or Influence?

People control their own behavior (unless, of course, they are under the influence of drugs or hypnosis). It is very rare for one person to be able to control another. In most cases adults are responsible for their own actions.

On the other hand, people do influence each other's behavior. You may hear someone say, "He controls a large group of people" or "She has complete control over him." Your brother may say, "If you wash my car, I'll let you use it tomorrow." In these cases, people are influencing other people's choices in a game that could be called "threats and promises." Others may influence our behavior by limiting the choices available to us. When an instructor says you must either write a special report or take a final examination, he or she is limiting your choices. You must do one thing or the other—or else fail the course. You may consider this an avoidance-avoidance conflict. Better ways of influencing people are by example and by persuasion. People in authority—parents, employers, or instructors—influence more by what they do in certain situations than by what they say. Professionals have considerable influence. A counselor, for example, may be able to influence a student to continue to seek an education. And a doctor can influence a patient to adhere to a special diet.

Many popular books and articles about success make it seem as though one person can control another by following a few simple rules. But no one can completely control the behavior of others. Even so, you should not underestimate the ability of people to influence one another.

VALUES

From our discussion of motivation thus far, you can gain some idea of how complex human behavior is. We have also recognized that we cannot have everything we might want or avoid everything we might not enjoy. It is also apparent that there are some things we want to *be* and there are some things we want to *have*, or possess.

Those who responded to the crises of the 1993 floods in the Midwest were demonstrating priorities within their value systems.

The degree to which a person wants something is its **value**. You read earlier in this chapter that security is a basic motive. Although everyone wants some sense of security, it is clearly more important or more valuable to some people than to others. And even people who value security highly do not agree about what makes them feel secure. For some, security may relate mostly to money. For others, security may involve close family relationships, education, or religion. Many people want all these types of security. For them, the order of importance is itself a matter of values.

The extent to which values may differ is shown by the following:

Two women were visiting a small village in a developing country where medical help was not available. There they saw a missionary washing the body of a leper. One woman turned to her companion and said, "I wouldn't do that for a million dollars." The missionary looked at the woman with a calm expression and replied, "Neither would I."

Clarifying Values

Values clarification is an attempt to understand our values and their relative importance to us. This can help us to examine our behavior and decide whether what we do is consistent with what we say is important to us. Many people say that something has great value for them, but their behavior does not bear that out. For example, most people would put their health high on a list of values, yet they continue to do many things that are harmful to their health. People who do not have a clear sense of their values are often confused and purposeless and, therefore, not self-motivated. You should also keep in mind that you have somewhat different values at different times in your life. Parents may have some values that their children do not have, for example. You can gain a better understanding of your own values by ranking those on the following page according to their importance to you. The one that is most important should be ranked 1, and so on.

Kinds of Values

You may have noted that the values listed are not things that can be purchased, although they may involve such things. A material object that can be touched, and often purchased, has a **tangible value.** Tangible object are of value to us to the extent that they satisfy our needs or wants. Al may be looking at fishing equipment, a piano, and a typewriter. The monetary value of these objects depends on their price tags, but their value to Al is determined by his needs and wants. In the same way, a glass of water may have great value to someone who has had nothing to drink for two days. Marlene, who is a nurse, may put great value on her watch, even though it wasn't expensive. And a painting, which has little practical use, may be prized highly by someone interested in art. People may be willing to work or save a long time to obtain the tangible things they value highly. Or they may value an object only for its resale value in order to obtain something else that they need or want.

Many other values in life are **intangible;** that is, they are not material. Examples of intangible values include freedom, beauty, love, respect, and morality. You may have heard people say, "The best things in life are free." The list of values that you were asked to rank contained many intangible values.

✎ Rank Your Personal Values

	Rank
1 A comfortable life (a prosperous life)	*1*
Equality (brotherhood, equal opportunity for all)	___
10 An exciting life (a stimulating, active life)	___
2 Family security (taking care of loved ones)	*2*
Freedom (independence, free choice)	___
3 Happiness (contentedness)	___
Inner harmony (freedom from inner conflict)	___
5 Mature love (sexual and spiritual intimacy)	___
National security (protection from attack)	___
7 Pleasure (an enjoyable, leisurely life)	___
Salvation (eternal life)	___
Self-respect (self-esteem)	___
9 A sense of accomplishment (making a lasting contribution)	___
4 Social recognition (respect, admiration)	___
6 True friendship (close companionship)	___
8 Wisdom (a mature understanding of life)	___
A world at peace (freedom from war and conflict)	___
A world of beauty (beauty of nature and the arts)[7]	___

Everyone has both tangible and intangible values. Some people, however, may be interested mostly in acquiring possessions. Others may direct their lives toward acquiring knowledge, happiness, or some other intangible value.

According to Milton Rokeach, values also may be classified as being either terminal or instrumental. *Terminal* values are "desirable endstates of existence that people strive for."[8] Examples include a world at peace, equality, brotherhood, eternal salvation, mature love, inner harmony, and a comfortable life. *Instrumental* values, on the other hand, pertain to "desirable modes of conduct," such as honesty, forgiveness, independence, and competence.

Influences on Values

A number of influences begin to interact in the development of a person's values early in life. These include family, friends, religion, school and textbooks, entertainment, and the media. Our values change somewhat as we become adults, become independent, and become parents, or as a result of other important changes in our lives. Differences in values can result in communication problems and can interfere with family relations, work, education, and society.

We would probably agree that we would like to have our values understood by others; this suggests that we should also try to understand their values. The least one can do is at times to say in effect, "That is not important to me, but I recognize that it is important to you. I don't even understand why it is important to you, but I believe that it *is* important to you."

Besides the many forces we have already considered, other factors can influence your values. Advertisers try to influence you to value or want their products more than a competitor's products. Society at large (which is often referred to as "they") also influences you. Consider how easily new styles and fads are accepted. Even people who are confident that their values are independent are influenced by what others currently accept and value.

Regardless of what our values are or how they have developed, our values are our own. Others use various types of influence to try to get us to change our behavior, but they cannot control our values, or what is most important to us. A distinction between external influence and individual choice is expressed by Richard Thornburgh, former Attorney General of the United States. He explains,

> Sometimes we think of laws and values as the same. They're related, but they're not the same. We establish laws to codify certain rules and standards that allow us to live together as peaceful people. But it's our values that inspire our laws—not laws that establish our values. Laws tell us what we *must* do. Values summon us to what we *should* do.[9]

Although values do not change easily or readily, our values do change somewhat as we move along in life, as was indicated earlier. In fact, not only do individual values change, but the values of society, or people as a whole, change with the times. Joseph T. Plummer in an article, "Changing Values," refers to the direction of values in today's Western societies":

- The new focus on individuality is favoring high levels of creativity, flexibility, and responsiveness by organizations rather than bigness and consistency.
- People increasingly expect high ethical standards of employment, political figures, and advertisers.
- The greater value being given to experience is prompting the growth of travel, the arts, sports, and lifelong education.
- Health behavior is shifting from curing sickness to promoting wellness, seen most dramatically in a decline in smoking and red-meat consumption.[10]

All individuals in a society do not have the same values or standards of behavior, however. The more self-confidence you develop and the better you understand yourself and know your priorities, the easier it will be to live by your values—as long as they are not interfering with the values of others.

SUMMARY

Motivation is a combination of internal and external forces that cause individuals to act as they do. Although all behavior is motivated or caused, behavior is extremely complex. Not all elements of the cause-and-effect relationship can always be known, even to the individual.

Three motivation theories are commonly used to explain behavior: behaviorism, psychoanalysis, and humanism. Behaviorism emphasizes the effects of environment, psychoanalysis emphasizes unconscious motivation, and humanism recognizes environmental and unconscious influence, but emphasizes conscious decision making and self-control.

A further approach, referred to as Theory X and Theory Y, is related to motivation at work. According to McGregor, Theory X is based on the assumption that human beings will avoid work, if possible. Theory Y, on the other hand, is based on an assumption of natural interest in work as a satisfying experience.

There are a number of ways to classify motivational forces. It can be said that people have physiological needs and psychological wants. A more complex classification is found in Maslow's hierarchy of motives. According to Maslow's theory, people have needs of various degrees of importance. In this view, physiological needs or survival is most important, followed by safety, belongingness and love, esteem, and finally self-actualization—only after the other four needs are satisfied.

We also face motivational conflicts in life. That is, we want some things and experiences but want to avoid others. The four basic types of conflicts are approach-approach, approach-avoidance, double approach-avoidance, and avoidance-avoidance. An understanding of these four conflicts can help a person make better decisions in life.

It is important to understand both self-motivation and the motivation of others. Employers and educators, for example, value self-motivation, but are also concerned with how to motivate others. It is important to keep in mind, also, that people can control their own behavior but can only influence the behavior of others.

Values classification is an attempt to understand one's values and their relative importance. Values can be classified as being tangible or intangible and as terminal and instrumental. Even with the many influences on the development of values, people today are more independent in making value judgments.

The values of individuals, and even of societies as a whole, change somewhat over time, however.

The motives and values of individuals affect how they perceive their environment and opportunities. An understanding of the motives and values of others can help you see things from their point of view. Factors that affect perception and principles of perception, presented in Chapter 4, "Senses and Perception," will provide more insight into the relationship between motivation and perception.

Psychology In Practice

1. Identify a person you believe to be a self-actualizer. Ask that person to share with you experiences in developing his or her potential. Also ask the person about any failures or major disappointments and how he or she reacted to them.

2. Four different motivational theories were discussed in the chapter. It was mentioned that there are even more theories of motivation. Working in a small group, look up information on a theory not covered in this book and evaluate it according to your conclusions on causes of behavior. Present your evaluations to the class.

3. Attempt to determine the major influences in the development of your present values. Also determine whether you believe all of the influences to have been positive ones. Think aboout how you might avoid negative influences on your values in the future.

Learning Activities

Turn to page 387 to complete the Learning Activities and Enrichment Activities for this chapter.

Notes

1. B. F. Skinner, *The Behavior of Organisms,* Appleton-Century-Crofts, Inc., New York, 1938, p. 32.
2. Douglas McGregor, *The Human Side of Enterprise,* McGraw-Hill, New York, 1960.
3. Bernard L. Rosenbaum, *How to Motivate Today's Workers,* McGraw-Hill, New York, 1982, pp. 16–17.
4. Abraham H. Maslow, *Motivation and Personality,* 2d ed., Harper & Row, New York, 1970, p. 35. By permission of Harper & Row, Publishers, Incorporated.
5. J. Clinton Williams and George P. Huber, *Human Behavior in Organizations,* 3d ed., South-Western Publishing Co., Cincinnati, 1986, p. 116.
6. Jud Morris, *The Art of Motivating,* Industrial Education Institute, Boston, 1968, p. 22.
7. Sidney B. Simon, Leland W. Howe, and Howard Kirschenbaum, *Values Clarification,* Hart Publishing Company, Inc., New York, 1972, pp. 113–114.
8. Milton Rokeach, *The Nature of Human Values,* Free Press, New York, 1973, p. 7.
9. Richard Thornburgh, "Law and Values in a Changing World," *Vital Speeches,* January 15, 1991, p. 205.
10. Joseph T. Plummer, "Changing Values," *The Futurist,* January–February, 1989, p. 13.

4 Senses and Perception

Learning Objectives

After completing this chapter, you will be able to do the following:

1. Write a short paragraph pertaining to perception using terms from the chapter correctly.
2. Identify the sense or senses that a particular television commercial or magazine advertisement appeals to.
3. Suggest an appropriate functional use of colors based on the effects these colors have on people.
4. Suggest ways that individuals might protect themselves from the hazards of sound.
5. Give examples of how factors that influence perception have affected your perception.
6. Identify the principle of perception involved in a number of situational examples.

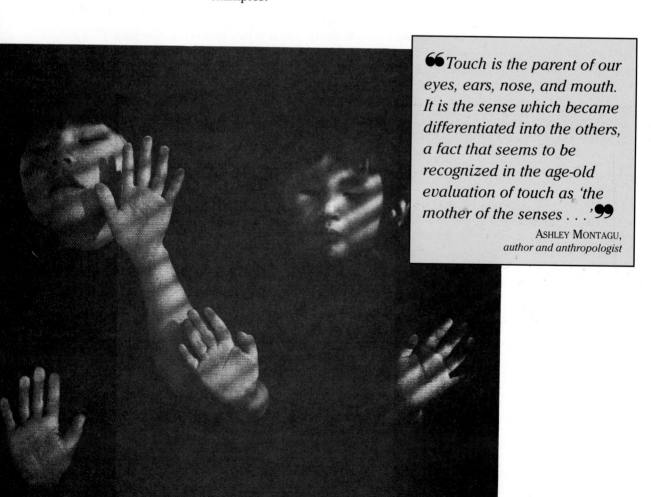

66 *Touch is the parent of our eyes, ears, nose, and mouth. It is the sense which became differentiated into the others, a fact that seems to be recognized in the age-old evaluation of touch as 'the mother of the senses . . .'* 99

ASHLEY MONTAGU,
author and anthropologist

Perception is directly related to all other areas of human behavior and is affected by our emotions, needs, expectations, and past experience, as well as other factors. **Perception** can be defined as awareness through the senses with interpretation by the individual. Two people may view the same scene, for example, and have different reactions. It is correct to say that we see with our eyes but that perception takes place in the mind. This would be similarly true of our other senses as well.

Conditions in the environment stimulate our sense organs and activate the sensory nerves. These messages are carried through the spinal cord to the brain, where we interpret or give meaning to our experiences. Numerous stimuli act on our senses at any one time, so our experiences become very complex.

This complexity is referred to by Walter J. Freeman of the University of California in the following:

> When a person glimpses the face of a famous actor, sniffs a favorite food or hears the voice of a friend, recognition is instant. Within a fraction of a second after the eyes, nose, ears, tongue, or skin is stimulated, one knows the object is familiar and whether it is desirable or dangerous. How does such recognition, which psychologists call preattentive perception, happen so accurately and quickly, even when the stimuli are complex and the context in which they arise varies?
>
> Much is known about the way the cerebral cortex, the outer rind of the brain, initially analyzes sensory messages. Yet investigations are only now beginning to suggest how the brain moves beyond the mere extraction of features—how it combines sensory messages with past experience and with expectation to identify both the stimulus and its particular meaning to the individual.[1]

Past experience and expectation are factors of perception that will be discussed later in this chapter.

LEVELS OF AWARENESS

It is impossible to be aware of everything that exists or is happening within yourself or in your surroundings at any given time. Of course, we would have no reason even to want to be aware of all of this all of the time. It would be disturbing and keep us from paying attention to our immediate concern.

Whatever you are thinking about or knowingly perceiving at this moment is your **conscious** level of awareness. You may be conscious of the room temperature, of whether you are hungry or thirsty, of whether the light is on or off, of discomfort of your left foot, of the time of day, and of the person next to you. Or you may be unaware of some of these conditions until they are brought to your attention. You are probably unaware of your breathing rate and of other conditions of your internal state of being and many characteristics of your environment. Our mind's allowing certain things to come to our attention while ignoring others is called **sensory gating.**

Your **preconscious** consists of things that you know but that you are not thinking about or aware of at the moment. There are many things that you know and are not thinking about, but that you could bring to your awareness or consciousness with little effort. If someone asked, for example, you could tell them where you were last night, or the names of your parents, or your favorite TV program. Your **unconscious,** because of its very nature, is more difficult to understand. In fact, we really don't understand much about the unconscious, but we know that it exists. It consists of the experiences, thoughts, and desires that would be disturbing to us if we were conscious of them. Remember Freud and the id in Chapter 2? Perhaps the clearest evidence of the unconscious is the fact that we dream. Scientists have concluded that dreaming has a function in contributing to our well-being by providing an outlet for urges and feelings. Because the id has more freedom in our dreams, we may have better self-control and be more content when we are awake.

ALTERED STATES OF CONSCIOUSNESS

Dreams themselves belong to what is known as altered states of consciousness. According to Atkinson, Atkinson, Smith, and Bem, "An altered state of consciousness is said to exist when mental functioning seems changed or out of the ordinary to the person experiencing the state."[2] They identify sleep, dreams, meditation, hypnosis, and mental states induced by drugs as this type of consciousness. A person who is temporarily knocked out or a person in a coma is also experiencing an altered state of consciousness.

Altered states of consciousness are sometimes intentionally induced for desired effects. Zen, Yoga, and transcendental meditation, for example, are used for relaxation and to relieve tension. Hypnosis is sometimes used in surgery and is increasingly used to help people overcome problems such as experiencing unwarranted fear, overeating, and smoking. There is also growing interest in the possible benefits of self-hypnosis, by which people can alter their own state of consciousness and learn to control their concentration and modify their behavior. However, no type of hypnosis should be attempted without professional supervision or guidance, for we still know relatively little about how the mind functions.

INCREASING AWARENESS

Biofeedback is a method of increasing one's awareness of what is happening inside his or her body. By means of electronic instruments, a person can become aware of his heart rate and blood pressure, for example. By paying

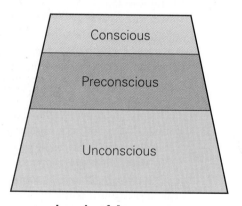

Levels of Awareness

attention to what he can do to raise or lower these body activities, he can improve his physiological functioning. The effectiveness of biofeedback is still controversial, however, and it is not extensively used. Better means of monitoring and controlling body functioning through behavior will likely be developed in the future.

It is not necessary to use unusual means to increase awareness. You can learn to use your senses more fully to enlarge and enhance your everyday experience. You can learn to notice and appreciate the simpler things in life. You also can develop appreciation for other, more complex experiences that involve the senses.

Harold Cook and Joel Davitz, in *60 Seconds to Mind Expansion,* give ways to increase awareness by making full use of your senses:

> What do you do with the moments in between? The 60 seconds, the minutes and occasionally the hours, of waiting and nothingness? Those pieces of time spent waiting for a train, a bus, or standing in a cashier's line—the restless moments that all of us have before the waiter brings the menu or while the gas tank is filling.
>
> For most of us, such moments are experienced as boredom, and when we are not unspeakably bored during these waiting times, we are simply irritated by them. But neither the boredom nor the irritation is inevitable, for it is precisely these moments that can be most useful to us. Instead of being helplessly idle in these in-between times, we can be stimulated, creative, and relaxed. Instead of viewing such moments as "trapped" time, they can be seen as "free" time—time in which we are free to develop our senses, expand our consciousness, and exchange nothingness for awareness.[3]

The person is experiencing an altered state of consciousness through biofeedback, whereby one becomes more aware of involuntary body processes in order to manipulate or consciously control them.

Besides being more aware of your own thoughts and environment, you also can be more aware of the perceptions of others, which may be different from yours. The following kinds of comments and questions can give you clues about other people's perception.

- "Let's leave. I don't see anything interesting here."
- "I have never seen such a beautiful sight. Don't you agree?"
- "I can't understand why that restaurant is so popular. The food is seasoned far too heavily."

What do you THINK?

"It is better not to be aware of some things in our environment because they might be disturbing to us." Can you think of exceptions?

SIGHT

Sight, or the **visual** sense, is, for many people, the most important and valued one. How and what you perceive depend on the visual capabilities of your particular eyes, your general physical condition, the amount of light entering your eyes, and environmental factors. If you can see clearly at 20 feet what a person with normal vision can see at 20 feet, you have 20/20 vision. However, if you can see at a 20-foot distance what a person with normal vision can see at 40 feet, you have 20/40 vision. You may also be aware that you have a "blind spot," the place where the nerves of your eye come together to form the optic nerve, where you have no vision. This does not cause a problem with our vision under ordinary circumstances.

Light and Dark Differences

Your eyes really function differently at night or in dim light than they do during daylight. This is because the *retina,* membrane at the back of the eyeball, has two kinds of cells. Daytime seeing is done with cells called *cones,* which are located in the center of the retina. Night seeing is done with the *rods,* which are on the outside edge of the retina.

You know from experience that it takes a little while for you to be able to see when you walk into a dimly lit room. If you go out into bright daylight a few hours later, the sun may blind you for a while. Light enters the eye through the *pupil,* the dark circle in the center of your eye; the *iris,* the colored part of your eye, expands or contracts to adjust to degrees of light or darkness. Since it takes a few minutes for one's eyes to adjust to light changes, it is advisable to be cautious when entering a situation with a major light difference.

Visual Hazards

Some of the most serious visual hazards relate to operation of motor vehicles, because of the speed involved. When a vehicle is moving at 55 miles an hour, it covers 80 feet per second. Good vision and quick reaction time are needed to avoid accidents. Young people rate high in both of these categories. Nevertheless, they have more fatal accidents because they take more risks.

Reaction time is slowed and depth perception distorted when a person has been drinking alcoholic beverages or using other drugs. In fact, alcohol is considered to be a contributing factor in at least half of all fatal traffic accidents. Other drugs also distort perception and judgment, thereby leading to accidents. Even antihistamines, found in some allergy and cold medications, can cause dizziness and drowsiness. The combination of alcohol and other drugs can be even more disastrous than either would be if used alone.

Other accidents are caused by people who have faulty vision at night even though their daytime vision may be normal. Visual perception hazards also result from glare and other environmental factors. Rain, snow, or fog, for example, can reduce visibility to a dangerous degree.

Still other visual hazards arise from glare, inadequate lighting, lack of eye protection when working with materials that produce fine particles that can fly into the eyes, misuse of contact lenses, or general poor health. Diabetes, for example, is the leading cause of new cases of blindness in the United States today.

Effects of Color

The science of color can be both fascinating and challenging. You may know that white light is a combination of all colors and that black is the absence of color. The primary colors in light are red, blue, and green. These are the colors used in creating color television. The primary colors in paint, however, are somewhat different. They are blue, red, and yellow. You may know from experience that they can be combined to form other colors.

Colors are also commonly used in language to indicate characteristics of behavior or moods. Note the meaning of the color in the following expressions: "She saw red!" "He has a yellow streak." "She looked at my ring with green eyes." "I felt blue yesterday." Colors also have meaning in such terms as "red tape" and "blackball." What other similar uses of color can you think of?

Color is also an important factor in marketing. Studies have shown that the same product will sell more in one color combination of packaging than in another. The following example came from June Leary, who writes,

> When a well-known orange juice manufacturer changed the primary color of its packaging from orange to black, sales figures climbed 25 percent. Although there was a previously unwritten rule that black was ineffective in representing food products, black made the packaging stand out from the sea of competitors and conveyed the sense of elegance and sophistication psychologically attached to the color.[4]

Specialists studying the effects of color have made important discoveries about the efficiency, comfort, and well-being of people in their surroundings. Business and industry have used these studies to relieve stress, reduce accidents, improve production, and contribute to employee satisfaction.

Some companies have used color to suit the individual preferences of their employees. A manufacturing business in Wisconsin allows its workers to choose the colors that their machines will be painted. Instead of the battleship gray so common in factories of the past, this firm's hydraulic presses are aqua or royal blue or whatever color the worker prefers. When a different employee is assigned to a machine, it is repainted to suit that person.

Examples of functional uses of color are the selection of blue-gray on machinery and worktables to relieve eye strain and of bright colors such as red, orange, and yellow for safety coding in factories. Hospitals often paint patients' rooms soft pastel colors to relax them or bright colors to stimulate them, depending on the effects desired. Schools use bright colors to stimulate participation and learning as well as to make them attractive. Visibility has been improved in classrooms by substituting green chalkboards for the old black ones, or blackboards.

What would you DO? If you intended to buy a car at a special sales event and you liked everything about a particular car but the color, what would you do?

Color Coding   Using specific colors to convey warnings or to provide information is known as **color coding.** Along with various shapes and printed messages, colors are being used in transportation systems, for example, to help people find rest areas, hospitals, and other facilities or points of interest. Faber Birren, a color consultant who helped develop the National Safety Color Code, points out that color speaks a universal language that everyone understands. Birren, as quoted in an article by Claire Schoen, says, "People respond to colors first, symbols second. We once ran a test to prove this: We let hundreds of people drive by a stop sign that was painted red but spelled 'Tops.' Everyone stopped but only two people noticed the misspelling."[5]

Color in Design and Decorating   Color can visibly enrich clothing and home furnishings. It also does unexpected things, which might be either exciting or disturbing. For example, a color used as a background can alter the appearance of another color placed before it. Or a color used in combination with one or more others can take on a different appearance. One color can appear quite different on different people, depending on the color of their skin, eyes, and hair. The suit that seemed to be one color hanging on a store rack may look a different shade when worn. A colored pillow on one sofa may look different when placed on a sofa of a different color. In short, the determination of color can seldom be considered apart from how and where it is to be used.

Lighting also affects colors. For example, blue-green in daylight may acquire a yellowish cast in artificial light. It is desirable, therefore, that wall paint and home furnishings be selected in the same kind of lighting as that in which they will be used.

Colors have some general characteristic effects. Yellow, orange, and red, for example, are considered warm colors; violet, blue, and green are cool colors. Dark colors make one appear slimmer than light colors. Dark colors make rooms look smaller. Black, white, beige, gray, and navy blue are basic colors, always considered to be in style. Despite individual preferences in color, people generally tire less quickly of basic colors; for this reason it is practical to choose basic colors when buying longer-lasting apparel such as coats and suits. They can also be accessorized easily with seasonably fashionable brighter colors. In the same way, home furnishings in basic colors can be accented with smaller, replaceable items in brighter colors that add contrast and interest.

HEARING

The **auditory** sense, commonly called "hearing," responds to a world of sound that affects us in various ways. The dull drumming of rain on a roof puts us to sleep, but the blare of an alarm clock wakes us up. We are entertained or relaxed by music or frightened by unexpected loud noises or recognizable warnings. We may be thrilled just by the sound of a loved one's voice. Or we may be turned off by a person with irritating or commanding vocal qualities. Sound also permits us to exchange verbal messages with one another.

Characteristics of Sound

There are many different kinds of sound, but what is sound? Vibrating changes in the air known as *sound waves* stimulate the auditory nerves in the ear. Impulses are then transmitted to the brain and are interpreted as **sound.** The number of vibrations per second is known as *frequency.* Most people cannot detect sounds with frequencies below 20 waves per second or above 20,000 waves per second. The point at which one hears sounds is called the **threshold of audibility.**

Pitch, loudness, and quality are characteristics of sound. *Pitch,* or the highness or lowness of tones, is determined by frequency. A low-pitched voice is more pleasant to most ears than a high-pitched one. *Loudness* is the strength of the sensation received by the ear and sent to the brain and is measured in decibels. *Quality* is a characteristic of musical tone but is also the feature that makes a friend's voice recognizable on the telephone. You know your friend's voice by its distinctive quality.

The difference between noise and music is that noise consists of irregular vibrations at irregular intervals, whereas music has regular characteristics. Any undesired or disturbing sound is also considered noise. A group of young people talking, laughing, and playing music at a party, for example, may cause neighbors to complain that they are making too much noise.

Hazards of Noise

Noise has become a serious pollution problem in today's world. The United States Environmental Protection Agency reports that over 16 million Americans have suffered some degree of hearing loss because of noise. The danger can result from a single loud blast or from a prolonged period of noise.

A wide variety of noises bombard our ears in modern society. Jets and helicopters, loud music, construction and street repair, sirens, and combinations of household appliances all take their toll. Such noise not only causes loss of hearing but also creates stress that contributes to accidents, decreased productivity, and irritability. Normal conversation is around 60 decibels in loudness. Sound twice that loud can be harmful or detrimental to hearing. It can also contribute to physical reactions such as headaches and nausea.

The Occupational Safety and Health Act (OSHA) has set limits on the amount of noise allowable in a working environment.

The following are suggestions for protecting yourself from excessive noise:

- Avoid noisy environments as much as possible. Even if you like loud music, remember that it can damage your hearing.

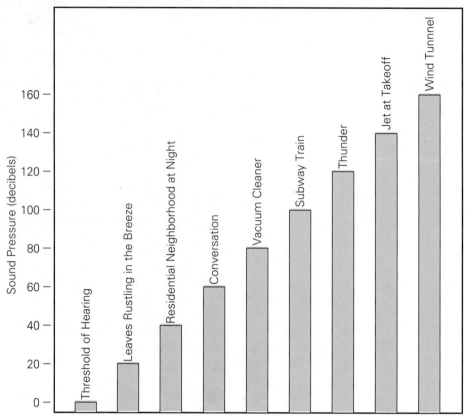

The Decibel Ratings for Various Common Sounds

Sound Pressure (decibels)

- Threshold of Hearing
- Leaves Rustling in the Breeze
- Residential Neighborhood at Night
- Conversation
- Vacuum Cleaner
- Subway Train
- Thunder
- Jet at Takeoff
- Wind Tunnnel

- Take noise breaks. If you can't avoid noisy environments, get away from the noise at intervals, if possible.
- When purchasing appliances, check their noise level. Manufacturers are responding to customer concerns about noise in the home.
- When renting an apartment or buying a home, check the acoustics and also the general environment at different times of the day and night.

Remember that noise can cause stress and other problems in addition to being hazardous to hearing.

Sound Control and Use

Scientific control of sound, or *acoustics,* is an important consideration in the construction of auditoriums to eliminate interference or to enhance sounds. Sound is also being reduced or absorbed in offices, factories, schools, and other types of buildings. Even homes are being designed to reduce or control sound.

Some sounds are beneficial, and a background of music in offices and hospitals, and even schools, has proved to reduce tension. This music should be soft and without vocal accompaniment, of course. You have probably had the experience of hearing music while you were on hold on a telephone line. Music

A worker in an automobile assembly plant wears special equipment to protect herself against hearing loss.

in places of business also has the psychological effect of making the listeners feel that someone cares about them; this is a morale booster.

Science has produced ultrasound, or ultrasonic waves, at vibrations too high to be heard by human beings. Ultrasound is used for a number of medical procedures. Manufacturers also use ultrasound to detect cracks in castings. These are only a few of the growing list of applications. Another scientific development is sonar, a device or system using the reflection of sound waves. Two of its many uses are detecting submarines and determining the depth of water in oceans.

✎ *Quiz Yourself on Sound*

Sound does not travel in a vacuum. The speed of sound depends upon the density of the substance through which it travels. See whether you can match the number of feet per second sound travels through the following three substances:

_____ 1. water   a. 16,400 feet per second

_____ 2. steel   b. 4,700 feet per second

_____ 3. air   c. 1,087 feet per second

Answers are on page 90.

TOUCH The sense of touch is known as the **cutaneous** sense. Receptors, or cells in the skin that respond to stimuli, give us sensations of heat, cold, pain, and pressure. Each touch sensation affects specific pinpoint skin areas and does not affect other areas. Receptors that respond to cold do not respond to heat, pain, or pressure, for example. Experiments have been conducted to determine different points of the skin that are sensitive to each of the four cutaneous sensations. Doctors and dentists freeze pain receptors in the body so that the patient does not feel pain during treatment or surgery. The term "painless dentistry" has arisen from this practice.

Through the sense of touch one can also distinguish thickness, flexibility, and texture. Experience makes it possible to identify metal, wood, paper, fabric, and plastic by touch alone. Sightless people have highly developed abilities to distinguish objects by touch, for they must often rely on this sense.

The skin responds to humidity and air movement as well as to temperature and the other sensations mentioned previously. Thus you feel hot, the wind is brisk on your skin, or the high humidity makes you feel uncomfortable. People have learned to control these factors indoors, however. Furnaces, air conditioners, humidifiers, and dehumidifiers help to keep us comfortable and efficient at work or at home.

Pain

A new approach to understanding and reacting to the sense of pain has developed in recent years. Dr. John J. Bonica is credited with establishing the nation's first pain clinic in 1960. Since then, pain control centers, including the Pain Management Center at the Mayo Clinic in Rochester, Minnesota, have arisen throughout the country. These pain clinics have medical directors and employ a number of specialists, including nurses, physical therapists, and psychologists.

The basic goal of a pain clinic is not so much to eliminate pain—an objective that is often impossible—but to help a person prevent pain from being the main focus of life. A patient who has been helped might typically say, "I still have pain, but my whole life no longer centers on pain." Such a person has learned to manage pain. Dr. Lorenz K. Y. Ng, a neurologist and psychiatrist at the Washington (DC) Pain Center, is quoted in an article entitled "Coping with Chronic Pain" as saying, "We need to reward wellness—to focus not on relieving pain but instead on restoring function. The focus shifts from passive to active, from cure to care, from pills to skills."[6] Methods used to help people with pain to learn to live more relaxed and constructive lives include physical and occupational therapy, biofeedback, walking, stationary bicycling, relaxation exercises, group therapy sessions, and gradual reduction of dependency on medication.

Although no one wants to live a life of pain, we should remember that pain serves a useful purpose. It tells us that something is wrong. We should attempt to learn the cause of pain, often with professional help. Then it can be determined what can be done to eliminate the cause, reduce the pain, or learn to live with it, if necessary.

Human Contact

It is becoming more evident that some caring physical contact is important to most human beings. Those who say they don't want to be around other people, much less touch them, or be touched by them, have probably been psychologically hurt and could be unconsciously protecting themselves from further hurt. Even a bumper sticker that asks, "Have you hugged someone today?" is displaying a worthwhile message.

TASTE

Taste, known as the **gustatory** sense, responds only to stimuli in a chemical state. We cannot taste salt or sugar, for example, until it has been dissolved in liquid.

Most tastes also involve smell. Experiments have tested the degree to which people can distinguish between taste and smell when one of the senses isn't working normally. It has been found that some people cannot distinguish between an onion and an apple if they cannot see or smell them. Thus taste, smell, and even sight are interrelated in eating. For example, something that has an unpleasant odor or appearance can spoil your appetite or desire to eat. Texture, which involves the sense of touch, is part of the total experience in eating such foods as pudding, a bagel, or peanut brittle. Even hearing can be a factor. The crunchy sound of celery or an apple or the sizzling sound of steak broiling can add interest to eating or spark our appetites. Temperature, too, can affect taste. Chocolate, for example, has more flavor when it is at room temperature than when it is very hot or very cold.

There are four basic tastes: sweet, sour, salty, and bitter. All others are said to be variations or combinations of these. The *taste buds* are groups of cells found in various areas of the tongue, mouth, and throat. Each taste has its particular area of the taste buds. Can you tell from your own experience where these are? What part of your mouth reacts, for instance, when you taste something sour? (The center of the tongue has little or no sensitivity to taste.) Because our tastes differ greatly, it is more reasonable and accurate for you to say that you don't like something than to say that it isn't any good. Other people may like the things you don't like. Thus, your taste is one more expression of your individuality.

SMELL

The sense of smell is more accurately called the **olfactory** sense. Like taste, smell is experienced only through chemical stimuli. Molecules of gas and vapors in the air enter the nasal passage, where moisture dissolves them. The olfactory nerve cells thus are activated, enabling us to experience smell.

Scientists have discovered that it is primarily the shape of molecules in the air that causes odor. Although it is difficult to classify basic odors, some common ones include camphoric, musty, floral, minty, ethereal, putrid, and pungent. Vapors and gases in the air can travel long distances, and you can be aware of odors originating many miles away. Odors are more noticeable at some times than at others, depending on atmospheric conditions. Many factories emit odors that are recognizable to nearby residents.

Have you ever walked into a room that had a strong odor and found that after a while you didn't notice the odor so much? This type of sensory adaptation is called **olfactory fatigue.** Although all the senses adapt to continued stimulation of a particular type, the sense of smell is especially adaptive. This can be dangerous! You may be inside a building where there is such a gradual increase in the smell of smoke or gas that you don't notice it immediately. If you do not check out a threatening smell before you become accustomed to it, you may forget it and suffer serious harm.

What is your EXPERIENCE? What part does smell play in your enjoyment of certain foods? Can you always distinguish smell from taste?

OTHER SENSES

What senses do we have besides the *exterior senses*—sight, hearing, touch, taste, and smell—that receive stimulation from the environment? We also have *interior senses* that involve body needs and sensations such as hunger, thirst, fatigue, and pain. In addition, we have a sense of movement called *kinesthesis,* with receptors in the muscles and joints. A sense of *rhythm* belongs to this type. We have a sense of balance, or *equilibrium,* which is controlled by the inner ear. And we have a sense of *nearness,* particularly important to sightless people, who sense that they are approaching obstacles. (This awareness is the result of changes in vibrations and air pressure caused by people or objects nearby.) Some of us have a better sense of *direction* than others. We also have a sense of *depth,* an awareness of deepness or distance, which has been shown to be present even in infants.

Our sense of *time* is associated with cues such as daylight and hunger. We can become so interested in what we are doing that we ignore the usual reminders, however, and lose all sense of time. An 8-year-old boy playing baseball after school does not have the same sense of time as the parent who is preparing the evening meal. And who can explain the inner alarm that wakes some people just before the alarm clock goes off, even when it is set for an unusual hour?

FACTORS THAT AFFECT PERCEPTION

What you perceive and how you interpret the sensations your senses receive are affected by a number of factors in your personal world. Especially important are physical disabilities and environmental conditions. Such factors as your past experiences and your level of attention also influence your perception.

Physical Abilities or Limitations

The abilities or limitations of the sense organs can affect perception temporarily or permanently. What you perceive through any of the senses depends first of all on what you are capable of perceiving. Some examples of physical limitations follow.

The diver is acutely aware of a sense of movement (kinestheses) as well as rhythm and equilibrium.

Impaired Hearing   You may hear inaccurately or may fail to hear something that is said because you have permanent hearing damage or impairment. Some problems can be reduced with a hearing aid, however. Others may be temporary, such as a wax buildup that temporarily interferes with one's hearing.

Color Blindness   It is difficult for you to know whether you are perceiving the world around you in the same way that others are. Many people go through life without realizing that they are colorblind, for example. Others discover during testing for a driver's license or military service that they are unable to distinguish between colors as most other people can. Color blindness is just one example of a visual problem with perception. Those who wear glasses are attempting to improve their perception of the world.

Illness or Cold   A temporary change in physical condition can affect all the senses. Your eyes may become more sensitive to light; your sense of hearing, taste, or smell may be dulled because of a cold; your body may feel unusually hot or cold when you have the flu. You may even be more sensitive to pressure and other sensations because of ill health.

Numbness from Cold Temperatures   When your blood does not circulate properly, your sense of touch or feeling is temporarily affected. If you live in a climate where the temperature falls below zero, you are familiar with the numbness of your hands and feet that results from being exposed to cold temperatures. You may temporarily lose feeling in your fingers and toes.

Sensitivity to Stimuli   Some people are more sensitive to tones than others are. Perhaps you can hear high notes that others do not detect. Other people may be more irritated by certain types of noise than you would be. Some people are able to identify differences in the tastes of cheeses and wines much better than others. Still others are more sensitive to changes in temperature or pressure. Each of us has a range of sensitivity to stimuli, which can be an advantage or disadvantage depending on the circumstances and our purposes. It may be desirable for us to learn to appreciate eating cereal with less or no sugar, for example, but it may be a disadvantage not to be able to detect "something wrong" with food that may indicate contamination.

Environmental Conditions

Not only your sensory abilities but also environmental conditions affect your perception. It is usually the total effect of all environmental conditions, rather than a single stimulus, that affects perception. A few examples of such factors are briefly discussed here.

Lighting—Intensity and Color   Artificial lighting at night, of course, affects what you can see, but types of lighting have different effects. Color is also a factor in total sensory response. People have become much more conscious of this factor since color TV has become common. Or you may not like a certain food because you do not like the color of it. Other examples of light and dark differences and the effects of color were given earlier in this chapter.

Glare of Lights and the Sun   The glare of the lights of an oncoming car can be temporarily blinding and extremely hazardous. For this reason most people who drive are careful to dim their lights when meeting another vehicle at night. Another example of glare is the sun shining on a lake or on snow, causing discomfort unless you are wearing dark glasses.

Fog and Smoke and Storms   Environmental conditions can also be hazardous, especially at night when ordinary visibility is reduced. It can be a rather eerie feeling to be closed in by fog or smoke, which drastically limits your ability to see and therefore to function normally. Sandstorms, snowstorms, and blinding rain can also be treacherous, and caution warnings should be heeded. One's own judgment must also be a factor.

Distracting Noises   As mentioned in the discussion of the sense of hearing, a particular sound may be a distracting noise to you but not to someone else. Or the same sound may be disturbing or pleasing to you, depending upon how you interpret its meaning or what else you are attempting to do at the time. Even a favorite TV program can be disturbing, for example, if someone else is watching it when you are trying to study for a test or concentrate on a project. Other distracting noises can block out sound. For instance, you may not hear the doorbell or telephone if your stereo volume is high.

Setting or Background   An important factor in a photograph is the appearance of the main subject against the setting or background. What is not noticed at the time the picture was taken may become conspicuous later. Perhaps you have heard someone say, "Why didn't I close that closet door?" or "Why didn't I move that old wagon?" Other settings can improve the appearance of something or how it is perceived. For example, the backyard can either add to or detract from the appearance of a house. Background is also an important factor in advertising in attempts to make a product or service look desirable.

Past Experience

Your perception is also influenced greatly by your past experience. Recognizing an object can give meaning to something you have never seen before. And whether you immediately like or dislike something or someone can be closely related to your past experience. Although our earlier experiences can give us guidelines for reacting appropriately in new situations, they can also interfere with our evaluating a new situation objectively.

Recognition of the Familiar   Recognition of what is familiar is a factor affecting how you perceive and how you react to what you perceive. Although the idea is interesting, it could be extremely frustrating if we awoke to a new world every day. You know the way to school or work, what kind of a car your friend drives, and where to look for particular items in a store. When you meet a

"She's having problems somewhere on the outskirts of Cleveland."
Reprinted from *The Saturday Evening Post.*

particular animal or person, you may react appropriately with joy, fright, or unconcern. Because of recognition and interpretation of the familiar, much of the activity of our lives becomes simplified and routine and we can concentrate on what is immediately important to us.

Association of New Stimuli with the Familiar   If you had never seen or used an electric toaster, it isn't likely that you would recognize one. But knowing what a toaster is, you are likely to associate even the most modern models with your concept of this type of appliance. This kind of association also works in recognizing what is old because of some similarities to what is new. If you visited a museum and saw a toaster from the 1700s, you would probably recognize it as a device for toasting bread. We form opinions or expectations in new situations by this type of association with what is familiar. If we let a single characteristic form the basis for our reaction, however, this type of association can be harmful. We might assume that a particular person is honest, for example, because she has a resemblance to a person whom we trust but find out that she is dishonest in actual experience with the person.

Association with Established Likes and Dislikes   During your lifetime thus far, you have developed a number of likes and dislikes. You may like the color green and dislike purple without being able to explain why. In some cases, at least, such responses are associated with pleasant and unpleasant experiences. If you had to wear a purple jacket that you didn't like for two years, you might have developed a dislike for that color. Or you may meet a person for the first time and immediately like that person for no particular reason of which you are aware. In many such cases you may be making an unconscious association of this individual with someone else you have liked and admired.

Set: Needs and Wants

Certain perceptual experiences are influenced by what you expect, or are **set** to perceive. What you focus your sense on in the vast perceptual world is also determined by your particular needs and wants.

Expectations   You often see or perceive what you expect to perceive. If someone says to you, "Sit in this chair and just see if it isn't the most comfortable chair you have ever sat in," you anticipate a particular type of experience. You are more likely to feel relaxed than if you had not been told what to expect.

Immediate Needs and Wants   Another type of set perception pertains to your needs and wants. If you want a new car, you notice cars on the sale lots, on the highway, and in parking lots more than you ordinarily would. If you are thirsty, you may notice a drinking fountain in a park before you become aware of anything else. We have the ability to concentrate on what might satisfy an immediate need, ignoring much else that would ordinarily come to our attention.

Beliefs, Prejudices, and Values   When you meet someone, you may pay more attention to what that person is saying and perceive him or her as an acceptable person if you both are of the same religion or have similar values. On the other hand, prejudice may be aroused by another characteristic about which you are biased.

Attention Factors

A number of factors are known to gain and hold attention and are therefore used extensively in advertising and display. They can also be effectively used in talking to a group or in other situations when we desire the attention of others. These are change, repetition, intensity, contrast, and novelty.

Change   Lights that flash off and on, for example, capture our attention better than a light that remains on continuously. You will notice a change in the sound of an engine or a signal more than if it maintains the same sound you generally hear.

Repetition   The element of repetition is evident in many television commercials and other types of advertising. Key phrases and the name of the product are repeated a number of times to gain attention and make an impression. We respond to this type of exposure to sights and sounds more than most of us realize.

Intensity   The intensity factor is used in a number of types of perception. A sound that one might not pay attention to is made louder; a smell that might go unnoticed is made stronger. We may tolerate a certain degree of pain, but a sudden stabbing pain will usually cause a noticeable reaction.

Contrast   The factor of contrast is widely used in advertising and in window displays. Dark velvet is frequently used as a background for jewelry because the contrast makes the jewelry look brighter and more attractive.

Novelty   Novelty has always been an effective attention getter with curious human beings. There are always customers to hear, taste, and see the new and different. Promotion people in every business search constantly for ways to use this attention factor to their advantage.

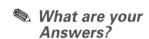 **What are your Answers?**

1. Divide 24 by 1/2 and add 16. What is your answer?_____

2. How many animals of each species did Moses have on the ark? _____

3. Take $7 away from $20. How many dollars do you have? _____

Answers are on page 91.

PRINCIPLES OF PERCEPTION

Perception was one of the earliest subjects in the study of human behavior. Wilhelm Wundt experimented with perception in the first psychological laboratory, established in 1879. Perception is still one of the most important and most interesting aspects of human behavior because we are using our senses in some way all of the time.

Our knowledge of how the senses and the nervous system operate and of the factors that affect perception can be combined into principles of perception, or basic rules about how perception functions. Although it is true that we as individuals hear, see, smell, taste, or feel the same things quite differently, there are some principles underlying what we perceive and why or how. Some of these were included in the discussion of the different senses, although they may not have been stated as such. In addition, six others are explained in the following sections.

Constancy

Constancy means that we tend to maintain established perceptual concepts and images. That is, we have a tendency to continue perceiving something in the same way even though it may have changed. Even though a particular food you eat frequently has been "improved" and changed slightly, you may not notice the difference. Your friend approaching you from a distance is the same size to you as always. You may not notice something different about your brother's appearance because you have a predetermined idea of what he looks like. It is not suggested that, because of the principle of constancy, we never notice changes in others or in our environment. We know from our own experience that we do. But you have probably also had the experience of not noticing a change that can be explained by the principle of constancy.

Figure-Ground

The principle of *figure-ground* is involved in much of our visual experience. Every time we are focusing on a particular thing, the rest of the surroundings becomes background. The wall is background for the clock that you may look

How many faces do you see?

From *Introduction to Psychology*, Fifth Edition, by Clifford T. Morgan and Richard A. King, Copyright © 1975 McGraw-Hill, p. 342.

at occasionally. If someone comments on the color of the wall, we may pay attention to the wall itself and ignore the clock. If you look at the figure opposite, you may recognize one or the other element of the figure-ground image but not both at the same time. We usually notice that which is most meaningful to us or that which looks familiar. The background may distort or emphasize certain figures. Figure-and-ground contrast is used for emphasis in advertising and display. Background may also distort certain features as well as emphasize them.

Totality (Gestalt)

Another principle is often referred to as either the *gestalt* or the totality principle. In fact, "gestalt" is a German word that means "unit" or "whole"—a number of stimuli are perceived as having a relationship to one another in making up a meaningful whole. You hear a melody rather than a series of individual notes. You see a painting rather than individual objects and colors. Parts of a machine are more meaningful if you can see where they belong in relation to other parts and the whole machine. This makes diagrams, blueprints, and maps more meaningful and helps us make more sense out of our work experiences and other activities.

 What would you SAY? If someone should ask you, "How can the whole be more than the sum of the parts," what would you say?

Camouflage

You are probably familiar with *camouflage* and some of its uses. This principle becomes very important when you are trying to protect yourself from an enemy. You try to blend in with your surroundings so as not to be noticed. This principle can also be helpful in making unsightly, but necessary, objects less conspicuous. Garbage cans can be camouflaged by painting them the same color as the building they are near. As you may have concluded, camouflage is essentially the opposite of figure-ground.

Closure

Closure is the tendency to complete or close the gaps in what is perceived. What you are accustomed to perceiving or expect or want to perceive may be a determining factor here. We might be surprised if we knew how often we actually believe we heard people say what we wanted them to say rather than what they did say! Rumors are also examples of how closure operates in what one hears. Some people (not *us*, of course) may hear part of a statement or conversation and complete it in their minds quite differently from the way it is actually expressed. If this inaccurate version is passed along from one person to another, it becomes even more distorted.

Closure can also involve what one sees. Three persons describing an athletic event may give conflicting accounts of what happened. Yet each person describing the event may be sure of what he or she saw. People not only see what they want to see or expect to see, but they jump to conclusions using partial or inaccurate evidence.

Conditioning

Becoming accustomed to an experience is also involved with perception and judgment. You sense the speed you are traveling or estimate the weight of a package because of previous similar experiences. You know where the church chimes are coming from partially because you know where they are supposed to be coming from.

An advantage of *conditioning* is that we can get accustomed to environmental conditions that otherwise might be disturbing to us. People can become acclimated to hot or cold weather, for example. Others get used to working in a very noisy situation. It should be kept in mind, however, that becoming accustomed to something does not mean that it may not be harmful. Even though some persons may become conditioned to working in a noisy environment, it can still be harmful to their hearing, for example.

ILLUSIONS

Some of the foregoing factors and principles are involved in illusions. An **illusion** is a misinterpretation of the stimuli your senses are receiving. Since illusions are deceiving, they are often deliberately used to create desired effects. People can try to make themselves appear slimmer by wearing vertical lines. Decorators make rooms look larger with color, wallpaper, design, and furniture arrangement. Makeup and hairstyles can be used to accent a person's best physical features and minimize weak points. It is interesting to try to figure out why your senses are deceiving you. It is important to keep illusions in mind when you are making major purchases, to guard against being deceived.

You have also had experience with illusions involving motion. The "phi phenomenon" is what makes alternating lights in a sign appear to be a moving arrow, for example. By stroboscopic motion, a series of images on film appear as a movie. A further illusion is called induced movement. This explains the

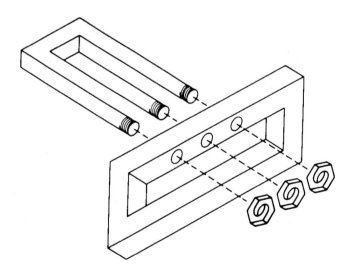

Try to find the source of the middle bar.

sensation you sometimes have of moving when you are sitting in a parked car and the car next to you starts to move.

PARA-PSYCHOLOGY

Parapsychology deals with psychic phenomena or beyond normal experiences or happenings. **Extrasensory perception** (ESP) belongs to this realm of psychology. It is the ability to perceive objects or know about happenings without the normal use of the senses. Three types of extrasensory perception are described below.

Telepathy is defined as the ability to transmit ideas from one person to another without any usual means of communication. It is often referred to as "mind reading." Although one occasionally may hear or read about reports of mind reading, it isn't likely that you have the skill or will meet anyone who has.

Clairvoyance is an awareness of objects or their location without the usual use of one's senses. People who are believed to have this ability have been contacted, on occasion, by law enforcement departments or families looking for missing persons. Their success has not been overwhelming; if it were, we would have fewer missing persons.

Precognition is an ability that modern-day prophets claim to have. It is the ability to know in advance that something is going to happen. Many predictions are made every year by people who are credited with having this kind of foresight. Such predictions are often made at the beginning of a new year. Some of these predictions come true, of course. There are differing opinions on whether some people have the ability to know accurately what will happen in the future.

Reprinted from *The Saturday Evening Post.*

Not a type of extrasensory perception but often included with the discussion of telepathy, clairvoyance, and precognition is **psychokinesis,** or mind over matter, because it is an out-of-the-ordinary experience. Some people claim to be able to control or move objects without the usual means of handling them. A person may attest to having the ability to close doors or move a tray of glasses across the room without touching them, for example.

ESP: Yes There Is; No There Isn't

The arguments over the reality of extrasensory perception will probably never be settled. First, an experience that is outside the realm of ordinary experience is very difficult to study and prove. Also, because much of what is claimed to be extrasensory is often deception or even fraud, any authentic example of ESP could be looked upon with skepticism. Still, there are those who are convinced that they or others have extrasensory perceptual abilities. The scientific approach, on the other hand, is that unless something can be proved, it cannot be accepted as truth or reality. The debate goes on.

SUMMARY

Perception consists of experiences of the senses, or sensation, and interpretation of these experiences by the individual. The functioning of the senses is highly complex, but a basic understanding can help you use your senses more effectively and avoid hazardous conditions.

There are three levels of awareness: the conscious, preconscious, and unconscious. Consciousness can also consist of altered states such as sleep, dreams, meditation, hypnosis, and mental states induced by drugs. The five exterior senses are sight, hearing, touch, taste, and smell. But there are also other senses referred to as interior senses. These include a sense of movement known as kinesthesis, and senses of rhythm, equilibrium, nearness, depth, direction, and time.

A number of factors can influence perception and make seemingly identical experiences quite different for individuals. These factors include physical abilities and limitations, environmental conditions, past experiences, needs and wants, and attention factors. Also, a number of principles of perception determine consistency in how human beings perceive. These principles are constancy, figure-ground, totality (or gestalt), camouflage, closure, and conditioning. Although it is quite natural to assume that others have the same sensory experiences and perceptual interpretations as you do, such is not the case.

The most controversial realm in the area of perception is parapsychology. There are those who claim that extrasensory perception (ESP) is a respectable science, those who aren't sure, and still others who discredit it completely.

How you perceive the world is related in some respects to emotions, the subject of Chapter 5.

Answers to Quiz Yourself on p. 77.
1. b
2. a
3. c

Answers to What Are Your Answers? on p. 85.

1. 64. You may have divided 24 by 2. But to divide by a fraction you invert it and multiply. That means you multiply 24 by 2, which gives you 48, and add 16, to get 64.
2. None. It was Noah's ark, not Moses'. This is an example of seeing what you expect to see.
3. You have the $7 you took. The question is, How many dollars do you have? not, How many dollars are left? The question is differently phrased than it usually is, hence the possible confusion.

Psychology In Practice

1. Identify ways in which principles of perception apply to your major area of study. (You may want to consult your major instructor about this.) Remember that perception involves all of the senses. Determine whether any of the principles contribute to possible hazards or problems.

2. Do your own investigation about extrasensory perception. Check library books and references, and interview several people about their beliefs on the subject. Try to keep an open mind until your investigation is completed. Then draw a conclusion and explain what influenced you to come to that conclusion.

3. Obtain more information about OSHA and find out how a particular industry protects its employees from noise and other perceptual hazards. Working in teams of two or three, design an ad for this industry—something to tell employees the company is looking out for them.

Learning Activities

Turn to page 393 to complete the Learning Activities and Enrichment Activities for this chapter.

Notes

1. Walter J. Freeman, "The Physiology of Perception," *Scientific American,* February 1991, p. 28.
2. Rita L. Atkinson, Richard C. Atkinson, Edward E. Smith, and Daryl J. Bem, *Introduction to Psychology,* 11th ed., Harcourt, Brace Jovanovich College Publishers, Fort Worth, 1993, p. 19.
3. Harold Cook and Joel Davitz, *60 Seconds to Mind Expansion,* Pocket Books, New York, 1976, p. 13.
4. June Leary, "How Color Can Influence Your Life," *Security Times,* Summer 1988, p. 42.
5. Clair Schoen, "Color—It Talks, "*House and Garden,* March 1979, p. 152.
6. Susan M. Menke, "Coping With Chronic Pain," *Consumers' Research,* July 6, 1985, p. 33.

5 Emotions

Learning Objectives

After completing this chapter, you will be able to do the following:

1. Identify examples of both pleasant and unpleasant emotions and suggest how a person might have more experiences involving pleasant emotions and fewer experiences involving unpleasant emotions.
2. Determine whether descriptions of the physiological effects of fear are correct or incorrect and revise each incorrect response to make it a correct response.
3. Propose methods by which particular fears of individuals might be lessened or overcome.
4. Identify characteristics of fear and anxiety, give an example of each, and explain why fear can be useful—whereas anxiety is not.
5. Give an example from your experience or observation that involved justifiable anger and explain what you believe would have been constructive reaction to the incident.
6. Describe a situation in which one person is jealous of another, explain what you believe to be the cause of the jealousy, and suggest how the jealous person might deal with or overcome this emotion.
7. Write definitions of types of love, according to Erich Fromm, and then explain why you agree, or disagree, with Fromm's classifications of love.

66 *To love is the greatest of human experiences and sooner or later we all realize that without it life is empty and meaningless. Love is always worth the effort, even if it brings confusion, uncertainty and pain in the process. A loving relationship should be a celebration all its own.* 99

LEO BUSCAGLIA,
educator and counselor

A robot would make a very uninteresting roommate, co-worker, marriage partner, or substitute for a person in any other human relationship. Although robots can even have computerized brains, they have no emotions, or feelings. Although a robot cannot become angry or jealous, neither can it appreciate you or show you affection.

An essential part of being human is having emotions. An **emotion** is a complex feeling that begins with some type of mental experience, such as a memory, imagination, an idea, a desire, or awareness of reality or a threat. This leads to physiological changes and possible changes in behavior. There is, thus, a complex relationship among emotional, physical, and mental behavior. No behavior is based only on one or another of these. Rather, behavior can be mainly physical (such as running), or mainly mental (such as working math problems), or mainly emotional (such as cheering at the hockey game). It is more accurate to say that emotion is a particular combination of mental and physical behavior than that it is a distinct type of behavior in itself.

An emotional response, then, begins in the mind and may result in fear, love, or any other emotion that affects our body functioning in some way. You may "get the chills," for example, when a friend tells you about a frightening experience. Or you may perspire when you are in a stressful situation, or your heart may beat more rapidly when you see someone you love.

Further insight into understanding emotion comes from Robert Zajonc, director of the Institute for Social Research. He explains,

> All emotional experiences involve a sudden and vigorous change in the nervous system; we are *always* in a state of emotion, and what we know of emotion is simply a change from one state to another. Some stimuli, such as strong sensory events, are intrinsically capable of evoking emotional reactions. But *any* stimulus can become emotional under particular circumstances: The harmless ticking of a clock is felt as a real threat if we believe it is connected to a bomb fuse.[1]

Our emotions play a role in most of our activities as human beings. The abilities to solve problems, to adjust to new situations in life, to develop relationships with others, and to maintain our well-being all involve the emotions or are affected by them.

Since emotions can be an underlying cause for behavior, they are closely related to motivation. Even our perceptions can be affected by emotions. Thus, a basic understanding of emotions is helpful in understanding other areas of our lives.

In some ways it is easy to discuss emotions because everyone has feelings—another term for emotional experience. Yet the attempt to understand emotions can be quite complex, because feelings may be deep-seated and may involve a combination of emotional responses. Emotions also may be difficult to understand because by nature they interfere with clear thinking. An underlying source of emotional experience may even be unconscious.

DEVELOPMENT OF EMOTIONS

How are emotions first experienced and expressed in a human being? Are emotions instinctive? Are all human beings born with certain emotional responses that are the same? It seems obvious that emotions are a part of human nature. All normal human beings seem to develop a wide variety of emotional responses, even though most emotions are not apparent at birth. Babies show only a kind of general response that later develops into specific emotional responses.

You may have heard it said that newborn infants have two fears: fear of falling and fear of loud noises. These are not real fears, however, as infants have no understanding of any possible danger. They do seem to be startled by noises or by a falling sensation. They show this by flinging out their arms. But such responses can more accurately be interpreted as a disturbance to the nervous system rather than fear. As will be discussed later in the chapter, fears are learned.

Newborn infants also display "emotional" reactions to discomfort caused by hunger, pain, or wet clothing. These first emotionlike responses are basically reactions to unpleasantness. During the first few months of life, infants learn to react to pleasant feelings by smiling, by making sounds, or by making body movements that indicate a sense of well-being or pleasure. In the first few years they learn more specific responses such as fear, joy, love, and possibly even jealousy.

The development of emotions varies somewhat with the individual and continues throughout life. We learn to express our emotions in specific ways that become somewhat automatic. For example, we usually react immediately and in a habitual way to something that frightens us. Such emotional habits begin to be formulated early in life and are carried over into how we react to friends, employers, and others. We learn to control our emotions, as well as personal ways of expressing them to some extent.

There is some evidence that a person can be born with a disposition to react intensely to frustration. Do you recall the reference to temperament in Chapter 2? Heredity should not be blamed for a bad temper, however. Thus, someone might say, "Zach inherited his father's terrible temper." The fact is that Zach has learned from his father to express frustration and anger in this way. As a result, expression of his emotions in relating to others becomes part of his personality.

CLASSIFICATIONS OF EMOTIONS

Emotions can be classified in various ways. Some psychologists use the two terms that describe emotions shortly after birth: unpleasant and pleasant. They would classify such emotions as fear, anger, jealousy, envy, guilt, and grief as being unpleasant; love, trust, peace, gratefulness, and enthusiasm would be classified as pleasant.

An emotion that is not a daily experience for most, but part of a full life is another emotion called joy. Letty Cottin Pogrebin describes such an experience as "an exquisite moment" in the form of a question, "Have you ever known one of those perfect moments of bliss when you felt happy, healthy, strong, well-loved and utterly at peace with the world?"[2]

Others subdivide pleasant emotions into lower and higher categories. "Lower pleasant" emotions are associated with basic physical needs such as eating, exercise, and sex. "Higher pleasant" emotions come from a sense of achievement, from a feeling of contributing to others, and from natural beauty and aesthetic experiences. The higher pleasant emotions involve greater mental reaction, understanding, and appreciation than the lower ones do. For example, people learn to appreciate various forms of art and classical music.

You may have read or heard that there are three basic emotions: love, fear, and anger. People who classify emotions in this way identify all other emotional responses as variations or degrees of these three.

Another psychologist, Nathan A. Fox, of the University of Maryland, refers to primary emotions as joy, interest, fear, disgust, anger, and sadness.[3] A third source, *Psychology: Principles and Applications,* by Stephen Worchel and Wayne Shebilske, identifies basic emotions as love, joy, (surprise), anger, sadness, and fear.[4] These are subdivided into dozens of more specific emotional experiences. We can conclude that emotional experiences are difficult to describe and to classify.

Most methods of classifying emotions are too simple. Many experiences are a combination of pleasant and unpleasant experiences. A person who is leaving her present job for a promotion may say, "I have mixed emotions about leaving. I am excited about the new career challenge, but I will miss daily contact with the people I have worked with." You may have had the same kind of feelings at some turning point in your life. Agreeing about how to classify emotions is not as important as understanding how our emotions affect our lives and the lives of others.

Other feelings that we can experience besides the ones already mentioned are annoyance, shame, bitterness, tenderness, loneliness, courage, and resentment. There are probably hundreds more. It is natural for human beings to have a wide range of feelings about themselves, others, and various aspects of their lives.

PHYSIOLOGICAL EFFECTS OF EMOTION

What happens to your body functioning when you are emotional? What changes in your physical being are you aware of when you are angry? How would you describe your total experience when you are thrilled about something that has happened to you? What physical sensations do you have after an intense emotional experience?

Actually, anger and fear affect your body in much the same way—by preparing you for "fight or flight." The pupils of your eyes dilate or enlarge, your heart beats faster, your blood pressure rises, your breathing speeds up, hormones are released into your bloodstream, your mouth becomes dry, and your hands perspire. These are typical physical effects of either anger or fear. Since your brain is not receiving its normal supply of oxygen, it, too, is affected. You may not be able to think as clearly and quickly as usual. In fact, people can become so irrational during violent anger that they do things they never would do under normal circumstances.

When the emotional reaction is anger, people are more likely to fight—either physically or verbally—than they usually would be. And because of the muscle tension and energy-giving hormones that accompany anger, a person is able to strike with more force than usual. If the emotional reaction is one of fear, people are prepared for escape or self-defense. People really can run faster when they are scared. They also have more strength in an emergency. You may have read about people who performed "impossible" feats to save themselves or others. One mother was able to lift an automobile off her child, who was pinned under a wheel. The hormones released in her system gave her the strength she needed in the emergency. After an intense emotional experience, one may feel weak. The muscles and limbs may feel limp before the body returns to normal.

Emotional Experience

Mental Experience	Physiological Change	Change in Behavior
▪ Memory ▪ Idea ▪ Desire ▪ Awareness of Reality ▪ Threat ▪ Imagination	▪ Eyes dilate ▪ Heart beats faster ▪ Blood pressure rises ▪ Breathing speeds up ▪ Hormones are released ▪ Mouth becomes dry ▪ Hands perspire	▪ Determined by the emotions and the individual

All emotions affect our body functioning and sensations in some way. Joy gives sensations of lightness or exhilaration, whereas grief gives sensations of dullness and heaviness. Although an emotional experience begins with a mental experience, even a mistaken idea, there is a physiological involvement in one's reaction.

The polygraph, or lie detector, measures the physiological effects of emotion. It should be noted, however, that one cannot be required to take a lie detector test and that the results usually are not considered to be reliable enough to be accepted as evidence in court. In fact, many who have studied the polygraph and its use (and misuse) warn us against its weaknesses. It can only record how you are reacting to the experience; it does not know whether you are lying. Leonard Saxe, a professor of psychology involved in a 1983 study of polygraph validity, reported that we cannot rely on it to detect lying. According to a 1986 report in *Discover,* "The polygraph doesn't detect lies; it merely records such telltale signs of anxiety as increased pulse, breathing rate, and perspiration. You might be lying, or thinking of family problems, or just faking."[5]

Because of limitations of the polygraph and some misuse, Congress passed the Employee Polygraph Protection Act in 1988. The law makes it illegal to use the polygraph to screen job applicants or investigate employees, with some exceptions.

Nation's Business offers the basic elements of the law as:

The Employee Polygraph Protection Act prohibits the use of polygraphs for pre-employment screening by most private-sector employers. (Exempted are security-service firms and pharmaceutical manufacturers, distributers, and dispensers.)

The act permits limited testing of employees as part of workplace investigations, but only under strict regulations.

In addition to indicating sadness, one's eyes can reflect excitement, arousal, and even boredom.

No employer can legally screen employees randomly or periodically.

The act specifically outlaws employers' use of polygraphs, deceptographs, voice-stress analyzers, psychological-stress evaluators, and other devices used to judge a person's honesty.[6]

 What would you DO?   If you were asked to take a polygraph test, what would you do?

You are probably aware that the appearance of one's eyes changes with emotional state. When a person is excited or intensely aroused, the pupils widen. When someone is experiencing something negative or dull, the pupils get smaller. This information may be interesting or somewhat useful. But we must always be cautious in using a single factor as a basis for judging the complex reaction of another human being. Tears, for example, can indicate grief, joy, or even that one has been peeling onions.

The eyes can express our feelings in other ways also. Actors, for example, can make their eyes sparkle by thinking of an exciting experience, or they can make their eyes look sad by thinking somber thoughts. Arousal of their emotions produces biochemical changes that are reflected in their eyes.

FEAR   Everyone has experienced the sensation of fear. It is normal, and even sensible, to have fears. Since fear is an unpleasant emotion, you might conclude that people would be better off without it. However, you should recognize that there are very real dangers in the environment, and you are wise to fear them. By recognizing hazards and the threats they pose, you can avoid them and protect yourself.

What would you SAY? If a friend of yours commented that she had never had any fears, what would you say?

Fear or Anxiety?

Fear can be exaggerated and can cause needless discomfort and ineffectiveness. But fear also can be realistic and can be directed toward protecting ourselves. A limited amount of tension that produces anxiety or apprehension can help us to perform at our best. On the other hand, anxiety can become a destructive habit. It can interfere with the ability to react realistically and effectively to a situation.

Anxiety will be discussed further, along with stress, in Chapter 8, "Coping with Stress." However, it will be helpful to compare fear and anxiety at this point in our study. Note the following differences:

Fear	Anxiety
Reaction to a specific, known, immediate threat	Prolonged concern about a vague, potential type of threat
Intense physiological reaction in preparation for fight or flight	Moderate but continuous physiological disturbance

Childhood Fears

You may no longer fear something you were afraid of when you were a small child. Children perceive their environment differently from adults. They therefore have fears that they will outgrow when they see things differently later in life. For example, small children may be afraid of a dog that is much bigger than they are. Children may also be afraid of thunder and other things they do not understand. They need a sense of security and therefore may fear being alone. Since it is common for human beings to fear the unknown, and since there are more unknowns in a child's experience, children are likely to have more fears than adults.

Some fears result from associations known as **conditioning.** A person becomes afraid of something that is associated with an original fear. A child who has to climb some stairs to the residence of someone who abuses him while his parents are away may become frightened of climbing any stairs by the combination of those experiences. Childhood fears that have resulted from such conditioning can be very difficult to dispel because it is not always known what the original fear stimulus was. Often adults have fears they do not really understand. Some such fears are the result of conditioning; the associations made earlier in life are no longer remembered.

Later Fears and Anxieties

Another time of life that presents a whole new set of fears is adolescence, or the teen years. During this time, tremendous physical and psychological

"You gotta' admit, Bernice, your fear of flying makes it darned hard to get to Capistrano every year."

Reprinted from *The Saturday Evening Post*.

changes make an adolescent feel insecure. Individuals are more self-conscious during the teen years than at any other age. They, therefore, may have fears about their abilities and the impressions they make.

As adolescents enter young adulthood, they also are likely to experience a sense of insecurity, this time as a result of the independence they desire. Along with independence comes anxiety about career success and a future life-style. These experiences will be discussed further in Chapter 11, "Life-Span Development."

Adults are likely to have both fears and anxieties but should be able to recognize them for what they are. Adults generally are better able to deal with their particular fears or anxieties. Some do, however, develop anxiety disorders, which will be discussed in Chapter 8, "Coping with Stress."

Controlling and Using Fears

It has been mentioned that many childhood fears are simply outgrown. Others can be overcome with the help and understanding of parents or other adults. A child who has learned to fear dogs, for example, can unlearn that same fear by a series of nonthreatening, pleasant experiences with a puppy or grown dog.

When people recognize what they are afraid of, they can take steps to protect themselves. For example, someone afraid of automobile accidents can take steps to reduce the threat of accidents. Someone else, perhaps fearful of the injury to children from idle machinery, can remove from reach some of the dangerous equipment. People can also remove themselves from danger. A person in a hazardous job who recognizes his or her fear can control that fear by seeking a less dangerous job.

Some people who have performed acts of courage readily admit that they were afraid but—in spite of their fear—performed the dangerous acts because they felt they had to. Still other types of courage involve constant risks, such as exposure to possibly harmful elements in research or the hazards that are inevitable in law enforcement. People choose to take such risks for personal reasons or because of dedication to a cause.

The eruption of Mount Pinatubo in the Philippines created a fearful natural disaster. In one of the century's most major volcanic explosions, two cubic miles of superheated ash were pumped into the atmosphere.

Here are some suggestions about how to deal with or overcome fears:

- Admit that you have fears.
- Do not be ashamed of or apologize for your fears.
- Understand your fears as specifically as possible. Try to identify exactly what it is that frightens you.
- Realize that fears can help you protect yourself from real dangers.
- Remember that the actual threat in a fearful situation is often exaggerated.
- The more competent you become in taking care of yourself, the fewer threats you will face and the fewer fears you will have.

"Do the thing you fear" is recommended for those who are afraid to resume a particular kind of activity because of a recent accident. The longer a person waits to go back to normal activity after an accident, the greater the chance that the fear will magnify and that future behavior will be affected. It is important to remember, though, that a person should never be forced to do what he or she fears. Forcing is likely to deepen the fear and make the problem even worse.

Phobias

Practically everyone has at least one abnormal, illogical fear. Such fears, which are out of proportion to any actual threat, are called **phobias.** These can range from relatively mild, but disturbing, fears to severe phobic anxiety. This term comes from the Greek word *phobos,* meaning "fear." *Hemo* is from the Latin word for blood, for example, so "hemophobia" is a fear of blood.

According to Edna B. Foa, a clinical psychologist, "The most frequent phobia—an intense, almost paralyzing fear— is "agoraphobia," from the Greek word *agora.* It literally means fear of the marketplace. But agoraphobics are not afraid of crowded or open places per se. Rather, they fear their own anxiety, so that every place that can cause them anxiety tends to be avoided."[7]

📝 *Quiz Yourself on Phobias*

See whether you can determine which abnormal fear each of the following phobias refers to. Write the letter of the definition next to the phobia it describes.

E 1. Androphobia
D 2. Claustrophobia
G 3. Hydrophobia
a 4. Acrophobia
H 5. Gynephobia
C 6. Phobophobia
f 7. Thanatophobia
B 8. Pyrophobia

a. Fear of height
b. Fear of fire
c. Fear of being afraid
d. Fear of closed spaces
e. Fear of men
f. Fear of death
g. Fear of water
h. Fear of women

Answers are given on page 110.

Treatment of Phobias

The basic idea underlying most treatment for phobias is to gradually expose the person to the anxiety-causing situation until the person begins to feel more

"Aha! Here it is—arachibutyrophobia: The fear of peanut butter sticking to the roof of the mouth."

Reprinted from *The Saturday Evening Post.*

comfortable. It is also important in such therapy that the individual with the phobia willingly consent to the treatment; otherwise anxiety may be increased, rather than decreased. The length of time that one is involved in the anxiety-producing experience can gradually become increased. A person with agoraphobia, for example, may sit in one's own yard with a friend watching other people go by; on another day she may take a short walk down the block with someone she feels comfortable with; at a later time, she may go all around the block; she can gradually go to familiar places close to home with someone else until she begins to feel comfortable enough to go away from home alone. Overcoming a phobia is not simple, but it is important to realize that most phobias can be overcome with the desire and time to do so. Some individuals can even overcome phobias on their own. Their feeling that they are in control helps reduce anxiety for them.

What do you THINK?   Do you think anyone reacts to danger without fear? Can you give examples to support your answer?

ANGER

How do you feel when you are angry? What do you do? Anger and the ways of expressing anger—like other emotional responses—are learned. Children who have temper tantrums, for example, have learned that such behavior gets them what they want. If the behavior continues to be effective, they will learn to utilize temper displays as adults.

What Makes People Angry?

Anger is a feeling of frustration that results from a situation that is not the way we think it should be or that we believe is wrong or unfair. Some people become angry most often with other people. Others are more likely to be angered by machines that don't work right or by things they can't find. It has also been shown that people are more likely to become angry when they are tired or hungry or when they are upset for some other reason. You may have found this to be true from your own experience. We sometimes refer to a person we expect to be easily angered at a particular time as "irritable."

Feelings of anger, at times, are to be expected in people who are seriously involved in their work and who care about what is happening. Anger, like fear, can be a justifiable and even a desirable emotional response. If nothing ever bothered people enough to make them frustrated or emotionally upset, much less would be accomplished in our schools, businesses, and communities. However, we should attempt to make our anger constructive.

Controlling and Using Anger

Anger can be suppressed, displaced, and destructive, or expressed openly, directly, and constructively. Anger is ordinarily thought of as a negative, unpleasant emotion, and it can be a very destructive force. Many people feel frustrated today because they believe problems in society are out of control. They are angry and are expressing these feelings in destructive ways. Anger, for whatever reason, is often suppressed or held in by persons who either feel it is wrong to be angry or are afraid of the consequences of expressing their anger. In other instances it is expressed in an inappropriate direction or displaced. If people did not make some attempt to control their anger, there would be much more violence in the world than we now have. But since there are increasing amounts of violence and aggression, it seems that many people are not trying to understand and control their anger—or, at least, are not being very successful in their attempts.

People who are frequently (some even constantly) frustrated and hostile are also endangering their own well-being. An article entitled, "Can Your Mind Heal Your Body?" has the following to say about chronic anger or hostility and one's physical well-being.

> Hostile people have frequent bouts of anger that put them in a near-constant state of stress. For example, they may pound on the door when the elevator is slow in coming and lash out when things go even slightly wrong. In hostile people, too, the body appears to respond to stress with an exaggerated increase in hormones that can raise blood pressure and accelerate other physiological processes that can damage the heart. There's also some evidence that hostile people often smoke and drink too much.[8]

Controlling anger, or any other emotion, can be carried to extremes, however. A person may become so filled with emotion that illness or an outburst of irrational behavior results. To avoid this, we can exercise some control in how we reach to whatever could cause us to become angry. Many of us would admit that we are more disturbed by trivial inconveniences than we should be.

Following are a few suggestions about how to react to frustration and use anger for constructive purposes:

- Learn to understand yourself and what bothers you to the point where you become angry about it. Then find out what you can do about it—and do it. Learn to solve problems. Chapter 6, "Attitudes" and Chapter 7, "Thinking and Problem Solving," will help you improve your ability to do this.
- Calm down after you have become angry. Give your body a chance to return to its normal condition. Then exercise to relax tense muscles. Instead of slamming doors and breaking things, take a walk, do some manual work, or engage in other physical activity. In the past, chopping wood and scrubbing clothes on a washboard were good ways to work off emotional tension. Automatic machines now perform much of the manual labor of the past, and that is one reason why people today are more tense. To provide more opportunity to vent anger with physical work, one family keeps a hammer in the garage near a box of cans for recycling. Whenever a member of the family becomes angry, he or she goes out into the garage and smashes some cans. This activity accomplishes two things: the anger is released, and the cans are ready to go at collection time.
- Concentrate on something else. Occupy your mind with something that demands your attention. Do something that gives you pleasure or satisfaction. Substitute a pleasant emotion for the unpleasant emotion. A hobby or special interest can be of value at emotional times. Hobbies require action and give a person a sense of satisfaction.

Aggression

Aggression is usually thought of as behavior that is intended to hurt someone or to violate the rights of others for one's own advantage. Although aggression is generally recognized as a major problem in human behavior, there is not complete agreement about the cause of aggression. Some say it is inherited; others say it is learned and is influenced by the environment. Still others say that aggressive behavior or the lack of it is caused by biochemistry and that it can be influenced significantly by drugs or even by diet.

There is also evidence that violence and aggression on television promote similar behavior in children and immature adults who are given to imitating others. Immature people have difficulty distinguishing between what is fantasy and what is real. Parents, television producers, and educators are working to reduce the harmful effects of television on young and immature viewers.

Ashley Montagu, an international authority on growth and development, says that aggression is not instinctive. Instead, he says, "to some extent behavior is always the expression of the interaction between genetic tendencies and environmental influences."[9]

In speaking about aggressive behavior of young people classified as juvenile delinquents, Montagu maintains:

> The juvenile delinquent is the product of a delinquent society, in which parents, teachers and the community have forgotten, if they have ever known, what it is to be human and what the needs of a growing human being are, the need, especially, for love. No child who was ever adequately loved ever became a delinquent or a murderer. Aggressive behavior is frequently the response to the frustration of the need for love, as well as a compelling attention to that need.[10]

Aggression seems to be caused by frustration and results in an individual's striking out at others in an attempt to release this frustration. Victims of the aggressive behavior may not be the cause of the frustration, however. Sometimes the cause of the aggression is within an individual. He or she may have a desire for power and control, which often results from an underlying feeling of insecurity.

LOVE

Every human being wants love. People would be happier and the world would be more peaceful if a definition of love were not necessary—if everyone knew from experience what love is. Probably all of us are aware, however, that there are different kinds of love. You will recall the importance of a positive, realistic self-concept, or self-love, discussed in Chapter 2. This is the basis for the other kinds of love. People who do not feel good about themselves have difficulty establishing loving relationships with other people.

Erich Fromm, in his book *The Art of Loving,* discusses different types of love and their relationship to one another. The types of love he identifies are brotherly love, motherly love, erotic love, self-love, and love of God.[11] Brotherly love might be interpreted as respect for and acceptance of other human beings in general as having worth; the concept of motherly love could be expanded to mean parental love, including "fatherly love," and even love for other members of one's family; erotic love is more commonly spoken of as romantic love, usu-

A young couple share an affectionate hug on a busy city street.

ally what is meant when a person says, "I am in love"; self-love primarily refers to a realistic, favorable self-concept; and love of God could include whatever an individual's belief would be about a Supreme Being or a higher universal power.

Another book entitled *Why Am I Afraid to Love?* by John Powell, gives us his thoughts on the meaning of love, some of which are as follows:

Whatever else can and should be said of love, it is quite evident that true love demands self-forgetfulness. If there are many people who use the word and claim the reality without knowing the meaning of the word or being able to love to any great extent, this is the test: Can we really forget ourselves? There are many counterfeit products on the market which are called love, but which in fact are falsely named. We can sometimes label the gratification of our needs "love"; we can even do things for others without really loving. The acid test is always the probing question of self-forgetfulness.

Can we really locate the focus of our minds on the happiness and fulfillment of others? Can we really ask not what others will do for us, but only what we can do for them? If we really want to love, then we must ask ourselves these questions.

We must become aware that we are capable of using people for our own advantage, for the satisfaction of our deep and throbbing human needs, and be deluded into thinking that this is really love. The young man who professes to love a young woman may often be deceived in thinking that the gratification of his own egotistical urges really constitutes love. The young woman who finds the voids of her own loneliness filled by the companionship and attention of a young man may well mistake this emotional satisfaction for love. Likewise, the mother and father who anxiously try to promote the success of their children can easily rationalize their desire for the vicarious experiences of success and convince themselves that they are loving parents. The critical question always remains that of self-forgetfulness. Does the young man or woman, the mother or father really forget himself and his convenience and emotional satisfaction to seek only the happiness and fulfillment of the beloved? These are not merely theoretical questions. The fact of the matter is that for most of us, our own needs are so palpable and real to us that it is enormously difficult for the seed to fall into the ground and die to itself before it can live a life of love.[12]

Love is caring about another human being's happiness as much or more than about one's own. Love can give meaning and purpose to one's life, regardless of whether the love is returned. It is like saying, "I cannot be happy unless you are happy first." Love is unconditional; we do not say, "I'll love you if . . . ." We love another person for himself or herself, not for what is done to us or for us.

HATE

Probably the most negative emotion of all is hate. It is the opposite of love, yet has characteristics in common with love. To **love** means to care deeply for a person and to wish that person every good. To **hate** means to dislike a person intensely and to wish that person harm. Both emotions require a deep involvement with another person. In fact, there are times when people feel as though they hate someone they love. However, this could be described more accurately as resentment for being hurt.

Hatred does not seem to have any useful purpose. In fact, it can have harmful effects—even on the person who hates. The time and energy spent hating someone could be used for a constructive purpose. And hatred can be damaging to a person's overall well-being. A person may rightly be disgusted or angry with the behavior of someone else, but it is always difficult to justify the desire to harm another.

OTHER EMOTIONS

People can experience a wide variety of emotions besides the ones already discussed. Some other emotions that deserve our attention are envy, jealousy, guilt, and grief.

Envy

Envy is wishing that you could have what someone else has or be what someone else is. People who are envious experience displeasure at the success, happiness, or achievement of another. They may avoid doing anything that would help those they envy—even if they also ultimately harm themselves. Without doubt, envy can be considered a negative emotion. It usually does the envious person as much harm as it does the person envied. As discussed in Chapter 2, "Self-Concept and Personality," people who have a favorable self-concept are more concerned with their own self-development than with a useless feeling such as envying someone else.

Jealousy

An emotion with some of the same characteristics of envy is jealousy. The basic difference between the two is that the jealous person already has what is desired but is afraid of losing it. Jealousy, then, results mainly from feelings of insecurity. A person who is afraid of losing the love of another person may even act in such a negative, suspicious way that he or she causes the very loss that is feared.

It is not a good feeling to be jealous; neither is it good to feel that someone else is needlessly disturbed about what we say or do.

✎ *Quiz Yourself on Jealousy*

1. Do I feel as if our relationship is threatened if my best friend tells me (he or she) is going to a social event with someone else? _Some times_

2. Do I feel as if our relationship is threatened if my (boy friend, girl friend, or spouse) tells me about an interesting person (of my own sex and age) whom (he or she) met recently? _YES_

3. Do I feel as if our relationship is threatened if my (boy friend, girl friend, or spouse) compliments someone on (his or her) appearance or achievement? _NO_

4. Do I become suspicious and feel threatened if I don't know where my (friend, girl friend, or boy friend) is or what (he or she) is doing most of the time? _YES_

5. Do I have a tendency to give my (boy friend or girl friend) "the third degree" about where (he or she) has been or what (he or she) has been doing if I have been out of town for a few days? _NO_

6. Do I feel unloved and uncertain of our relationship if my (boy friend, girl friend, or spouse) does not tell me frequently that (he or she) loves me? _NO_

7. Do I insist on knowing what my (girl friend, boy friend, or spouse) has been talking about if I see (her or him) talking to a person of the opposite sex? _YES_

Yes answers to more than one of the above questions are an indication that you should work on eliminating feelings of jealousy.

How does one work on excessive feelings of jealousy? Even though jealousy is considered a negative emotion, it is natural and understandable to a degree. There is a difference, also, between being interested in what another person is doing and investigating for our own sense of security. Since jealousy is anxiety about a relationship, the following suggestions could be helpful.

- Work on developing a more positive self-concept. This is easier said than done, but all of us have personal worth and deserve to feel good about ourselves.
- Do not allow any one individual to become the only important person in your life. You can be involved in a number of types of activities and meet many interesting people.

- Remember that there are different kinds of love. There is a difference between platonic love (friendship with a person of the opposite sex) and romantic love. It is also true, however, that friendship can grow into romantic love.
- Realize that a meaningful, lasting relationship must be based on trust. A general feeling of mistrust toward others may indicate a lack of confidence in oneself. It may also be related to disappointing experiences we have had with others that have no connection with our present relationship.
- If possible, get to know the person or persons about whom you are jealous. You will gain a better understanding of the situation and may also find them to be friendly and interesting.
- Don't feel sorry for yourself or look for sympathy. This can be more damaging than supportive to a relationship. Become a more interesting person.
- Talk about your feelings instead of pouting or making accusations and threats. One could say, "I felt really uncomfortable when you seemed to ignore me while you were talking to Jeff after class."

Jealousy in work relationships can also be self-destructive. It interferes with a person's self-confidence and productivity, and it can cause disharmony in the work environment.

 What would you SUGGEST? If someone you know quite well and like, talks as if he's jealous of his friend and asks for your opinion, what would you suggest?

Guilt

Guilt is an emotion that is directed toward oneself rather than toward others. In a sense, we are all guilty. Each one of us has made mistakes and may even have done something on purpose that we shouldn't have done. Or we may not have done some things we should have done. It is usually of value—for oneself and others—to admit our wrongdoings and to attempt somehow to make up for them. But it can be useless, and even harmful, to exaggerate our wrongdoing and to live with constant feelings of guilt.

"Nobody knows how much suffering, and even tragedy, has been triggered by needless feelings of guilt, one of the commonest, yet most powerful, emotions that rule our lives," says Lester David in an article from *Family Health*.[13]

It can be even more intolerable for an individual to harm another person severely and to *lack* any feelings of guilt or remorse. It is an individual's responsibility to establish a realistic sense of rightness and wrongness and to know what guilt *is,* without being overshadowed by it. There is nothing more useless than trying to undo what has been done. We can, however, use our feelings of guilt to stimulate ourselves to correct our mistakes and to become better persons.

Grief

The emotion of grief is based on a keen sense of loss, usually associated with the death of a family member or other loved one. That type of loss is the most difficult emotional experience most people encounter. We also face difficult situations in somehow attempting to be supportive of others who are experiencing the loss of a loved one. Lois Duncan, whose daughter was killed in a random shooting when she was 18 years old, has used her experience to offer suggestions in "Helping Friends Who Grieve." She says, "It's better to do something klutzy than to do nothing—and the kindest words are often the simplest." She adds, "What helps is the little things . . . replenishing groceries, cashing checks, returning library books. Most of all, caring enough to help others bear the unbearable."[14]

In addition to grief associated with loss through death, other types of separation can also cause great emotional pain. Divorce, even when it is a preferred change, can cause grief for either or both partners. Even a baby weaned from the breast or bottle may experience a sense of loss. A high school athlete who graduates and no longer is part of the team, or a family that moves to another city, away from friends, may experience a sense of loss that can be classified as grief. Since these types of experiences require further understanding and adjustments, they will be discussed again in Chapter 8, "Coping with Stress."

EMOTIONS CAN ENRICH LIVING

Are most of our feelings negative or causes of displeasure? It would seem that way, from the amount of emphasis that has been put on anger, fear, envy, grief, and other such emotions. Although these emotions would fall into the unpleasant category, some of them—such as anger and fear—can also be useful. Appropriate reactions to these two emotions can contribute to a fuller, more enriched life.

We can also have feelings of contentment and peace. These feelings occur when we have no major frustrations and are comfortable with ourselves and our lives. We can at least occasionally experience joy, that total sense of well-being sometimes referred to as a "natural high," when an experience or situation is all we might hope it to be.

To enjoy life you should also understand your moods, or periodic shifts in how you feel. You know, for instance, that the way you feel affects the way time seems to pass. If you are depressed, time seems to pass very slowly. On the other hand, if you are enthusiastic about what you are doing, time seems to pass quickly. You can almost measure how much you are getting out of life by the pace at which hours, days, and years seem to pass. Whenever people, young or old, say that the days just fly by and they never get all the things done that they would like to do, it is likely that they are emotionally stable and able to solve their problems to their satisfaction.

There can be so much emphasis on controlling emotions and on what not to do with regard to unpleasant emotions that a person may be tempted to suppress all emotion and become a human robot. But life consists of laughter and tears, emotional ups and downs. We will not experience the satisfaction, and even joy, of achievement if we are not willing to take some risks. We would miss opportunities to improve our personal lives and situations in our workplaces and communities if some things did not frustrate, or anger, us enough to move us to constructive action. *The person for whom life is an exciting experience has learned how to make the joys of living far outweigh the disappointments.*

What do you THINK? Do you think there might be times when it would be best not to express how you really feel? If so, what would be your reason?

SUMMARY

Emotions make the difference—between human beings and machines and between living and merely existing. Emotional behavior is not a separate type of behavior. It is a particular combination of mental and physical behavior. Basic emotions have been classified as love, fear, and anger. The many variations of these emotions are classified as pleasant or unpleasant. However, there are many different types of emotions, including envy, jealousy, guilt, grief, and joy.

The physical effects of emotions are evident in fear and anger. For example, the pupils of the eyes enlarge, the heart beats faster, blood pressure rises, breathing speeds up, hormones are released into the bloodstream, digestion slows down or stops, muscles become tense, the mouth becomes dry, and the hands perspire. These physical effects, causing a decrease in oxygen to the brain, can result in irrational behavior.

Fears are learned and therefore can be unlearned or overcome. Many childhood fears result from a lack of understanding or from conditioning. These can be eased as time passes. Fears carried over into later life, however, can be more difficult to cope with. Fears that are out of proportion to the actual threat involved are known as phobias. Understanding the basis of fears and phobias is the first step to overcoming them.

Everyone experiences a degree of anger, at least occasionally. Anger can be harmful to oneself and to others, but it also can motivate and lead to constructive behavior.

There are many definitions of love—one of the basic and most interesting of the emotions—and many types. Erich Fromm refers to brotherly love, motherly love, erotic love, self-love, and love of God. Unconditional love is the most unselfish type of love because it does not involve "ifs."

Now that we have studied the emotions, we will consider how our feelings are involved in attitudes, the subject of Chapter 6.

Answers to Quiz Yourself

1. e	**3.** g	**5.** h	**7.** f
2. d	**4.** a	**6.** c	**8.** b

 Psychology In Practice

1. Read an article or a book about a particular emotion and how it affects one's life. Develop several personal guidelines for enriching your life through emotional experiences

2. Over a three-day period, keep track of evidence of pleasant and unpleasant emotions you observe in others. Note how people express these emotions and how others react to them. Plan a role-play with another student to present to the class.

3. Find out more about the polygraph and the voice-stress analyzer. Determine whether you believe these are appropriate instruments for drawing conclusions about whether individuals are telling the truth. Be able to offer reasons for your belief.

Learning Activities Turn to page 397 to complete the Learning Activities and Enrichment Activities for this chapter.

Notes
1. Robert Zajonc, "The Face As Window and Machine for the Emotions," *LSA Magazine,* University of Michigan, Fall 1990, p. 17.
2. Letty Cottin Pogrebin, "Is Fear Holding You Back?" *Family Circle,* February 18, 1992, p. 38.
3. "Seeking the Source of Emotions," *Science News,* September, 1989, p. 175 (reference to Nathan A. Fox in article).
4. Stephen Worchel and Wayne Shebilske, *Psychology: Principles and Applications,* Prentice Hall, A Simon & Schuster Company, Englewood Cliffs, NJ, 1992, pp. 432–433.
5. "The Truth About Lie Detectors," *Discover,* March 1986, p. 26.
6. "How to Comply with the Polygraph Law," *Nation's Business,* December 1989, p. 36.
7. "Phobias: How to Keep Your Fears Under Control," *U.S. News & World Report,* interview with Edna B. Foa, November 23, 1981, p. 69.
8. "Can Your Body Heal Your Mind?" *Consumer Reports,* February 1993, p. 112. (Report is largely adapted from the book *Mind/Body Medicine,* Consumer Reports Books, Fairfield, OH, 1993.)
9. Ashley Montagu, *The Nature of Human Aggression,* Oxford University Press, New York, 1976, p. 309.
10. Ibid., p. 323.
11. Erich Fromm, *The Art of Loving,* Harper & Row, New York, 1956, p. 46.
12. John Powell, *Why Am I Afraid to Love?* Argus Communications Company, Chicago, revised, 1972, pp. 17–20.
13. Lester David, "The Many Faces of Guilt," *Family Health* Magazine, July 1977, p. 22.
14. Lois Duncan, "Helping Friends Who Grieve, "*Reader's Digest,* November 1991, p. 29.

6 Attitudes

Learning Objectives

After completing the chapter, you will be able to do the following:

1. Match terms from the chapter with the correct definitions.
2. State what you believe to be the main influence on the development of particular attitudes.
3. Describe a possible difference in attitude between a teenager and parent pertaining to the use of money, and explain what you believe to be the reason for the difference.
4. Explain how reasonable prejudgment differs from prejudice.
5. Describe an example of behavior resulting from prejudice and state what you believe to be the causes of the prejudice.
6. Compare definitions of discrimination and prejudice and compare the effects of each on individuals.
7. Identify what you consider to be an important work-related attitude, in addition to those included in the chapter.
8. Describe a person whose attitudes and behavior may not be in harmony and explain whether you think the person should change the attitude or the behavior and why.

> 66 *We cannot cast out pain from the world, but needless suffering we can. Tragedy will be with us in some degree as long as there is life, but misery we can banish. Injustice will raise its head in the best of all possible worlds, but tyranny we can conquer.* 99
>
> JAMES A. MICHENER
> *author*

Probably nothing is more fundamental to what you are and what you do than attitudes. An **attitude** is a readiness to act; it involves both thinking and emotion. It is a tendency to respond in a particular way to an object, a person, a group, or even an idea. A person can hold many attitudes, and they can be favorable or unfavorable. Even not caring at all about something is an attitude, called **apathy.**

We have a tendency to believe we are more **rational,** or thinking, than we probably are. In other words, most of us tend to believe we use our minds more than our feelings in reacting to other people, situations, and events. What we think affects how we feel, and how we feel affects what we think. An attitude or a reaction may seem to be based on reason but in reality may be based largely on an emotion such as fear or jealousy. What we feel can become so interwoven with what we think that we may be unable to understand our response to a particular person, event, or thing.

In a discussion of a controversial issue such as capital punishment, you would probably hear such statements as "I think deliberately killing another person is always wrong" or "I feel each state should have the right to make its own laws." People often interchange the expressions "I think" and "I feel" when expressing their attitudes. However, it would be more accurate to say, "My attitude is . . ." This would indicate that both the ideas and the feelings of the speaker are involved. We should try to understand the difference between our thoughts and our feelings, and we should say what we mean.

Note also that even our thinking is not always clear and logical. Even if we could always separate our feelings from our thoughts or beliefs, the result might not be sound thinking. There are many different reasons why we think or believe as we do. And there are many reasons why we feel as we do.

"I'm undecided, but that doesn't mean I'm apathetic or uniformed."

Drawing by C. Barsotti; © 1980 *The New Yorker* Magazine, Inc.

INFLUENCES ON ATTITUDES

The many attitudes you now have were learned. They were acquired over a period of time, and they were influenced by at least four different factors: your family, your peers, your experience, and your culture.

Your Family

You did not inherit your attitudes, even though the members of a family often have similar ideas and beliefs. For example, the members of a family may have similar attitudes about exercising or about watching television. This happens because children learn their attitudes from their parents. Of course, parents do not say, "Today we are going to teach you an attitude about television." Instead, attitudes develop in a more gradual and subtle way. Neither the child nor the parents may even be aware that an attitude is being taught. Suppose, for example, that the parents say things like, "I'm too busy to watch the junk on television. It rots your mind." Their child will learn a different attitude about television than if they say, "I really enjoy watching television after a hard day. It gives me a break and helps me to relax."

Children learn by watching others and imitating them. If parents and older children hold strong attitudes about something, a young child is likely to develop similar attitudes. Many attitudes are learned in the home. Your feelings about spending or saving money or about treating older people politely are likely to be influenced by your family life. Also, your family is particularly influential when it comes to religious and political attitudes.

Your Peers

Although your family will doubtless have a lasting effect on how you think and feel about many things, it is seldom the only strong influence on your attitudes. By the time children reach adolescence, other people their own age—their **peers**—become an important influence on their attitudes and values. Because young people during these years are psychologically breaking away from their families, being accepted by peers becomes extremely important. Thus, the attitudes of most young people are affected at least for a while by friends and ac-

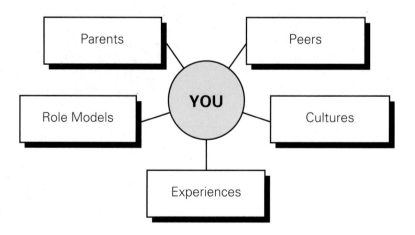

quaintances of their own age. More will be said about the influence of both family and peers in Chapter 11, "Life-Span Development."

Role Models

Every child has role models—older persons he or she admires and would like to be like. A young person's evaluation of such a role model might not be realistic, but whatever he thinks the person stands for affects the development of his attitudes and behavior, nonetheless. Sometimes the role model is an older brother or sister, a parent, or other relative. At other times he or she might be a film star or an athlete. Michael Jordan, former Chicago Bulls basketball star, is aware that he is a role model for others. He says, "The good part about being famous is being able to help people. The hard part is every day you have to be in a good mood, because that is what people expect. You learn to get good at it."[1] He wants his influence on others, particularly on young people, to be positive. One doesn't have to be especially talented or famous to be a role model, however. It should also be remembered that those who are models or examples for others aren't necessarily displaying attitudes and behavior that are desirable or acceptable. They may not even be aware that they are models for the attitudes and behavior of others.

Your Experience

Your direct experience also influences your attitudes. If you have had many bad experiences in a particular situation, you are likely to develop a negative attitude toward it. For example, if Roger has had poor luck fishing on Perch Lake several times, he is likely to have a negative attitude toward fishing there.

" I THOUGHT A DOG WOULD CHEER HIM UP. "

Reprinted from *The Saturday Evening Post.*

On the other hand, if Louise has had a good time every time she visited her friend in Denver, she will doubtless develop a favorable attitude toward that city as well as toward her friend. These are examples of how experiences affect our attitudes.

The type of work we do can also influence our attitudes to some extent. This is especially true if the work limits our contact with other people. A marriage counselor, for example, who works mostly with couples having problems, may develop unrealistic, negative attitudes toward marriage. Since most jobs limit the types of experiences we have, our attitudes often are affected by our occupations. However, we should not assume that all people who hold particular jobs have particular attitudes. It is a mistake to think that, for example, all teachers or all salespeople or all plumbers have similar attitudes.

What would you SAY?

Suppose a prospective employer asks you in an interview, "Who or what influenced you to choose the occupation for which you are now applying?" What would you say?

Your Culture

Another influence on attitudes is the culture in which one grows up. People in different parts of the world traditionally have had different attitudes toward family relationships, work, education, leisure time, and death, for example. In the global community, discussed in Chapter 1, we now have a more multicultural society, and there is an attempt to preserve some values and customs of one's heritage as well as to appreciate the attitudes and values of others. An article in *Time* entitled "America's Changing Colors," notes, "During the 21st Century racial and ethnic minorities will collectively outnumber whites for the first time. The 'browning of America' will affect every aspect of society."[2] New attitudes will develop and some changes of attitudes will be required if we want to live in harmony with one another.

ATTITUDES AND BEHAVIOR

One reason it is valuable to understand attitudes is that they are closely related to behavior. You will control your own behavior better if you understand the attitudes that affect what you do. You also will understand the behavior of others better, and you will be better able to predict what someone else might do in a a given situation. Finally, by understanding your attitudes, you can see how others are trying to influence your behavior by attempting to change your attitudes.

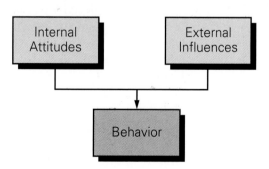

Attitudes sometimes are expressed openly in various types of discussion groups or in conversations. But more often they are revealed only indirectly. It is important to understand attitudes because certain attitudes are expected to lead to certain types of behavior. Thus we act toward others according to what we assume their attitudes to be. For example, if someone believes you have an attitude of trust toward others, that person will expect you to enter into relationships more readily than would a person who is suspicious of others.

Even though attitudes usually precede behavior, they also can result from behavior. Behaving or acting in a certain way can lead you to develop a particular attitude. For example, if you make a special effort to accept other people—even though they may have characteristics quite different from yours—this will cause you to become more tolerant. In the same way, by acting enthusiastic about your work or some other activity, even though you may not feel that way at first, you can develop an enthusiastic attitude.

Attitudes and behavior do not always agree. What you say and do may contradict what you think and feel. A phrase as simple as "thank you" can be sincere or can express sarcasm and discontent. Your expressions and gestures may emphasize or contradict the actual words you are using. Thus you may agree to work on your day off, even though you had other plans and think the request is unfair. Disagreement between attitudes and behavior will be discussed further later in this chapter.

The relationship between attitudes and behavior can be confusing, because they influence each other. Moreover, we may not always know exactly how that influence works. Since attitudes *do* affect behavior, it is helpful to know the attitudes of others. Remember also that others are "reading" your attitudes and are reacting to you accordingly.

In Chapter 3, "Motives and Values," we discussed the difference between controlling and influencing others. If you agree that we can only influence, not control, the behavior of others, you can see that it is even more difficult to control what others think and feel. Someone in authority may have considerable influence over what others do (and don't do) in a particular situation. Such a person may be able to encourage or discourage certain types of behavior. But a person who says "I insist that you respect me," will get nowhere. Respect is an attitude. It is based on our opinion of another person and on our feelings toward that person. Although an attitude of respect or disrespect is reflected in what we do, no one can force us to have that attitude. People may be able to influence our behavior, but they cannot control our thoughts and feelings.

POSITIVE AND NEGATIVE ATTITUDES

A common way of classifying attitudes is to think of them as positive or negative. People who habitually display negative attitudes toward their jobs and the world are called **pessimists.** Those who see the brighter, more positive side of life are called **optimists.** In reacting to the same experience, both types will perceive it differently. Thus, a pessimist might consider a job transfer to be an undesirable change that probably would cause disappointments and problems. An optimist, however, would see the situation as a new opportunity and challenge. In both cases, attitudes would affect the person's perception.

In fact, a job transfer probably would cause some problems, such as finding a new place to live. But an optimist focuses on the desirable aspects of the

situation, and a pessimist pays more attention to the negative aspects. Interestingly, very few people view themselves as pessimists. Most people tend to believe that they are viewing the situation as it really is.

An appropriate theme for attitude improvement might be "Accentuate the positive; eliminate the negative." Examples of positive attitudes are tolerance, enthusiasm, optimism, confidence, and conscientiousness. Examples of negative attitudes are revengefulness, pessimism, suspicion, apathy, and uncooperativeness. We must first recognize our negative attitudes if we want to eliminate them.

Low self-esteem can contribute to negative attitudes toward oneself as well as toward others and the world in general. Cherie Carter-Scott coined the term *negaholism* and describes it as, "a syndrome in which people unconsciously limit their own innate abilities, convince themselves that they can't have what they want, and sabotage their wishes, desires, and dreams."[3] Although it isn't likely that your attitudes are that self-defeating, it is important to keep in mind that our attitudes do affect our behavior and what we achieve in our lives.

A fictional example of negative thinking is included in "Say Yes to Yourself." According to authors of *Beyond Negative Thinking*,

> A traveling salesman gets a flat tire on a dark, lonely road and then discovers that he has no jack. He sees a light in a farmhouse. As he walks toward it, his mind churns: "Suppose no one comes to the door." "Suppose they don't have a jack." "Suppose the guy won't lend me his jack even if he has one." The harder his mind works, the more agitated he becomes, and when the door opens, he punches the farmer and yells, "Keep your lousy jack!"[4]

You can choose to be an optimist. Advantages of developing a more positive attitude are further explained by Martin E. P. Seligman in *Learned Optimism*. He maintains,

> Life inflicts the same setbacks and tragedies on the optimist as on the pessimist, but the optimist weathers them better. As we have seen, the optimist bounces back from defeat, and, with his life somewhat poorer, he picks up and starts again. The pessimist gives up and falls into depression. Because of his resilience, the optimist achieves more at work, at school, and on the playing field. The optimist has better physical health and may even live longer. Americans want optimists to lead them. Even when things go well for the pessimist, he is haunted by forebodings of catastrophe."[5]

It is easier for most people to control what they say or do than to control their attitudes. Although attitudes and behaviors affect each other, acting in a particular way can gradually affect how one feels. As mentioned earlier, by acting enthusiastically about your work or about other activities—even though you may not feel that way at first—you can develop an enthusiastic attitude toward them. You also can lessen feelings of discouragement by working at something constructive or creative. If a certain aspect of your work becomes discouraging, the time spent on more satisfying tasks can help restore a positive, confident attitude.

Attitude Surveys

Various types of surveys to determine attitudes of society in general, or different segments of society, toward major issues are common. An example of atti-

Reprinted from *The Saturday Evening Post*.

tude surveys conducted in today's society is a USA TODAY/CNN/Gallup Poll, in which there was a comparison of attitudes of gun owners and non–gun owners toward gun control. Of the gun owners, 57% favored stricter gun laws, 36% wanted no change, and 6% wanted less stringent laws. Of the non–gun owners, 82% wanted stricter control and 13% want no change.[6] One must be careful in interpreting results of polls not to confuse cause and effect. In other words, do the non–gun owners want stricter control because they do not own guns, or do they not own guns because they are in favor of stricter control? Similar attitude surveys are periodically conducted pertaining to gay rights, abortion, taxes, and other current issues.

Although there are different ways that a survey can be structured, many are set up like the questions in the following self-evaluation, called "Quiz Yourself on Your Attitudes Toward Smoking." This self-evaluation contains only a few typical questions; therefore, it would not necessarily be an accurate determination of your attitudes.

It must also be remembered that attitudes are what one thinks and feels and are not behavior. Although an attitude often leads to behavior similar to that attitude, there can be a variety of reasons for having a particular attitude. A person who does not smoke, for example, may be opposed to certain regulations to restrict smoking.

Although there are not right or wrong answers to these questions, notes at the end of the chapter will be helpful to you in interpreting your responses.

Further questions concerning attitudes and possible attitude change will be found later in the chapter.

"Sorry, that opinion is incorrect."

Reprinted from *The Saturday Evening Post*.

✎ *Quiz Yourself on Your Attitudes Toward Smoking*

Determining your response to each of the following questions can give you a better understanding of attitudes in general and your attitudes on this particular issue. This a self-evaluation, but you may want to compare your attitudes with others in the class.

1.	Should smoking be prohibited in all public buildings?	yes	not sure	no
2.	Does everyone have a right to smoke where he or she chooses?	yes	not sure	no
3.	Do some people have the right to ask others not to smoke?	yes	not sure	no
4.	Are you in favor of an increased tax on cigarettes to help pay for health insurance?	yes	not sure	no
5.	Are your attitudes toward smoking the same as that of your friends?	yes	not sure	no
6.	Are your attitudes toward smoking influenced by either your smoking or nonsmoking behavior?	yes	not sure	no

Notes on Quiz Yourself are on pages 133–134.

Prejudice

Prejudice is an attitude that seriously affects the lives of many people. The word **prejudice** means "judging before"; it is prejudging without having adequate information or reason. We develop attitudes over a period of time without being fully aware of why we think and feel the way we do. Or we may develop an attitude as a result of a single especially favorable or unfavorable incident. In either case such attitudes may lack justifiable foundations.

As you know, it is possible to be prejudiced either in favor of something or against it. If an employer believes that the only people qualified to work for her are those who graduated from her alma mater, she is prejudiced in favor of these graduates. If another employer believes that all people who belong to a certain religion are unreliable, he is prejudiced against this group. In both cases, prejudice or prejudgment is being made by the employers without adequate information.

The word adequate is an important part of the definition of prejudice. In reality it is necessary to prejudge every day. You decide to buy a new product without knowing exactly how well it will serve your purposes. You may ask a new acquaintance for a date without knowing exactly how the person will act. You may enroll in flight school without knowing whether you have the aptitude or even a realistic desire to learn to fly. However, the more information you have about a product or a person, the greater the chance that your prejudgment is sound. Whether a given amount of information is adequate for making a prejudgment depends upon the amount of information that is available and the difficulty or complexity of the activity.

Stereotyping

"Men are all alike." "Teenagers all act the same." "All salespeople are alike." These statements are examples of **stereotyping,** or assuming that all members of a particular group conform to the same pattern and react in the same way. Although members of a group often have characteristics in common, there is no group in which all members are alike.

What Causes Prejudice?

Why do so many people prejudge without adequate information? There are a number of reasons. Common causes of prejudice are lack of information, misinformation, fear of the unknown, lack of understanding, and blind loyalties. Some prejudices arise from a basic feeling of inferiority. Thus, people may try to make themselves look and feel better by making others appear inferior to them.

Prejudiced people usually hold very strong opinions. They are likely to have a number of prejudices because they are narrow-minded and often are not interested in acquiring adequate information. This makes it difficult to reduce prejudice. Since prejudice is an unsupported attitude, prejudiced people cannot be expected to be reasonable about examining their attitudes. They are also often insecure and distrustful in their relationships with others.

Most people try to justify their prejudices by devising what they think are acceptable reasons for them. One difficulty in eliminating prejudices is that the cause of the prejudice lies within a person.

The following questions were among those posed by *Christopher News Notes* as a self-examination on prejudice:

> How do I react when I hear about an example of racism? Do I seek revenge? Do I see all people of a particular race in a bad light because of the actions of a few?
>
> Do I welcome others of different races or backgrounds?
>
> Do I respect the languages and customs of others?
>
> Do I know the contributions various races and ethnic and religious groups have made to this country?
>
> Do I join in negative remarks about a person or persons of a specific racial, religious, or ethnic group or do I refuse to participate?[7]

Most people try to justify their prejudices by devising what they think are acceptable reasons for them. One difficulty in eliminating prejudices is that the cause of the prejudice lies within the individual who is prejudiced.

DISCRIMINATION

Prejudice is an attitude; **discrimination** is behavior. Discrimination is behavior—usually unfair and harmful—toward an individual because he or she belongs to a particular group. A person may be discriminated against because he or she is a Democrat, a Methodist, a Native American, a manager, a union member, a homosexual, or a member of any other group, for example; she may be discriminated against as a female. People are also discriminated against because they are too old or too young, too thin or too fat, or too anything. Discrimination ranges from simple avoidance to verbal criticism to hostility and violence. There are laws against discrimination in housing, employment, club

A woman ably performs work once thought to be suited only to males.

membership, school attendance, and many other areas of living. However, problems often arise in efforts to adhere to these laws. Consider the following example.

> The Reliable Construction Company had neither employed a female construction worker nor had any females applied for work with the company. Karen applied to work for the company when it was looking for thirty workers to build a new community health center. Because the building was funded in part by federal money, the superintendent of the project was fearful of losing the contract if he showed sex discrimination in hiring workers. As a result, he reluctantly hired Karen. However, she discovered by the end of the first week on the job that none of the male construction workers wanted to work with her. In an effort to make Karen quit, the superintendent assigned her more than her share of heavy manual labor.

A well-known male who has spoken out against discrimination and sexual harassment of women in the workplace is Bernard Shaw, a CNN news anchor. He objects to females being referred to as "Honey" or other terms of familiarity. He also refers to lower pay and fewer management opportunities for women. "My point in all this is simple," he says. "We must change. We must change now! Our attitudes must change and change in basic ways." He continues, "We must change so that those who study what we did, correctly conclude that our society matured and affirmed that a woman does not have to out-man a man to be respected and—respectable."[8]

The late Ralph J. Bunche, an author of the United Nations Charter, was sometimes the object of prejudice, but he felt none in return. He once said, "I have a deep-seated bias against hate and intolerance. I have a bias against racial and religious bigotry. I have a bias against war, a bias for peace. I have a bias which leads me to believe that no problem of human relations is ever insoluble."[9] The problems related to prejudice and discrimination are still not completely solved, however.

Eliminating discrimination is a complicated process. In 1965, President Lyndon B. Johnson signed an executive order establishing **affirmative action** guidelines. These required businesses receiving government contracts to hire, or at least attempt to hire, representative numbers of women and minorities. Other businesses, organizations, and institutions have also developed affirmative action plans.

New problems arose, however, including charges of **reverse discrimination** against white males. As a result, in 1978, the Supreme Court heard a reverse discrimination case and ruled that a California medical school illegally discriminated against Allan Bakke, a white male, in favor of minorities. The Court did not rule against affirmative action as a whole, however.

In 1986, court rulings pertained to firefighters in Cleveland and sheet-metal workers in New York. The Supreme Court ruled that federal judges may set goals and timetables requiring employers guilty of past discrimination to hire or promote specific numbers of minorities, even if these people have not personally experienced discrimination. Then, in 1987, the Court upheld the hiring of a woman as a dispatcher by Santa Clara County, California, even though a male was considered slightly more qualified. Because a woman had never held such a job in that county, the Court considered her hiring as affirmative action.

It has been noted by Peter Brimelow in "The Spiral of Silence," that white males aren't as likely to protest against reverse discrimination as much as members of other groups may fight against discrimination. He attributes this to male psychology itself. These victims seem really to have believed that real men don't cry. A considerable number did not even mention their disappointment to friends, relatives or fellow workers.[10]

Obviously, laws cannot completely eliminate discrimination. Such attempts, along with attempts to avoid and reduce attitudes of prejudice, improve the equality of opportunity for all, however.

A basic social problem is to eliminate and prevent prejudice itself, rather than to concentrate only on control of the results of prejudice. Because of better education and a more mobile population, in which people come into contact with many other people, there is a lessening of some kinds of prejudice. There is less religious prejudice, for example, than there was a generation ago. Most religions are moving toward a better understanding and acceptance of one another. Members of various denominations are learning how much they have in common, whereas previously they were aware mostly of differences. Knowledge usually reduces any kind of prejudice.

We all use reasonable discrimination in making choices every day. Whenever we choose one thing instead of another, we are discriminating. Some of it may be unwise but not necessarily unfair. It is unfair discrimination resulting from prejudice that is a serious social concern.

William B. Allen, Commissioner of the U.S. Commission on Human Rights, gave a speech in 1991 in which he declared that we must learn to "live in a world, in a country, where people can see black, white, and anything at all, without seeing a problem, where people can refer to color because color is no longer an issue."[11]

WORK-RELATED ATTITUDES

How do your attitudes affect your work? How do they affect your education (which, for the time being, *is* your work)?

Because most people have to work whether they like it or not, people have a wide range of attitudes toward their jobs. To the question, How do you like your job? typical replies might be:

"I'm glad I am able to work and that I have a job."
"I couldn't ask for a job I'd like better; it's a real challenge."
"It's okay, I guess; I've never thought much about it."
"I like my job. If I didn't like it, I would try to find one I did like."
"Who likes any job? Work is work."
"I don't like the work itself so much, but it's a good company and I like the people I work with."

You might say, "If I do my job, what difference does it make what my attitude is?" The answer is that your attitude toward your job affects the quality of your work. If you don't take pride in your work, your performance may not meet the requisite standards. In specialized fields, in which many people may work on the final product, a careless attitude by one person can cause the final product to be inferior. An expensive motor can be rejected because it has one flaw caused by one person who didn't care.

How your attitude influences others is noticed by your boss and by others who are in a position to affect your future. Arlo may think, "I have kept my job for fifteen years, so I must be considered a good employee." However, he may never know what opportunities or benefits he has missed because someone decided he did not have the right attitude.

A widely used book by those who realize that positive attitudes are important on the job is Elwood Chapman's *Your Attitude Is Showing*. He tells us, "A positive attitude is essential to career success for many reasons." He then goes on to say that:

- When you are positive you are usually more energetic, highly motivated, productive, and alert. Thinking about negative things too much has a way of draining your energy. Put another way, a positive attitude opens a gate and lets your inner enthusiasm spill out. A negative attitude, on the other hand, will keep the gate closed.
- First impressions are important on the job because they often have a lasting effect. Co-workers you meet for the first time appear to have little radar sets tuned in to your attitude. If your attitude is positive, they receive a friendly, warm signal, and they are attracted to you. If your attitude is negative, they receive an unfriendly signal, and they try to avoid you.
- A positive employee contributes to the productivity of others. A negative employee does not. Attitudes are caught more than they are taught! Both negative and positive attitudes are transmitted on the job. They are

This mother has family responsibilities to be met before she goes to her job outside the home.

picked up by others. A persistently negative attitude, like the rotten apple in the barrel, can spoil the positive attitudes of others. It is very difficult to maintain a high level of productivity while working next to a person with a negative attitude.

- Co-workers like you when you are positive. They like to be around you because you are fun. This makes your job more interesting and exciting, because you are in the middle of things and not on the outside complaining. When you are negative, people prefer to stay clear of you. A negative person may build good relationships with a few other people (who are perhaps negative themselves), but such a person cannot build good relationships with the majority of employees.
- The kind of attitude you transmit to management will have a great deal to do with your future success. Management constantly reads your mental attitude, even though you may feel you are successful in covering it up. Supervisors can determine your attitude by how you approach your job, react to directives, handle problems, and work with others. If you are positive, you will be given greater consideration when special assignments and promotion opportunities arise.[12]

Where Work Attitudes Begin

Attitudes toward work begin very early in life — long before a child is expected to work. As with other types of attitudes, children are influenced by their parents' attitudes toward work. Today, however, outside influences also begin at an earlier age than in the past. Children in elementary schools are learning more about careers and career choices, and such information is provided in depth in high school. The goal is to encourage realistic attention to career opportunities over a period of years, as well as to promote the development of constructive attitudes toward work. Recognition of the fact that work is a major part of life should not be something that comes as a shock upon graduation from high school.

After deciding what you want to do in the way of work, the next step is to prepare yourself for it. Most jobs today require some specialized training. Many young people who have dropped out of high school "to get a job" have found that there aren't many jobs for which they are qualified. In addition, they cannot foresee their working a lifetime at the unskilled jobs that are available. Perhaps a negative attitude toward school caused them to drop out and seek a job. But a realistic encounter with the job market may cause a change in attitude that will result in further occupational education and training.

After you prepare yourself through education and training for a particular type of work, the next step, of course, is actually to get the job. You must be not only personable and persuasive but also skilled enough at a particular type of work to get the job, and then you must do the job well enough to keep it. Both you and your employer must be interested in developing your skills so that your value to the company increases. Attitude is an important factor throughout. Being able to do a particular type of work is expected, but that is only the beginning of your evaluation as an employee.

Some students in vocational and job training programs are impatient with courses that do not seem to train them directly in their major skills. But experience has shown that those who have favorable attitudes toward themselves, other people, and life in general become the most sought-after employees. It is not unusual for an employer to say something like "Let people with basic skills and constructive attitudes come to our company, and we'll give them the special training and opportunities they need. People who have the right skills but negative attitudes soon become a nuisance to us — and often discredit themselves."

Important Work Attitudes

Many managers and personnel directors consider attitudes more important than any other factor when hiring employees. What are these attitudes? Some of them are identified in the following sections:

Loyality to the Company   Loyalty begins with interest and caring. Personnel managers naturally expect that employees are interested in satisfying their own needs, but they are looking also for people who will show an interest in and feel loyal to the company. Employees are expected to have a high regard for the company or organization they work for, without being negative about competitors or past employers. A person can be interested in the company from the beginning of employment and have intentions of being loyal, but a feeling of loyalty and pride in the organization you work for usually takes some time.

Willingness to Work   Although it would seem obvious that someone looking for a job wants to work, employers know this is not always the case. An employer is not likely to hire someone who answers the question, "Why do you want to work for our company?" by saying, "Well, I need something to do," or "I could really use the money."

Willingness to Learn   Students completing work-related courses have the right to feel competent and to believe they are qualified for a job in the area of their major. You are being naive, however, if you do not realize that you still have much to learn. New employees must be willing to learn about the functioning of a particular business or industry. They must be willing to become more skilled through practice and to benefit by association with those who have more experience. Willingness to learn includes receptiveness to constructive criticism. We cannot learn if our attitude is that we have nothing to learn.

Willingness to Work with Others   Teamwork is required in today's workplace. Although individuals may have different skills and responsibilities, it is only when everyone is working together toward common goals that the company or organization is productive and profitable. Also, situations may arise that require temporary substitutions or helping out beyond one's immediate responsibility. Although union contracts or licensing may limit what employees are allowed to do outside their own jobs, an overall attitude of helpfulness makes the organization run more smoothly, and improves morale.

Respect for Supervisors, Co-workers, Customers, and Clients   Respect is an attitude rather than behavior. It consists of what one thinks and feels toward others. No one can demand that you respect him or her, for example. What others can do is demand that we treat them the way they want to be treated or accept the consequences over which they have control. Remember the discussion of control and influence in Chapter 3? Respect should not involve believing that others are superior human beings with greater human rights. It recognizes the dignity and needs of others and our relationship to them under specific circumstances. Respect recognizes the uniqueness of each individual and accepts his or her ways — as long as this does not interfere with the rights of others or with the organization's productivity or goals.

Positive Attitudes Toward Change   You will recall, or can review, a number of types of change related to the world of work discussed in Chapter 1. Although some resistance to change can be expected, especially when we are not sure how it will affect us, change is inevitable in all aspects of life today. This can require new learning and some adjustments; it can also keep our work lives interesting and challenging. There aren't very many people today who would be willing to do the same repetitive job for twenty-five or thirty years, as was often the case in the past. Not only can we be receptive to change but we can be among the most valued employees who help bring it about.

These are some of the attitudes most frequently mentioned by employers. A person needs the skills to do the job, but it has been said that "Attitude is more important than aptitude." It is easier to teach individuals something new if they have the attitudes that are discussed above.

 What would you SUGGEST?   If a good friend asked you, "How can I improve my attitude toward my work?" what would you suggest?

CHANGING ATTITUDES

We would be much less concerned about attitudes if it were not possible to change or to influence them. Even so, it can be a frustrating experience to try to change the attitudes of others.

People change their attitudes only after they perceive situations differently. This doesn't ordinarily happen easily or quickly. But to believe that attitudes cannot be changed is a negative attitude in itself. A challenge toward attitude examination and changes is offered to us in a book entitled, *How to Love Every Minute of Your Life.*

> Often, our beliefs, prejudices and opinions insulate us from perceiving the potential for growth and creativity that is inherent in every problem confronting us. By hanging on to our beliefs, we maintain painful cycles of confusion and ineffective behavior in the face of the many opportunities for growth that our life presents to us. In order to break these cycles, it is first necessary to become aware of and to set aside our beliefs and to begin to examine our lives in the light of our own experience.[13]

Earlier in this chapter you were asked to examine your attitudes toward smoking restrictions. Following are a few more questions pertaining to attitude change. As with the questions pertaining to smoking, there is no way to accurately score your responses. Notes at the end of the chapter will help you in evaluating your responses.

✏ *Quiz Yourself on Attitude Formation and Change*

Following are questions to consider in an examination of your attitudes. They require careful thought, but your answers can be helpful in understanding your attitudes.

1. Do I resist new ideas or change?	yes	not sure	no
2. Is it difficult for me to admit I am wrong?	yes	not sure	no
3. Am I tolerant of the ideas of others? Do I really listen to and consider their opinions?	yes	not sure	no
4. How long have I held particular attitudes? Have my attitudes become habits?	yes	not sure	no
5. How recently have I had new experience or acquired new information related to certain attitudes?	yes	not sure	no
6. How are my attitudes affecting my studies, my work, and my relationships with others?	yes	not sure	no

Notes on Quiz Yourself are on page 134.

Attitudes Can Change with Time

Attitudes, like values, can be expected to change over time. In part, this results from having new experiences and developing new understanding. As Mark Twain put it: "When I was a boy of fourteen, my father was so ignorant, I could hardly stand to have the old man around. But when I got to be twenty-one, I was astonished at how much he had learned in seven years!"

One parent recalls a conflict of attitudes between herself and her parents when she was a teenager. Evidently they disagreed about how much independence the girl should have at the age of 16. She recalls thinking, "When I get to be a parent and have a 16-year-old daughter, I will allow her as much independence as she wishes." Now, as a parent, she can remember her earlier attitude, but she no longer thinks and feels that way. Because of her age and new point of view, her attitude has changed.

The attitudes of most older adults are relatively stable. They may not change much for the rest of a person's life. There are several reasons for this. Some older people may simply be stubborn. Others may have more knowledge than younger people but are not continuing to learn at the same pace as younger people, so their attitudes may not be challenged so much. Their attitudes at this time may be the result of earlier changes. They have become satisfied now with their ideas and feelings on many subjects. They have established their ideas about politics, religion, economics, and many other subjects, and they are not likely to change. This is called cognitive consistency. It has been found that many married couples over the years maintain similar

A father and daughter exchange views and perhaps move closer toward mutual attitude adjustment.

attitudes and values. Avshalom Caspi, who conducted a study of couples, explains that they did not *grow* more alike; instead they *remained* moderately similar in attitudes and values across 20 years. He believes shared experiences such as work, recreational, and religious activities maintain similarities.[14]

In addition, older people may not have as much contact with as many different people as they did when they were younger. They have settled down socially, so there are fewer people influencing their attitudes. Finally, the attitudes of older people may become so much a part of what they are that to change their ideas and feelings would be damaging to their sense of security. We will look at this idea more closely in Chapter 8, "Coping with Stress."

Where Does Change Begin?

If a change in either attitude or behavior is desired, where does one begin? Most often it is suggested that attitudes be changed first, since they tend to result in certain kinds of behavior (as discussed earlier). But some people say that attitude changes should begin with a behavior change. This, they say, will encourage a more natural, permanent behavior change. Consider the approach taken by Daryl J. Bem in *Beliefs, Attitudes, and Human Affairs:*

> There is now sufficient evidence to suggest that under certain conditions, one of the most effective ways to "change the hearts and minds of men" is to change their behavior. In fact, this may even be easier than the other way around. Conventional wisdom suggests that goodwill campaigns and brotherhood weeks may convince people to discriminate less, but there is better evidence that suggests making people discriminate less may convince them to have goodwill and act like brothers. Most people agree that the question, "Why

do you eat brown bread?" can be properly answered with, "Because I like it." I should like to convince you, however, that the question, "Why do you like brown bread?" frequently ought to be answered with, "Because I eat it."[15]

Attitudes and Personality

Since attitudes are underlying factors in our reactions to others, they must be closely related to our personalities — our typical ways of expressing what we think and feel. However, personality involves how we behave or act as a result of our attitudes. A person may think that other people are basically honest and may feel no threat from them. Therefore, he or she will act toward others in a relaxed, trusting manner.

There are many ways to describe someone's attitudes and behavior. We may consider a person to be outgoing, sincere, considerate, self-centered, stubborn, suspicious, belligerent, humane, defiant, inflexible, enthusiastic, and so on. The willingness to change one's attitude is related to one's basic personality. A person who has a poor self-concept may be influenced more easily than someone who is confident, for example. Other people may be narrow-minded or stubborn and may be unable or unwilling to see things from another point of view. Again, we can see the relationship between attitude and perception.

 What do you THINK?   Can one regard one's own unwillingness to change as loyalty or dedication and yet regard someone else's unwillingness to change as stubbornness? What do you think?

Agreement Between Attitudes and Behavior

Not only do attitudes and behavior affect one another but it is important for an individual's attitudes and behavior to agree or be in balance. Sometimes two attitudes can be in conflict with one another, or attitude and behavior can be in conflict. When such a conflict exists, a person is said to be experiencing cognitive dissonance. A person can become so disturbed that either the attitude or behavior has to be changed.

For example, a person may have a charitable attitude and yet never really do anything to help others. Such a person either has to perform charitable acts or admit to not really being charitable. Another person may have favorable ideas and feelings about being clean and orderly but still be careless about personal appearance and possessions. To feel comfortable, this person must change either the behavior or the attitude about order and cleanliness. In a sense, it is important not only to practice what you preach but also to practice what you believe. You sometimes can be frustrated by a situation or by your overall life-style without quite realizing that the problem is caused by a conflict between your attitudes and behavior.

Or a person may attempt to justify behavior in spite of its inconsistency with his or her belief. Henry Gleitman, author of *Basic Psychology,* refers to this as attempting to maintain a "favorable self-picture."[16] This is a type of rationalization that you will read about in Chapter 8, "Coping with Stress."

Drastic Experiences

Although attitudes do not change readily after a person reaches adulthood, sometimes a single drastic experience can cause complete attitude reversal. Someone who has never bothered with seat belts, for example, may see a tragic accident that changes that attitude for life. Or someone may be skeptical about the value of a proper diet until a medical condition that changes that attitude develops. Most of us, however, do not have to face such drastic situations, so our attitudes may change only slightly and gradually unless we make a serious effort to change them.

Outside Influences

Some common methods of changing attitudes are used in advertising, sales promotion, and other persuasion techniques. One technique used in advertising is called **association.** In this, a product or service is shown with something else we already accept, or it may be presented by a celebrity in order to persuade us to transfer our favorable attitude toward that person to the product being sold. We would like to believe that we make up our own minds, but advertisers know they have tremendous opportunities to influence our attitudes and buying behavior. Indeed, they spend millions of dollars trying to do so.

Association and other persuasion techniques can be used by any group or individual seeking to change attitudes. The efforts may be aimed at the general public, at a smaller group such as a club, or at an individual. As an individual, you should be aware of such techniques and what those who use them are trying to accomplish.

The most extreme method of changing attitudes is called **brainwashing.** This is an attempt to change a person's thinking and feelings completely, causing him or her to reject former loyalties and adopt a new point of view. Brainwashing has occurred mostly in prison camps during wars, but cult groups and others have also been accused of using the technique. The basic principle involved is to isolate the individual from what was previously meaningful and important. Next, the person's basic needs are not satisfied until the new attitude is accepted. Only then is the person permitted to sleep or eat. This technique obviously requires that the brainwashers totally control the environment. In such circumstances it is difficult or impossible for the individual to realize what is happening or to resist the influence being exerted. Of course, people vary in how readily they react to such influences and pressures, but the process seems to be very effective with some people.

WHAT'S YOUR ATTITUDE? On what basis do you judge the attitudes of others? Some people openly express their beliefs and ideas in various types of discussion groups and in conversation. Others may have similar attitudes but do not share their ideas and feelings readily.

For most people it is easier to share ideas than feelings. There are some, however, who are willing to express their feelings, at least to a few other persons. The willingness or unwillingness to share thoughts and feelings was discussed in Chapter 2, "Self-Concept and Personality."

In many instances attitudes are revealed by indirect clues, such as facial expressions and body posture, often referred to as body language. Our thoughts and feelings are revealed in these ways even when we do not realize it. Attention or lack of it is also an expression of attitude. If you have a negative attitude about an experience you are having, it probably shows in some way. It is important to realize, however, that facial expressions and body language can be misinterpreted. Thus, someone who is simply not very expressive may be considered apathetic or even aloof. We are not always accurate in determining the attitudes of others, yet we often react toward them as though we knew what they believe and feel. This chapter should have made it clear that attitudes are difficult to determine or change. A little tolerance goes a long way — on the job and in every area of living.

SUMMARY

Attitudes influence us more than we sometimes realize. An attitude involves both what we think and what we feel about a person, an object, a situation, or an idea.

Attitudes are learned. Major influences on the development of attitudes are your family, your peers, role models, your experience, and your culture.

Behavior and attitudes are related. Certain attitudes usually result in similar behavior. But it is also possible for behavior to lead to the development of an attitude.

One way to classify attitudes is to see them as positive or negative. Those who are usually cheerful and positive toward work and life are called optimists; those who habitually display negative attitudes are known as pessimists.

Prejudice is prejudging without having adequate information or reason. Discrimination is unfair treatment that results from prejudice. Reverse discrimination is discrimination against white males in favor of women and minorities, usually as a result of affirmative action.

Work-related attitudes begin to develop very early in life. The attitudes of your parents and your teachers and your part-time work experiences have undoubtedly influenced your attitudes toward work. Desirable work attitudes include willingness to work, learn, and work with others. They also include loyalty and respect for supervisors, co-workers, customers, and clients. Further, it's important to have positive attitudes toward change.

Attitudes become relatively fixed as a person becomes older, but they can be changed through self-understanding, motivation, and sincere effort. Our attitudes affect everything we do. They even affect our ability to think and solve problems, which is the subject of Chapter 7.

Notes on Quiz Yourself on Your Attitudes Toward Smoking
Although there are no right or wrong answers, the following notes may be helpful in interpreting your responses. You may want to compare your responses with other members of the class or friends.

1. Since smoking is now prohibited in public buildings in some states and communities, there is support for this position. Even some people who smoke may be opposed to smoking in public buildings. Others may disapprove of smoking but do not wish to prohibit others from smoking under certain conditions. Do you think your attitude is related to whether or not you smoke?

2. A Yes answer to the question indicates a disregard for the rights of others. Most people today would probably answer No to this statement.

3. Those who answer Yes to this question will often qualify it according to the place and conditions involved. Most would agree one has the right to ask others not to smoke in their automobiles and homes. Laws prohibiting smoking and policy of the establishment would be additional factors. The well-being and rights of individuals affected would also be factors. Some smokers, in referring to a public place not restricting smoking would respond, "If my smoking bothers you, you can move." Would this be your attitude?

4. Since nonsmokers would not have to pay the tax, it is likely those who disapprove of smoking would favor the tax. Other nonsmokers, as well as smokers, would consider the tax an unreasonable way to discourage smoking. They might claim that smoking and its effects, in most cases, should not be controlled by governments.

5. The question pertains to how attitudes are acquired. Consider the influence your friends or peers have on your attitudes. Also consider, of course, the influence you may have had on their attitudes.

6. This question pertains to the relationship between attitudes and behavior. They affect one another.

Notes on Quiz Yourself on Attitude Formation and Change

The following notes are intended to give you a better understanding of attitudes. There are no right or wrong answers to the questions.

1. Since we are living in a rapidly changing world, we should be willing to at least examine our attitudes to determine if they are still valid or appropriate. A change in behavior can often lead to a corresponding change in attitude. Since it is easier for most of us to change what we do than what we think or feel, some changes can begin with how we act.

2. Being unwilling to admit that we are wrong usually indicates a weak self-concept. This can keep us from being open-minded, from learning, and from examining our ideas, feelings, and behavior. We are thus not being fair to ourselves as well as to others.

3. Lack of tolerance leads to some of the same problems as resisting change. Lack of tolerance of others is often due to an inferiority complex. This, of course, is also related to a poor self-concept. When people feel good about themselves, they are more accepting of others.

4. The longer one holds an attitude, the more difficult it can be to change. What we think and how we feel, as well as what we do, can become habits. And we know that habits can be difficult to change. The first step in changing a habit is becoming aware of it and its possible negative effects.

5. Although we needn't be examining our attitudes on a daily basis, we should be willing to adjust our ideas and feelings if new experiences or information warrant it. New experience includes an evaluation of the experience. People who hesitate to have new experience are leading lives that are not as interesting as they could be.

6. Since our attitudes affect our studies and work, we can improve what we accomplish in these areas by developing more optimistic, constructive attitudes. Nobody enjoys being around others who consistently have negative attitudes. Such attitudes can definitely interfere with our relationships with others, which includes relationships at work.

Psychology In Practice

1. Try to identify a group against which you might have been prejudiced. Find out as much about the group and several members of the group as you can. Does your evidence indicate that your beliefs have sound support, or can you see ways you were, or still are, prejudiced?

2. Work on having a more positive attitude toward everyone you associate with and all your experiences for at least three days. Either share the results orally with the class or write a brief description of the results.

3. Working in small groups, investigate the subject of brainwashing. Try to find an example of brainwashing associated with a cult. Determine whether you think you could be brainwashed. Write a brief opinion paper that represents the group's findings.

Learning Activities

Turn to page 401 to complete the Learning Activities and Enrichment Activities for this chapter.

Notes

1. Jim Naughton, *Washington Post,* reprinted in "Personal Glimpses," *Reader's Digest,* October 1990, p. 181.

2. Naushad. S. Mehta/New York, Sylvester Monroe/Los Angeles, and Don Winbush/Atlanta, "Beyond the Melting Pot," *Time,* April 9, 1990, p. 28.

3. Cherie Carter-Scott, *Negaholics: How to Recover from Your Addiction to Negativity and Turn Your Life Around,* Villard Books, New York, 1989, p. 18.

4. Joseph T. Martorano and John P. Kildahl, "Say Yes to Yourself," *Reader's Digest,* May 1990, p. 157, condensed from their book, *Beyond Negative Thinking,* Insight Books (a division of Plenum Publishing Corporation), New York, 1989.

5. Martin E. P. Seligman, *Learned Optimism,* Alfred A. Knopf, Inc., New York, 1990, p. 207.

6. Dennis Cauchon, "Poll: Owners Favor Gun Laws," *USA TODAY,* March 17, 1993, p. 1A.

7. "Healing the Hate: What You Can Do About Racism," *Christopher News Notes,* July/August 1990.

8. Bernard Shaw, "Our Attitude About Women," *Vital Speeches,* February 1, 1993, p. 247.

9. "A Man Without Color," *Time,* December 20, 1970, p. 34.

10. Peter Brimelow, "The Spiral of Silence," *Forbes,* May 25, 1992, p. 77.

11. William B. Allen, "Why I Am Still Black," *Vital Speeches,* May 1, 1991, p. 430.

12. Elwood Chapman, *Your Attitude Is Showing,* 6th ed., Macmillan Publishing Company, New York, 1991, p. 21–22.

13. Gay Hendricks and Carol Leavenworth, *How to Love Every Minute of Your Life,* Prentice-Hall, Inc., Englewood Cliffs, NJ, 1978, p. 7.

14. B. Bower, "Adult Attitudes: Share and Share Alike," *Science News,* February 22, 1992, p. 116.

15. Daryl J. Bem, *Beliefs, Attitudes,* and *Human Affairs,* Brooks/Cole, Monterey, CA, 1970, p. 54.

16. Henry Gleitman, *Basic Psychology,* W. W. Norton & Company, New York, p. 313.

7 Thinking and Problem Solving

Learning Objectives

After completing this chapter, you will be able to do the following:

1. Distinguish between recognition and recall by determining which is involved in a number of situational examples.
2. Identify stages of cognitive development and associate an approximate age and mental ability with each stage.
3. Indicate how factors affecting memory could be applied to learning a specific skill in your major area of study.
4. Give an example of common-sense problem solving from your own experience and explain how components of common sense were involved.
5. Apply the chapter problem-solving formula to an actual or a hypothetical problem.
6. Suggest possible sources of advice or assistance for examples of transportation problems at different times in your life.
7. Suggest two possible solutions to a problem that might confront a young married couple and indicate which of the solutions you believe to be the better one and why.

> **66** *A person who never made a mistake never tried anything new.* **99**
>
> ALBERT EINSTEIN
> *scientist*

hink! When you think, what really happens in your brain? You might answer, "I never thought about it." If you have thought about it, but still don't know what is happening in your brain when you think, you are not alone. Although more has been discovered about the brain and its functions in recent years, it still is not known exactly how our brains perform when we remember, solve problems, or imagine new experiences. Fortunately, we can do these things without having to control or understand the processes consciously. However, we can learn to think more logically, remember more accurately and longer, and think more creatively. This ability could remove some of our frustration and make our lives more interesting.

The term *cognition* is frequently used in discussions of learning and thinking. It can be defined as the mental activity involved in processing, storing, and retrieving information.

Richard E. Mayer, in *Thinking, Problem Solving and Cognition,* explains that thinking includes three basic ideas:

1. Thinking is cognitive, but is inferred from behavior. It occurs internally, in the mind or cognitive system, and must be inferred indirectly.
2. Thinking is a process that involves some manipulation of or set of operations on knowledge in the cognitive system.
3. Thinking is directed and results in behavior that "solves" a problem or is directed toward a solution.[1]

What Mayer is saying can be interpreted as: Since we don't know what other people are thinking, we infer, or suppose, what they are thinking by their behavior. We use knowledge in the process of thinking. And finally, there is purpose to thinking. We think about a situation in order to decide what to do or how to solve a problem. We need mental ability to gain knowledge but we wouldn't have much to think about without knowledge. If you are serious about your present education and continued learning, you must be interested in gaining more knowledge and improving your ability to think and problem-solve.

A **problem** involves a situation that offers a choice of actions, and it therefore requires a decision about what should be done. A young person graduating from high school, for example, must decide whether to get more education or look for a job. Or a job opens up for someone who then faces the problem of getting there each day. The choices may include using public transportation such as a bus or train, driving, joining a carpool with other employees, or moving within walking distance of the job. If young parents work outside the home, they then have the problem of child care. The parents can share the responsibility if they work different hours; they can find a child care center that suits their needs; or they can explore other possibilities.

THE BRAIN   The human brain is considered the most mysterious mechanism in the universe. The structure of the brain is complex because of its millions of neural connections, and its various parts control specialities of human experience and behavior. We are concerned in this chapter, however, with only the parts of the brain involved with mental abilities and processes. The functioning of the brain may never be completely understood, but knowledge and

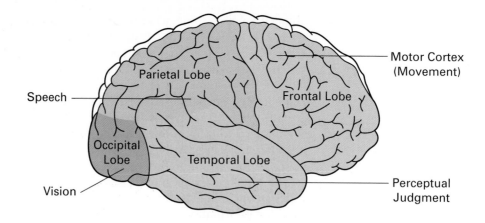

understanding are continuously increasing. At least be assured that you do have a brain and that it serves you in amazing ways.

Functioning of the Brain

We may partially understand the brain and its functioning in terms of the four lobes, which are primarily involved in experiences of the senses. We must remember that all experience comes to us through our senses. We wouldn't have much to think about without perception—sensory stimulation and interpretation. The illustration above shows the general location of the lobes of the brain.

There are also structural divisions of the brain identified as the hindbrain, the midbrain, and the forebrain. Although every part of the brain is essential to leading a normal life, it is the forebrain that will receive our attention in this chapter, as this is the area we use for thinking and problem solving.

It is the cerebral cortex that gives us the ability to speak, think, problem-solve, learn, and remember. It consists of two hemispheres that have numerous folds, or fissures, resembling a walnut. The two hemispheres are connected by a network of nerve fibers called the corpus callosum, which is essential to the interaction of the total brain. The illustration on page 139 shows a cross-section of the brain with the locations of the hindbrain, the midbrain, and the forebrain.

Two Brains?

Considerable popular attention have been given in recent years to whether a person is right-brained or left-brained. Studies have shown that the left side of the brain is more involved with language, logic, and mathematical ability, whereas the right side of the brain is more involved in our artistic, creative abilities, for example. The right side of the brain is believed to be more holistic, specializing in forming mental images or maps. The left hemisphere, on the other hand, might provide specific instructions for following the map. The right brain forms an overall image of a person; whereas the left brain would be more involved in noting specific features of the person's face and remembering his or her name.

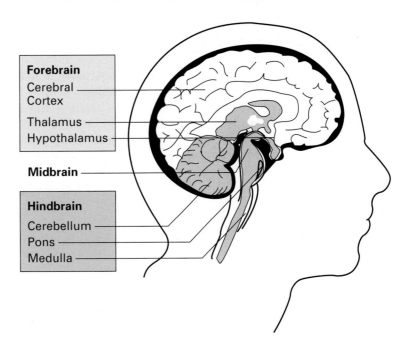

Forebrain
Cerebral Cortex
Thalamus
Hypothalamus

Midbrain

Hindbrain
Cerebellum
Pons
Medulla

Although the two hemispheres of the cerebral cortex do have such differences, scientists today are reminding us that the concept has been oversimplified. Rod Plotnik discusses this in the third edition of his *Introduction to Psychology:* "It is a popular notion that some of us primarily use the programs in our right hemispheres, which are characterized as involving images, creativity, and intuition, while others primarily use the programs of their left hemispheres, which are characterized as involving language, reason, and logic."[2] He refers to the work of Jerre Levy, a biopsychologist, who has done extensive research pertaining to the functioning and interaction of the two hemispheres.

Jerre Levy herself states:

> The two-brain myth was founded on an erroneous premise: that since each hemisphere was specialized, each must function as an independent brain. But in fact, just the opposite is true. To the extent that regions are differentiated in the brain, they must integrate their activities. Indeed, it is precisely that integration that gives rise to behavior and mental processes greater than and different from each region's special contribution."[3]

Since we do not have external controls, or switches, to operate our brains, it is reassuring to know that the brain itself knows how to function.

Sex Differences in the Brain?

Are there differences in the brain that affect the way males and females think? Do males and females have differences in kinds of mental abilities? The questions have been asked for generations but we still don't have all the answers. Many people, generations ago, just "knew," with no need of scientific proof, that the answer was, "Of course men and women think differently." A generation ago, many individuals, particularly feminists, strongly objected to even suggestions that they weren't the same as men, except for obvious physical differences. But scientists search for the truth, even if it isn't what they hope to find. They admit that studies aren't always in agreement and that the truth is often difficult to establish.

What are these scientists saying today about sex differences in the brain? There is limited recent research that points to some differences. Doreen Kimura, who has studied the subject extensively, has written an article in the *Scientific American,* in which she attributes differences to the effects of sex hormones in brain organization. These occur so early in life, she says, "that from the start the environment is acting on differently wired brains in girls and boys." She notes further "Major sex differences in intellectual function seem to lie in patterns of ability rather than in overall level of intelligence (IQ)."[4] Men, on the average, are better at spatial tasks, following a route, and on mentally manipulating an object in some way. Women, on the average, are better at such things as language skills, recalling landmarks on a route, and at some manual tasks requiring precision, according to recent research.

In considering sex differences in brain functioning, we are again cautioned not to overgeneralize and oversimplify. There are many differences and degrees of differences within each sex. Also, similarities in mental abilities of the sexes are greater than any differences that have as yet been identified. Finally, what each of us thinks may be more important than understanding exactly how we think.

A Human Computer?

The brain has sometimes been referred to as a "human computer." Although we know how electronic computers operate, we still are not certain how the human computer, or brain, operates. We can observe some similarities and differences between the two, however. Both the human brain and the electronic computer can store information and relate it in meaningful ways. The electronic brain, or computer, makes few mistakes if it is in working order and is given the right information and the right instructions.

Without doubt, computers will have additional capabilities in the future. The actual and potential problem-solving abilities of computers, similar to what would be considered intelligence in humans, is called *artificial intelligence*—a fascinating but highly controversial subject. Advances in any tech-

FRANK AND ERNEST by Bob Thaves

FRANK & ERNEST reprinted by permission of NEA, Inc.

nology are not accomplished by people who are quick to say, "It can't be done," however. Most people do not expect computers to surpass the intricacies and range of mental abilities of the human brain. A computer may not be expected to have imagination with which to be creative or an unconscious with which to dream, for example.

What would you SUGGEST? If you could make a suggestion to computer scientists for an ability you would like a computer have, what would it be?

STAGES OF COGNITIVE DEVELOPMENT

The Swiss psychologist Jean Piaget extensively studied the development of mental ability and identified four stages of **cognitive** or mental development. These stages with some of the characteristics of each stage are shown in the following list:

Sensorimotor Stage (Birth to 2 years)

Develops *self*-awareness as being separate from the rest of the world; recognizes objects and realizes that objects do not cease to exist when they are out of sight.

Preoperational Stage (2 to 7 years)

Develops some ability to remember and look forward to future events; pays attention to only one or two characteristics of an object rather than all (a 3-year-old child, for example, may think of an orange in terms of its color only, ignoring that it is also round, slightly rough, tasty, and fragrant); is not capable of mentally retracing a series of steps to reach a conclusion.

Concrete Operations Stage (7 to 11 years)

Can retrace thoughts; can consider more characteristics of objects; is capable of looking at a problem in different ways; can retain understanding of amount or mass even though shape may change (can understand, for example, that an amount of liquid remains the same when it is poured from a bottle of one shape to one of another).

Formal Operations Stage (12 years and up)

Can consider various solutions to a problem; can ponder consequences of action; can use reason and logic in problem solving; can think about **abstractions,** or ideas that are not directly related to specific objects (can think of the idea of justice without relating it to a specific situation).[5]

The age ranges for each of the stages are average and may vary with individuals. We can see, however, that the ability to do various types of thinking is developmental. This is an important factor in elementary education, but should also be useful to parents or anyone else associated with children. Children who are encouraged to use their mental abilities as they develop and who are allowed to solve some of their own problems are learning to become more effective problem solvers as adults. They learn to solve difficult problems by first solving fairly simple problems. Thus ability to solve problems depends both on development of mental abilities and on learning experiences. By the time young people begin high school, they have developed the ability to evaluate possibilities for their futures.

INTELLIGENCE OR INTELLIGENCES?

Does a person have a certain degree of intelligence or does he or she have degrees of different kinds of intelligences? It used to be generally thought that intelligence pertained to how "smart" a person was without recognizing different types of mental ability. We now know that intelligence varies not only in degree but also in kind from one person to another. Two people may have the same **intelligence quotient (IQ),** or score on an intelligence test, and yet their ability to solve particular kinds of problems or perform certain tasks may be quite different. One person may be good at word meanings and relationships; another may be outstanding in mathematics.

Howard Gardner in *Frames of Mind* discusses the "prerequisites of an intelligence." He says, "To my mind, a human intellectual competence must entail a set of skills of problem solving—enabling the individual *to resolve genuine problems or difficulties* that he or she encounters and, when appropriate, to create an effective product—and must also entail the potential for *finding or creating problems*—thereby laying the groundwork for the acquisition of new knowledge."[6] He identifies different kinds of intelligence as *linguistic, musical, logical-mathematical, spatial, bodily-kinesthetic,* and *personal intelligences.*[7] Linguistic intelligence pertains to ability to use and understand language. A person having this type of intelligence reads and writes with ease and may also be adept at learning new languages. Musical intelligence may pertain to learning to play a musical instrument or interpreting and perhaps even composing

These students are utilizing logical-mathematical intelligence as they participate in an after-school chess club.

music. Logical-mathematical intelligence is related to solving problems that involve step-by-step reasoning or mathematical relationships. Spatial intelligence helps a person visualize three dimensions, for example in reading blueprints. Bodily-kinesthetic intelligence pertains to mastery over the motions of one's body, which could be evident in gymnastics or dexterity required in one's work. Personal intelligence refers to understanding of oneself and understanding of others. A person may have a number of these intelligences or may excel in one while being only average or below average in others.

Today there is less emphasis on the measurement of mental ability and more concern with motivation and learning opportunities. Your desire to learn, in most cases, is more important than your score on an IQ test. The extent to which one learns and develops her or his abilities depends also, in large measure, on the environment in which one lives. If Angela grew up in a family that followed and discussed current events, she is likely to have more motivation to develop her mental abilities than someone whose family has lived only in their own small world of interests and problems.

LEARNING AND MEMORY

You have been learning since you were born, and you will continue to learn all your life. Learning results in a relatively permanent change in behavior. We

This teacher of jazz dancing is demonstrating and communicating bodily-kinesthetic intelligence.

must consider all types of behavior, however, including physical and emotional as well as mental. **Learning** may involve the acquisition of knowledge, the understanding of facts and principles, the development of skills, or the shaping of attitudes and values. An educated person has developed learning in each of these areas. Career education programs are usually planned carefully to include all types of learning.

There are many ways to learn besides taking formal courses. We can learn from experience, from observation and listening, and from independent study. Activities of the human brain that show evidence of learning include interpreting, recognizing, associating, and recalling. Rhonda, for example, interprets the dark screen on a television set as a burned-out transistor, thus giving meaning to clues that she perceives. Upon examination of the set, she recognizes, or identifies, the transistor that is burned out and needs replacement. She associates, or compares, the present task with a similar lab activity. She recalls, or remembers from previous learning, where the transistor for replacement is located. The brain may perform these four activities in any order or even all at once.

Memory is the ability to retain, or hold, knowledge or learning. Like most mental activities, it is more complex than we might expect even if it involves something we know very well. An article in *Psychology Today* states, "It is now widely accepted that memory is not stored in a single cell, but is spread out over an extensive neuronal network."[8]

It is generally believed that there are three stages in the memory process. The first stage is referred to as *sensory register* and lasts only a fraction of a second when we are aware of something but do not give it further attention. You are using sensory register when you scan a newspaper, looking for a particular item, for example.

The second stage is referred to as *short-term memory* and probably lasts less than a minute. This involves information we want to use for only a brief pe-

Reprinted by permission of the artist, Harley L. Schwadron.

riod of time. You may look up a number in the telephone directory, for example, and remember it only long enough to dial it. Some authorities in memory are now substituting the term working memory for short-term memory. According to Alan Baddeley, one of these authorities, "The term working memory refers to a brain system that provides temporary storage and manipulation of the information necessary for such complex cognitive tasks as language comprehension, learning, and reasoning."[9]

Learning that we do, in contrast, involves the third stage, or *long-term memory*. We not only want to learn certain things, but we also want to be able to recall them at appropriate times. Long-term memory consists of two basic types identified by Endel Tulving in *Organization of Memory*.[10] These are semantic memory and episodic memory and are described by A. Christine Parham in *Psychology: Studying the Behavior of People* as:

> *Semantic* memory is the part of long-term memory that consists of information, facts, and general, nonpersonal knowledge. It is sometimes said to be like a dictionary or encyclopedia because information is stored semantically in terms of meaning. Semantic memory forms the basis for comprehension, thinking, reasoning, and decision making. *Episodic* memory is the part of long-term memory that consists of the chronologic record of a person's personal experiences. It is sometimes said to be like the person's diary—an autobiographical record. The requirement for episodic memory is merely to have an experience and form a long-term memory of it. Episodic memory is particularly affected by rehearsal or repetition.[11]

To recall something from your memory, without clues, can be more difficult than to recognize an idea or information with the aid of a sensory stimulus such as sight, sound, taste, touch, or smell. For example, if you were asked to name the capitals of the fifty states, you might find it difficult to recall all of them. But if you were given a matching exercise with the states in one column and the capitals in another, you would be more likely to match them correctly.

Other evidence of the function of memory can be seen in relearning. Even when previous learning cannot be recalled or is recognized only faintly, it is easier and faster to relearn the material than it was to learn it in the first place. When people say they have poor memory, they are not speaking accurately. Memory is not something a person has or doesn't have. Memory is an ability that can be developed, and it can be improved.

Memory

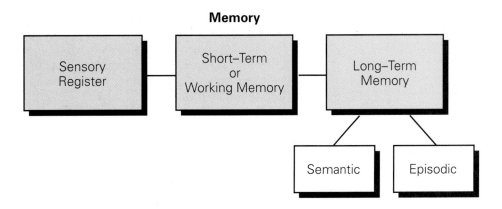

INTUITION AND INSIGHT

Intuition is often associated with problem solving, but what is it? Daniel Goleman and others in *The Creative Spirit* explain their understanding of intuition:

> Our intuition draws directly on the vast storehouse of information which is an open book to the unconscious but to some degree closed to consciousness. That is why, for instance, courses preparing students to take the Scholastic Aptitude Test advise that if we are stumped by a question, we should make our guess the first answer that seems right. Indeed, experimental studies have shown that first hunches generally form the basis for better decisions than those decisions made after rationally working through the pros and cons. When we trust our intuition, we are really turning to the wisdom of the unconscious."[12]

Some of us may know from experience that we cannot always rely on intuition as an approach to problem solving. When it is successful, it is referred to as intuition; when it isn't, it may be called a "bad hunch."

Insight refers to deep understanding of a situation that is difficult to analyze or explain, but nevertheless is helpful in making judgments and decisions. Dennis Coon in *Essentials of Psychology: Exploration and Application* defines insight as, "A sudden reorganization of a problem causing the solution to seem self-evident."[13] Perhaps you have had the experience of mentally wrestling with a problem for quite a while and all of a sudden, like a flash, the solution pops into your mind. "I've got it!" might have been your reaction. Insight also involves the unconscious and is often referred to as wisdom. The more knowledge and experience one has, the more likely he or she is to have insightful solutions to problems.

CONTRIBUTORS TO LEARNING AND MEMORY

We remember only a small part of what we learn. Many factors determine what we learn and how well or how long we remember it. The more factors involved in a particular learning experience, the better it will be remembered. A few of these factors include motivation, meaningfulness of skill or material, attention, association, and repetition.

Motivation

How well you learn and remember depends greatly on your reasons for doing so. If you are quite confident that your learning skills will help you get the kind of job you want, you are likely to learn well. You remember the name of a person to see about getting a job if you really want the job. Or, you remember your friend's birthday because that person is special in some way. When you have reasons for remembering something, you are also likely to make use of the following additional factors.

Meaningfulness of Skill or Material

It is easier for you to remember something if it makes sense to you, if you understand what you are trying to learn. Something learned by strict memorization, or *rote learning,* is often not understood and, therefore, cannot be applied and is easily forgotten. You could memorize nonsense syllables that have no meaning for you or formulas you do not understand. But you would not remember them as well as material that has meaning and usefulness for you.

Attention

You remember better if you give careful and undivided attention to what you are doing. You can be so involved mentally in a project or work that is interesting or important that you are quite unaware of other things that are taking place around you. A young man who is concentrating on troubleshooting an engine may not notice that others are putting away tools or that he is hungry; he may not even hear a whistle blow. But when he does leave his work and later returns, he will remember what he has already tried and tested.

Association

When you use association, you relate what you want to recall to something else easily recalled. You often can remember the names of people if you associate them with the way the people look, or the kind of work they do, or the place where you were or the thing you were doing when you met them. You may not recognize Joan's cousin, whom you met only once, unless you see her with Joan, whom you know well.

There are many interesting—and sometimes silly, but effective—ways to remember by association. You may have relied on the following rhyme to help you remember how to spell some words:

> *i* before *e,* except after *c*
> or when sounded like *a*
> as in *neighbor* and *weigh*

Such a technique, called a **mnemonic device,** is intended to assist memory. Another mnemonic device is the word *HOMES* for remembering the Great Lakes: *H*uron, *O*ntario, *M*ichigan, *E*rie, and *S*uperior. Do you know of other such memory aids? Why not develop a mnemonic device of your own for something you want to remember?

Repetition

Performing an activity over and over in the same way helps you to learn and also to remember what has been learned. It was mentioned earlier that you remember your friend's telephone number because you have reason to remember it. Another factor that helps you remember the number from day to day is using it often. Mentally going over a procedure, as well as actually doing it, helps one to remember. The use of repetition, or practice, is one of the techniques involved in on-the-job training programs. Trainees, for example, often learn how to operate a machine by repeating the process over and over again. When people set up their own practice sessions, they find that spaced, shorter sessions give them better results than longer practice periods. A person practicing information processing, for example, will show greater improvement from practicing an hour a day for six days than from practicing six hours one day but none the next five.

Another type of repetition that aids memory is known as overlearning. To overlearn is to review mentally or orally what you have already learned in order to assure greater retention. Although it may not be interesting to review what you already know, experiments have shown that it is an effective memory technique. Students who review their mathematics equations every week will easily remember them throughout the course.

Many books and articles have been written on improving memory, and many gimmicks are advertised as being useful for that purpose. Remember, however, that you are the one who has to improve this ability. Techniques can be learned and can be useful, but success is dependent largely on the factors we have just considered.

What do you THINK?

Would you agree with, "The more you know the easier it is to learn more"? Why or why not?

EXPERIENCE AND COMMON SENSE

The knowledge or skill gained from being engaged in an activity is referred to as experience. We can learn from experience how to solve problems and also how to avoid problems. Experience teaches us not to repeat an activity that has brought undesirable results. Yet it is impractical for us to experience everything firsthand. Some things are obviously best learned through the experience of others. From their experience we learn not to risk swimming alone in unknown bodies of water because of current and depth hazards, for example. Neither do we knowingly test the consequences of lighting a flame near explosive vapors nor expose ourselves unnecessarily to radiation or high-voltage lines.

A common difficulty in benefiting from the experience of others is the great amount of conflicting suggestions and advice available. When you want to change jobs, buy a car, or even arrange for a date, you can usually get more advice than you can use or may want. On the other hand, advice based on the experience of others can save time, money, pain, and even your life. To profit from this source of experience, you must be able to evaluate suggestions and decide what advice you can use and in what way you can use it.

Every normal human being possesses a type of problem-solving ability known as common sense. A definition of **common sense** might be the ability to make use of past experience to prevent or avoid a problem or to react to a situation that demands immediate attention. According to this definition, a person using common sense is able to:

- identify danger and take necessary precautions for the protection of life,
- identify possible hazards to equipment or property,
- consider probabilities in cause and effect,
- engage available human resources, and
- make appropriate use of available tools and materials—improvising, if necessary.

As learning experiences vary from one individual to another, so do uses of common sense in any given problem situation. Common sense might be credited with solving the following problem.

What would you SUGGEST? A truck became wedged in an underpass. Most of the suggestions offered by bystanders involved damage to either the underpass or the truck. What would you suggest? A workable solution is on p. 158.

It would be worthwhile for everyone to remember that others do not have the same type or degree of common sense that he or she has. People cannot be expected, therefore, to react to a problem in the same ways. It can be very frustrating to a new person on a job to be expected to know how to handle situations with which he or she has no knowledge or experience. Although it is true that those who live and work in similar environments often have similar common sense, many problems require more than that type of everyday problem-solving ability.

GUIDELINES TO PROBLEM SOLVING

The following guidelines to problem solving can be helpful to a person in a situation requiring analysis, evaluation, decision, and action, when an immediate solution is not required.

Define the problem.

Look at the total situation.

Identify problems related to the major problem.

Determine possible causes of the problem and related problems.

Consider as many solutions as possible.

Consider sources of advice and assistance.

Evaluate plus and minus factors of each solution.

Decide on a solution.

Take the first active step.

Reevaluate the effectiveness of the solution.

Each of these guidelines is discussed in the following pages, along with some specific examples. A similar approach and procedure can be used to solve your own problems.

Define the Problem

This first step in problem solving is often the most difficult but is also the most important. Defining the problem is difficult because many people do not look at themselves or their situations objectively. They are likely to blame someone else for their troubles or to emphasize the wrong factor. Thus to really solve a problem, you must determine all the facts and conditions as distinctly and clearly as possible.

Look at the Total Situation

The gestalt principle of perception, discussed in Chapter 4, applies to this early stage of problem solving. Although the situation may be complex and you may not be able to deal with all aspects of it at the same time, it is helpful to see the total picture. You must relate the various aspects of the situation to the overall problem by looking at the total situation and determining what things you can—and want to —change.

Identify Related Problems

A complex problem usually includes a number of interrelated smaller problems. These problems could pertain to time, money, energy, motivation, abilities, or relationships with others. Such problems must be identified and assigned an order of importance in solving the main problem. Also, solving one of the minor problems sometimes leads to solving the major problem.

Determine Possible Causes

In a situation involving a complex problem it is not always simple to distinguish between cause and effect. In fact, an effect of one problem may cause another problem in the total situation. The following questions must be considered at this stage of problem analysis: If two things are happening in sequence or at the same time, is one related to or causing the other? Is an identified cause of a problem the sole cause or only one of a number of causes? What may at first seem to be the obvious cause may not be the underlying cause of a problem at all. All possible cause-and-effect relationships must be considered.

Consider as Many Solutions as Possible

Visualize your problem as being solved. Compare your situation now with what you want it to be. Then consider as many ways as possible to arrive at the desired change in your situation. Think of as many possible solutions as you can before deciding which to use. The first solution that comes to mind may not be the most effective. You might use individualized brainstorming as discussed later in this chapter to think of solution possibilities.

Consider Sources of Advice and Assistance

For a number of reasons it is often advisable to seek advice and assistance in problem solving. Because it is difficult to see yourself and your problem objectively, someone else can often help you define your problem more accurately. Also, because of special knowledge or experience, others may be able to suggest solutions that you would fail to consider on your own. Not to be overlooked, either, is the moral support you can receive in making your decision and taking necessary action. Students, counselors, and financial aid personnel, found in nearly every community and technical college, can also help with both academic and personal problems. Advice from your family and friends, who have a special interest in you, is also worth consideration. A further value of sharing your problems with others is that often, in just talking about a situation, you view it in a different perspective and may come up with your own solution.

What a person does in this step of problem solving depends on the particular problem, on the types of advice and assistance available, and on the preferences of the individual. It is not suggested that you run for help whenever you encounter some difficulty. But it can be just as unwise to ignore available sources of advice and assistance.

Evaluate Plus and Minus Factors of Each Solution

The approach-avoidance conflicts discussed in Chapter 3 were really situations presenting problems. It may be a good idea at this time to review these conflicts. Almost every decision you can make has both positive and negative factors or characteristics. How you weigh these factors depends on your circumstances and values. What might be a plus factor to one person could be a minus or at least a neutral factor to you. The cost of buying a computer, for example, may be a minus factor to one person, whereas to another a computer would be well worth the immediate cost or possible payments. The plus factor of its usefulness could outweigh the minus factor of cost. It is essential to keep your needs, abilities, and values in mind in evaluating possible solutions. One should also consider the effects of a decision on others and one's relationships with them. Note the involvement of motivational conflicts discussed in Chapter 3.

Decide on a Solution

After thoughtful consideration and investigation of all the previous guidelines in problem solving, you must decide which solution you believe would be most effective and practical. Not only must a solution work, but it must also be practical in terms of the time, cost, and effort involved. If you are having serious trouble with your car, for example, the most effective solution to your transportation problem would be to buy a new one, but that may not be practical in terms of your financial situation.

Take the First Active Step

When a solution has been decided upon, you must take action to put the solution into effect. The first step in this procedure should be taken as soon as possible or practical. For example, if you decide that you are going to contact a credit union about a loan, look up the telephone number or address and make the contact as soon as possible.

Reevaluate the Effectiveness of the Solution

Some decisions in life are somewhat more permanent, such as getting married or buying a house. Others also have a degree of permanence, for example, attending a particular school, starting a new job, or even buying a car. It is difficult but not impossible to make changes after action has been taken in light of such decisions. In many other situations, it is relatively easy to reevaluate or change a decision if a solution proves ineffective. It is important in such cases to follow through by reevaluating solution effectiveness. A person who makes a practice of evaluating decisions and their results not only solves problems more effectively but also foresees and prevents additional problems that others may overlook.

CREATIVE THINKING

To be creative is to be imaginative and original in developing new works of art, products, services, uses of materials, or ways of doing things. Creative thinking is not a new approach to problem solving. An example from ancient times involves Hammurabi, king of ancient Babylon, who was concerned about getting people to a water supply. He solved the problem by realizing that it would be more practical to find a way of getting the water to his people. Through this type of thinking and problem solving, the concept of a canal was developed.

You may have noticed that many new foods, styles, materials, and processes are not completely original but are combinations or variations of things already familiar in some form. Other innovations simply make things smaller or larger than they were. The minicalculator is an example. Another is the adult-size tricycle used by older people who do not feel secure on a bicycle or a moped.

Everyone can do creative thinking and problem solving. We can all learn to use the abilities of our right brain more fully. We can learn to perceive characteristics and relationships that otherwise would go unnoticed by others. Creative thinking is not just a magic bursting of ideas in the minds of especially gifted individuals. Even though some people have more natural creative talent than others, we can all be creative in some ways.

To be creative is to be original. The objectives of creative people are usually to express themselves, to make life more interesting, and to seek improvements in their surroundings. The world is constantly presenting its inhabitants with new problems, and human beings are also constantly seeking new or better solutions to old problems. Some of the best future solutions will be the result of creative thinking.

Characteristics of Creative Thinkers

Although creative thinking is not as structured as traditional problem solving, creative people have demonstrated that they have several characteristics in common. If we want to become more creative, it may help to try to develop these characteristics.

Questioning Attitude   Creative thinkers wonder why things are the way they are and how they might be changed and improved. New ways of doing things, after all, are often just variations or adaptations of old ways. Two stimulating questions used by creative workers are, How can present methods be changed or combined for an improved effect? and What materials can be substituted for those that are costly, scarce, ineffective, or dangerous in some way? Individuals who consider such questions frequently in their work and other activities find that they are generating new ideas. Periods of waiting can be used to perceive one's environment in new ways, boring tasks can become stimulating, work can become highly challenging, and all of life can become extremely rewarding.

Self-Confidence   To be creative means, in a sense, to be different. Creative people are looking for new ways to do things. Their ideas and even their products are often criticized by others who are less imaginative or who are reluctant to change their ways. This resistance does not bother creative persons. They have confidence in their individuality and in their ability. When they do make mistakes or develop "duds," they can laugh at themselves and try something else. They are not embarrassed or stifled by criticism from others and can evaluate their work's worth. They are their own critics to a large degree.

Flexibility   It doesn't disturb creative people as much as it does others if things go wrong. They can adapt to new methods and even think of better ones. They can go without what others might consider necessities or substitute new uses for existing products. Neither do they feel the need to function according to fixed schedules. Variations in when and how they do their work, if within the requirements of the job, help them to break out of fixed patterns of time and procedure. They are generally less disturbed by what others may consider inconveniences.

Ability to Concentrate   Creative thinkers give their undivided attention to their projects. They may sometimes appear inattentive, but their minds are occupied with the task at hand, and they are not distracted by other environmental stimuli. People who have developed the ability to concentrate may at times be totally unaware of what is going on around them.

Persistence   Many people who are creative explain that they cannot be creative at will. This is partly because the unconscious mind is involved in the creative process. Some creative people become familiar with the problem and what they want to achieve. Then, they let the problem rest, giving their unconscious minds an opportunity to solve it.

There are many variations in how creative people work. Sometimes they get an inspiration for a complete piece of work or project at once. Or creative people may develop ideas as they get further into their work. In any case, creative people do not give up easily, do not lose confidence in their ability, and make fuller use of both their conscious and unconscious mental abilities than most of us do.

 What would you SAY?   If someone were to ask what you considered the outstanding characteristic of a creative person, what would you say?

 **Quiz yourself on Connecting Dots**   The problem is to connect all the dots by drawing no more than four straight lines without lifting your pencil or pen from the paper.

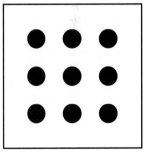

The answer is on page 159.

Brainstorming

Creative thinking can also be done by a group. One type of group creative thinking has been made popular by Alex Osborn and is called **brainstorming.** With this approach, a group of people get together and spontaneously pool as many ideas as possible about a given problem. Following are Osborn's rules for a brainstorming session during the period when ideas are being presented:

- Criticism is not allowed. This will come later when the ideas are evaluated.
- The wilder the idea, the better. It is easier to discard or modify ideas than to think of new ones.
- Quantity is more important than quality—the more ideas, the better.
- Combinations and variations of ideas are welcome. One idea leads to another. Some brainstormers refer to this association of ideas as "hitchhiking."[14]

It is also profitable to engage in your own brainstorming to solve some of your problems. Simply follow the rules for brainstorming, jotting down ideas as fast as you can think of them, without evaluation or self-criticism. Then look at your ideas more critically to see whether any of them have merit.

Lateral and Vertical Thinking

Edward de Bono, a well-known British author of works on thinking and problem solving, has developed a type of problem solving that he calls lateral thinking. This type of thinking involves taking different viewpoints and approaches to problem solving. Sometimes we have difficulty solving a problem because we are viewing it in the same way we have approached similar problems in the past. Lateral thinking is different from vertical thinking, or logical thinking, which proceeds step-by-step in a given direction.

A writer who attended one of de Bono's lateral thinking seminars describes the following problem often used by de Bono.[15] What would your explanation be?

"OKAY, TURN RIGHT AND THEN RIGHT AGAIN AND WE'LL BE OUT.."

Three worms, a mother, father, and baby worm, crawl partway up a little hill and then crawl into it at different points. Upon coming out on the other side, the baby worm looks back and says, "I see only two holes."

Check de Bono's explanation on p. 159.

The writer quotes de Bono in saying, "Whatever you're thinking about, there will be things you'll take for granted." A lateral thinker does not take for granted things that interfere with different approaches to solving a problem.

Another example used by de Bono pertains to the fish-processing industry in England. The old way of filleting fish was to pull the meat from the bones. One day a worker suggested that the process be reversed. His suggestion was tried and it worked, and removing the bones from the meat became the improved method.

In brainstorming, discussed earlier, lateral thinking is used in the first part of a session to break out of mental ruts and to generate new ideas. Vertical thinking is then done to see whether any of the ideas will work. Many problems in business and industry have been solved this way. The method has also been used to improve products and develop new processes.

QUALITY CIRCLES

A relatively new approach to problem solving on the job is known as a **quality circle.** This type of group is concerned with more than problems, however. Those using this approach are trying to prevent problems from happening in the first place. The quality circle originated in Japan but is now widely used in the United States and other countries. The book *Quality Circles: How to Make Them Work in America* gives us the following definition:

> A quality circle is a small group of employees and their supervisor from the same work area, who voluntarily meet on a regular basis to study quality control and productivity improvement techniques, to apply these techniques to identify and solve work-related problems, to present their solutions to management for approval, and to monitor the implementation of these solutions to ensure that they work.[16]

Some of the characteristics of quality circles are the following:

- Quality circles are small. The best size is about eight members.
- All members come from the same shop or work area.
- The members work under the same supervisor, who is a member of the circle. The supervisor does not issue orders or make decisions. The circle members, as a group, draw their own conclusions, and make recommendations.
- Participation is voluntary. Everyone in a shop or office has an opportunity to join or not, to quit the circle, or to rejoin.
- Circles usually meet once every week on company time, with pay. They usually meet in a meeting room away from their normal work area.
- Circle members, not management, choose the problems and projects they will work on. They can request information or assistance from technical specialists or management, however.

A quality circle group are exchanging ideas with obvious interest and commitment.

- Circle members receive advice and guidance from an adviser who attends all circle meetings but who is not a circle member.
- Presentations are given to managers and technical specialists who normally make a decision on a proposal by the circle.
- Circles exist as long as the members wish to meet. This may be for months or years, solving numerous problems, or for a short period of time, dealing with a specific problem or need.

Results of quality circles include improved morale and loyalty to the company or organization, increased teamwork among employees, and improved productivity and quality of the product or service. They are also known to reduce grievances, lost time, accidents, absenteeism, tardiness, and resignations.[17] For these reasons they are popular among employees at all levels as well as among managers and owners of businesses. Team problem solving will be discussed further in Chapter 13, "Human Relations at Work."

LIFE AND PROBLEM SOLVING

Problems are a part of life. You have already faced many problems in your life and you undoubtedly face some right now. You will become more effective — and, therefore, happier — if you become a better problem solver.

There are variations from person to person in what is perceived as a problem, what can be considered as possible solutions, and what is selected as the best solution. Individual needs, abilities, opportunities, and values all influence one's decision and course of action in solving problems.

You may think that if you could remove all problems from your life, you would be a happier person. And it is true that fewer health, financial, family, or social problems would make life more secure and satisfying. There is constant effort being made by individuals and society, therefore, to prevent or solve such problems.

Not having any problems, however, would essentially leave you with no choices in life, which would be dull and uninteresting. In fact, life consists of a constant stream of problems, some of which are not really undesirable. Sometimes we even create problems for the enjoyment or challenge of solving them. Athletic contests, puzzles, and many games are problems that have been created for the purpose of trying to overcome the obstacles and "win."

We will be able to continue to learn as long as we live, barring brain injury or disease. Our brains will not wear out or use up their potential for "storing knowledge" or developing understanding. And we can learn to use our mental abilities more fully and creatively. Although the full extent of our mental abilities is not known, it is suspected that we use only a portion of our brain power. This does not necessarily mean that we are mentally lazy, but it does suggest that we have mental abilities that we have not yet learned to use or are not using effectively. Most of us have greater mental potential than we will ever develop or use to our advantage.

Take a problem-solving approach to life. Not only will your life become safer and more financially sound, but it will be more challenging and interesting.

What do you THINK?

It has been said that good judgment comes from experience — and that experience comes from poor judgment. To what extent do you think parents, teachers, and employers should allow others to make mistakes in learning in order to solve problems and develop good judgment?

SUMMARY

People can learn to develop and use more of their mental abilities despite the fact that they do not understand completely how their brains function.

A problem is a situation in which some change is desired, there is some choice of possible solutions, and a decision must be made about what action to take. Since life brings problems for all of us, effective living consists of effective problem solving. A person who learns to think and reason effectively in solving problems will lead a stimulating and productive life.

Research indicates that the right and left hemispheres of the brain have specialized abilities but that they function together in a whole-brain system. Recent research also seems to confirm that there are sex differences in the biology and functioning of the brain. Both of these brain-related subjects are controversial, however.

According to Jean Piaget, ability to think and problem-solve is developmental. He has identified four stages of this development: sensorimotor, preoperational, concrete operations, and formal operations. Abilities range from the recognition of objects in the sensorimotor stage to abstract thinking in the formal operations stage.

It would be more accurate to refer to human intelligences or kinds of mental abilities, rather than intelligence in general. Kinds of intelligence include linguistic, musical, logical-mathematical, spatial, bodily-kinesthetic, and personal.

Memory is the ability to retain knowledge or learning. Three stages in the memory process are sensory register, short-term memory, and long-term memory. There are two basic types of long-term memory: semantic and episodic. Mental activities involving learning and interpretation are recognition, association, and recall. Factors that contribute to learning and memory are motivation, meaningfulness of skill or material, attention, association, and repetition.

People can solve problems more effectively if they employ the following guidelines to problem solving: define the problem, look at the total situation, identify problems related to the major problem, determine possible causes of the problem and related problems, consider as many solutions as possible, consider sources of advice and assistance, evaluate plus and minus factors of each solution, decide on a solution, take the first active step, and later reevaluate the effectiveness of the solution.

A degree of common-sense problem-solving ability results from experience in living. People have developed common sense when they can identify danger and take necessary precautions for the protection of life, identify possible hazards to equipment or property, consider probabilities in cause and effect, engage available human resources, and make appropriate use of available tools and materials — improvising, if necessary.

Although creativity is generally thought of as a talent, anyone can become a more creative thinker. Characteristics of creative thinkers are a questioning attitude, self-confidence, flexibility, ability to concentrate, and persistence. A popular type of creative problem solving is known as brainstorming. This type of creative thinking, in the first phase, stresses quantity rather than quality of ideas, expression of wild ideas without criticism, and combination of ideas. In the second phase these ideas are evaluated to determine whether they are workable.

Another relatively new type of group problem solving is the quality circle. In a typical quality circle, all employees of a particular department, including the supervisor, meet regularly to discuss how to improve productivity and quality of products or service, as well as related problems. Suggestions are then passed on to administrators, who consider their implementation.

Since not all problems can be solved and not all situations can be changed to one's complete satisfaction, people often find that they themselves must change. They must learn to accept or adjust to situations and conditions that cannot be changed as they would prefer. Adjusting to changes that are natural or inevitable in life is essential for harmonious living. This is the subject of Chapter 8, "Coping with Stress."

Answers to What Would You Suggest? on p. 149
One bystander suggested letting some of the air out of the tires. The height of the truck was thereby lowered and the vehicle moved out without damage to the truck or underpass.

Solution to Dots problem on p. 153

Many people assume that they have to draw a square formation or that the lines may not fall outside the dots. There are also other possible solutions. Can you think of any?

Answers to Quiz Yourself on p. 155

According to de Bono, the baby worm can't count. An effective lateral thinker does not make assumptions that would narrow thinking — in this case, the assumption that the baby worm could count.

Psychology In Practice

1. Check your school or community library for a book or videotape on memory. Select a resource that explains the "loci," "peg," or a similar method, for improving one's memory. Use one of these methods to remember something you are currently studying in one of your courses or in your work.

2. Brainstorming can be fun, and it is also very effective in problem solving. If you belong to a club or some other organized group, suggest that the group brainstorm how to raise money to go on a trip or to a convention.

3. Identify six problems or related parts of one problem someone might have that involve health, finances, a family situation, or work. List them according to the order in which you think they should be solved. If you think some have equal priority or must be solved at the same time, be able to explain why.

Learning Activities

Turn to page 405 to complete the Learning Activities and Enrichment Activities for this chapter.

Notes

1. Richard E. Mayer, *Thinking, Problem Solving and Cognition,* W. H. Freeman and Company, New York, 1992, p. 7.
2. Rod Plotnik, *Introduction to Psychology,* 3rd ed., Brooks/Cole Publishers (a division of Wadsworth, Inc.), Belmont, CA, 1993, p. 81.
3. Jerre Levy, "Right Brain, Left Brain: Fact and Fiction," *Psychology Today,* May 1985, p. 43.
4. Doreen Kimura, "Sex Differences in the Brain," *Scientific American,* September 1992, p. 119.
5. Richard I. Evans, *Jean Piaget: The Man and His Ideas,* E. P. Dutton and Company, Inc., New York, 1973, pp. 15–27.
6. Howard Gardner, *Frames of Mind,* Basic Books, Inc., New York, 1983, p. 60.
7. Ibid., pp. 73–77.
8. Beth Livermore, "Build a Better Brain," *Psychology Today,* October 1992, p. 41.
9. Alan Baddeley, "Working Memory," *Science,* January 1992, p. 556.
10. Endel Tulving and W. Donaldson, eds., *Organization of Memory,* Academic Press, New York, 1972, cited in: A. Christine Parham, *Psychology: Studying the Behavior of People,* South-Western Publishing Company, Cincinnati, OH, 1988, p. 233.

11. A. Christine Parham, *Psychology: Studying the Behavior of People,* South-Western Publishing Company, Cincinnati, OH, 1988, p. 231.

12. Daniel Goleman, Paul Kaufman, and Michael Ray, *The Creative Spirit,* a Dutton Book, Penguin Books USA, Inc., New York, 1992, p. 131.

13. Dennis Coon, *Essentials of Psychology: Exploration and Application,* 5th ed., West Publishing Company, St. Paul, MN, 1991.

14. Alex Osborn, *Applied Imagination,* Charles Scribner's Sons, New York, 1963, p. 84.

15. Kevin McManus, "How to Think Sideways," *Forbes,* December 20, 1982, p. 152.

16. Philip C. Thompson, *Quality Circles: How to Make Them Work in America,* AMA-COM, American Management Association, New York, 1982, pp. 3 and 4.

17. Ibid., p. 11.

8 Coping with Stress

Learning Objectives

After completing this chapter, you will be able to do the following:

1. Give an example of ways a person might adapt to experiences in life that require major adjustments.
2. Suggest orientation information or experience that would be helpful to a new employee.
3. Determine areas of living that would require adjustment because of job-related situations.
4. Explain how a family might cope with their total situation following a job layoff and unemployment.
5. Explain why you believe (or don't believe) a person experiences the five stages of coping with the approach of his or her own death, according to Dr. Kübler-Ross.
6. Identify the coping mechanisms employed in a number of incidents describing defensive behavior.
7. Give suggestions a young adult might use in learning to live independently.

> **66***God grant me the serenity to accept the things I cannot change Courage to change the things I can And wisdom to know the difference.***99**
>
> REINHOLD NIEBUHR
> *pastor and educator*

What do you do in a situation that is not the way you would like it to be? Marcy may say, "Change it." Aaron may say, "Accept it." Jerry may say, "Learn to adjust to it." We have to be able to do any of these things, but first we have to decide which is most appropriate.

Because even the best problem solvers cannot always get the results they want, they also must be able to accept what they cannot change or adjust. They must make some changes in themselves and in their behavior to fit unchanging situations. The ability to solve problems, to accept what we cannot change, and to make adjustments in ourselves, as appropriate, is called **coping.** This is something we have to do throughout life. Chapter 7, "Thinking and Problem Solving," should be helpful in the coping process. Without the ability to cope, our personal lives and those of people in general would be burdened with problems. We would also experience excessive stress and its harmful effects.

MAJOR ADJUSTMENTS IN LIFE

As long as we live we will have to cope with change. Even though some of the changes will be desirable, we will still need the ability to adjust. Some of the situations during our lifetimes that will challenge our ability to cope are discussed in the following sections. Although each of us may not personally experience all of these, we will be faced with situations with which we must cope from the beginning of our lives to the end.

Early Experiences

Leaving the security of the mother's womb and entering the entirely different environment of the outside world is the first major adjustment a human being must make. Although no one recalls his or her entry into the world, there has been much concern in recent years that the birth process has been a shocking, disturbing experience for newborns. Instead of being spanked into a new world of bright lights and noise, many infants today are undergoing "birth without violence." This involves softer lighting and a quiet, relaxed setting. The baby is laid against the mother's body so that both may experience a sense of warmth and security immediately after the delivery. This method is an attempt to ease the baby's adjustment in moving from the warmth and security of the mother's womb into the outside world.

For many children, the next major change may involve absence from the parents for hours at a time while they work. Day care centers have been established almost everywhere, and their trained personnel teach and care for children from infancy to school age. Most children adjust quickly to this change and even enjoy their experiences at the centers.

For other children, the beginning of school is the first time they are away from home for any length of time. Parents' attitudes and the examples of older brothers and sisters influence how well a young child makes this adjustment. Even at this early age, a child's self-concept affects how this new experience is approached. The degree of success in adjusting to school life later influences how the child will adjust to future changes.

There also are other reasons why young children sometimes have to make adjustments. There may be a change of position in the family with the arrival

PEANUTS reprinted by permission of UFS, Inc.

of a new brother or sister. For a first child who has been the center of attention, this adjustment can be quite difficult. Hospitalization during the early years can be another situation that requires adjustments. Today, both parents and the hospitalized child receive special attention to make this adjustment as pleasant as possible.

Adolescence

The teen years, or **adolescence,** are filled with complex psychological and physical changes. The young boy or girl must adjust to the physical change of becoming an adult, known as **puberty.** Some young people are very self-conscious about their body changes. They may also have relatively low self-esteem, and therefore acceptance and approval are important to them. They need to have the opportunity to communicate their feelings and to feel that they are understood. They have this need even though parents may feel that their adolescents do not want to communicate with them and are even somewhat rebellious. When there is too much adolescent-parent conflict, some young people leave home; others are asked by their parents to leave or are "kicked out." Some troubled teens often turn to drugs or even suicide. They do not realize that help is available and that they can learn to manage their lives.

Adolescents must cope with increased responsibility and independence. Even though young people may look upon these changes as desirable, there are likely to be some confusing and disturbing times for them. They must strive to achieve individual development while being influenced strongly by their peers.

Although there are numerous difficulties in leaving childhood and approaching adulthood, the teen years can also be exciting and challenging. In fact, many teenagers do not experience major problems and conflicts. For both them and their parents their transition to adulthood is a good experience.

Independent Living

Many young adults today are living on their own while they attend school or after they have taken a full-time job. They often share apartments or, in some cases, a house. If you are living this way, you know about the adjustments that are required. Along with added independence comes the responsibility of running a household, including cooking, cleaning, and paying the bills. In order to

do this, young adults must learn coping skills; they must manage both time and money. There also may be adjustments in learning to live with other people who have different habits and values.

Many young adults in speaking of their experiences in independent living tell of unexpected problems, such as noise complaints from the people downstairs or plumbing problems. They frequently can also laugh about some of their "challenges" such as trying to live three days at the end of the month on two dollars or using too much soap in the automatic washing machine at the laundromat. You may have heard the expression "Experience is a good teacher." Someone else has responded, "Considering what it costs, experience *should* be a good teacher." The main idea is to keep learning through experience that is not too costly or harmful to oneself or others.

Marriage

When a couple get married, there are more adjustments than are immediately obvious. Each person must give up some independence and must consider the needs and wishes of another person in making decisions. On the other hand, it is easier to accept disappointments if the person you love is pleased or benefits in some way. It is also easier to adjust to changes involved with your job or other activities when you have the support of an understanding marriage partner.

One obvious adjustment required in marriage involves the use of money. The young couple probably have saved to make basic purchases for their home; they may also have received gifts to meet other needs. But the day-to-day and month-by-month expenses of maintaining a home can bring unexpected problems and bills. An important requirement in making these adjustments is to avoid blaming each other for problems.

Other adjustments in married life involve personal habits and shared living space. The use of time may result in too much togetherness or too little privacy. Relationships with each other's friends and family also require both persons to adjust.

When "two become three," further adjustments are required. A couple may want children and may rejoice when their first child is born, but there still will be some major adjustments to make. Although these can be difficult or sometimes disturbing, patience and caring can increase the love and joy in the home—and can ease the problems of coping.

Some couples who have been married for years claim they have never had a quarrel. This is unlikely; it certainly cannot mean that the couple have never had a disagreement. No two people think and act exactly alike. Instead, one person probably has continually given in to the other. This may maintain a peaceful marriage, but it is not likely to be a happy one.

When two human beings care about themselves and about the many things that happen in life, they have differences. People have emotions, and feelings are not always expressed with appropriate control. In a good marriage, both partners should be able to express themselves, either rationally or, sometimes, emotionally. Further, each person should be able to admit making a mistake and say, "I'm sorry." It isn't the disagreement so much or how it develops that is important, but how it is settled. Disagreements can be worked out satisfactorily through a problem-solving approach, or settled by compromise or thoughtful consideration of the other person.

Most young married couples—even though they are very much in love and are sexually attracted to each other—are faced with sexual adjustments. Enjoyment of sex by both people is not as automatic as they might have imagined. The desire to please the other person, which is the essence of love, is an important factor. The intimate experience of sexual relations can also reduce frustrations caused by other problems in the life of a young couple.

When a marriage does not last, there are further adjustments to make. Children may have an especially difficult time, particularly if conflicting loyalties make them feel torn between the two parents.

Illness or Disability

Fortunately, not everyone has to make the crucial adjustments that involve coping with the effects of a major illness or disability. Probably only those who have had this experience, or those living or working directly with people who have, can understand how difficult these adjustments are. There is much more involved than simply adjusting to a different kind of activity or to limited activity. One's previous activities affect the problems of adjustment. An athlete, for example, may have more difficulty in adjusting to a disability than a person whose work and interests require less physical activity.

Attitude toward the total situation is important in the adjustment process. Brad, who broke both legs in an automobile accident, keeps asking, "Why did this have to happen to me?" Amy, who had a similar accident, expresses a different attitude: "I'm fortunate that I'm alive—that my chances of walking again are excellent." Disabilities will be discussed further in Chapter 10, "Exceptional Persons."

JOB-RELATED ADJUSTMENTS

A person who likes other people, who can get acquainted easily, and who has human-relations skills has valuable job-related assets in these traits. People function and work in groups in much of our modern world, and harmony is extremely important for production. Liking your boss, co-workers, and work is a factor in reducing absenteeism and even accidents. If you are not disturbed by irritations and tensions, you can give more attention to your work and will have a better safety record. You will learn more about interaction on the job in Chapter 13, "Human Relations at Work." Constant changes in the world of work require adaptation and adjustment to such factors as automation, technological development, increased specialization, variations in work schedules, and even transportation to and from one's job. Job-related situations are discussed in the following sections.

The New Employee

When beginning a new job, a person has a number of adjustments to make at once. This can be frustrating to the conscientious person who begins the job with good intentions. Most companies and businesses have some type of job orientation that helps new employees become acquainted with their employer, co-workers, and job. This may be just an interview and a walk around the department, or it may be an extensive program of on-the-job training lasting several weeks.

Some of the things a new employee will want to know are, Who is my boss? From whom do I receive instructions? If I work for more than one person, do their standards and expectations vary? What are the priorities when work accumulates? How can I avoid misinterpretations of instructions? What supplies and equipment are available?

A new employee may also have questions pertaining to work done by workers on another shift, use of equipment and tools, break and lunchroom policies, absenteeism, safety measures, or union policies. Becoming a part of the company or business will require related adjustments.

A few suggestions to a new employee may be:

- Be friendly; introduce yourself to others.
- Be willing to learn; observe; listen.
- Be yourself but try to adjust to company and employee policies and practices.
- Be patient; it takes time to adjust to a new situation and responsibilities.
- Show appreciation to those helping you get started in various ways.
- Maintain your self-confidence; you will soon feel comfortable in your job and as a part of the organization.

 What would you SUGGEST? If a friend confides in you that she is having difficulty adjusting to a new job, what would you suggest?

Working Hours

Working shifts is a common employment situation that may require adjustment. Many night workers have had to learn to sleep during the day while other people are at work. A job with rotating shifts poses a particular adjustment challenge; as soon as a person adjusts to one shift, a change must be made to another.

There are also some people who have great difficulty in adjusting to anything except a traditional workday. It is now recognized that some people are basically day people and others are night people. Each person seems to feel and function best during some part of the twenty-four-hour day. If employees and the companies they work for recognize this and have some flexibility in scheduling working hours, it can be to their advantage.

An increasingly popular concept of time spent on the job is called **flextime.** Under this arrangement, employees can choose their own hours to work as long as they establish a schedule. A schedule may consist of working a split shift or starting earlier or later than usual. There are usually certain "core hours" that everyone is expected to work. But flexibility is allowed in scheduling around these hours. Many large companies and businesses are satisfied with the results of flextime. People plan their schedules according to other responsibilities, transportation arrangements, or personal interests. This recognition of individual needs has resulted in greater commitment to work responsibilities and, in many cases, in greater productivity.

Changes in Supervision and Procedures

You may have become well adjusted to your job and total work situation only to be faced with changes in supervision and procedures. A new supervisor means a different person, and new human relationships always require adjustments. In another instance, the management of a company may plan and adopt new policies and procedures. Many of the actual changes, however, are made by their employees. It can be particularly difficult to accept and adjust to changes that are decided by someone else and that you do not understand. This is one of the reasons why management and labor often work together to determine necessary changes and to make smooth adjustments.

Job Change

It is estimated that a young person starting out in the working world today may change jobs six or seven times. Each of these new situations will call for many adjustments. Young people may stay with the same company and be promoted to another position or even transfer to a new location, or they may go to work for another company or for themselves. It is not unusual today for a person to receive new training to enter a different line of work. Many of tomorrow's jobs do not exist today. Career education is concerned not only with what you learn but whether you continue to learn and to adjust to changes in your work.

Changing the **status quo,** or existing conditions, is always a bit disturbing, even when the change is desirable. Better adjustments can be made when the people who are affected are informed ahead of time about changes to be made. Remember that any change requires an adjustment period. Therefore, the total effect of the change cannot be determined by an immediate reaction.

Unemployment

Unemployment, for whatever reason, is another situation that calls for a number of adjustments. These adjustments can relate to such factors as income and spending, self-esteem, relationships with others, use of time, further education or retraining, and personal responsibilities.

How Well Would You Cope?

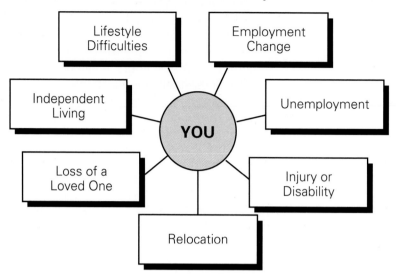

Unemployment compensation and other types of insurance can prevent unemployment from becoming a financial disaster. If there is another income in the family, that money will likely have to be budgeted more closely. Spending, even for necessities, may have to be restricted. This requires understanding and willingness to make adjustments by all members of a family.

Suppose you have lost your job, or could sometime in the future. It is not pessimistic to recognize that job security is not as assured as it was in earlier years. If you do lose your job you may be somewhat embarrassed, even if your unemployment is due to no fault of yours. Talking about your problems with friends and others who are interested can release tensions, lead to temporary solutions in meeting responsibilities, and ease other adjustments. Others may also be able to give you leads to another job.

You will also have to adjust to a change in those with whom you have daily contact. You may miss some of the people you worked with. You will also have more contact with other members of your family. If you are married and your spouse works, you may have additional responsibilities pertaining to household chores and child care. Whatever your particular situation, adjustments will have to be made in related changes in human relationships. This can be trying, especially when added to other aspects of unemployment.

How to use extra time on your hands in a constructive manner can be an additional challenge. You can become very discouraged and may feel useless unless you can occupy yourself in satisfying activity. You may want to catch up on some well-deserved rest and relaxation. You may also adjust to unemployment by actively job hunting, learning new skills, making home repairs, or helping others. Not having to maintain the schedule required of your former job may be welcome and give you flexibility in a number of activities. Yet it is advisable to develop a schedule of functioning that will provide you a sense of purpose and accomplishment. At least planning what you are going to do each day, even if each day's activities vary, will keep you feeling better both physically and mentally.

Options for further education and retraining are available to all age levels today. The class you are taking now doubtless is made up of individuals from a variety of age groups and work-related backgrounds. It is common to return to school for a variety of reasons. An injury may prevent a person from continuing in former work, a change in lifestyle may give a person time that he or she didn't have earlier, a change in responsibilities may require preparing for employment, or a person may need retraining for a new line of work because of loss of a job. Many adults going back into education may lack self-confidence at first, but most soon realize that they can still learn, and their motivation usually makes them highly successful students.

It is important for an unemployed person to evaluate his or her current total situation. Drastic, impulsive decisions should be avoided. In some cases a person may decide to sell his or her home and move to another part of the country where the employment situation is more promising, but that should not be done without careful consideration of all factors involved. Above all else, unemployed persons should keep confidence in themselves and their potential and be realistic and responsible.

Retirement

It comes as a surprise to many people that they must adjust to retirement, but retirement can be another difficult adjustment in one's life. Unless they have prepared for their days of free time by developing new interests or can participate in activities in which they can make a contribution, retired persons may experience disappointment and serious maladjustment. New types of activity must replace their former work if retirement is to be enjoyed.

These retirees are enhancing their smooth transition from fulltime employment by participating in the preparation of meals for the homeless.

You probably know of people who have made relatively smooth transitions into retirement and perhaps others who had some difficulties. This topic is not discussed in more detail here as not many readers of this book are at that stage of life. Remember, however, to someday make preparations for your retirement and to expect to make some adjustments when the time comes. In the meantime, for those of you soon to enter the workforce as fulltime employees in careers you have chosen, look forward to many years of challenging, satisfying work. Remember self-actualization at the peak of Maslow's heirarachy in Chapter 3? Your best opportunity to develop your potential is likely to be through your work.

DEATH AND DYING

For the vast majority of people, adjustments to death and dying will be the most difficult. Coping with death must occur on both a mental and an emotional level. This pertains to one's own death as well as to the deaths of others.

I Am Mortal

Children today are not sheltered so much from death as they were in the past. One reason for this is that adults themselves are learning to cope with death more effectively. They therefore can be more realistic in helping children to understand both life and death. Even the death of a pet can often be used as an opportunity to help a child learn that living things die.

Quite early in life one learns that human beings die. One must come to say, "I am a human being; therefore I will die." That is the mental aspect of recognizing and accepting death. A person can say, "I am mortal," however, without learning to deal with death on an emotional level. It is natural to fear the unknown and to avoid involvement with what is feared. Yet it must be done.

Acceptance of death in a personal sense takes time. Even if we accept the idea of death and our own mortality, we may regard our own death as extremely remote. This is not to suggest that we should be thinking continually about death or dying. But we should not avoid the issue either. We must accept it as a reality. Then we can give attention and energy to experiencing life more fully.

Acceptance of Death

Dr. Elisabeth Kübler-Ross has contributed notably to our understanding of the psychological aspects of dying. After interviewing hundreds of dying patients, she concluded that there are five stages to approaching one's own death.[1] According to Dr. Kübler-Ross dying patients generally go through these stages, or some variation of them, between the time when they learn about a terminal illness and the time they die.

The first stage is *denial.* The dying person refuses to believe that death is near. Relatives and friends may also try to deny the inevitable, either to protect the dying person from the truth or because they cannot accept the truth themselves. The second stage is *anger.* Once the reality of dying has been recognized, the person reacts in protest and anger, asking "Why me?" The patient may be angry with doctors and nurses, with relatives, and even with God. A person in this stage of approaching death may express anger at anyone who is well and at anyone who tries to help.

After the anger stage, for most people comes a period of *bargaining*—either with God or with whatever power the person believes in. Such bargains take the form, "If I get well, I will lead a better life" or "If I could only live until . . . I would dedicate my life to . . . " The actual bargains depend on the values, past experiences, and personality of the individual. There are some who claim that their bargaining, to some extent, was successful. But in most cases the dying persons realize their bargaining does not work.

Depression is the stage following bargaining. By this time the patient realizes death is near. But emotional acceptance is not yet possible. It is heartbreaking to lose a loved one, but it can be many times harder for the dying person to cope with the idea of losing everyone and everything on earth. The opportunity to express this loss can be helpful to the patient. Those who care about the dying person should be willing both to talk and to listen.

The fifth and final stage of dying is *acceptance*. The dying person learns to accept death without undue fear and bitterness. Just how a person reacts in this stage varies with the individual. Some want to do whatever they can as long as they are able. They may want to see friends and relatives. Others may wish to spend more time alone or with someone close, to prepare for the death they have now accepted.

The conclusions of Dr. Kübler-Ross concerning the five stages have been challenged by later researchers on death and dying. As is so often the case in further studies on a subject, critics of Kübler-Ross claim that the stages are not that predictable or do not necessarily occur in a particular sequence. Robert Kastenbaum is one of the researchers frequently referred to in this challenge. Kastenbaum has found that reactions to knowledge of one's own impending death can vary from acceptance, to apprehension of the unknown, to real terror.[2] Since people have different personalities, live their lives differently, and have widely different beliefs about the purpose of life, it can be expected they would also have different attitudes and behaviors related to death. One's age is also considered an important factor in reaction to approaching death. Dr. Kübler-Ross herself should not be criticized about her conclusions as much as perhaps those who have overgeneralized what she was communicating about death and dying. She at least is credited with bringing the formerly taboo subject of death and dying into the open so that greater understanding could develop and feelings could be expressed.

There have been a number of relatively recent efforts to make dying a less painful experience. Hospices, or homelike places where dying persons spend their remaining days, have become common. At these hospices dying patients are treated with loving attention and dignity. The members of one's family are allowed to visit at any time. Personal belongings and even pets are sometimes permitted. The patients in hospices are given the care they need, but in an environment that resembles their own home.

Another great help to people who are suffering from a terminal illness is a group called "Make Today Count." This group was founded by Orville E. Kelly when he learned he was dying of cancer. The group's national headquarters is in Burlington, Iowa. Kelly's message was "I do not consider myself dying of cancer, but living despite it. I do not look upon each day as another day closer to death, but as another day of life, to be appreciated and enjoyed."[3] Make Today Count, Inc., is a nonprofit organization for persons with life-threatening

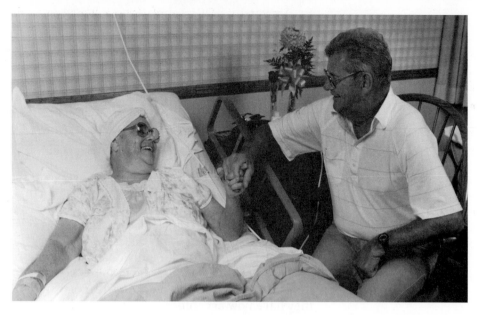

A hospice provides dying patients an environment of loving attention and dignity.

illnesses, their family members, and other interested persons. There are no dues for membership, as the group depends on contributions. Another support group for people experiencing severe difficulties is "I Can Cope." Such groups help the individual by giving him or her contact with others who are experiencing similar difficulties and by teaching ways to cope.

Loss of a Loved One

It would be a good idea to review the discussion of grief in Chapter 5, "Emotions." There will be further consideration here of how grief affects those who lose a loved one and how we can give some support to relatives or friends who are experiencing such a loss. It was noted in Chapter 5 that a person can experience grief because of a number of different losses. It doesn't necessarily have to relate to the death of a loved one. Our discussion here, however, primarily relates to a sense of loss due to a death.

Grief affects people differently because of the differences in their personalities, coping skills, and their relationships with the person who has died. A person may have a number of ambivalent feelings, including anger, sorrow, relief, guilt, loneliness, or sadness. He or she will also experience the physiological effects of emotion and may have difficulty sleeping, eating, and generally taking care of oneself. A person may experience confusion and even have hallucinations of hearing or seeing the person who is no longer present. Some people resort to the use of coping mechanisms, which are psychological crutches that help us deal with situations when our regular coping skills are not adequate. It is of value to know that experiences such as these are within the normal range of reactions to loss, but also to recognize that individual experiences vary in type, degree, and duration.

University of Chicago's Froma Walsh, in a *Psychology Today* interview, states,

> In healthy families and well-functioning families there is a sense that death is part of the life cycle and that it's inevitable. Healthier individuals and families tend to be more accepting of death as part of the life cycle. Given the life cycle, the most painful and unjust deaths are early death, untimely deaths. The death of a young adult or a kid is inherently unjust, doubly difficult because it reverses the life cycle.[4]

Support to Others

It is natural to want to do something for our relatives or friends who are having difficulties—in this case experiencing grief. Yet we often feel quite helpless in this type of situation. What can we do? What can we even say? In "Grief is Not a Sign of Weakness," the authors, a grief counselor and the president of a grief support group, give us the following suggestions:

- Stay in touch—don't expect the bereaved person to call you.
- Listen without giving advice, unless asked.
- Don't make blanket statements like "You're young, you'll get married again," or "You can have another baby."
- Don't say, "I know how you feel"; grief is individual.
- Mention the dead person's name.
- Remember important occasions such as a wedding anniversary or the date of death.
- Don't say, "Don't cry"; rather, accept and share the tears.
- Don't expect the bereaved to be the same person again.
- Realize that the grief and pain never will be totally gone.
- Learn about grief and the grief process.
- Share your friend's or relative's bereavement.[5]

 What would you SAY? Suppose you unexpectedly run into a person you know who has recently experienced the loss of a spouse. What might you say to show the person you are aware of his or her grief and that you care?

COPING MECHANISMS

Human beings attempt to protect themselves psychologically as well as physically. If someone harms you physically, you may want to fight back or you may try to protect yourself in some way. This is an expression of your need for self-preservation.

Attempts to protect yourself psychologically are expressions of the need for self-esteem. If necessary, you use **coping mechanisms,** or unconscious behavior patterns that help you maintain a favorable self-concept. Although coping mechanisms are relatively immature ways of handling a situation, they serve as psychological crutches when an individual cannot handle a problem in a conscious, reasonable way. Since they are behavior patterns, or habits, regular reliance on certain coping mechanisms develops into personality traits of an individual.

Everyone uses coping mechanisms to some extent. None of us is so mature or so capable in all situations that he or she never has need of a psychological crutch. When you are using a coping mechanism, you are unaware of the real cause of your behavior in adjusting to an undesirable or threatening situation. However, the effects upon you and others are real.

The following are common coping mechanisms that people use to protect themselves psychologically.

Daydreaming

Everyone daydreams; your mind is never completely inactive. **Daydreaming,** or fantasy, as it is also called, is the simplest form of unconscious mental activity. The mind wanders freely from one topic to another when you are daydreaming.

You may use daydreaming as an escape because reality is too uncomfortable, and changing reality can be too difficult. Another person may feel inadequate in social situations and have fantasies about being popular and more capable. Daydreaming often interferes with effective life, work, and self-improvement. It can also be harmful in other ways. If your mind wanders while you are driving a car, you may have a serious accident; if working with mechanical equipment, you may damage it or injure yourself.

Daydreaming, on the other hand, can lead to creative thinking. Thomas Edison was considered a daydreamer by his teachers, but he was a creative, constructive dreamer who patented more than 1,100 inventions in his lifetime. Daydreams can also give a vision of self that may motivate actual achievement.

Most daydreaming is harmless and can temporarily relieve frustration and provide mental relaxation. If you use daydreaming as an escape, however, you are employing a defense reaction. The question is not, then, whether you daydream, but when, and to what extent, and why.

Rationalization

The expression "Don't kid yourself" is based on our tendency to rationalize. Some psychologists say our biggest task in life is to establish a satisfactory self-image and then to protect that image. **Rationalization** is one of the mental devices used to accomplish this. A student may not feel like studying for a test, so she rationalizes, "I probably wouldn't study the right things anyway." You may neglect to return an item borrowed from a friend by rationalizing, "He's probably glad to have it out of his way."

PEANUTS reprinted by permission of UFS, Inc.

Two familiar types of rationalization are often called "sour grapes" and "sweet lemon." When a person fails to obtain something he wanted, he may say, "I really didn't want it, anyway." This would be like saying, "The grapes are sour, anyway." On the other hand, when one has to accept something he didn't want, he may rationalize by thinking or saying, "It's not so bad, after all." This is the "sweet lemon" reaction. This type of defense mechanism prevents us from being too disappointed by whatever happens to us.

When we rationalize we do what we want to do and then interpret it as the best action or an acceptable action. Rationalization, or excuse making, stands in the way of honest evaluation of behavior. It can also interfere with our achievement by making us satisfied with inferior performance.

Regression

A person who uses **regression** returns to an earlier form of behavior. A young man who suffers a decrease in income, becoming once again financially dependent on his parents, may return to the behavior of a child in relying on someone else to make his decisions for him. An adult who generally acts in a mature and responsible manner may regress to having a childish tantrum when a relationship with someone else doesn't go his or her way.

Other forms of regression are wanting to be pampered when ill or hurt, showing off to get attention, or pouting when not getting your way. The person who regresses is temporarily rejecting the "hard cruel world" and seeking the greater security of childhood.

Fixation

Fixation is a coping mechanism that resembles regression in the sense that the person is acting younger than his or her age. In regression there is a temporary turning back to earlier behavior. In **fixation** a person develops psychologically to a certain point and then stops or "fixes" personality development there. This can happen in late adolescence when an individual is breaking the last bonds of childhood dependence and becoming an independent adult. A person who has a shattering experience at that time, such as the breaking of an engagement or failure in some other important venture, may refuse to enter the final doorway to the adult world, preferring to remain dependent on others. Such a person never really grows up psychologically, even while continuing to grow older in years.

Displacement

One of the most troublesome of the coping mechanisms is displacement. There is a three-part relationship in **displacement,** involving: (1) the person who is frustrated, (2) the person or thing that is the cause of the frustration, and (3) the innocent third party onto whom the frustrated person transfers or displaces the frustration. When something is bothering you and you don't know what you can do about it, you often displace your frustration onto someone else. If you have trouble with your car or do poorly on a test, for example, you may displace your frustration by being critical of a friend.

Anyone would readily admit that this is unreasonable behavior. Yet everyone probably uses displacement to some degree at least occasionally. If you acquire an understanding of this kind of behavior, you will have a better chance of becoming aware of it in yourself and others. And recognition of a personal weakness is the first step in self-improvement. If you can recognize displacement in yourself, you can make a greater effort to determine the cause of your frustration and find a constructive, or at least harmless, method of releasing tensions.

If you recognize the behavior of someone else toward you as displacement, you can better control your reaction and avoid further complications. Suppose your supervisor is worried and upset about a problem at home. Until the problem is solved, the supervisor may be tense and irritable, perhaps blaming the employees in your department for minor things that ordinarily would be taken in stride. If you are a victim of displacement and can recognize this type of behavior, you can try to be more tolerant and understanding; you may even try to help the frustrated person do something about the problem. It would be a mistake to assume that all anger and criticism are displacement, however. To take the attitude "It can't be me; something else must be the problem" will block the path of effective problem solving and adjustment.

Projection

In **projection** you defend yourself psychologically by accusing others of having the personality weakness that you yourself have. You may at some time have heard someone reprimand another person for being irresponsible, extravagant, or selfish, when it was obvious to you that the person is describing himself or herself. The person using projection, however, is unaware of why the reprimand or accusation is made. If you are quite certain that criticism of you is really only defensive behavior, you may ignore or tolerate it without becoming upset. As with displacement, however, you must be careful that you are not being defensive in assuming innocence.

Repression

Repression should not be confused with suppression, which is not a coping mechanism. **Suppression** is a conscious control of one's behavior to avoid hurting someone's feelings or causing a problem for oneself. Suppression is sometimes referred to as tact and is necessary for effective human relations. Repression, on the other hand, is unconscious and is a coping mechanism. **Repression** is pushing into your unconscious what is frightening, contrary to your moral standards, or unacceptable to you for some other reason. There are some ideas or desires that people cannot consciously tolerate, or the memory of an experience may be so frightening or disgusting that they "forget"; they are no longer conscious of the experience. These repressed ideas and memories in an emotionally disturbed person are sometimes revealed during therapy. It is believed that the unconscious mind influences our feelings and behavior even though we are not aware of what is thus affecting us. Repressed ideas or feelings may also be activated in dreams, in which the dreamer has no conscious control.

Denial of Reality

Rather than facing a situation squarely and determining how to cope with it, some people resort to **denial,** a refusal to accept the situation as real. This way they can at least temporarily avoid the pain and fear of dealing with the actual circumstances. Thus students may deny that they are failing a course and therefore not worry about it. When they do fail, they may deny that it is important. Some people deny that they have a drinking problem or that they are showing favoritism in their relationships with others. Denial, like many other coping mechanisms, is an unconscious attempt to live with oneself and a potentially threatening situation. People who use denial are deceiving themselves more than others. They are coping with the situation in a self-defeating, nonproductive way.

Identification

Another common coping mechanism is a type of behavior called **identification.** In this defense reaction a person's identity is associated with that of another person who is greatly admired. Small children do this by pretending to be their current heroes. This type of behavior is also common in adolescence, when young people may be dissatisfied with themselves and may be striving to become something more than or different from what they are.

Identification limits one's behavior. Parents sometimes attempt to relive their youth through the lives of their children, for example. This is disturbing to young people, who want to live their own lives. The parents are also depriving themselves of fully experiencing a stage of life that should be satisfying and complete in itself.

There are also variations of identification. In **imitation** a person acts like another person, because he or she feels inadequate or has low self-esteem. This behavior usually has undesirable effects because the imitator is playing a role and neglecting his or her development as a unique individual.

Such imitation is in contrast to **emulation,** which is a conscious attempt to improve oneself and is therefore not a defense mechanism. In emulation one admires characteristics of another person and attempts to develop similar characteristics in his or her own way. Behind every successful person there are probably several people who have influenced and inspired that person's self-actualization or self-development in this way.

Compensation

Nobody is perfect. Everyone has personal weaknesses in ability and self-development. If some circumstance or disability prevents a person from being successful at something she would like to do, she may compensate by trying something else that she knows she will be able to do. **Compensation** is a type of unconscious substitution that helps a person to experience success and have a good feeling about herself or himself. A person who would like to be an athlete, but lacks the ability, may compensate by becoming a referee, for example. We should not conclude from this, however, that all referees are thus compensating. Some of them have been successful athletes in the past, and others may never have wanted to be an athlete in the first place.

Conscious substitution of goals, as well as some coping mechanisms, can help us experience success in life. There have been many instances in which what was accepted as next best turned out to be the best for someone. A strong desire to do something is often related to one's having the potential to accomplish a goal. If physical disabilities or environmental circumstances stand in the way of developing potential, however, it is reasonable to substitute another objective or goal. For example, a young woman who would like to become a model, but isn't tall enough for most assignments, may choose a career in fashion design, instead.

EFFECTS OF COPING MECHANISMS

It can be concluded, after considering the preceding coping mechanisms, that some of them are relatively harmless unless carried to extremes. Daydreaming is an example. Other coping mechanisms can help one to make a better adjustment to oneself, to others, or to the situation or environment. Compensation is an example of this type. Displacement, on the other hand, is an example of a coping mechanism that indicates maladjustment and that can interfere with purposeful living and effective relationships with other human beings.

After learning about coping mechanisms, we must be careful not to interpret practically all behavior that we observe in others as the use of coping mechanisms. Certain types of behavior are coping mechanisms more because of *why* people act that way than because of *what* they do. And it is very easy to misinterpret why people do what they do.

The use of coping mechanisms is usually an immature, inadequate way of coping. But they do reduce anxiety that might otherwise cause more serious problems. They may be only temporary reactions, until a person learns how to solve problems or adjust more effectively. Ways of reacting become habits, however, which are not easy to change.

NEUROSIS

Maladjustment and excessive anxiety in one or more respects is known as **neurosis.** This difficulty in coping may be the result of conflicts and frequent frustrations or personal inadequacies. Persons with neuroses may have repressed fears or aggressive feelings from childhood experiences that they are no longer aware of as such but that influence their present behavior.

There are identifiable symptoms of neurotic behavior. If an adult is neurotic about safety and has an excessive fear of the dark, for example, that behavior is *immature* and childish. Andrea is 35 years old but must have a light on in her room at night and carries a large flashlight in her handbag at all times "in case the lights go off."

Second, neurotic behavior is *excessive* as a reaction. Although there is always some possibility that lights will go off, Andrea takes more than ordinary precautions. Her reaction is out of proportion to the actual threat.

A third symptom of neurotic behavior is that it is *persistent* or typical of the person's usual way of reacting. Andrea has this excessive anxiety about the dark whether she is in her own home or in an environment where she could be confident that others would adequately take care of the situation if the lights would go off. Andrea's excessive fear is a *phobia,* as discussed in Chapter 5.

Unless a person receives some type of therapy, a phobia can be a lifetime maladjustment.

Another person may be excessively self-centered and neurotic about appearance. Alvin is checking his apparel or hair every few minutes to see that everything is exactly as it should be. Physical appearance is important, but after normal attention to personal cleanliness and appearance, Alvin should be confident about his appearance and concentrate on what he is doing. If he fails to moderate his abnormal behavior, he will not be efficient on the job or even interesting as a person.

Fortunately, most neuroses are minor, and many people with neuroses manage to cope satisfactorily even though it requires extra effort and may cause them some discomfort. Severe problems and psychological disorders, will be discussed in Chapter 9, "Wellness."

STRESS

Physiological disturbance and psychological frustration caused by unmet and external pressures, real or perceived, are called stress. This human condition often results from a sense of threat or personal inadequacy. Environmental factors, such as pollution, noise, crowding, and climatic conditions, also cause undue stress.

Such causes of stress are called stressors. In a very real sense, however, it is not external factors and situations that produce stress. It is the individual's perception of these and the individual's reaction and inability to cope effectively that cause stress.

Life also provides us with opportunities for "good" stress, or what Dr. Hans Selye, probably the world's leading authority on stress, calls **eustress.**[6] This kind of stress is created by excitement, enthusiasm, and anticipation of desired circumstances or events. The type of stress to be considered further here, however, is stress according to the preceding definition—the kind that causes us problems and therefore requires more of our attention.

Dr. Hans Selye explains that human beings react to stress with three stages of adjustment, which he refers to as the **general adaptation syndrome.** These stages are alarm, resistance, and exhaustion.[7] The *alarm* stage involves physiological changes similar to those associated with emotion. The heart beats faster, hormones are released from the endocrine glands, breathing becomes faster, muscles become tense, pupils dilate, blood sugar level increases, and digestion slows. The body's resources are becoming mobilized.

During the *resistance* stage there is an effort to adapt to the stress. If the cause of the stress is removed or is handled in a satisfactory way, body functioning returns to normal. Otherwise, resistance to the stress continues and intensifies. If the stress continues over a period of time, *exhaustion* is experienced, with the person becoming less able to deal with the stress in a constructive way. The exhausted individual may experience psychosomatic

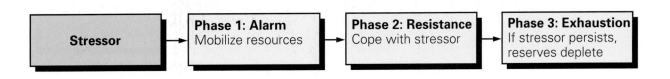

illness consisting of headaches, ulcers, high blood pressure, or other stress-related physical problems. Knowing more about stress and how to avoid or react to it can protect us from this final stage of exhaustion. The rest of this chapter should be useful in this respect.

It is estimated that the cost of work-related stress runs into billions of dollars of year. Problems caused by, or at least made worse by, stress, are excessive absenteeism, decreased productivity, disgruntled workers, conflicts between employees or between employees and their supervisors, fatigue, depression, and other physical or psychological problems.

Businesses and other organizations are concerned about reducing stress in the workplace. The Northwestern National Life Insurance Company, for example, has developed a workplace stress test for use by American companies to determine stress levels of their employees. Items pertain to such topics as management practices, training procedures, workloads, workspace and equipment, layoff practices, and benefits.[8]

It may be helpful to determine one's exposure to stress over a period of time—for example, a year—by using a readjustment rating scale developed by T. H. Holmes and R. H. Rahe. It must be kept in mind that all persons do not react to similar events and situations in the same way; therefore, your rating cannot be an absolute measure of the stress you have experienced and its possible effects. Nevertheless, the scale is widely used and does give a person some understanding of the effects of potentially stressful situations. Notice that the scale shown on page 181 has some events that are definitely undesirable, some that are relatively neutral, and still others that are desirable. Even these interpretations, however, depend somewhat on the individual.

Evaluation of the test consists of adding all of the scores for the events you have experienced in a given period of time. The meaning of a total score also depends somewhat on the individual, but for the average person the higher the total the more susceptible that person is to the exhaustion stage, psychosomatic illness, and stress-related physical problems.

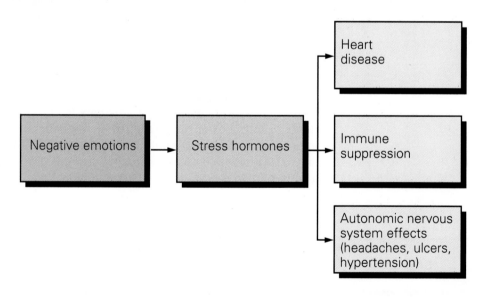

The Social Readjustment Rating Scale

Life Event	Mean Value (Average Value)
Death of spouse	100
Divorce	73
Marital separation	65
Jail term	63
Death of close family member	63
Personal injury or illness	53
Marriage	50
Fired at work	47
Marital reconciliation	45
Retirement	45
Change in health of family member	44
Pregnancy	40
Sex difficulties	39
Gain of new family member	39
Business readjustment	39
Change in financial state	38
Death of close friend	37
Change to different line of work	36
Change in number of arguments with spouse	35
Mortgage or loan for major purchase	31
Foreclosure on mortgage or loan	30
Change in responsibilities at work	29
Son or daughter leaving home	29
Trouble with in-laws	29
Outstanding personal achievement	28
Spouse begins or stops work	26
Begin or end school	26
Change in living conditions	25
Revision of personal habits	24
Trouble with boss	23
Change in work hours or conditions	20
Change in residence	20
Change in schools	20
Change in recreation	19
Change in church activities	19
Change in social activities	18
Mortgage or loan for lesser purchase	17
Change in sleeping habits	16
Change in number of family get-togethers	15
Change in eating habits	15
Vacation	13
Christmas	12
Minor violations of the law	11

Reprinted with permission from Thomas H. Holmes and R. H. Rahe, "The Social Readjustment Rating Scale" in *Journal of Psychosomatic Research*, 11, 213–218. Copyright 1967, Pergamon Press, Ltd.

ZIGGY Copyright © 1990 ZIGGY AND FRIENDS, Inc. Dist. by
UNIVERSAL PRESS SYNDICATE. Reprinted with permission. All
rights reserved.

INABILITY TO COPE

It is not so much what happens to a person, however, as how he or she reacts that determines the seriousness of the situation. One of the most tragic results of the inability to cope is suicide. People who commit suicide perceive their situation as being hopeless or intolerable. Some of the most common causes of suicide are depression, drug abuse, personal expectations that are unreasonably high, inability to live up to what one perceives as expectations of others, revenge toward members of one's family or another person, sense of loss or rejection, or even need for attention.

The inability either to solve a problem or to adjust to it leads some people to escape from life itself. Others may lead suicidal lives. They may drive recklessly or engage in other life-threatening behavior. The problems that cause some people to take their lives are no worse than the problems many other people have. The difference is in the individual's *reaction* to the problem.

A person who is thinking about ending his or her life is confused and needs help. Suicidal persons need to know that they can be accepted for what they are and that they can change themselves and alter their situations if they choose. It can also be helpful for others to be familiar with identified clues to possible suicides. These include previous attempts, threats to take one's own life, extreme depression, drastic changes in behavior or personal hygiene, or giving away valued possessions. Whatever the cause or causes, a suicidal

The young woman has experienced stress to the point of despair.

person needs, and in most cases wants, help. There are crisis- and suicide-prevention centers in most communities of moderate or large size where those who feel the need can turn. Inability to cope can also result in mental illness, which is considered in the chapter, "Wellness."

WAYS TO REDUCE STRESS

Although some stress is desirable in our lives, we also know that we can experience much undesirable stress or distress. We must not only be able to recognize such stress and be aware of its possible effects, we should have constructive ways of avoiding and reducing it. Consider the ways you can apply the following suggestions to yourself and your particular situations.

Become a Better Problem Solver You will recall from the previous chapter that the ability to problem-solve is part of the definition of coping. Since the better we cope, the less stress we experience, it follows that we can prevent some stress and reduce other stress by improving our ability to problem-solve.

Accept Your Limitations It is important to understand ourselves as we really are, as discussed in Chapter 2, "Self-Concept and Personality." It is much easier to agree with this than to apply it, however, as with many other aspects of personal psychology. If we expect too much of ourselves or are perfectionists, we are bound to create undue stress for ourselves. We should know and accept our limitations, our humanness, and be able to handle disappointment in our own performance. This does not mean that we shouldn't strive to do our best and to improve. But it does mean that we should realize that we are not perfect.

Know Your Priorities It is true that human beings have many needs and wants in common, but our individual values have an order of importance that

✎ Quiz Yourself on Stress Symptoms

WHAT ARE YOUR STRESS SYMPTOMS? This scale measures the minor physical and emotional symptoms that indicate difficulty in dealing with everyday stress. During the past month, how much of the time were the following statements true for you? Place a checkmark in the appropriate column.

	Most of the Time	Some of the Time	Almost Never
1. I felt tense, nervous, anxious, or upset.	_____	_____	_____
2. I felt sad, depressed, down in the dumps, or hopeless.	_____	_____	_____
3. I was low in energy, exhausted, tired, or unable to get things done.	_____	_____	_____
4. I couldn't turn off my thoughts at night or on weekends long enough to feel relaxed and refreshed the next day.	_____	_____	_____
5. I had difficulty falling asleep and/or staying asleep, and didn't feel rested when I awakened.	_____	_____	_____
6. I found myself unable to sit still, and had to move around constantly.	_____	_____	_____
7. I felt discouraged, pessimistic, sad, self-critical, inadequate, or guilty.	_____	_____	_____
8. I was so upset that I felt I was losing control of my feelings.	_____	_____	_____
9. I have been preoccupied with a serious personal problem.	_____	_____	_____
10. I have been bothered by vague body aches and pains, nervous indigestion, or jitters.	_____	_____	_____
11. I have been in unpleasant situations that I felt helpless to do anything about.	_____	_____	_____
12. I felt tired in the morning, with no energy to get up or face daily activities.	_____	_____	_____

To Score: Total your checkmarks in each column. Enter here: _____ _____ _____

Allow 2 points for Most of the Time
      1 point for Some of the Time
      0 points for Almost Never

Total Score _____

A total score of 10 or more indicates a need to take active steps in order to improve coping.

Source: Dennis T. Jaffe, *Healing from Within*, Knopf, New York, 1981. Used with permission of the publisher.

is our own. Since we do not have the time or money or energy to do or have everything that may have some value for us, we have to be selective. If we try to do more than is reasonable for us, we are going to experience stress. Knowing your priorities, or the order of importance to what you want, will help you to avoid stress. Although we should consider the effect of our values on others, it is important for each of us to establish our own values and priorities. Continually trying to please others can be stressful.

Accept the Realities of Life   This pertains not only to our own limitations, as discussed previously, but also to realities such as working for a living and experiencing difficulties in life. We should try to find the type of work that we can find satisfying, but it is unrealistic to resent the fact that we have to work at all. In fact, there is much evidence in our society that not working can be more stressful than working. Also, if we expect some difficulties and disappointments in our lives, as is true of everyone's life, we will be better able to cope with such experiences.

Avoid Too Many Changes in Your Life at One Time   The social readjustment rating scale earlier in this chapter presents evidence of the fact that too many changes in a given period of time, even though some of them are welcome, can create stress. Although we do not have control over everything that happens to us in life, we can selectively delay some changes if we have recently experienced considerable other change. We can give ourselves a chance to adjust and adapt to some changes before becoming voluntarily involved in others. Circumstances that may be very disturbing to us at first can become almost negligible after a while. We can become accustomed to situations that at first seem barely tolerable.

Learn to Relax   We can avoid some stress and reduce what we cannot avoid by learning to relax. There are a number of ways we can do this. What may work best for one person may not be effective for another. Some people find "doing nothing" in the sun very relaxing, for example, although others may find it stressful. Some find relaxation in music; others prefer meditation, a form of relaxation achieved when they sit in a comfortable position, breathe slowly and deeply, and repeat a mantra, a meaningless word, or the word *one* to free their minds of other thoughts and concerns. Progressive relaxation, another type of relaxation, involves step-by-step relaxation of various muscles of the body. People may begin, for example, flexing their fingers and relaxing each hand. They then move on to the arms, the shoulder, and so on, to the toes. Another technique useful to some people is **biofeedback.** With biofeedback, a person monitors her body functioning with the use of a machine until she learns what type of behavior reduces her blood pressure, heart rate, or other body functions. There are numerous other types of relaxation. Everyone should be able to find an activity or nonactivity that promotes relaxation.

Give Attention to Others   Too much attention to oneself and one's own concerns can cause stress. One of the best ways of avoiding or reducing stress, therefore, is to give attention to others. That is not the only reason for giving attention to others, of course. Regardless of one's reason, however, getting one's mind off one's own problems can be an effective technique for relieving stress. Tiredness from constructive activity and involvement with others is not nearly as stressful as fatigue caused by tension and stress.

Let Go of Prejudices and Grudges   Although prejudices and grudges are by definition directed at others, they often cause the greatest problem for those who carry them. If you can free yourself of unreasonable attitudes toward others and learn to forgive and forget, you will be doing yourself a greater favor than anyone else. Even if you think you are justified in not wanting to be associated with another person, do not cause yourself a further problem by building a barrier between yourself and that person. Those who maintain, "She doesn't bother me; I don't have anything to do with her" are being bothered by maintaining that attitude more than they realize.

Be Organized, Yet Flexible   It can be stressful not to have some plan or structure to our activities. It can be reassuring and relatively relaxing, on the other hand, to have goals and a plan to achieve them. But it is also important to be flexible, to be able to adjust our plans if circumstances suggest such. Those who feel they must follow through on an original plan even though it is no longer practical or even desirable are setting themselves up for a stress-related problem. Too much rigidity in our behavior can be as stressful as disorganization.

Don't Try to Change Others   There is a difference between trying to influence others to change and trying to control them. Those who are involved in a stressful situation with others often ask, "How can I make him (or her) change?" If they are trying to do the impossible, they are only asking for stress. If we really believe that another person would be better off if she or he changed in some way, we should try to influence that person to want to change. We should recognize, at the same time, that everyone is entitled to and responsible for his or her own life. People, therefore, have a right to be the kind of persons they are as long as they are not interfering with the rights of others.

Communicate; Talk Out Your Stress   Some problems involving others can be avoided if we make our needs and situations known to them. We should also be aware that some problems are basically misunderstandings, which communication can rectify. Talking about how we feel can also give us insight into why we feel the way we do and help to reduce stress.

Learn to Recognize Job Burnout   Although we can become "burned out" in any situation, one of the most serious problem area is work. **Burnout** is generally thought of as a reaction to excessive stress over a period of time, leading to feelings of helplessness and apathy and making one unproductive. To avoid burnout, it helps to know the reasons for what we are doing and to experience a sense of achievement. We also need some variety in our work as well as in the rest of our lives. We need vacations and ways of refreshing ourselves so that we do not become victims of this undesirable condition.

Find Ways to Release Tension   It was suggested earlier that we should be realistic. It would be unrealistic to think that we can avoid all tension and undesirable stress. Tension, in this sense, refers to physiological stresses and strains. Physical exercise and activity help to release such tension. Some people resort to aggressive behavior in an unconscious effort to reduce tension. This, of course, is not condoned. Others, who have better understanding of themselves and better control, find harmless or even constructive ways of getting rid of such tension. Participation in physical work or sports helps to reduce tension, for example.

Live One Day at a Time   *Can* you live more than one day at a time? In spite of this obvious limitation, we can create unnecessary and undesirable stress for ourselves by worrying about problems that may never materialize. We should have goals and plans, but we also need to adjust those when circumstances warrant it. If we know our priorities and can adjust them when necessary, we will avoid much of the stress common in modern living. We will not only accomplish more, but we will also enjoy life more.

Keep Well   Wellness is the theme of the next chapter, and we will consider ways of maintaining wellness. It will be noted here, however, that exercise, adequate sleep, proper nutrition, and mental health attitudes help to avoid and reduce stress.

What would you DO?   If you felt that you were under too much stress from a combination of studies, work, and personal responsibilities, what would you do?

SUMMARY   Coping consists of the ability to problem-solve, to accept what we cannot change, and to make adjustments in ourselves. Since even the most effective problem solvers cannot solve all problems to their satisfaction, they must adjust to situations that are not what they would like them to be. They can also learn to accept what they cannot change. Even changes that are desirable require some adjustment. Coping is therefore a constant part of life.

Some experiences in life that often require major adjustments are school entry, adolescence, independent living, marriage, divorce, illness or disability, and retirement. Job-related adjustments involve the new employee, working hours, changes in supervision and procedures, job change, unemployment, and numerous other situations.

Death and dying and grief involve some of the most difficult adjustments in human life. Understanding the related experiences can be helpful. We can also learn to be supportive of others who are facing death or experiencing grief.

Coping mechanisms are unconscious psychological devices used to maintain self-esteem and to adjust to unpleasant realities in life. These include daydreaming, rationalization, regression, fixation, displacement, projection, repression, identification, denial of reality, and compensation. The results of the use of coping mechanisms can range from the relatively harmless to useful to the seriously harmful, depending on how the coping behavior affects those who use it and their relations with others.

Inability to cope effectively causes excessive tension and stress. Hans Selye refers to the body's reaction to stress as the general adaptation syndrome. Too much stress in a given period of time can lead to serious problems or psychosomatic illness. A social readjustment scale has also been used to alert people to too much stress in their lives. Inability to cope can even lead to mental illness or suicide.

Businesses and other organizations are recognizing the problems created by stress in work situations and are taking measures to reduce stress.

A person can learn to cope more effectively by becoming a better problem solver, preparing for demanding experiences, accepting what cannot be changed, and learning to use a limited amount of stress to advantage. There are a number of suggestions that one can apply to avoid or reduce stress in his or her life.

A person who has learned to cope effectively has taken a basic step toward total wellness, the subject of the next chapter.

 Psychology In Practice

1. Write an autobiography including a description of the major adjustments you have had to make in your life. Include a final paragraph explaining what you have learned about coping that may help you to deal with situations in the future.

2. Ask three people you know who have recently started on a job about their job-related adjustments. Attempt to identify people who have started on different kinds of jobs. Compare similarities and differences.

 3. Brainstorming is a creative problem-solving technique discussed in Chapter 7. Set up a brainstorming session with other members of the class on how to reduce stress in the lives of students.

Learning Activities

Turn to page 411 to complete the Learning Activities and Enrichment Activities for this chapter.

Notes

1. Elisabeth Kübler-Ross, *On Death and Dying,* The Macmillan Company, New York, 1969. Copyright 1969 by Elisabeth Kübler-Ross.

2. Robert Kastenbaum, *Dying and Death: A Life-span Approach;* in J. E. Birren and K. W. Schaie, eds., *Handbook of the Psychology of Aging,* 2nd ed., Van Nostrand Reinhold, New York, 1985. Referenced in Garry L. Martin and J. Grayson Osborne, *Psychology: Adjustment and Everyday Living,* 2nd ed., Prentice Hall, Englewood Cliffs, N. J., 1993, p. 327.

3. Orville E. Kelly, *Make Today Count,* Delacorte Press, New York, 1975.

4. Froma Walsh, "Loss Loss Loss," *Psychology Today,* July/August 1992, p. 90.

5. Catherine Thompson and Barbara E. Moore, "GRIEF Is Not a Sign of Weakness," *USA Today,* July 1991, p. 93.

6. Hans Selye, *The Stress of Life,* rev. ed., McGraw-Hill Book Company, New York, 1976, p. 74.

7. Ibid. pp. 36–40.

8. The NWNL Workplace Stress Test, Northwestern Life Insurance Company, copyright 1992, in Barry L. Puce and Rhonda Brandt, *Effective Human Relations in Organizations,* 5th ed., Houghton Mifflin Company, Boston, 1993, pp. 511–514.

9 Wellness

Learning Objectives

After completing this chapter, you will be able to do the following:

1. Plan a day's menu for yourself including recommended servings from each of the categories of the Food Guide Pyramid; then compare your eating for a typical day with the menu you planned.
2. Describe how you could become more physically fit; or if you are pysically fit, explain how you achieved that state of fitness.
3. Explain the difference between drug abuse and drug addiction and give an example of each.
4. Explain the difference between an obsession and a compulsion as components of Obsessive-Compulsive Disorder and give what you believe to an example of each.
5. Identify a habit desirable for your wellness and set up a plan for establishing it as a personal habit.
6. Identify an undesirable habit you have and set up a plan for breaking it.

> **66** *Your body was built to be exercised. If an owner's manual came with your body at birth, its basic instruction would be three words long:*
> *MOVE IT—REGULARLY.* **99**
>
> ART TUROCK
> *fitness consultant*

189

What does it mean to be "well"? It has come to mean much more than not being sick. You may have heard the expression "wellness revolution," popular in the last decade. This has included an emphasis on total wellness, with the individual assuming greater responsibility for his or her total state of wellness.

According to Jane Myers, 1990–1991 President of the American Association for Counseling and Development, "Wellness refers to the maximizing of human potential through positive life-style choices."[1]

You may have heard the term holistic health in discussions on wellness. John and Muriel James give us an explanation of the origin of this approach to wellness in *Passion for Life*. They write,

> Vitality and an eagerness to live are best observed in people who are healthy. The word health comes from the Anglo Saxon root *hal*, which means both whole and holy. The word *holistic*, sometimes spelled wholistic, was first used in the 1930s by Jan Christiaan Smuts, former premier of South Africa. Today it has become increasingly popular in the fields of medicine and psychology. A healthy approach to life emphasizes the wholeness and health of body, mind, and spirit.[2]

More specifically, holistic health involves a balance among the different components of well-being such as physical health and fitness, mental health, stress management, environmental safety, emotional stability, vocational competence, social effectiveness, and spiritual harmony. When an individual is experiencing a problem in one of these areas it affects his or her total well-being. Some of these topics have already been discussed, and others will be discussed further in later chapters. Social effectiveness, for example, will be considered in Chapter 12, "Interpersonal Relationships."

NUTRITION

What we eat, or don't eat, affects our total well-being. If we eat too much or eat too much of certain foods, we gain weight. If we don't eat a well-balanced diet, we become more susceptible to illness or certain diseases. Too much sugar or caffeine can have negative effects on how we feel. Insufficient amounts of certain vitamins can cause problems, and even disease. Overuse of vitamins can also have detrimental effects. As we become adults and are more responsible for our wellness than we have ever been before, it is not enough to eat just

FRANK & ERNEST reprinted by permission of NEA, Inc.

because we are hungry or because some things taste good. We should know and apply basic principles of nutrition. Eating well-balanced meals of nutritious foods is a major factor in our total wellness. Most of the foods that are good for you are common and relatively inexpensive. Poor eating habits are primarily due to eating what we like rather than what is best for our health.

Nutrition refers not only to the characteristics of food itself but also to how the body handles it. It includes the process of digestion and distribution of nourishment. Your body has basic needs that can be fulfilled by an adequate diet. Otherwise some kind of vitamin or mineral supplement may be required to maintain good health.

It is important to recognize that malnutrition can be caused by a number of factors. It is not just those people who don't have enough food to eat who have nutrition problems. In fact, millions of Americans who can afford to eat well suffer from malnutrition.

Nutrients

Nutrients are substances required for body functioning. Proteins, carbohydrates, fats, vitamins, and minerals are such essentials. A minimum amount of each is need for energy, growth, tissue maintenance and repair, and to keep the systems of the body functioning properly. While water and fiber are not nutrients in the strictest sense, they are also essential to physical well-being.

The following descriptions of nutrients will give you a better understanding of nutrients and their roles in good health.

Protein   Protein forms the foundation of every living cell in your body. Since your body is constantly using protein, it must be replaced to maintain good health. The bones, muscles, skin, hair, and nails all need protein. Some body energy is also derived from protein. The best sources of this nutrient are meat, poultry, fish, cheese, milk, eggs, and beans.

Carbohydrates   Carbohydrates are the body's main source of energy. They are found in grain products, such as bread and cereal, sugar, honey, and starches. When the body does not have an adequate supply of carbohydrates, proteins and fats are used up. Carbohydrates are needed so that protein can be used to rebuild the body rather than to supply energy.

Fats   It may occur to some people that it would be well to eliminate fats from the diet. This is not true. Stored fat can be used as an emergency energy supply. Fatty tissue helps retain body heat and protects the vital organs and other parts of the body from injury. We should avoid an excess of animal fat in the diet, however.

Vitamins   A regular intake of vitamins is essential to good health, and a well-balanced diet will supply the vitamins you need. Cereal, milk, and some other foods sometimes have vitamins added. Many people also choose to take care of possible deficiencies in their diets with a daily vitamin supplement. Even so, the diets of many people are deficient in vitamins they should have. A well-balanced diet is, in most cases, the best solution.

Minerals   A sensible daily diet can also provide needed minerals. All protein foods, for example, contain some minerals. Milk and milk products are rich in calcium. Sources of iron, an important ingredient of blood, are liver, green leafy vegetables, and raisins. In addition to calcium and iron, our bodies need phosphorus, iodine, magnesium, copper, zinc, and a number of other minerals. A daily vitamin supplement also often contains minerals.

Fiber   Although fiber does not have nutrient value, it is important in elimination of body waste. Common sources of fiber are whole-grain breads and cereals, popcorn, apples, peas, and broccoli.

Water   The human body is about 65 percent water. Constant replacement of this body water is essential. In fact, a person can live without food longer than without water. A week without water could prove fatal, but one can survive for weeks without food.

A Balanced Diet

A balanced diet means that we daily obtain nourishment from combinations of different types of foods. The original four basic food groups you may have learned about in earlier education have been modified due to better understanding of body needs and more awareness of health factors related to our diets.

The Federal Food and Drug Administration now requires food labeling containing nutrition facts on almost all food products. The new labeling is easier for the ordinary consumer to understand than has been the case in the past. Also, to help us with our nutrition needs, The U.S. Department of Agriculture/U.S. Department of Health and Human Services now recommends a Food Guide Pyramid as a guide to daily food choices. The recommended amounts in each of the six categories are shown in the illustration of the pyramid below.

The Calorie Count

As mentioned earlier, energy is supplied by proteins, carbohydrates, and fats. A **calorie** is a measure of the energy supplied by what we eat and drink. One pound of weight is equivalent to 3,500 calories. One of the ways often suggested for determining whether you are overweight is by what is called the pinch test. Pinch a fold of skin and fat at your waist or the underside of your upper arm. If you are pinching more than an inch, you are probably overweight.

To some extent you can vary the balance between the calories you eat and the calories you use. If you eat 500 extra calories today, you can eat a little less tomorrow and get a little more exercise. It's a good idea occasionally to look at a chart indicating the number of calories certain foods contain and the number of calories that are used up by certain activities. A cup of string beans contains only 25 calories, whereas a cup of macaroni and cheese contains 350. Twenty potato chips contain about 150 calories—and that's without dip. On the other hand, walking briskly for a half hour uses up about 170 calories. Swimming and running burn up over twice that many. A combination of diet control and exercise is needed for weight reduction and the maintenance of wellness.

Food Guide Pyramid
A Guide to Daily Food Choices

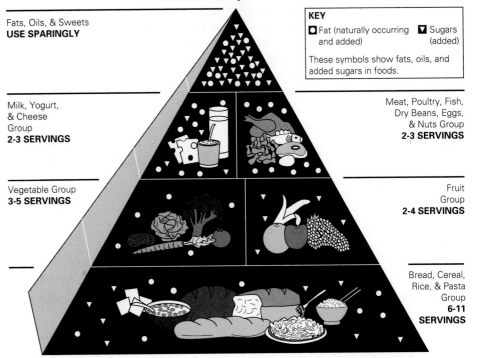

Fats, Oils, & Sweets
USE SPARINGLY

KEY
□ Fat (naturally occurring and added)   ▼ Sugars (added)
These symbols show fats, oils, and added sugars in foods.

Milk, Yogurt, & Cheese Group
2-3 SERVINGS

Meat, Poultry, Fish, Dry Beans, Eggs, & Nuts Group
2-3 SERVINGS

Vegetable Group
3-5 SERVINGS

Fruit Group
2-4 SERVINGS

Bread, Cereal, Rice, & Pasta Group
6-11 SERVINGS

Source: U.S. Department of Agriculture/U.S. Department of Health and Human Services.

In our discussion of both nutrients and calories, we should also consider what is called *nutrient density,* or the amount of nutrients contained in a food in proportion to the number of calories. A 12-ounce can of regular cola contains 150 calories, for example, but has little or no nutritional value. An equal amount of skim milk, on the other hand, contains protein, minerals, and vitamins and is only about 120 calories.

There has been increased concern in recent years about health problems related to red meat, animal fats, and other food products. The nutrition section of a Health Guide in the *U.S. News & World Report* compares a change in thinking related to protein, for example. According to this special issue on health:

> The old thinking: You can't get too much protein. Generous servings of lean meat, chicken or fish each day are key to a healthy diet. Grains, vegetables, and legumes are fine as side dishes.
> The new thinking: Too much protein could be killing us. Meat, chicken and fish are out as main courses; vegetables, fruits, legumes, and grains are in. No more than 3 ounces of animal protein a day.[3]

Although this "new thinking" may seem extreme to some of us, there is a definite shift in eating habits, especially a decrease in the consumption of red meat and animal fats.

Those who have become more conscious of nutrition are also reading food labels more carefully. We can now check nutrient content, calories per serving, various types of fat content, and sodium, as well as other ingredients. Restaurants are also providing their customers with information on calories and fat content of various menu items.

It can be confusing and sometimes deceiving to ordinary consumers, like most of us, to pay attention to what we are eating and drinking and their effects on our well-being. But no one should be expected to be more responsible for what we do to and for our bodies than we ourselves. We must also remember that our physical conditions affect other aspects of holistic health.

✎ *Quiz Yourself*   How many calories do you think the following food items have? Select the numbers you believe to be correct and then check them with the answers on p. 220.

		a.	b.	c.
1.	One small baked potato	a. 60	b. 210	c. 90
2.	4 ounces broiled hamburger	a. 325	b. 450	c. 575
3.	1 frankfurter	a. 150	b. 80	c. 260
4.	1 fried egg	a. 70	b. 100	c. 180
5.	1 cup vegetable soup	a. 220	b. 85	c. 110
6.	1 cup string beans	a. 25	b. 75	c. 120
7.	1 cup macaroni and cheese	a. 110	b. 230	c. 350
8.	$\frac{1}{4}$ head lettuce	a. 35	b. 80	c. 10
9.	20 potato chips	a. 220	b. 150	c. 340
10.	$\frac{1}{3}$ pint chocolate ice cream	a. 190	b. 80	c. 310
11.	6 ounces orange juice	a. 64	b. 90	c. 50
12.	6 ounces yogurt (lite)	a. 80	b. 28	c. 100
13.	$\frac{2}{3}$ cup rice (minute)	a. 60	b. 120	c. 45
14.	1 soda cracker	a. 4	b. 20	c. 12

Suggestions For Healthful Eating

Individual needs, life-styles, and values vary, and they all affect our eating habits and wellness. The following guidelines should at least be considered in maintaining wellness, however. Doesn't everyone want to be well?

- Watch your eating habits. It is recommended that you eat only when seated at a table, lunch counter, or wherever for you is a regular place to eat.
- Do not eat just for something to do. Also avoid eating when you are angry or nervous, but not really hungry.
- Take your time when you eat. We can often eat less but enjoy eating more. Give your attention to your enjoyment of your food, rather than eating while you are reading, watching TV, or doing something else.

- Avoid too much caffeine, found in coffee, tea, cola, and chocolate. There are 100 milligrams (mg) of caffeine in a cup of regular coffee, and it is recommended that we do not exceed 200 to 300 milligrams a day.
- Avoid crash or fad diets. The basic idea is to have an understanding of nutrients, calories, and sensible eating habits. It is better to learn to live and eat differently than to try to lose a large amount of weight in a short period of time.
- Learn to shop wisely. We probably all watch prices, but we should also read labels. On a label, the first ingredient listed is present in a greater amount than any of the other ingredients.
- Avoid junk food. Don't even buy junk food. If you are in the habit of eating such food and snacks, cut down, at least.
- Learn to cook. One of the reasons why Americans eat so much junk food is that they don't know how to cook or don't bother to. Anybody who can read this book can learn to cook.
- Follow the basic guidelines in the Food Guide Pyramid, including a good supply of fiber.
- Avoid excessive salt, sugar, saturated fats, red meat and preservatives such as nitrates in meats.

A young woman is preparing a nutritious meal using fresh vegetables and the guidance of a cookbook.

- Drink more water, including a glass of water before or with a meal. Six to eight glasses of water daily are recommended, in addition to water we consume in other drinks or foods.

Will there come a time when all of the nutrients we need will be available in pills? Can you imagine yourself so busy that you would prefer a handful of nutrient capsules as your daily diet? Would such a diet provide you with better health? Read what an article entitled "Can You Survive by Pills Alone?" in *Time* has to say on this subject:

> Call it the Jetson diet: a futuristic feast of prefab pellets containing all the nourishment any 21st century citizen would want. It makes for a nice cartoon fantasy, but could people really eat this way? Not a chance. Real food is here to stay.
> Multiple-vitamin pills do not contain the fiber, carbohydrates, and proteins necessary for maintaining the body and giving it energy. Such nutrients can be put into pills, but they would have to be taken in such large quantities that they would be impractical—not to mention tasteless—substitutes for real food."[4]

Eating is a human experience that most people enjoy. We shouldn't just "live to eat," but on the other hand, most of us want more than to "eat to live," or to provide for our nutritional needs in the simplest way possible.

What will you DO?   What will you do to improve your eating habits as a result of the information, and reminders, discussed in the nutrition section of this chapter?

ORAL HYGIENE

Wellness includes the condition of one's mouth, gums, and teeth. A diet that is appropriate for good health generally also contributes to good oral hygiene. You have probably heard since you were a small child that too many sweets cause cavities. The National Institute of Dental Research has more to say on this subject:

> It is important to limit your consumption of foods and beverages high in sugar content—not only in amount, but in number of times you eat them during the day. If you eat sweets, it's best to have them as dessert after a well-balanced meal. Snacking should be kept to a minimum and confined to foods that don't promote decay such as nuts, popcorn, raw fruits and vegetables, and sugar-free drinks. Remember that each time you eat sweets, harmful bacteria produce acid in the mouth for at least 20 minutes. It is this acid that causes tooth decay.[5]

And have you heard lately that it is also important to brush your teeth regularly and correctly and to use dental floss to remove plaque, a sticky film that contains bacteria? Drinking fluoridated water is also highly recommended. Where fluoride has not been added to the water supply, fluoride in the form of drops, tablets, and mouth rinses is usually available.

Regular checkups by a dentist are important, as many problems are not noticeable until they are painful and serious. Such checkups usually include oral prophylaxis, a term dentists use for professional teeth cleaning to remove calculus, which is hardened plaque, and possible stains. *Peridontal disease,* or gum disease, very common in adults, can also be identified in early stages through regular visits to a dentist. Signs of this disease may be bleeding gums, gum tenderness, swelling, or loose teeth. Dental hygienists, who usually perform the oral prophylaxis in dental offices and clinics, have been known to remind patients, "Ignore your teeth and they'll go away!"

Implants and restorative dentistry are increasingly used instead of dentures with adults who have lost teeth or need extensive dental attention. Sealants, a plastic film or resin, are quite commonly used today to protect the molars of children.

Good oral hygiene, like many other aspects of wellness, depends not so much on learning more about what is beneficial or harmful as on developing habits that promote wellness.

PHYSICAL FITNESS

We would probably all like to be physically fit. Many of us look at others who appear to be physically fit and wonder whether they really had to do what we think we would have to do to *become* physically fit. Many of us ride nearly everywhere we go and take elevators or escalators instead of climbing the stairs in buildings. Work is more sedentary than it used to be, requiring less physical activity. Americans generally have become spectators rather than participants. Leisure hours are often spent watching television and walking to the kitchen for snacks. There are numerous values, however, to our becoming more physically fit, if we recognize that there is room for improvement.

Posture and physical fitness are related: One affects the other. Poor posture can cause cramping of internal organs, interfere with circulation, and produce muscle strain. Good posture, on the other hand, is easier and more natural when you have proper weight distribution and good muscle tone and coordination. When people are confident that they look good, they have a favorable self-concept and, consequently, feel better about the rest of the world, too. They are happier and easier to get along with wherever they may be.

What Is Physical Fitness?

Fitness Fundamentals, developed by the President's Council on Physical Fitness and Sports, states,

> Physical fitness is to the human body what fine tuning is to an engine. It enables us to perform up to our potential. Fitness can be described as a condition that helps us to look, feel, and do our best. More specifically, it is:
>
> The ability to perform daily tasks vigorously and alertly, with energy left over for enjoying leisure-time activities and meeting emergency demands. It is the ability to endure, to bear up, to withstand stress, to carry on in circumstances where an unfit person could not continue, and is a major basis for good health and well-being.
>
> Physical fitness involves the performance of the heart and lungs, and the muscles of the body. And since what we do with our bodies also affects what we can do with our minds, fitness influences to some degree qualities such as mental alertness and emotional stability.[6]

Four basic qualities are usually associated with physical fitness. They are flexibility, muscular strength, muscular endurance, and cardiorespiratory endurance. Flexibility is the ability to move one's muscles freely, with a full range of motion. Muscular strength refers to the ability to apply force for a relatively brief period of time. Muscular endurance is the ability of a muscle, or a group of muscles, to continue applying force against a fixed object. Push-ups are often used, for example, to test endurance. Probably the most important component of fitness is cardiorespiratory endurance. This pertains to the ability of the circulatory system to supply adequate oxygen and nutrients to the body over a sustained period of time. The process involves taking oxygen into the lungs, distributing it to the muscles, and getting it back to the heart and then to the lungs to begin the cycle again.

Another term often associated with physical fitness is motor fitness. Motor fitness refers to the physical abilities dominated by the kinesthetic, or muscle sense, including balance, flexibility, agility, strength, power, and muscular endurance. It is motor fitness that plays an important part in the coordination necessary for playing games and sports, maintaining balance on slippery sidewalks, standing on a bus or subway, and moving with ease.

Starting Your Own Physical Fitness Program

There are many physical fitness programs. An exercise program called aerobics, developed by U.S. Air Force doctor Kenneth H. Cooper, has become very popular. **Aerobics** is a physical fitness program of exercises that stimulate heart and lung functioning. A major objective of the program is to increase the supply of oxygen to all parts of the body in order to improve and maintain physical fitness. Numerous other aerobic exercise programs have been developed.

Anyone can develop a personal physical fitness program. Basically it is a plan for understanding your current state of wellness and physical fitness, setting realistic goals for the condition you would like to attain, and developing a schedule of activities that will help you to attain those goals.

Unless you know your current state of health and fitness, it is recommended that you have a checkup and approval of a physician before beginning a rigorous fitness program. In determining realistic goals, it is a good idea to review existing fitness programs to get ideas about how often certain types of exercises or activities should be done and how long it takes to get results. In most cases, vigorous exercise for thirty minutes at a time three or four times a week is recommended. It is also recommended that one start with stretches of the muscles that are used most. Both a warm-up and a cool-down period are important each time you engage in your physical fitness activities.

One of the problems with most of us is that we want too much too soon in terms of results and are discouraged if we don't perceive the benefits of the program in a short period of time. Keeping a chart of your activities and progress helps to keep your fitness program organized and consistent. This is an important factor in achieving results. A progress chart also encourages you to continue toward your goal. Those who are physically fit at the present time should remember that it is easier to maintain good health and physical fitness than to attempt to regain them later in life.

Some activities appropriate for a physical program are discussed briefly in the following sections.

Running   Everybody—just about—is running. Some of those who aren't are talking about starting. It is an inexpensive, stimulating way for millions of people to relax and keep themselves in shape. Most people who run speak with favor of the psychological as well as physical benefits of running. It is not quite as easy as it looks, however. There are cautions about exposure to heat or cold or overexertion. Anyone thinking about becoming a serious runner should check with a reliable source for advice about how to run or jog safely.

Walking   Not to be overlooked is the value of the common and natural exercise of walking. It increases one's cardiorespiratory fitness and helps keep a person trim. Walking can be both relaxing and invigorating; it can also take us to some of the places we want to go. Although it is preferable to have comfortable shoes with good support, walking does not require special equipment. In addition to being a good basic physical fitness activity for all of us, walking has other advantages. Some additional benefits attributed to regular walking are that it can lower blood pressure, help lose weight, relieve back pain, and generally improve how a person thinks and feels.

Swimming   Although swimming does require a place to swim, it is considered one of the best forms of exercise. It involves all of the major muscles of our arms, legs, and body trunk and contributes to total body development and well-being. If you are serious about swimming for physical fitness, you should swim in a facility that has lanes so that you can swim without interference. Your goal might be to swim continuously for twenty to thirty minutes. The crawl stroke is considered excellent, but a variety of strokes should be used. People of any age, and even people with disabilities, can swim and benefit from this activity. It is not necessary to belong to a health club to be able to swim during most of the year. Many schools and public facilities have indoor pools. To benefit from swimming as an exercise, one doesn't necessarily have to swim all year long. Other types of exercise can be substituted when swimming is not practical.

Jumping Rope   In earlier days, jumping rope was mainly a children's activity or a training exercise for boxers and athletes. In recent years, however, it has become a widely popular fitness exercise, included in many organized fitness programs. It is also a good exercise for those who cannot leave their living quarters or do not care to. Selection from among its numerous forms can suit it to the interests and stamina of the individual.

Since jumping rope can be very strenuous, someone with a health problem should not begin this exercise without a physician's recommendation. Even a person in good health should start working out gradually. Ten minutes of vigorous rope jumping can be equivalent to thirty minutes of jogging. As with all exercises, there should be three phases: a warm-up period, a workout, and a cooling-off phase.

Sitting   For those who are involved in work that requires many hours of sitting, there are even exercises that can be done in a chair. Such exercises include "jogging in your chair" by first raising one heel as high as possible and then the other, at the same time raising your arms in a bent position and rocking rhythmically forward and back as in walking. Even a class could well begin with a moment of such jogging. That might jog our mental powers a bit, also.

Many people combine keeping physically fit with relaxation and enjoyment. Team sports, racketball, and cross-country skiing serve all these purposes for growing numbers of people. It is important to keeping physically fit that an exercise program be regular.

What would you SUGGEST? If a friend asked you, "How can I get more exercise when I just don't have the time for a fitness program?"

THREATS TO WELLNESS

In spite of a better-educated public and advances in medicine, threats to wellness are increasing. Some of the major ones are discussed in this section.

Stress

The effects of undue stress and some ways to use a reasonable amount of stress were discussed in Chapter 8, "Coping with Stress." We know that too much stress, particularly over a period of time, can cause illness. This shows how emotional, mental, social, and physical aspects of a person's life affect one another.

Physical illness caused by or made worse by emotions and stress is called **psychosomatic illness.** This type of illness is not imaginary. It causes very real pain, and the person can become seriously ill. But the cause of the illness has been tension or another unpleasant emotional experience over a period of time. The resulting stress can cause chronic headaches, backaches, muscular pains, circulatory problems, and ulcers. Some physicians believe that at least half the patients in their waiting rooms have health problems caused by stress. Dr. Hans Selye, referred to in Chapter 8, calls this type of stress "distress." Common signals of harmful effects of stress include pounding of the heart, feelings of overall exhaustion, inability to sleep well or to relax, and a general feeling of frustration. These, in turn, can lead to more serious physical problems. Persons experiencing such problems often seek relief in increased smoking or alcohol or drug abuse, which only worsen their difficulties.

Drug Abuse and Addiction

You are no doubt aware of the importance of prescribed drugs to wellness. Not all drugs are bad for us; nor are all drugs good for us. Sometimes it is not the drug itself but abuse of the drug that has harmful effects. *Drug abuse* is the use of a drug for other than medicinal purposes. It includes the use of illegal drugs but also the overuse and misuse of prescription drugs. In addition to possible physical harmful effects, there can be a psychological dependence that interferes with a person's ability to function at school, at work, or as a member of a family. *Drug addiction* refers to a physiological dependence on drugs or a particular drug. A person who is addicted to a drug usually needs help in breaking the dependence that is grossly interfering with his or her wellness and life. All such misuses of drugs can cause physical as well as mental, emotional, financial, and social problems.

Drugs can be classified in a number of different ways. They are commonly broadly classified as depressants, stimulants, hallucinogens, narcotics, inhalants, and cannabis sativa. A brief description and some examples of each of these classifications follows:

Depressants   Drugs belonging to this classification are commonly referred to as "downers" as they slow the activity of the central nervous system. Barbiturates and tranquilizers are examples of depressants. Although depressants and antianxiety sedatives are legal and are often prescribed, they can become addictive. Overdose can result in coma or death.

Stimulants   These drugs are essentially the opposite of depressants and are commonly referred as "uppers." They tend to increase the activity of the central nervous system. Amphetamines, cocaine, and crack belong to this group. Crack, a smokable form of cocaine, delivers a much greater impact than "snorting" cocaine and can cause death from heart or respiratory failure. Caffeine is also a stimulant and is relatively harmless if used in moderation. Expectant mothers are advised not to use it, however, because of possible harmful effects on their unborn babies.

Hallucinogens   Lysergic acid diethylamide (LSD) is probably the most commonly known drug of this classification. Hallucinogens are so named because they cause perceptual distortions or hallucinations. Those who use them are usually seeking a sense of euphoria, but in some cases they cause frightening perceptual experiences or violent reactions that can lead to death.

Narcotics   Opiates is another term for this classifications of drugs, as they are derived from the opium plant. Opium, morphine, codeine, and heroin are narcotics. Although some of these drugs do have legitimate medicinal purposes in relieving pain, they can become addictive, and overdose can also cause death.

Inhalants   Chemicals that are inhaled or "sniffed" to get high belong to this category. Such chemicals are found in paints, lighter fluids, glues, aerosols, and insecticides. These products are readily available, and adolescents are the largest users. Many users are simply after fun and adventure without realizing the dangers involved. Effects, however, can include liver and kidney damage, brain damage, or even death by instant heart failure.

Cannabis Sativa   Marijuana and hashish, which belong to this category, are derived from the hemp plant. Marijuana consists of crushed stems, leaves, and flowers of the plant, whereas hashish is its dried resin. Both are smoked. Among possible adverse effects are perceptual distortions, short-term memory loss, and interference with the reproductive system. Marijuana is sometimes classified as a hallucinogen.

According to the Department of Health and Human Services, "Contrary to many young people's beliefs, marijuana is a harmful drug, especially since the potency of marijuana now available has increased more than 275 percent over the last decade. For those who smoke marijuana now, the dangers are much more serious than they were in the 1960s."[7]

Alcohol and nicotine are also drugs that can be addictive and are discussed separately in the following sections. These drugs, in addition to marijuana, are sometimes referred to as "gateway drugs," as they are believed, in some cases, to lead to the use of drugs described above.

It is important to recognize that drugs do not affect all persons in the same way. In a publication entitled *A Guide to Commonly Abused Drugs,* the effect of any drug is related to the following factors:

- the expectations of the user
- the setting in which the use takes place
- the amount of the drug taken
- how often it is taken
- the user's personality
- the body weight of the user[8]

Drug abuse and addiction continue to be a major problem in the United States and throughout the world. It is important that we all be knowledgeable about drugs and their effects. Education is not the only answer, however. Illegal drug traffic is a major concern, and more effective apprehension and prosecution of dealers is essential. Also, the use and abuse of drugs by individuals is partly attitudinal. Many do not accept the reality that drugs can ruin their lives, because their attitude is, "I can handle what I'm doing." Evidence proves, however, that most cannot.

 What would you SUGGEST? What are some additional ways drug abuse could be reduced in today's society?

Alcoholism

Alcohol is not only a drug: It is considered by many to be the most abused drug in America. One of the reasons is that, to some extent, it is socially acceptable to "drink." Many people use alcohol as a temporary escape from the problems and stresses of everyday life.

There is a difference between problem drinking and **alcoholism,** which is an illness whereby a person has a compulsion to consume alcohol. There are millions of alcoholics in our society today, and each of them contributes to problems and suffering for many more.

The Alcoholism Council of Greater New York defines alcoholism as:

A complex illness caused by a combination of physical, cultural, and psychological factors. Alcoholism can be identified whenever drinking consistently interferes with daily life: job, family, and health. Warning signals include blackouts (amnesia), withdrawal symptoms (shaking, hallucinations), morning drinking, or gulping of drinks. At the levels consumed in chronic alcoholism, ethanol (alcohol) is toxic to most of the organs and systems in the body, including the brain, liver, kidneys, pancreas, blood and the respiratory and cardiovascular systems. Alcoholism's physical toll can lead to death—but alcoholism is treatable and the alcoholic can fully recover.[9]

Alcoholism, like other illnesses, has some specific warning signals. Any one or more of the following signs may indicate a drinking problem:

- Family or social problems caused by drinking
- Job or financial difficulties related to drinking
- Loss of a consistent ability to control drinking
- "Blackouts," or the inability to remember what happened while drinking
- Distressing physical and/or psychological reactions if you try to stop drinking
- A need to drink increasing amounts of alcohol to get the desired effect
- Marked changes in behavior or personality when drinking
- Getting drunk frequently
- Injuring yourself—or someone else—while intoxicated
- Breaking the law while intoxicated
- Starting the day with a drink

If any of the above warning signals apply to you, you should seriously evaluate your drinking and your life-style. If others have been trying to convince you that you have a problem, it is time to start listening to them. One of the biggest difficulties in identifying one's own problem is the tendency to use denial. Admitting that one is an alcoholic is the first step toward controlling the problem.

Alcoholics Anonymous (AA) has helped many persons solve their problem and change their lives. This organization consists of recovering alcoholics who admit their individual helplessness. They openly place their trust in God and in support from one another. Al-Anon and Al-a-Teen groups are for family members of alcoholics. These groups help families to understand the alcoholic and to cope with their own situation.

The topic of drug abuse could be an extensive study in itself. Also, there is still much that is unknown of the long-term effects of a number of drugs. Extensive research is being conducted, and it can be expected that we will know more about the effects of drugs in the future.

Smoking

Is it possible for anyone not to know that smoking is a threat to health? Many people have learned to use denial—to ignore the warning on their packages of cigarettes, however. Most public places do not permit smoking. Others allow people to smoke only in designated areas. Some restaurants have moved from having smoking and nonsmoking sections to becoming totally nonsmoking establishments. This is intended primarily to protect the rights of nonsmokers. There is increasing evidence that "passive smoking," or breathing smoke-filled air, can be a health hazard also. According to the American Lung Association, nearly 400,000 Americans die each year from the effects of cigarette smoking. This number may decrease in the future, however, as more individuals decide to quit smoking or not to begin.

Even though nicotine in cigarettes is addictive, there is probably no one who could not quit smoking if he or she really wanted to. The critical factor is determining that you want better health for yourself and those who share your environment. Many people quit on their own—with varying degrees of difficulty and success. Some programs involve hypnosis; others advocate wearing nicotine patches. Those who wear such patches should be aware that there are additional health hazards if a person smokes while wearing them. In spite of everything, the motivation of the smoker is usually the determining factor. The smoker faces an approach-avoidance conflict. Does he or she want to quit smoking enough to endure what is entailed in becoming a nonsmoker?

Smokeless tobacco has been substituted for cigarette smoking by some people. However, that, too, can be hazardous. Its use can lead to oral cancer, which is painful, disfiguring, and disabling, and can be fatal.

Sexually Transmitted Diseases

Sexually transmitted diseases, or STDs, are diseases of the sex organs that eventually affect the whole body. Syphilis and gonorrhea were once the most common types, and they still affect millions of people every year. More recently, however, several new types of STDs have been identified. They are nongonococcal urethritis (NGU), and type 2 herpes simplex.

STDs are spread by direct sexual contact. They are found most frequently in an age group ranging from the early teens to the late twenties. There may be no early symptoms of the disease, and even when there are early signs of possible STD, they may disappear. This does not mean the disease is cured, however. In nearly all cases, STD needs treatment in order to be cured.

It is extremely important that STDs be recognized and treated properly. Minors can now be treated for STDs without parental knowledge or consent.

Health and medical personnel urge those who suspect they have an STD to contact a doctor, school nurse, or public health agency. They will not be punished or even embarrassed unnecessarily. It is also important to give the names and addresses of others with whom there has been sexual contact, as these people must also be treated for the disease and prevented from spreading it further. Because people needlessly fear seeking medical help or hesitate to give the names of others involved, a disease that can be controlled has become an epidemic. Syphilis and gonorrhea can be cured with penicillin. Other antibiotics are effective in most cases of NGU. There is promising research being conducted for the treatment of type 2 herpes simplex.

All types of STDs should be given medical attention as soon as they are suspected. Untreated venereal disease can result in damage to the nervous system, mental illness, and sterility; it also can endanger unborn children.

AIDS

"Your condition has been diagnosed as acquired immune deficiency or AIDS," is a statement none of us ever want to hear. The risk is increasing, however. According to the Center for Disease Control in Atlanta, there were 200,000 cases in the United States at the beginning of 1992, with over half that many related deaths. Predictions were that the next 100,000 cases would come four times as quickly as the first. The epidemic began in the early 1980s, with 100,000 cases reported by 1989. The next 100,000, the Center for Disease Control points out, took a little more than two years. In 1992, John Lee Clowe, M.D., the president of the American Medical Association, reported that one million Americans are infected with HIV, which causes AIDS.

Dr. Clowe made the following observations on this dreaded disease:

AIDS/HIV. A disease so complex, researchers the world over have spent billions of dollars—and still haven't been able to unlock its deepest mysteries. It's a disease that doesn't discriminate by age or gender. Social or economic standing. Geography or national wealth.

And this is what's most chilling: AIDS is so deadly, that by its very diagnosis the patient faces what literally is a death sentence.

The United States hasn't experienced anything quite like it since the great Spanish flu epidemic killed 200,000 of our people in 1918.

Because AIDS is so uniformly fatal—and so uniformly expensive—it is having a profound impact on our health delivery system.[10]

What Is AIDS?

Acquired Immune Deficiency Syndrome (AIDS) is caused by the human immunodeficiency virus (HIV). One can carry the virus for a long period of time without being aware of it, as it takes an average of 10 years for AIDS to develop after one is infected. AIDS results in a weakening and finally a destruction of the body's immune defenses. It is the immune system of our body that defends us against disease. In later stages of AIDS, the individual is no longer able to combat even a mild illness or infection, and death results.

How Is AIDS Acquired?

The most common means of acquiring AIDS is through sexual intercourse with someone who has the HIV virus or by using drug-injection needles that have

An individual remembers a victim of AIDS whose name has become a part of the Memorial Quilt.

been contaminated by infected blood. Pregnant women who have HIV can also transmit the disease to their unborn babies. In the past, some hemophiliacs developed AIDS after receiving transfusions of blood containing the HIV virus. Since 1985, however, all blood has been screened before transfusions, so that this risk no longer exists. AIDS, it is widely agreed by medical authorities, is not transmitted through kissing, shaking hands, using public restrooms or swimming pools, from food handlers, or through casual contact with a person who has AIDS.

What Are the Symptoms?

It may be difficult to identify the symptoms of this disease. Some resemble symptoms of other ailments. For example, a person with swollen glands and a fever may be believed to have some other infectious illness. Other symptoms may include excessive tiredness, pink or purple blotches or bumps, sore throat, easy bruising, bleeding from any area of the body, or severe headaches. Some people who are HIV positive may not have any of these symptoms, at least not for many years. In the meantime they may be infecting others with the virus. Those who suspect that they may have been exposed to HIV should be clinically tested.

Who Are the Victims?

According to the Center for Disease Control in Atlanta, the largest number of persons with AIDS have been homosexual or bisexual men and drug addicts who share needles. Of the newer cases, a growing number involve heterosexual transmission. The increase is slight but is expected to grow. Heterosexual individuals who have multiple sex partners are passing HIV to others. Married persons who are having extramarital sexual relations are infecting their spouses. And as mentioned earlier, unborn babies may develop AIDS from their mothers-to-be. AIDS is becoming a disease that potentially could claim anyone for a victim.

Everett Koop, M.D., former Surgeon General of the United States, has stated, "Many people feel that only certain 'high-risk groups' of people are infected by the AIDS virus. This is untrue. Who you are has nothing to do with whether you are in danger of being infected with the AIDS virus. What matters is what you do."[11]

The news we have had about AIDS in recent years is not encouraging. There is an increase in the number of cases and deaths, and there is still no preventive vaccine or cure. There are those who are optimistic about finding ways to prevent, control, or cure AIDS, but we must be realistic about the current dangers of this disease to individuals and society.

Everyone should be knowledgeable about AIDS. School health services and public health departments can provide further information about this life-threatening disease, as well as preventive measures.

What would you SAY? If a co-worker confided to you, "I don't want any contact with a person who has AIDS."

Anorexia Nervosa and Bulimia

For reasons that are not entirely understood, there has been an increase in eating disorder diseases in today's society. **Anorexia nervosa** is often referred to as the "starvation" or "dieting disease." It occurs most often among teenage girls and young women who go on diets and carry losing weight to a dangerous, and sometimes fatal, extreme. This disease cannot be completely covered here. The key element in the disease—the one from which most of the other symptoms and signs stem—is what is called "distorted body image." As strange as it may seem to others, victims of anorexia nervosa see themselves as undesirably fat even when they are dangerously thin. We should be aware that dieting can be carried to extremes.

Bulimia is another eating disorder, in which the individual goes on eating binges and then takes laxatives or induces vomiting. The individual, as with anorexia nervosa, has an uncontrollable fear of becoming fat. Both anorexia nervosa and bulimia are most common among adolescent girls and young women. The onset of these illnesses is often related to emotional stress. Therefore treatment should address both the physical and psychological aspects of the problem. Anyone who has either of these eating disorders needs professional help.

Other Threats

Among the numerous other threats to wellness in today's world are various environmental hazards such as pollution of water, soil, and air. Asbestos is known to cause problems with our lungs. Cholesterol is believed to cause heart disease. Food additives are suspected of causing cancer. There is also growing concern about overexposure to radiation. It is obviously impossible to avoid all threats to our total well-being. However, it seems sensible to avoid or counteract the factors that seem most dangerous or potentially harmful.

 What do you KNOW? Do you know of any serious threats to wellness that were not mentioned in this section? If so, how might they be avoided or counteracted?

PROPER TREATMENT

Although we can do much to maintain our wellness, we are limited in our abilities to test and treat ourselves. There are various types of self-diagnostic kits on the market for measuring blood pressure, blood sugar levels, and other conditions or problems. Although these have their merit, they should supplement, rather than substitute for, professional attention.

Alternative medicine is a term you may be hearing more, as it seems to be gaining in favor. Such practices include hypnosis, acupuncture, biofeedback, and other activities not considered standard medical procedures in the past. Mind/Body medicine is also receiving increased attention. Practices and treatments related to this approach include maintaining a positive attitude, using meditation and relaxation techniques, and participating in support groups that involve sharing of experiences and feelings. Authors of an article on mind/body medicine in *Psychology Today* have this to say:

Although many questions remain to be answered, we believe mind/body approaches can and should become more widely used as a regular part of medical care for several reasons:

- The physical and emotional risk of these techniques is minimal, while the potential benefit is high.
- The economic cost of most mind/body approaches is low; many can be taught by paraprofessionals and involve no high-tech interventions.
- These techniques can and should be used along with standard medical care. They are not alternative measures, but can be applied in the context of conventional medicine, rather than standing in opposition to it.

More and more people are looking for medical care that takes into account their thought and emotions as well as their overt medical problems—in short, mind/body medicine.[12]

A book by Bill Moyers of PBS has also drawn attention to this approach through a television series in 1993 and his companion book, *Healing and the Mind.*

Emphasis on maintaining wellness can avoid some illnesses but must also be realistic. There are times when a person has an illness or disease that requires professional advice and treatment. Family practice, a relatively new area of medicine, is concerned with preventive care as well as the health problems of the individual. Most clinics also have a number of specialists to diagnose and take care of particular problems.

It is impossible to clearly and easily state what is proper treatment in all cases. You should become knowledgeable about your condition, be aware of your choices, and take personal responsibility for decisions. The Clinton administration health care plan promises to make it possible for all Americans to be covered by health insurance and to accomplish wellness or receive the treatment that is needed.

What would you DO? If you observed disturbing signs of poor health in a friend, what would you do?

MENTAL HEALTH

We should not take our mental health for granted any more than we should take our physical health for granted. Although mental health is not necessarily the same for everyone, there are some common characteristics. Individuals are usually considered mentally healthy if their behavior falls with a normal range and if they are reasonably well adjusted and happy. But what is normal?

What Is Normal?

Do you consider yourself normal? Most people do. But what is a normal condition and what is normal behavior? The answer can be important to each of us in evaluating our state of wellness. It can also be important to professional people in suggesting and applying treatment for types of abnormality. It should be kept in mind that the difference between **normal** and **abnormal** is largely a matter of degrees of certain types of behavior rather than completely different

kinds of behavior. Some fear is normal, for example, but fear of being among people one does not know can be abnormal.

One way to determine what is normal is by comparing one's behavior with that of others. It is normal to make some mistakes in judgment and to have some apprehension about failure. It is normal to experience some anxiety about starting a new job. But it is also normal to look forward to a vacation after you have been working on your job for a year. A range of behavior can be expected of normal human beings.

Another way to evaluate the normality of behavior is to consider what is typical of a particular individual. What is usual for one person may be very unusual for another. A still further method of determining what is normal is first to identify or define what is abnormal. Anything else, then, can be accepted as normal. It is abnormal to feel tired all the time or to "see things" that aren't there. We must have an understanding of what is normal in order to detect what is abnormal. But since the range of normality contains so many variations and degrees, it is sometimes easier to recognize what is outside the range of normal behavior.

Common characteristics of mentally healthy individuals include the following:

- accepts oneself; has a positive, realistic self-concept
- can cope with situations in one's life
- gives reasonable attention to total wellness
- can effectively problem-solve and make decisions
- understands one's fears and apprehensions
- expresses emotions in acceptable, constructive ways
- is responsible toward others
- is basically content but is motivated to become more self-actualized

PSYCHOLOGICAL DISORDERS

Psychosis, a term for mental illness, is declining in use in today's society. It is being replaced by more specific terms referring to psychological disorders. Therefore, the term psychological disorder will be used in our discussion of these types of problems. *Psychological disorders* refer to the difficulty or inability to adapt to the realities of life. They include behavior usually considered abnormal in society, such as thought disturbances and difficulty in understanding oneself and relating to others. Psychological disorders are usually identified as the following types: *anxiety disorders, somatoform disorders, dissociative disorders, mood disorders, schizophrenia disorders,* and *personality disorders.* David G. Myers, in *Exploring Psychology,* gives us an explanation for the classifications:

> In both medicine and psychology, diagnostic classification seeks to describe a disorder and to predict its future course, as well as to facilitate research about its causes and treatment. Indeed, naming and describing a scheme for classifying psychological disorders is the American Psychiatric Association's Diagnostic and Statistical Manual of Mental Disorders (Third Edition-Revised), nicknamed DSM-III-R.[13]

Actually this publication, revised in 1987, includes over 230 disorders.

Anxiety Disorder

Generalized anxiety disorder, panic disorder, phobic disorder, and *obsessive-compulsive disorder* are the primary types of anxiety disorders. Each is briefly described below:

Generalized Anxiety Disorder A chronic overwhelming feeling of anxiety characterizes this disorder. It is sometimes referred to as "free-floating anxiety" as it is difficult to determine what might be causing feelings of persistent nervousness and discomfort, both emotional and physical. It includes the characteristics of anxiety discussed in Chapter 5, "Emotions."

Panic Disorder A person with a panic disorder experiences severe psychological symptoms such as heart pounding, a sense of choking, and dizziness. The attack comes on suddenly, and although it may only last a few minutes, it can be a terrifying experience. The cause is usually unknown, but it is believed that both hereditary and psychological factors can be involved.

Phobic Disorder Phobias were also discussed in Chapter 5, "Emotions," and were defined as abnormal, illogical fears. Phobias can be relatively mild and not too disturbing or they may be severe and extremely frightening. It is the more severe phobias that would ordinarily be considered a phobic disorder. Common types of phobic disorders relate to ordinary things, such as fear of cats, water, people, and public places. This last type, fear of public places, is called agoraphobia, and is one of the more common types of phobic disorders.

Obsessive-Compulsive Disorder As is indicated by the name of this disorder, it involves two subtypes. An **obsession** is an irrational thought that a person is "hung up on" and is unable to dismiss from his or her mind. Obsessive-compulsive disorders can be relatively harmless, such as continuing to think about a particular person for no apparent reason, or they can be extremely disturbing. It is common, for example, for obsessions to pertain to violence or unacceptable moral behavior.

Compulsions involve uncontrollable repetition of behavior or rituals. The behavior has no rational purpose, but the person seems to be unable to stop the behavior, nonetheless. A very common type of compulsion is an excessive washing of one's hands. The merit of having clean hands cannot be denied, but persons with a compulsive disorder go beyond what would be considered practical and can't seem to restrain themselves. Obsessive behavior can lead to a compulsion in the sense that persons who are obsessed with cleanliness will relieve some of the related anxiety by compulsive washing of the hands.

Somatoform Disorder

Common examples of this disorder are **conversion** and **hypochondria.** With conversion, often referred to as hysteria in the past, a person loses a physical ability even though there is no physically related cause. The condition is caused by emotional stress and is not necessarily permanent, but the individual usually needs professional help to overcome the disorder.

You probably have heard the term **hypochondriac,** but it is not always used correctly. Persons with this disorder think they have serious physical problems even though they may be in relatively good health. They interpret any minor disturbance as related to an illness, often associated with something they have recently heard about or seen on a television program. Hypochondriacs have a tendency to disbelieve results of medical tests and professionals.

Dissociative Disorder

Amnesia, sometimes referred to as psychogenic amnesia, is one type of this disorder. A person who experiences amnesia may lose his or her identity to the extent that they do not know who they are or any of the details of their past experience or lives. Amnesia is usually considered to be a reaction from emotional stress to the point at which those afflicted psychologically escape from their identities and responsibilities. Amnesia has been an element in considerable fictional writing, but in reality it is not common.

Multiple personality is a second dissociative disorder that has been the subject of books and movies, often based on actual cases. Two such examples are *Sybil* and *The Three Faces of Eve.* As is implied by the name of the disorder, such persons have two or more distinct personalities. Usually these personalities are in sharp contrast to one another. One may be very shy and proper, for example, and the other may be nonconforming and bold. The personalities may be unaware of one another, but each may reveal itself without any particular warning or explanation.

Mood Disorder

Major depression, often simply referred to as depression, and bipolar depression, are the most common types of this disorder. Although it is normal to have moods—to feel much better psychologically at some times than others—persons who experience major depression have an uncontrollable sense of sadness, fatigue, have difficulty in performing ordinary daily activities, and have a general sense of feeling that life is not worth the effort. Sometimes this type of depression is brought on by a traumatic event such as a death in the family and is referred to as *reactive depression.* This type of depression usually passes with time, although counseling may help the individual make the adjustment required. In contrast, depression can also be "inner," without being related to any specific experience in the person's life. This type of depression is usually more severe and longer lasting than reactive depression.

Physiological problems are also usually present with depression, such as difficulty in sleeping, and eating. There is still some debate about the causes of depression, as with many other psychological disorders, but it often has both a psychological and biochemical basis. Severe depression that is not recognized and treated often leads to suicide.

Bipolar, or **manic-depressive,** disorder consists of extreme mood swings from experiencing feelings of high enthusiasm and energy to the type of despair described above. These mood changes tend to run in cycles and are not directly related to what the person is doing or what is happening in his or her life. Bipolar disorders are relatively rare, but can cause extreme difficulty for a person attempting to function in a consistent, constructive manner.

Schizophrenic Disorder

Schizophrenia has sometimes been confused with multiple personality disorder because it involves a "split" in thought and emotions. The person becomes disoriented and may have delusions or false beliefs about his or her identity. Persons with this disorder may also have hallucinations, often hearing voices that give them orders or ridicule them. The major classifications of schizophrenia are *disorganized,* whereby behavior is incoherent, bizarre, or silly, and generally inappropriate; *catatonic,* whereby behavior ranges from unresponsiveness to extreme hyperactivity; *paranoid,* whereby a person generally has delusions of persecution, but may also have delusions of grandeur; and *undifferentiated,* whereby behavior does not fit the other classifications. Approximately half of the people admitted to mental hospitals have schizophrenic disorder, but treatment, including new drug therapy, is increasingly encouraging.

Personality Disorder

With this disorder, persons experience difficulty adapting to their personal lives and interactions with others. They have difficulty coping with life in ways that are generally considered within a normal range of behavior. *Antisocial personality* is one of the most common types of this disorder. Antisocial, in this sense, does not mean avoiding social interaction with others, as one might suspect. Instead, it consists of behavior that is irresponsible, aggressive, and often in violation of the rights of others.

TREATMENT OF PSYCHOLOGICAL DISORDERS

Many people who receive treatment for mental or psychological disorders are able to return to normal productive lives. It is also encouraging to know that many functional disorders can be prevented. People can learn to accept themselves, to adjust to others and situations, and to face problems realistically. There is increased emphasis, therefore, on mental health and the prevention of disorders. Also, a promising number of new drugs that are effective in helping to control psychological disorders have been developed in recent years.

Recovery depends on the nature and degree of the disorder, as well as the patient's desire to return to normal functioning and good mental health. It also, of course, depends on the quality of the treatment and care the person receives. In addition to assistance that is available from local and state agencies, treatment facilities include hospitals, outpatient clinics, and halfway houses. Many communities also provide housing for relatively independent living that is supervised by a mental health agency. In spite of these opportunities, however, it is believed that thousands of persons with psychological disorders live in the streets, suffering physical deprivation as well as the effects of the disorder itself.

There are a number of proven methods of treating psychological disorders. Treatment usually begins with a physical examination, including gathering of background information about the individual, such as work, personal activities, and medical and family history. The examination may also include laboratory tests. Types of treatment may include **biochemical** therapy (the use of prescription drugs), **electroconvulsive therapy** (ECT or electric shock, which is controversial but is sometimes used for severe depression), or a number of types of **psychotherapy.** With psychotherapy, emphasis is placed on the psychological, rather than the physical or chemical, treatment of the disorder, although some medication may be prescribed to treat disturbing symptoms during the process. The therapist and patient develop a trusting, open relationship so that the patient feels comfortable expressing himself or herself freely. Together they develop ways for the individual to learn more realistic coping skills.

Group therapy is often used with other types of therapy. Individuals with common disorders have the opportunity to interact with others and come to discover that their problems are not unique. Members of the group feel

Counseling often is most successful when both a young person and parents participate.

relatively safe in sharing experiences and expressing themselves. Although there are various types of independent support groups, this type of treatment as therapy is under the guidance of professionals.

The type of treatment used depends on the diagnosis of the disorder, the particular specialization of the therapist, and the preference of the patient or guardian. Clinical psychologists and psychiatric nurses provide various types of therapy, but most treatment is administered under the direction of a psychiatrist.

Misunderstanding about what a psychiatrist is and does is common. A psychiatrist is a physician who has specialized in the branch of medicine that diagnoses and treats persons with mental or psychological disorders. Those who go to a psychiatrist should not be judged to have a severe psychological disorder any more than a person who goes to an internal medicine specialist should be judged to have a serious physical illness. There are many degrees of all types of disorders. Many people recognize that they need professional help to maintain or restore the kind of mental health that will contribute to making their lives less stressful and more meaningful as a whole.

Getting Help

Any problem involving one's general wellness can be handled more easily if attended to at an early stage. Many health problems result from negligence; ignoring problems only makes them worse. When you are in need of help or advice with regard to any health problem, do not hesitate to seek help. People you respect and trust can usually give you some direction. These might include members of your family, friends, teachers, members of the clergy, or counselors. Another person can view your situation more objectively. He or she can help you make a wise decision and can also give you support. The final responsibility for your well-being is yours, of course.

It may help to know that the American Hospital Association has issued a leaflet entitled *A Patient's Bill of Rights.* These rights include the right to be told about an illness and its treatment, the right to refuse treatment within legal limits, and the right to receive proper care and information about costs. You have the right to care about what is happening to you. You have the right to expect others to care also. Most persons working in health professions are dedicated to their work. It is seldom necessary to insist on one's rights.

Giving Help

It is not always easy to give or suggest help to a person who seems to need it. Sometimes people refuse to admit that they have a problem, especially if the problem involves drug or alcohol abuse or mental health. The following suggestions may be helpful:

1. Suggest a change in routine. Perhaps the person needs a change of pace or a vacation. Some people may need more relaxation. Others may need more meaningful activity.
2. Remind the person that no one is perfect. Discuss the value of living one day at a time, without excessive concern about the past or future and without excessive demands of oneself.

3. Encourage the person to see a doctor, a member of the clergy, or some other professional person.

Be patient. Be a good listener. Your suggestions will be accepted only if they are offered in the right way at the right time. Avoid being too pushy in trying to help others. People often have fears that make action difficult, or they may not be quite ready to do what you think they should. Too much pressure at the wrong time can do more harm than good. Knowing that others care and are available to talk or to help out in other ways is often what a person needs.

It can be difficult to recognize the need for outside help. For one thing, an illness may develop gradually. Neither the ill person nor others may be aware of the degree of change. Behavior that is generally considered abnormal—such as experiencing hallucinations—requires attention, however. Also, a drastic change in what would be considered normal in the habits of a particular person may be a sign of an impending serious illness. No one has perfect mental health at any one time; maintaining such perfection is no more possible than experiencing perfect physical health at all times. There are various degrees of mental health. A person who has most of the characteristics of a normal person is mentally healthy. Lacking one or two characteristics may cause problems but does not make a person mentally ill.

HABITS

Although we may admit that we are creatures of habit, it isn't likely that we even know what all our habits are. A **habit** is a pattern of behavior that has been repeated until it becomes automatic. If a habit is something we do without thinking, it is understandable that we may not be aware of all our habits.

You hear about good and bad habits. It is more correct, however, to consider how a habit affects a particular person. What may be good for you may be harmful to someone else. Vigorous exercise is good for a healthy person. It may be fatal for one with a heart problem.

Breaking Habits   To break a habit one must first be aware of it and be motivated to change the behavior pattern. Even then, people who want to break a habit may have to make several attempts until they discover or work out the method that will be effective for them. They will also probably receive much advice. Some successful habit breakers advise, "Don't taper off unless this is recommended by medical authorities because of physiological effects. Decide you are going to quit a particular habit and do it. Don't allow yourself to 'one more time' your undesirable habit. Begin and don't make exceptions."

Sometimes outside help is needed or at least is beneficial in breaking habits. Doctors are attempting to help people who seriously want to give up smoking. People meet in groups, are shown films of the harmful effects of smoking, and are then advised on how to break the habit. The degree of commitment to breaking a habit can be a deciding factor. Once individuals announce, so to speak, that they are going to do something, they suffer lack of esteem if they don't live up to that claim.

Others may advise, "Take your habit breaking one day at a time." This is one of the successful techniques used by Alcoholics Anonymous. The recovering alcoholic resolves not to take a drink today and makes the same resolution again tomorrow.

Breaking a habit as part of a group who have the same objective has proved successful for many. This is one of the methods used by weight-losing groups. Members have the common habit of eating too much or eating the wrong foods. By working at their common problem together, they make a commitment they feel obliged to fulfill. They also give one another moral support and encouragement.

As with all human behavior, habits are complex. The real reason for certain types of habitual behavior may have to be identified and dealt with before the habit can be successfully changed. Esther has a habit of eating too much too often, not because she is hungry but because she is lonely and frustrated. Habit analysis must determine such motives.

A number of stimuli or related activities are involved in a habit. Smoking, for example, involves taking out a cigarette, lighting it up, inhaling, blowing smoke, tapping ashes, and perhaps making miscellaneous gestures with the cigarette. All of these are part of the habit. So a person not only has to overcome a craving for the cigarette, but in a sense must also substitute another activity for the smoking routine.

Since many habits are a sequence of activities, one of the ways to break a habit is to avoid the first step that triggers the sequence into motion. Understanding how habits were formed in the first place helps one to understand how a situation may be changed or stimuli removed to promote the breaking of a habit.

Components of Holistic Health

Forming New Habits   More attention is usually given to habit breaking than to new habit formation. An undesirable habit such as biting your fingernails can be quite conspicuous. It takes more careful analysis to determine what new habits could be beneficial.

Sometimes breaking an undesirable habit and forming a desirable habit can be accomplished together. A desirable habit can be substituted for an undesirable one. Eating raw vegetables can be substituted for eating sweets, for example. Substitution is useful in habit breaking because, as already mentioned, related activity is an integral part of the habit. But unless you substitute a harmless or beneficial activity, you may discover you have just substituted one undesirable habit for another.

If you desire to form a new habit, you should begin immediately or as soon as possible. If you prolong the time between deciding to do something and doing it, you often begin to make excuses for yourself. You may rationalize that this really isn't important anyway. But remember—the formation of new habits takes special effort at first; after a while, new habits can become as easy to follow as the old poor habits were.

What do you THINK?   In your opinion, why do people continue habits that they know are hazardous to their health?

YOUR JOB AND WELLNESS

Your wellness is not strictly your own business. Your wellness is of concern to many others even if you don't have a communicable disease. You would expect someone selling you health or life insurance, for example, to be interested in your physical condition. But prospective employers are also concerned about the health of the people they hire. Because businesses cannot operate properly with a reduced number of employees, absenteeism due to illness is of major importance to employers. Sick leave and replacement training are also costly. Even employees on the job who don't feel well can be a hindrance to effective operation. For these reasons you will be asked to indicate the condition of your health on most job applications; you may even be required to have a physical examination, including tests for drug use, before you are hired. You will also be required to follow safety regulations in your job environment and to report illness and injury. And these are government regulations pertaining to health and safety measures.

Hazards on the job also include unsanitary working conditions and noxious fumes or waste particles in the air. Injuries to the back and hands are also common. Hazards to the eyes and ears were discussed in Chapter 4, "Senses and Perception," and are often associated with one's work. Stress, discussed earlier in the chapter, is also considered a major factor in wellness related to one's work.

An article in *USA TODAY* entitled "Job Stress: America's Leading Adult Health Problem," places the cost of job stress at more than $200,000,000 annually. The article has the following to say:

The nature of job stress varies with different occupations, but affects workers at all levels. Some of the major sources that have been identified are:

- Inadequate time to complete a job to one's satisfaction
- Lack of clear job description or chain of command
- Little recognition or reward for good job performance
- Inability or lack of opportunity to voice complaints
- Lots of responsibility, but little authority
- Inability to work with superiors, co-workers, or subordinates because of basic differences in goals and values
- Lack of control or pride over the finished product
- Insecurity caused by pressures from within or without due to the possibility of takeover or merger
- Prejudice because of age, gender, race, or religion
- Unpleasant environmental conditions (smoky or polluted air, crowding, noise, fear of exposure to toxic chemicals or carcinogens)
- Chronic commuting difficulties
- Concerns related to responsibilities for employees
- Not being able to utilize personal talents and abilities effectively or to full potential
- Fear, uncertainty, and doubt[14]

Numerous examples can be found today of the concern of business and industry for the wellness of their employees. Besides health insurance and in-house doctors, nurses, and counselors, many companies have extensive fitness facilities and programs. Frequently employers also provide help for those with problems of alcoholism, drug abuse, or emotional stress. Job-related burnout is also recognized as a problem today and both employers and employees are giving attention to prevention or remedy. Burnout consists of extreme physical and emotional fatigue resulting in loss of interest in one's work and in a general reduction of efficiency.

Employee assistance programs serve smaller companies whose structure and budget do not allow special services of their own. The interest in employee wellness is not for the exclusive benefit of the company; there is obvious growing interest in employees as human beings with personal lives and responsibilities. The Family Leave and Medical Act, passed in 1993, recognizes such responsibilities. It provides for eligible employees to receive up to 12 weeks of unpaid leave per year following birth or adoption of a child or to care for a seriously ill child, spouse, or parent. All 12 weeks need not be taken at once. Most companies can make accomodations for their employees to take advantage of this act as needed.

BALANCES

The need for balance in our personal lives and in society was discussed in Chapter 1, "Psychology in Our Changing World." Keeping well requires a number of balances. We need a balanced diet. We need a balance of activity and rest. We need some stress to function at our best, although too much stress can make us ill. You may have heard "All things in moderation; nothing in excess." This saying applies to wellness in many respects.

A realistic attitude is a balance between what we would like to be and what is reasonably possible. Self-image, too, can help us become and stay healthier.

Those who think of themselves as being the kind of person they want to be are more likely to take care of themselves.

SUMMARY

Wellness, or holistic health, involves a complex interrelationship among physical health and fitness, mental health, stress management, environmental safety, emotional stability, vocational competence, social effectiveness, and spiritual harmony.

We can keep ourselves well in a number of ways. What we eat is of vital importance. The essential nutrients and appropriate selections from the Food Guide Pyramid should be included in our daily diets. There should also be a balance between calorie intake and energy use in order to maintain desired weight. Oral hygiene is also an important part of total wellness and in some respects is related to our diets.

Physical fitness can improve our wellness in a number of ways. The four basic qualities of fitness are flexibility, muscular strength, muscular endurance, and cardiovascular endurance. Any reasonably healthy person should be able to keep physically fit through a variety of activities: Popular ones are sports, exercise programs, running, walking, and swimming. There is also emphasis today on aerobics to stimulate heart and lung functioning. Many combine exercise and recreation. Improved appearance is also a result of weight control and physical fitness.

Among the threats to wellness in today's society are stress, drug abuse and addiction, alcoholism, smoking, sexually transmitted diseases, AIDS, and eating disorders. Improper treatment can also be a threat to maintaining or regaining wellness.

Mental health is a vital component to holistic health. If the behavior of individuals falls within a normal range of behavior and if they are well adjusted and happy, they are usually considered mentally healthy. Mental health varies with individuals, but there are some common characteristics related to this aspect of wellness.

Psychological disorders refer to difficulty in adapting or inability to adapt to the realities of life. They are commonly classified as anxiety disorder, somatoform disorder, dissociative disorder, mood disorder, schizophrenic disorder, and personality disorder. Treatment of psychological disorders includes biochemical therapy, electroconvulsive therapy, and a number of types of psychotherapy, including both individualized and group therapy. Many people with psychological disorders are treated as outpatients rather than being institutionalized as in the past.

Business and industry are becoming increasingly concerned about the wellness of their employees. This is to their benefit, as it reduces costly absenteeism and replacement training. But there is also evidence of sincere interest in wellness among employees as human beings with personal lives and responsibilities. The Family Leave Act of 1993 also recognizes this.

We should all be interested in maintaining a high level of total wellness. To some extent this requires breaking harmful habits and developing desirable ones. We also need balances in diet, exercise, and other activities.

Disabilities will be discussed in the next chapter, "Exceptional Persons."

Psychology In Practice

1. Develop a physical fitness program that you believe would be realistic for you. Use a physical fitness book or guide as a reference. Do not follow the plan, however, unless you are confident that you can do so without risk.

2. Present some information to the class about a wellness hazard not discussed in the chapter. Public health officials or other agencies may be able to give you pamphlets or display materials.

3. Check on organizations or agencies within your area that offer wellness services and materials to the public. Obtain available pamphlets and information from one of them and, with a fellow student, present your findings to the class.

4. Find out what you can about types of treatment for mental illness and psychological disorders in your area. Determine, to the best of your ability, some of the problems in helping those with such disorders become mentally healthy and functioning members of the community.

Learning Activities

Turn to page 415 to complete the Learning Activities and Enrichment Activities for this chapter.

Notes

1. Jane E. Myers, "Wellness As the Paradigm for Counseling and Development: The Possible Future," *Counselor Education and Supervision,* March 1991, p. 183.
2. John James and Muriel James, *Passion For Life: Psychology and the Human Spirit,* A Dutton Book, Penquin Books USA Inc., New York, 1991, p. 70.
3. Doug Podolsky, "Eat Your Beans," *U.S. News & World Report,* May 20, 1991, pp. 70–71.
4. Reported by Janice M. Horowitz/New York, Elaine Lafferty/Los Angeles, and Dick Thompson/Washington, "The New Scoop on Vitamins," *Time,* April 6, 1992, p. 56.
5. *Tooth Decay,* National Institute of Dental Research, Bethesda, Maryland (no date, no page).
6. *Fitness Fundamentals: Guidelines for Personal Exercise Programs,* Developed by the President's Council on Physical Fitness and Sports, Department of Health and Human Services (no date), p. 2.
7. *Turning Awareness Into Action,* U.S. Department of Health and Human Services, Public Health Service, Washington, D.C., rev. 1991, p. 56.
8. *A Guide to Commonly Abused Drugs,* Winters Communications, Inc., Tampa, FL, 1989, p. 2.
9. *A Health and Fitness Guide to Alcohol,* Alcoholism Council of Greater New York, New York (no date, no page).
10. John Lee Clowe, "The Changing World of AIDS," *Vital Speeches,* December 15, 1992, p. 135.

11. C. Everett Koop, *The Memoirs of America's Family Doctor,* Random House, New York, 1991, Appendix A.

12. Daniel Golemann and Joel Gurin, Mind/Body Medicine—At Last," *Psychology Today,* March/April 1993, p. 16.

13. David G. Myers, *Exploring Psychology,* Worth Publishers, Inc., New York, 1990, p. 338.

14. Paul J. Rosch, "Job Stress: America's Leading Adult Health Problem," *USA TODAY,* May 1991, pp. 43–44. Reprinted from *USA Today Magazine,* May copyright 1991 by the Society for the Advancement of Education.

10 Exceptional Persons

Learning Objectives

After completing this chapter, you will be able to do the following:

1. Explain the difference between disability and handicap.
2. Compare the meanings of quantitative and qualitative and give an example of quantitative differences in characteristics of exceptional persons.
3. Explain how you would react to a situation involving a relative and his retarded brother.
4. Identify three suggestions you should follow in communicating with a person who is deaf.
5. Describe what you should *not* do when meeting a blind person using a cane and when meeting a blind person with a guide dog.
6. Indicate four factors that parents should consider in caring for a disabled child and the rest of their children.
7. Give two suggestions for modifying behavior, resulting from negative societal attitudes and prejudice, toward disabled persons.
8. Identify two disadvantages a twelve-year-old girl living in a poverty section of a large city might have, and suggest how they might be reduced or overcome.
9. Suggest how three of Buscaglia's guidelines could be followed in continuing your relationship with a classmate who must use a wheelchair as a result of a spinal injury.

> **❝In spite of** disabilities, *everyone has the* ability *to make his or her life meaningful.*❞
>
> MAGGIE MCKAY
> *speech pathologist*

Every human being is unique. This uniqueness was discussed in Chapter 2, "Self-Concept and Personality." Not all of us are exceptional, however. Although we may have used this term in our everyday language, as in saying, "That movie was exceptional!" the term has a different meaning in this chapter. "Exceptional," according to the authors of *Human Exceptionality: Society, School and Family,* is "an individual whose physical, mental or behavioral performance deviates substantially from the norm, either higher or lower."[1] Although many exceptional persons have disabilities or psychological problems, the definition also includes those who have special abilities or talents.

The following major classifications of exceptional persons will be discussed in this chapter: the gifted or talented; the mentally retarded; the physically disabled; the emotionally disturbed; the societally neglected and culturally disadvantaged; the deaf/hard of hearing; and those with visual impairments, speech and language disorders, and learning disabilities.

A number of persons have more than one impairment or disability. In addition, one disability may lead to another. Deafness, for example, often leads to language problems. A visual impairment usually limits experience and stimulation and thus can interfere with intellectual development. Other people may have separate physical and mental disabilities that affect one another and affect total performance.

HOW AM I INVOLVED?

You may have wondered as you approached this chapter, "Why should I know more about and better understand exceptional persons? How does this subject involve me?"

Consider some of these responses to the questions:

- It is possible that you are an exceptional person, yourself. If so, you may have recently acquired a disability and be in the process of adjustment. However difficult it may be, perhaps this chapter could help you make that adjustment. Or you may have been born with a disability, have already accepted its effect on your life, and now be in the process of getting education and training to make your life more productive and meaningful. If you are an exceptional person, you know how you are involved, but you can gain information and guidelines related to education, the world of work, and a quality life-style.

- A member of your family may have a disability, which affects all members of the family in some way. Most people in this situation want their spouse, parent, sibling, or other family member to have a meaningful life, but they also do not want to have to sacrifice their own goals and opportunities.

- You are certainly not encouraged to become a pessimist and think of all the tragic things that could happen to you, but it is realistic to recognize that you could be disabled yourself at some time. Ask someone who has acquired a disability to confirm that in most cases the disability was totally unexpected. Since many acquired disabilities are the result of accidents, you might be motivated to take precautions against such a misfortune. There are also ways to protect oneself from some illnesses that could result in a disability.

- It is also possible that you have, or will have in the future, a friend with a disability. It is important that we do not abandon a friend who has acquired a disability, but we sometimes have difficulty in understanding and accepting this change in a friend or in maintaining a mutually rewarding relationship. Everyone needs friends, and although those with disabilities often establish friendships with those with similar disabilities, they enjoy friendship with others, too. A disability is only one characteristic of a person's identity and personality.
- For those of you who will become parents someday, there is a slight possibility that you could have a child born with a disability. Three babies out of a hundred are born with a serious defect. Other children can acquire disabilities through illness or accidents. There are also adults who knowingly adopt or provide foster care for children who have disabilities. Some of you may already have children who are exceptional. You may want to share your experience with others. This could also help you gain further insight into your own situation as well as your relationship with your child and other members of your family.
- As the student that you are now, whatever your program, it is likely that you have some association with students who are exceptional in some way. These students want to be an integral part of the class or of their particular educational situation. Staying out of their way or merely opening doors for them is hardly an acceptance of them as co-learners or unique individuals. If you get to know some of them personally, you will doubtless find your own life enriched.
- It is almost certain that you will be working with individuals with disabilities when you enter the workforce. Relatively new legislation has opened up new opportunities in the world of work for those with disabilities. If one concentrates on a person's abilities rather than on his or her limitations, it can be surprising how quickly a disability can be almost completely overlooked in the workplace, especially by co-workers.

All of us can identify with at least several of these circumstances. How you react to this chapter will depend on which ways and to what extent you are involved.

DISABILITY OR HANDICAP?

The terms disability and handicap are often used interchangeably. The term handicap is used in laws, regulations, and services related to people who have disabilities. Let's consider an important difference between the meaning of the two terms, however. D. P. Hallahan and J. M. Kauffman, in a book on exceptionality, explain the difference as follows:

> [D]isability is an inability to do something, a diminished capacity to perform in a specific way. A handicap, on the other hand, is a disadvantage imposed on an individual. A disability may not be a handicap, depending on the circumstances. Likewise, a handicap may or may not be caused by a disability. For example, blindness is a disability that can be anything but a handicap in the dark. In fact, in the dark the person who has sight is the one who is handicapped. Being in a wheelchair may be a handicap in certain social situations, but the disadvantage may be the result of other people's reactions, not the inability to walk. Other people can handicap a person who is different from themselves (in

color, size, appearance, language, and so on) by stereotyping them or not giving them an opportunity to do the things they are able to do. When working and living with exceptional individuals who have disabilities, we must constantly strive to separate the disability from the handicap. That is, our goal should be to confine their handicap to those characteristics that cannot be changed and to make sure that we impose no further handicap by our attitudes or our unwillingness to accommodate their disability.[2]

WHAT DOES IT MEAN TO BE DIFFERENT?

As human beings we have both similarities and differences. We have unique strengths and weaknesses. We have different potentials in different areas. The idea that an exceptional person differs from a normal person only in having a different *degree* of an ability is a **quantitative** approach. This differs from the **qualitative** approach—more common in the past—in which a person with a disability was regarded as a different *kind* of person.

With the quantitative approach there is a tendency to avoid labeling and classifying people as different. However, sometimes these labels are needed to provide rehabilitation, appropriate education, facilities, and job opportunities for exceptional persons. When a difference is labeled it should be for the benefit rather than the disadvantage of those so labeled. It certainly should not cause further problems for them.

One of the criticisms of labeling a person as gifted or mentally retarded, for example, involves the self-fulfilling prophesy, discussed in Chapter 2. This term came into use following a study a number of years ago in which a group of school children were given an intelligence test. Thereafter, teachers of the students were told that certain children had greater potential for intellectual growth than the others. This was for the purposes of the experiment and was not true, however. When the test was given again later in the year, the children that the teachers had been told had higher intellectual potential scored higher. The conclusion was that the teachers' expectations, including their attention to these students, contributed to the rise in their scores. In this sense, the self-fulfilling prophesy means that you have a tendency to become what you are labeled or what others expect of you.

Although a label draws attention to a particular characteristic, it is only one aspect of that person. There are probably more similarities than differences. We should concentrate on similarities as much as possible.

People with a particular disability such as blindness or deafness are different from each other just as sighted and hearing people are. Some like to dance, fish, and swim, and others do not. Some do better in school and are more sociable than others. We enjoy spending time with some more than others and they with us. We must learn to look at them as people first and at their disability as a single characteristic.

The major classifications mentioned earlier in this chapter will now be further explained.

GIFTED AND TALENTED

We must be careful about putting human beings into categories. This is especially important in respect to mental ability. Test results are used with caution today, but this was not always true. Earlier in this century there was a great deal of emphasis on measuring mental ability. It is known now, however, that mental ability is very difficult to measure accurately. The results of mental tests are easily misinterpreted and misused. You will recall from Chapter 7 that there are a number of kinds of intelligence. A person who is low in one type may be high in others.

It is more realistic to identify those who fall below or above the average range of ability. This approach can be helpful to individuals, their families, educators, and those providing aids and services. We also need some kind of identification system so that persons who have exceptional mental abilities can qualify for legislative benefits.

Who Are the Gifted?

If we consider intelligence quotients (IQ test scores) ranging from 90 to 110 to be average, those with scores above 130 are usually classified as gifted intellectually. Although the term gifted referred in the past to those with superior mental ability, it now includes other types of ability such as talent in art, music, sports, business, mechanics, leadership, and creative activities. Some of the gifted have a number of special talents, but with others a particular talent may be their exceptional characteristic. There may be considerable variation within a type of talent also. Not all people who are creative, for example, are creative in the same way. The gifted comprise up to 5 percent of the population, depending on definition.

Problems Associated with Giftedness

At first it would seem that giftedness and talent may be the one area of exceptionality that does not have problems associated with it. For gifted and talented people, finding a job is generally not a problem, but finding employment that is adequately challenging can be. Additional problems associated with exceptional ability can include being very critical of others and oneself and resisting direction and pressure to conform. Also, because of their need for success the gifted and talented may become easily frustrated.

What do you THINK? An often-heard complaint is that there aren't enough people with strong leadership ability in our society. Do you think more attention to the gifted would solve this problem?

Some professionals have referred to the gifted as the most neglected segment of our population. There has been less legislation to benefit the gifted than other exceptional persons. Not all opportunities need come through legislation, however. Parents and teachers can do much to remove barriers to the development of gifted children. Many schools have developed programs that challenge the gifted, and grants and scholarships are available to those with superior talent and financial need.

MENTAL RETARDATION

Just as the highest range of intellectual ability is considered gifted, the lowest range is classified as mentally retarded. There are many different causes of mental retardation, some of which are related to hereditary or genetic factors, problems during pregnancy, birth complications, early childhood diseases, accidents, and environmental factors.

In 1992, the American Association for Mental Retardation adopted a new definition:

> Mental retardation refers to substantial limitations in present functioning. It is characterized by significantly subaverage intellectual functioning, existing concurrently with related limitations in two or more of the following applicable adaptive skill areas: communication, self-care, home living, social skills, community use, self-direction, health and safety, functional academics, leisure and work. Mental retardation manifests before age 18.[3]

Classifications of mental retardation vary, but typically include:

	IQ Level
Mild	55–70
Moderate	40–55
Severe	25–40
Profound	below 25

By far, the largest number of mentally retarded are within the mild range. Students within this range can usually learn at least basic skills in a regular classroom setting. Adults usually have developed adequate communication and social skills, and many of them are not readily recognized as mentally retarded. They can be functional, responsible members of society and hopefully are accepted as such without discrimination. Many of them are able to hold low-skill jobs.

Nearly one-third of those within the moderate range of mental retardation were born with Down syndrome, often called mongolism in the past. It is a genetic disorder that results from an extra 21st chromosome. Those with Down

In a community for those with Down Syndrome, a resident performs useful and meaningful work.

syndrome have characteristic physical features also. Their eyes have an upward slant and they have thickened eyelids, a broad nose, and a stocky body build, for example. Individuals with Down syndrome usually have loving, caring personalities and many families with a Down syndrome child attest to the joy the person has brought to their families, in spite of how devastated they might have felt with the initial diagnosis.

About half of those within the moderate range of mental retardation have some form of brain damage that could have resulted from a variety of causes. This group can learn daily living skills and can function reasonably well as members of a family. And, as with all other disabilities, it is important that they be given the opportunity to be as independent as possible and to have some sense of personal achievement. Sheltered workshops provide this opportunity for some moderately retarded.

The severely mentally retarded can learn to care for some of their personal needs, but in most cases they require close supervision for other tasks. They represent about 4 percent of all mentally retarded. Those who are profoundly mentally retarded are basically dependent on others. Their ability to learn is very limited and they need almost constant supervision. Only about 1 percent of the mentally retarded belong to this classification.

It is important to remember that mentally retarded persons do have feelings and want to be part of the normal stream of life as much as possible. Adults who are mentally retarded, especially in the upper ranges of the disorder, should not be treated as children, but should tactfully be given whatever assistance is appropriate for the individual and situation.

PHYSICAL DISABILITIES

Physical disabilities can be the result of a genetic abnormality or of prenatal complications, or they can be acquired later as a result of accident or disease. A disability can be relatively minor or so severe that the person cannot function without mechanical or human assistance.

Many acquired disabilities are the result of accidents or other injuries. Some of these occur in sports such as football, skiing, and hockey. Numerous others are the result of automobile, motorcycle, or other vehicle accidents. The more serious of such accidents cause spinal cord injuries that result in paralysis. To date, injury of the spinal cord that is severe enough to cause paralysis cannot be repaired. Other injuries may result in the loss of a limb or limbs. This is a traumatic experience for the victim, but there has been much success, and there is further promise, with artificial limbs. Some of these can be attached to a patient's nerves so that impulses from the brain can travel to the electronic apparatus in the limb, allowing lifelike use. There has also been some success with reattaching such body parts as arms, fingers, legs, and toes that have been severed in accidents.

Surely one of the most difficult types of adjustment involves a teenager or young adult who suddenly acquires a physical disability. Yet "difficult" does not mean "impossible." With time, usually some counseling and other psychological support, and with determination, acceptance can be achieved and new goals established. Even for those with a disability acquired at birth or early in life, the teen and young adult years can be especially difficult. Don Zimmerman writes of his feelings in those years in *Accent on Living,* a magazine about and

"We need to have a talk."
Reprinted with permission. © 1992 ACCENT ON LIVING.

for the physically disabled. Some of these people write articles themselves for the periodical, as Zimmerman did. He says:

> As a pre-teen, I do not recall ever thinking about it. Of course, I could not play as other kids played, and I spent more time with doctors and hospitals than most other kids, but that's just the way life went. My parents' positive attitude toward my difference certainly contributed toward my feeling all right.
>
> As a teenager, I hated it! One of the most vulnerable characteristics of that age group is their self-image. Looking in the mirror, they are never satisfied. I was too skinny, my hands were too twisted, and my spinal curvature was too severe. From the neck up, I thought I was reasonably handsome, but even the wave in my hair had to be combed just right.
>
> During my twenties, I felt much like the frog waiting for the princess to kiss him, so he could turn into a prince. Not a cute Kermit-like creature; it wasn't that easy being green. I know, however, that if people took the time to get to know me, my difference would sort of disappear, and I'd be more acceptable, and considered more "normal."[4]

The article goes on to say that the princess eventually kissed the frog in his marrying an understanding, accepting person who was involved in his care. Today, according to the article, Don Zimmerman is a consultant and conducts workshops on diversity and/or disability issues in corporate environments, public schools, and other groups.

All of us, those with disabilities and those with none, might take greater precaution. Avoiding needless risks, wearing seat belts and motorcycle helmets, driving at safe speeds, and following safety regulations on the job can reduce our chances of accidents that result in physical disabilities.

EMOTIONAL DISTURBANCES AND BEHAVIOR DISORDERS

Emotional development begins at birth, as discussed in Chapter 5, "Emotions." And emotional well-being is an integral part of total wellness as discussed in Chapter 9, "Wellness." Some factors can interfere with healthy emotional development, however, resulting in **emotional disturbance.** This can begin at a very early age, and it can be compounded by emotionally disturbing experiences throughout childhood and into adulthood. Such emotional problems, in turn, result in **behavior disorders,** or behavior that is not within the normal range of social and cultural expectations. Such behavior can be an expression of anxiety and frustration as well as evidence of other problems. This abnormal type of behavior is characteristic of a child over a period of time, but the child can be helped by specialists in behavior and education. The situation is much more complicated than punishing the child for not "behaving." In fact, punishment for behavior disorders may compound the problem. It should be remembered that the behavior of each of us reflects our way of coping. This is true also of those with emotional disturbance and behavior disorders even if their behavior is considered undesirable.

Emotional disturbances may be difficult to identify. For example, a young person who is considered "quiet" may have a serious emotional problem. Others may be constantly punished for aggressive behavior such as fighting, when that behavior is really an outlet for serious emotional disturbance. Although the behavior cannot always be tolerated, ignoring its causes does not solve the problem.

Not only is it difficult to identify emotional disturbances, it is also difficult to identify the causes underlying most emotional disturbances. In addition to the factors discussed previously, a biochemical imbalance or other organic factor may interfere with emotional stability. Some emotional disturbances result from nervous system disorders. Poor nutrition can also be a contributing factor.

Both neglect and abuse of children can cause emotional disturbance. If children do not receive attention and love, they are less likely to develop into emotionally healthy people. Child abuse is also a major cause of serious emotional problems. Although the physical effects of child abuse are more obvious, the emotional effects may be deeper and may last longer. Whether or not the words are actually spoken, abused children get the message that they are unwanted, bad, and not deserving of love. A broken home or a home in which family relationships are constantly in conflict may have disturbing effects on children. Youngsters who go from one foster home to another frequently lack a sense of security, which is essential to emotional well-being. Such children are unable to develop a sense of trust, so they do not experience close relationships with others.

Emotional disturbances in childhood often lead to juvenile delinquency during adolescence. Later crimes may represent an irrational striking out at society because of inner turmoil. The emphasis, it seems, should be on preventing emotional disorders by helping children develop in an emotionally healthy way. This includes developing a positive self-concept and acceptance of others.

SOCIETALLY NEGLECTED AND CULTURALLY DISADVANTAGED PERSONS

It might not be an exaggeration to say we are all disadvantaged in some respect. One might ask, "Is it possible for all to be given adequate opportunity to develop their potential, even though we believe each has the right to such opportunity?"

It is important that the term *culturally disadvantaged* be interpreted correctly. Nobody's ethnic culture is undesirable; in fact, one's native language, customs, and ethnic life-style are usually reasons for pride. It is claimed by some people that any ethnic-related disadvantage is created by society. At least it is apparent that a characteristic of an individual might be a disadvantage in one time and place but not in another. A language is foreign, for example, only where it is not generally spoken. For whatever reason, those from ethnic minorities and others have often been at a disadvantage in terms of education and other aspects of society. Such disadvantages may lessen in the future because we are becoming more aware of them, and thus more able to control the circumstances causing them.

It is idealistic to believe that the only thing those who have lived in poverty with little or no education need is an opportunity to become self-motivated, independent, and responsible members of society. It is difficult to change in a short time the thinking, values, and habits underlying a life-style. To take the position "That's the way they are; they'll never change" or to blame people for circumstances beyond their control doesn't solve the problem either. Even though most members of society today consider it inexcusable to live on welfare rather than work, if one is able and work is available, or to allow housing developments to deteriorate into slums, belief is not enough. The solution to such problems must begin with more people caring about themselves, their environment, and the well-being of others.

 What would you SUGGEST? How can the needs of the neglected and disadvantaged in our society be met without waste and abuse?

DEAF/HARD OF HEARING

What does it mean to live in a world of silence? Although you may enjoy some peaceful periods of quiet, your world would be quite different if you could not hear. Or perhaps you are a person who is hard of hearing. The use of the term hearing impairment is intentionally not used here as the May 1993 issue of *Deaf Life* notes, "The World Federation of the Deaf and other organizations agreed in 1991 that the term 'hearing impaired' was no longer acceptable usage, and that references should be to 'deaf/hard of hearing.'" It is the belief of the deaf, according to the article, that the label "hearing impaired" makes them "seem less independent, less capable, less human. The emphasis should be on the person, not the impairment; on what we are, not what we lack."[5] Although the term "hearing impairment" seems to have meaning and is not intended to be degrading, there is no reason that the request of the deaf/hard of hearing should not be respected.

Types and Degrees

There are two types of hearing loss—conductive and sensorineural. **Conductive** loss involves the outer or middle ear and can be helped medically or with a hearing aid. **Sensorineural** loss involves the inner ear and damage to the auditory nerve and cannot be cured. There are also degrees of hearing loss ranging from *slight* (which presents little difficulty under ordinary circumstances) to *profound* (the person responds to vibrations rather than to sounds). Many people have lost some hearing ability through illness or injury, but they still have *residual* hearing. All should make every effort to use whatever perceptual ability they have.

Communicating with Deaf/Hard of Hearing Persons

Many deaf persons can speech read well enough to understand much of what you may want to communicate to them. Those who work with the deaf and those with hearing problems would rather have you attempt to communicate with them than ignore them. The following suggestions from the National Technical Institute for the Deaf can be helpful:

To communicate with a deaf person in a one-to-one situation:

- Get the deaf person's attention.
- Speak slowly and clearly.
- Look directly at the deaf person.
- Maintain eye contact with the deaf person.
- First repeat, then try to rephrase a thought.
- Use body language and facial expression.
- Be courteous to the deaf person.

Learning to Communicate

Deaf/hard of hearing individuals can learn to communicate in different ways. These include several types of sign language and finger spelling, oral communication and speech reading, and what is called "total communication." Finger spelling is the use of fingers to form the letters of the alphabet when there isn't an appropriate sign. Proper nouns, for example, are often spelled out in this way. Otherwise signs are used to indicate whole words, ideas, and feelings.

With oral communication training and speech reading, some deaf persons learn to speak even though they cannot hear. Speech reading was more commonly referred to as "lip reading" in the past. Speech reading is a more accurate term as it includes not only watching the person's lips, but also his or her facial expressions, gestures, and other body language. Learning to speak, although deaf, requires determination, practice, and patience; yet some learn to speak so well that there is little indication that they are deaf.

"Total communication" involves a variety of communication methods. This a relatively new approach which includes all forms of communication in order to give the deaf person as much language competence as possible in a variety of situations. It includes finger spelling, sign language, gestures, speech, speech reading, and practice in reading and writing. The National Association of the Deaf supports the use of total communication, and it is now taught and used throughout the United States.

Further understanding of the deaf/hard of hearing is offered in "TIPS You Can Use in Communicating with Deaf People":

> Some deaf people are more easily understood than others. Some use speech only . . . or a combination of sign language, finger spelling, and speech . . . or writing . . . or body language and facial expression. You can communicate with deaf persons in several ways. And remember—they are more than willing to facilitate communication. The key is to find out which combination of techniques works best with each deaf person. Simply experiment to find out which method you feel comfortable with and works. Keep in mind that it's not how you exchange ideas, but that you do.[7]

Unless one notices a hearing aid or sees someone using sign language, it is impossible to know by looking at a person that he or she is deaf/hard of hearing. Moreover wearing a hearing aid does not necessarily indicate that a person can understand the spoken word. Such aids are sometimes worn by deaf people to amplify their own sounds and let them know how they are communicating, even though they cannot hear others.

VISUAL IMPAIRMENT

There was some discussion of vision in Chapter 4, "Senses and Perception." That unit included a discussion of visual hazards and protecting oneself from eye damage or loss of vision. This section centers on understanding and relating to the visually impaired, or blind.

Degrees of Impairment

Definitions of blindness or degrees of visual impairment are often determined by state and federal laws. Persons are considered legally blind, for example, if their vision is not better than 20/200 in the better eye with the use of corrective lenses or if their visual field is less than an angle of 20 degrees. In other words, if a person can see no more at a distance of 20 feet than someone with normal vision can see at a distance of 200 feet, he or she is considered blind according to law.

There are also lesser degrees of visual impairment. The American Foundation for the Blind estimates that as many as 65 million people in the United States have some kind of visual impairment. About 400,000 have no usable vision.

Understanding the Visually Impaired Person

According to the National Federation of the Blind, the real problem of blindness is not the loss of eyesight, but the misunderstanding of the condition that exists. To lessen this misunderstanding, the National Federation of the Blind provides the following information:

Where Are They Going? It is becoming more and more common for blind persons to realize that they can, and should, contribute to society and fulfill their responsibilities as taxpaying citizens along with their sighted peers. With this realization, blind people have found the confidence to venture out into the world and accomplish tasks which are considered quite ordinary by the average person. By using the simple alternatives to vision, blindness can be reduced from a severe handicap to a mere inconvenience . . .

The use of a long white cane or guide dog enables blind persons to travel anywhere they wish to go. They may be heading for their place of employment or the store, or they may be simply taking a daily walk. What ever the reason, it is becoming more likely that you will see blind pedestrians traveling alone.

How Is a White Cane Used? The blind person holds the white cane extended in front of him or her and swings it from side to side with the tip touching the ground so that objects can be detected. Many well-meaning sighted people want to warn a blind person when they see that the cane is about to come into contact with an object. You should not be alarmed, for the purpose of using a cane is to find such objects.

What Can a Guide Dog Do? A guide dog should be considered a tool and not a pet. It serves the same purpose as a white cane and is simply a different method of travel . . .

When approaching an object or a curb, the dog stops and the blind person investigates to determine the cause of the delay. It is a myth to assume that the dog is directing the master. The master is the boss and is directing the dog to their final destination.

Do Not Speak To or Touch the Dog! It is working and should not be distracted. If you wish to do so, you may speak to the dog's owner.

How Can I Assist A Blind Pedestrian? Many drivers have the impulse to exit their automobiles when they see a blind person crossing the street. The purpose in leaving the automobile is to assist the individual in crossing the street safely. This occurs because most drivers do not understand that blind pedestrians are crossing many streets and will continue to do so with or without assistance. If a blind person appears to be lost and in no danger, you should stay in your car . . .

It should be assumed that the independent blind traveler has had the necessary training to correct errors that may have been made in crossing an intersection . . .

If you are a pedestrian, and you are in doubt as to whether or not to assist a blind individual, you can ask the person whether help is needed. The person may simply wish to know the name of a particular street or may seek your help in crossing it. If such help is requested, let the blind person take your arm so that you can both move easily from one point to another. The blind person may not need help, but will appreciate the offer.[8]

SPEECH AND LANGUAGE DISORDERS

Our ability to communicate—or inability to communicate—affects nearly every aspect of our lives. As mentioned earlier, speech and language problems can result from other problems. Speech and language disorders can also lead to behavioral problems and to difficulties in school, at work, and in numerous other situations. It is encouraging, therefore, that many people of all ages are learning to overcome speech and language disorders or to communicate despite such disabilities. You may have a speech or language disorder yourself. One out of every twenty persons does. Or you may have had a disorder that has been corrected. Whatever your ability or disability, you *can* communicate with others.

Many think of speech and language as being very similar in meaning, but there is an important difference. **Speech** is the process by which sounds are produced. **Language** consists of the use of words and other symbols to express meaning. We use language to give others information, to ask questions, and to express our ideas and feelings. If we do this orally, we are using speech. If we do it through writing, we are using language, but not speech.

Articulation disorders, or problems with producing speech sounds, are the most common type of speech problem, according to the American Speech, Language and Hearing Association. Most articulation disorders are developmental in nature; this means that a child is learning to say sounds at a later age than normally would be expected. It usually involves the substitution of one sound for another or the omission of a sound completely. Once the problem has been identified, it can usually be eliminated with appropriate help or treatment.

Voice Disorders

Voice problems affect pitch, loudness, and quality and are often medical in nature. People who have cancer of the throat or who develop bumps call nodules or polyps on their vocal cords should have treatment and voice therapy, for example. Excessive air flow through the nose, called nasality, is also considered a voice disorder. Other voice disorders are psychological in nature, such as losing one's voice as a result of a traumatic experience.

Fluency Disorder

Stuttering is more accurately referred to as a fluency disorder. Fluency is smooth, easy flowing of speech. Difficulties related to fluency usually begin during preschool years and may last throughout life if not dealt with at that time. Dysfluency, or lack of fluency, is a problem adults learn to live with or control but rarely eliminate. Dysfluency is also situational in nature. Most dysfluent persons, for example, are fluent in some functions, such as singing or whispering.

A few suggestions for communicating with dysfluent persons follow.

- Look at them when talking to them and when they are talking, as you would with anyone else.
- Do not fill in words for them.
- Do not suggest ways to increase their fluency such as "slow down," "think about what you are trying to say," or "take a deep breath."

Language Disorders

The various types of language disorders are often related to perceptual abilities, to the functioning of the central nervous system, and to emotional adjustment. The problems themselves may involve meanings, word order, or other usage complications.

Language problems may be developmental in children or caused by injury to the brain in adults. Also, people who have strokes usually experience language problems, which may decrease as the brain heals or as proper therapy proceeds. However, many stroke victims experience some lasting difficulties. Perhaps you know someone who has suffered a stroke or head injury and has language difficulties. There are also some who through excellent therapy and heroic effects have remarkably recovered from strokes. Those of us who do not have such problems can imagine how very frustrating it must be to be unable to communicate one's needs, feelings, or ideas.

Identification of speech and language disorders can be difficult. Diagnosis and treatment are highly specialized and require time, patience, and practice, A team made up of parents or other family members and a variety of professional people can be most effective. Therapy can be given in a private clinic, a hospital, a school, or the home. The most important factor is motivation. Those with a disorder must want to improve their ability to communicate.

LEARNING DISABILITIES

In the not-so-distant past, children with various types of leaning difficulties were considered mentally retarded. Since learning disabilities are primarily the concern of educators, we will not discuss them in depth here. Yet, since education is so much a part of everyone's life, and since learning in various ways continues throughout life, we all can benefit from a basic understanding of learning disabilities.

Learning problems are unlike the other types of exceptionality discussed in this chapter. They are not caused by mental retardation, by visual or hearing impairments, or by emotional problems. Nor are learning disabilities caused by cultural disadvantages or the types of speech and language disorders discussed earlier. Nonetheless, they may be related to some of these other problems. And, again, a person may have more than one disability or type of exceptionality. People with learning disabilities, however, have normal or above-average intelligence. In fact, they may appear and act normal in every other way.

The term learning disability, as used in legislation and by educators, does not include all learning difficulties. It refers to serious differences between what a person is learning and what that person is considered capable of learning. For example, a young child may have undue difficulty with basic skills such as oral expression, writing, reading, and mathematics. A learning disability is more than a temporary learning problem.

It is difficult to determine who has a learning disability and who has a learning problem resulting from other causes. Brain damage, biochemical imbalance, poor educational experiences, and some environmental factors are believed to cause or contribute to learning disabilities. Much more research is being done in this area of learning. All children and young people with learning disabilities are entitled to specialized education to the extent that it is necessary.

What do you THINK?

Have you ever avoided communicating with a person with a disability? Do you think you would be more likely to communicate with a person with a disability now?

When a learning disability is recognized as such and a child is given the professional help he or she deserves, that child can be successful in school and develop the confidence and ability to be independent and successful in life.

FAMILIES OF CHILDREN WITH DISABILITIES

Every member of a family is affected by the disability of one of its members. As you may already know from experience, or as we shall conclude in our discussion, the effect is not necessarily negative. We must also keep in mind that members of a family, be they parents, siblings, grandparents, or other relatives, are also individuals. Each member of a family has his or her own way of reacting to the disability of a member. There are some common experiences that deserve attention, however.

Effects on Parents

Parents of a child with a disability usually are affected the most, both initially and during the lifespan of their child. The first reaction—whether a child's disability is congenital and obvious at birth, or becomes apparent during the early years, or results from an accident—is often one of shock and denial. "There must be some mistake," is a common reaction. Do you recall denial described as a coping mechanism in Chapter 8? Coping mechanisms help us deal with situations that are difficult to accept. They do not help us deal in a constructive way with the reality of situations, however.

Following initial shock and disbelief, many parents experience feelings of guilt, anger, and bitterness before they finally accept the reality of their child's disability. Learning to understand and accept the child with his or her disability is important not only to the stability of their own lives, but also to the child's growth and development.

Detecting a Problem   Some physical disabilities are present and obvious at birth. In other cases, however, it may be difficult for parents to recognize that their child has a disability. Some cases of mental retardation or visual impairment may not be suspected at first, for example. Sometimes a grandparent or friend, who do not see the child on a daily basis, will notice a child's problem before the parents do.

It is important, however, for parents to recognize that *something* may not be normal and that the child should be examined by the family doctor or some other professional. For example, the earlier deafness is detected, the better chance a child has to learn to communicate effectively despite the disability.

It is also well to keep in mind that children develop at different rates. A child of 14 months does not have to be doing exactly the same things as a neighbor's child of the same age.

Lifelong Responsibility   Parents, according to M. L. Hardman and others in *Human Exceptionality: Society, School, and Family,* go through a development

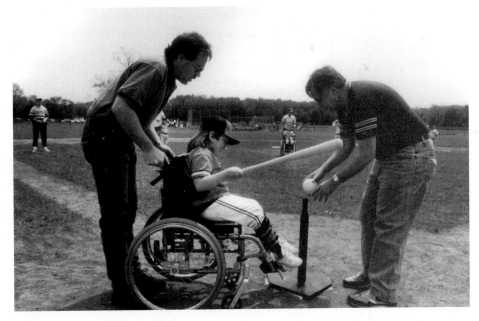

With the support of parents, teachers, and peers, handicapped children are able to participate fully in sports programs.

cycle in the process of raising the child to adulthood. The cycle includes the following phases:

1. The time at which parents learn about or suspect a disability in their child
2. The period in which the parents determine what action to take regarding the child's education
3. The point at which the individual who is disabled has completed his or her education
4. The time when the parents become older and may be unable to care for their adult offspring[9]

It is evident from these stages that raising a child with a disability can be a lifelong special responsibility. Not to be overlooked, however, is the love and joy that any family member can contribute to other members of his or her family. A person with a disability is no exception, as many parents and other family members verify.

Effects on Siblings

Having a brother or sister with a severe disability can be a difficult experience for many children. They may be angry that some of their personal freedom is lost due to the needs of their brother or sister. In some cases they may also feel cheated that their family cannot, or does not, take the kind of vacations that other families do. They may also experience loneliness or resentment because their parents cannot give them equal time and attention. Resentment can in turn lead to feelings of guilt. Embarrassment about a brother or sister's behavior may be a further dilemma, preventing them from inviting their friends to their homes. These are not inevitable consequences of having a disabled sibling, but they are relatively common. Children who are having such difficulties should be assured of their parents' love and helped to understand their families' relationships and responsibilities. It is constructive for some children who are having particular difficulty to receive counseling. No child should become a victim of another person's disability.

Effects on the Extended Family

The extended family, including grandparents and close relatives, often play valuable roles in assisting with the needs of a person with a disability. The initial psychological pain of grandparents may be twofold. They experience not only the trauma of knowing their grandchild has a disability, but they also identify with the pain their own son or daughter is experiencing. However, grandparents and other members of the extended family adjust and accept too, and usually become supportive in a number of ways. They can be extremely helpful as relief caregivers for parents and as loving, supportive companions to the children themselves. They may have more time to play games with children, for example, than do the busy parents.

Working It Out Together

It is difficult for parents to be objective about their children and to view them as they really are. It can also be difficult for parents to decide what is best for a child after they understand and accept the child's exceptionality. "If only we knew what would be best," they say. Parents will feel more satisfied if they receive information and advice from a number of reliable, trusted sources. Doctors, public health professionals, clergy, psychologists, teachers, and other parents of exceptional children all can provide insight into making decisions about what is best for a child.

With the health, community, and educational services that are available today, all but the very severely disabled may live at home as a part of the family. The home is considered the best environment, today, in almost all cases. Nonetheless, this requires adjustments in the life-style of all members of the family.

The effects of a child with a disability on a family depend somewhat on the already existing stability (or lack of it) of family relationships. If the family, for whatever reasons, already has internal conflict and stress, the psychological, financial, time, and energy demands may be more than they can cope with. The family unit may further deteriorate, often with members taking out their frustrations on one another (displacement). In some cases an already troubled family breaks up.

Other families, in spite of the same difficulties related to caring for a disabled child, may develop stronger bonds of love and support. Crises and difficulties in life can have a strengthening effect on those who have perseverance and are willing to do their best whatever the circumstances. Although we would not choose such experiences, they can contribute to the development of personality traits that will help us in future situations and in relationships with others.

All family members should be careful about becoming overprotective in ways that deny a disabled person the satisfaction of doing things independently. A person with a disability should not be the center of attention but should be rather a member of the family with responsibilities that fit his or her capabilities. An exceptional child should be given the opportunity to contribute in any way possible. Still, extra work and expenses are to be expected. Yet, despite (or perhaps because of) these obligations, some families have developed closer bonds and have learned to cooperate and consider one another. They have also experienced rewards and satisfactions that they might not otherwise have known.

EDUCATION MUST BE AVAILABLE

There have been a number of references to educational abilities, methods, and opportunities in the previous sections. Since everyone needs and is entitled to education, legislation pertaining to education of the exceptional will be considered briefly. Much has been accomplished in recent years in terms of educational opportunities for children and young people with disorders or disabilities.

Effects of Public Law 94-142

The primary factor underlying this progress has been the Education for All Handicapped Children Act, often referred to as Public Law 94-142.

This law was passed in 1975 and states that education must be available to all handicapped persons, up to 21 years of age. This is their fundamental right. In addition, children should be properly tested, and education should be made available in what the law calls "the least restrictive environment." In most cases this results in what is called **mainstreaming,** or placing the child in a normal classroom situation except for periodic individual work with a special education teacher or therapist, depending on the child's disability. The idea is to provide education appropriate to the child's needs that is as similar as possible to that of the average child. The opportunity to relate to other people of one's own age is considered important to learning and development. It also helps other children learn to understand exceptional persons better and to overcome prejudices.

Another way of providing education for exceptional persons consists of individual sessions with specialized teachers. The team approach, involving educators, parents, psychologists, and appropriate others, has also been successful in numerous cases. Residence schools (one of the major means prior to new legislation) are still considered best for some persons. Private tutoring is another approach to providing for the learning needs of some.

Adults with disabilities have a variety of educational opportunities in addition to physically attending colleges or other learning centers. In addition to correspondence courses, which have been available for many years, they are now able to take telecourses or interactive television (ITV) courses without leaving their homes. Although these courses are available to anyone who desires to take them, they are of particular value to persons with disabilities.

In addition to federal legislation requiring educational opportunities, many states have laws providing for programs and services for exceptional persons. In fact, the major part of the funding, in many cases, comes from the state. Financial assistance and services are also provided at the local level. Although there have been problems associated with Public Law 94-142 and its enforcement, it has had a positive effect on exceptional persons and their families. As a result, society as a whole has benefited.

Rights of Parents

The rights of parents of exceptional children are also protected by Public Law 94-142. They must consent to their child's testing and placement in programs, and they have the right to ask questions and receive explanations about methods and progress. As do all parents, they have the right to examine the school records pertaining to their child. It is important that parents have these rights, but they should also realize that many highly specialized people are involved in the total process of working with their child, and at times they may not be able to understand completely what is happening with the child and why.

The Human Factor

It takes more than laws to provide exceptional persons the opportunity to develop as well-adjusted, reasonably competent people. Unless those who are working with or associated with exceptional children care about them and what happens to them, much of the rest can be wasted. Not only their physical and educational needs but also their psychological needs must be met. They must be able to experience growth and achievement if their education is to accomplish its purpose.

This section about work does not specifically discuss gifted individuals, as finding gainful employment is not a special problem for them in today's society, although it may be difficult for some to find employment that is adequately challenging. The idea that all should develop their full potential applies to the gifted as well as to those with less mental ability or with disabilities.

Education and work are closely related. Anyone who desires to do anything but unskilled labor must have the education and training for other types of jobs. Some vocational education systems involve extensive evaluations before training so that each student can realistically select a type of occupational training.

Most exceptional persons—except the mentally retarded—have average or higher intelligence. With confidence, motivation, and opportunity, they have become some of the best students in higher education and some of the most competent people in the world of work. Employers generally report that disabled workers compare favorably or, in some cases, are superior to

Commitment, along with specialized equipment, enables even the most severely handicapped people to be employed.

nondisabled workers. They have high productivity levels and safety records, yet low absenteeism and less turnover.

The rights of persons with disabilities were recognized a number of years ago when the federal government passed the 1973 Rehabilitation Act. This law provided for the rights of the physically and mentally disabled in terms of jobs, education, health care, housing, and other services aided by federal funds. Although the provisions of this law offered those with disabilities greater freedom and opportunity than they had ever had before, over time it was found inadequate in a number of respects. A much more comprehensive federal law, the Americans With Disabilities Act (ADA) was passed in 1990 and went into effect in 1992. According to this act those with disabilities include the visually impaired, the deaf/hard of hearing, those with physical disabilities requiring use of wheelchairs, those with emotional disturbances or mental illness, those recovering from drug and alcohol abuse, persons recovering from physical problems, and persons with a physical scar. People who are disabled because of illegal drug abuse are excluded from coverage under ADA, but people who are currently undergoing treatment and are not using drugs or alcohol are covered. There are also limits on preemployment physical examinations. Job applicants must be offered a job on a conditional basis before being required to take a physical examination. If the person accepts the job offer, however, the employer may then require a physical examination, which could result in the job offer being withdrawn.

In a discussion of ADA and what it will mean to employers, an article in *Nation's Business* in April 1993 stated: "The disabilities law says employers must make 'reasonable accommodations' for job applicants or employees with disabilities as long as the candidate is able to perform the 'essential functions' of the job and the accommodation causes no 'undue hardship' to the company."[10] These terms are difficult to define, however, and exactly what they stand for will probably have to be determined by the courts. Employers will be required to provide access to their facilities, appropriate restroom accommodations, and other practical aspects of being able to work within a particular environment. But they will also have to find ways of custom-fitting jobs to persons with disabilities.

Although ADA is intended to expand work opportunities to those with disabilities, employers have some rights under the act also. Individuals need not be hired or retained if they present a direct threat to the health or safety of themselves or co-workers, for example. Also, if applicants cannot perform the job despite reasonable accommodations by the employer, they need not be offered the job.

Both educators and disabled persons themselves must realize that the job market is competitive and that the individuals must be able to do the work, with accommodations required by ADA, if they expect to be hired. Most vocational programs duplicate the actual job responsibilities and environment as closely as possible, thus making it easier to move into a job situation. Others work cooperatively with business and industry in on-the-job training programs, giving disabled persons a realistic opportunity to learn to do the work and adapt to other requirements.

Persons with disabilities can be found in practically every type of occupation in the workforce today. Examples are computer programmers, microelectric assemblers, telephone operators, consultants, laboratory technicians, and teachers. Work not only allows these individuals to become more financially independent but gives them a sense of worth that contributes to their self-concept and sense of achievement.

Employers in recent years who have made special efforts to provide opportunities to work to disabled individuals have received recognition from The President's Committee on Employment of People with Disabilities within the U.S. Department of Labor. Awards include the Distinguished Service Award, the Employer of the Year Award, and the Employers Merit Award. It is common, also, for communities to recognize employers who have given persons with disabilities more than ordinary employment opportunities.

A person with a disability may have more difficulty than another person pursuing a particular career, but it is important to remember that they are entitled to the same choices as everyone else. They have the right to choose what they want to do on the basis of their particular interests and abilities. They should base their decisions on job availability and growing fields of opportunity. They should be realistic about their strengths and weaknesses in making decisions. But so should everyone. Exceptional persons are individuals who are as different from one another as nonexceptional persons are. They have a right to try, to succeed, and even to fail.

 What do you THINK? In what ways does society as a whole benefit when persons with disabilities become more independent?

INFORMATION AND SERVICES

Most exceptional people would appreciate and benefit from numerous sources of assistance today but may not be aware of such services. It is not only the exceptional themselves who can obtain various types of services and materials; their families and teachers may also.

A few sources of information or assistance were mentioned earlier in the chapter. It is impossible to mention all of them, especially state and local agencies. Some sources of help are National Association of the Deaf, American Federation of the Blind, American Speech-Language-Hearing Association, Congress of Organizations for the Physically Handicapped, Association of Learning Disabled Adults, Paralyzed Veterans of America, Association for Handicapped Students, School to Work Transition Services, Employability Support Network, National Council of Independent Living Programs, and Recreational Mobility, Inc. Addresses of these organizations, and many others, are listed in the book *Yes You Can: A Helpbook for the Physically Disabled.*[11]

RELATING TO EXCEPTIONAL PERSONS

A number of suggestions have been given throughout this chapter for relating to individuals with particular disabilities. It is doubtful that anyone who does not have a disability would purposely cause those with disabilities further problems.

Societal Attitudes

Do those of us who do not have disabilities have biases and prejudices stemming from stereotypes of the disabled that cause them problems? Although

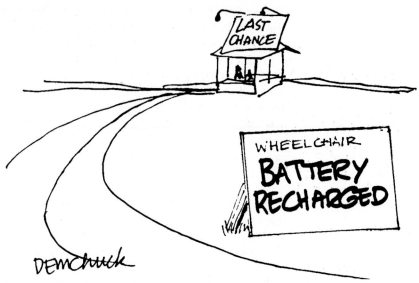

better understanding of and contact with individuals with disabilities has reduced bias and prejudice to some extent, many individuals with disabilities still consider societal attitudes a major hindrance to their freedom and opportunities for full participation in activities. It might be well for us to review the discussion of prejudice and discrimination in Chapter 6 and to examine how we relate to those with disabilities.

Buscaglia's Guidelines

The following guidelines offered by Leo Buscaglia, a widely known authority on human relationships and exceptional persons, are appropriate for our relationships with exceptional persons. He points out that "handicaps are made, not born." By following these guidelines, we can help prevent those with disabilities from becoming unduly handicapped and allow them to be less different.

- Remember that the disabled are their own persons, not yours. They do not belong to you, to your family, your doctor, or to society.
- Remember that each person who is disabled is different, and no matter what label is attached for the convenience of others, is still a totally "unique" person. There are no two retarded children who are the same, or no two deaf adults who respond and react in a similar fashion.
- Remember that the persons with disabilities are persons first and disabled individuals secondly. These persons have the same right to self-actualization as any others—at their own rate, in their own way, and by means of their own tools. Only they can suffer their non-being or find their "selves."
- Remember that the disabled have the same needs that you have, to love and be loved, to learn, to share, to grow and to experience, in the same world you live in. They have no separate world. There is only one world.

- Remember that the disabled have the same right as you to fall, to fail, to suffer, to decry, to cry, to curse, to despair. To protect them from these experiences is to keep them from life.
- Remember that only those who are disabled can show or tell you what is possible for them. We who love them must be attentive, attuned observers.
- Remember that the disabled must do for themselves. We can supply the alternatives, the possibilities, the necessary tools—but only they can put these things into action. We can only stand fast, be present to reinforce, encourage, hope and help, when we can.
- Remember that the disabled, like ourselves, are entitled to life as we know it. They, too, must decide to live it fully in peace, joy and love, with what they are and what they have, or to sit back in lacrimal apathy and await death.
- Remember that persons with disabilities, no matter how disabled, have a limitless potential for becoming—not what we desire them to become, but what is within them to become.
- Remember that the disabled must find their own manner of doing things—that to set our standards (or the culture's standards) upon them, is to be unrealistic, even destructive. There are many ways of tying shoes, drinking from a glass, finding one's way to a bus stop. There are many ways of learning and adjusting. They must find the best way for them.
- Remember that the disabled also need the world, and others, in order to learn. All learning does not take place in the protected environment of the home or in a classroom, as many people believe. The world is a classroom. All of humankind are teachers. There is no meaningless experience. Our job is to act as loving human beings with emotional Band-Aids always ready after a fall, but with new road maps at hand for new adventures!
- Remember that all persons with disabilities have a right to honesty about themselves, about you, and about their condition. To be dishonest with them is the most terrible disservice one can perform. Honesty forms the only solid base upon which all growth can take place. And this above all—remember that the disabled need the best you possible. In order for them to be themselves, growing, free, learning, changing, developing, experiencing persons—you must be all of these things. You can only teach what you are. If you are growing, free to learn, change, develop, and experience, you will allow them to be.[12]

QUALITY OF LIFE

It is important to remember that everyone has limitations. Some limitations are more obvious or more severe than others, so that special opportunities and extra effort are required. Persons who understand themselves and their capabilities and potential—as well as their limitations—are ready to progress toward self-actualization. That is within the power of almost every human being.

People with disabilities or victims of misfortune in life may never work out answers to the question, Why me? The answer, or acceptance without an answer, depends on one's total maturity and one's beliefs about the meaning of life. Thousands of people with disabling characteristics, however, say that they believe their lives have become more meaningful than they might have been under ordinary circumstances. Such people have turned from the Why me? approach to How can I develop and use my abilities to make my life meaningful? It bears repeating that an exceptional characteristic need not be a handicap. Helen Keller is an example of a person who did not let the fact that she was both deaf and blind stand in the way of leading a meaningful life and contributing to the needs of others. Franklin D. Roosevelt developed a physical disability as a result of polio when he was 39, but he went on to become governor of New York and to be elected president of the United States for four terms.

Nelson Rockefeller, who served as vice president of the United States, had extreme difficulty in learning to read. You may know that Thomas Edison, holder of over one thousand patents, was considered mentally defective by one of his teachers. Albert Einstein, the great scientist best known for his theory of relativity, did not speak until he was three years old and had difficulty in school. Perhaps you know of other examples.

Quality of Life Factors

What is meant by quality of life? Certainly the answer would vary for individuals, depending on their cultural background, beliefs, and personal values. R. L. Schalock and others have authored an article entitled: "Quality of Life: Its Measurement and Use." They identify three factors they consider essential to quality of life: environment control, community involvement, and social relations.[13] By environmental control they are referring to one's personal lifestyle and how much choice and control the individual has over such matters as freedom in use of living quarters and how one's time is spent.

 What do you SAY? Many exceptional people are successful because they try harder. "Would it require a disability to cause you to do your best?"

Residential Possibilities   Where and how do people with disabilities live today? Certainly there are more options than in the past when those with disabilities were either kept at home—often in seclusion—or sent to institutions. Today group homes, foster homes, and semi-independent apartments are available, even though individuals don't always have full choice as to which of these will be where they live. As indicated earlier, home with one's own family, in most cases, is most favorable to a person with a disability.

Social Interaction   Opportunities for close interpersonal relationships are also important to those with disabilities, as they are with all of us. Exceptional persons of this type need more than care and education and work opportunities. They need a social aspect to their lives—relationships where they are accepted for who they are as individuals and can feel comfortable in a variety of types of social interaction. It should be remembered, also, that those with disabilities have the same sexual needs and desires as those without their particular limitations. Many persons with disabilities fall in love, marry, and have families, and not necessarily with other persons with disabilities. It should not be assumed that those who have disabilities are less human than those who do not.

Recreation and Leisure   Persons with disabilities want to have fun and the joy of competition as much as anyone else. Some of the activities they enjoy, for example, are fishing, playing cards and other games, dancing, and participating in sports. You have probably heard of Special Olympics, athletic competition for the mentally retarded, founded in Chicago in 1968. In July of 1991 the eighth International Summer Special Olympic Games were held in the United States, with over 6,000 athletes participating. Some may not be aware that the Olympics in Barcelona, Spain, in the summer of 1992 also included wheelchair races. Of course there are many other recreational and athletic events that are exciting to the participants even though they do not get the publicity and recognition of Olympic competitions.

Choices

Having choices is considered by most people, disabled or not, to be essential to the quality of their lives. What would happen to your evaluation of the quality of your life, for instance, if your choices became more limited? Persons with disabilities should have as many choices as their particular abilities and situations will allow, as long as they don't interfere with the choices and rights of others.

It's Up to You!

For those of you who have experienced disabilities and may still be in the process of acceptance and adjustment, Helynn Hoffa and Gary Morgan, authors of *Yes You Can: A Helpbook for the Physically Disabled,* have this message for you: "What you make of your life has always been up to you. It still is. That hasn't changed."[14]

SUMMARY   Each of us is unique. We are not all exceptional, however. Exceptional has been defined as being different from the average to the extent that a person requires special education, facilities, or equipment to function in society. Major classifications of exceptional persons include the gifted or talented, the mentally retarded, the physically disabled, the emotionally disturbed, the socially neglected and culturally disadvantaged, the deaf/hard of hearing and those with visual impairments, speech and language disorders, and learning disabilities.

Attitudes toward and treatment of exceptional persons have improved in recent years. Legislation in the 1970s provided for broader educational and employment opportunities and ADA has expanded employment opportunities in the 1990s. The approach today is quantitative, meaning that exceptional persons are different in degree rather than being totally different kinds of people. Although the terms disabled and handicapped are often used in the same way in society, a handicap prevents a person from doing what he or she wants to do.

Those in the upper range of the population in intellectual ability are considered gifted; the lower range are considered mentally retarded. Mental retardation can be caused by hereditary (genetic) factors, problems during pregnancy, birth complications, early childhood diseases and accidents, and environmental factors.

Emotional disturbance is another type of disability. It can arise from organic causes, neglect of a child's psychological needs, or child abuse. Emotional disturbance usually results in behavioral disorders. A further classification of exceptionality pertains to those who are considered societally neglected or culturally disadvantaged.

People with visual impairment are also considered exceptional. There are a number of causes and degrees of each of these types of impairment. The lack of appropriate educational opportunities and materials has been a major problem for the visually impaired in the past, but many handicaps related to visual problems are being overcome today.

The greatest handicap related to those who are deaf/hard of hearing is usually difficulty in learning to communicate. There is emphasis today on total communication for the deaf, which includes finger spelling, speech reading, and speaking. Some speech and language disorders are not related to hearing problems. Still another type of exceptionality pertains to learning disabilities. Although other disorders may also cause problems with learning, a learning disability is not necessarily related to other types of disability.

Parents and families of exceptional persons must make difficult decisions and adjustments, but many find that the exceptional person has contributed to family unity and has brought special satisfactions and fuller meaning to their lives.

Public Law 94-142 provides for educational opportunities for exceptional persons, with limitations based on the individual disabilities. Many states also have laws governing programs and services for exceptional persons. Exceptional persons still have difficulty finding employment, but opportunities are increasing, not only because of federal legislation, but as employers are finding that exceptional persons can do many types of work as well as those without a disability. They are also dependable employees. Numerous agencies and other groups provide help to exceptional persons, their families, and the professionals working with them.

It is understandably difficult for anyone to adjust to a severe, permanent disability. First reactions may be similar to grief, involving both denial and anger. However, the lives of people who have made excellent adjustments can be an inspiration to others.

Exceptional persons also may be handicapped by societal attitudes and prejudices. Probably the most important point is to avoid stereotyping and needless labeling. Exceptional persons usually do not want people to relate to them differently. They are individuals who want to be accepted for the persons they are.

All persons, whether or not they are exceptional, grow and change throughout their lifetime. Chapter 12, "Interpersonal Relationships," should help enrich the lives of all of us, including exceptional persons.

Psychology In Practice

1. Make a special effort to be friendly with an exceptional person. Write a brief account of the experience and its effect on you and your ideas of exceptional persons and share it with the class.

2. Take turns with another person being blindfolded and experiencing what it is like not to have sight. Engage in everyday activities for at least twenty minutes. You should give necessary direction to one another while blindfolded so that you do not get hurt.

3. Talk to two exceptional persons who are employed and whom you know. Ask them when they have experienced problems because of people's attitudes toward their disabilities. Compare their responses and consider how such attitudes might be overcome.

Learning Activities

Turn to page 419 to complete the Learning Activities and Enrichment Activities for this chapter.

Notes

1. Michael L. Hardman, Clifford J. Drew, M. Winston Egan, and Barbara Wolf, *Human Exceptionality: Society, School, and Family,* Allyn & Bacon, Boston, 1993, p. 3.

2. Daniel P. Hallahan and James M. Kauffman, *Exceptional Children,* 5th ed., Prentice Hall, Englewood Cliffs, NJ, p. 6.

3. Michael L. Hardman et al., Appendix A, p. 429.

4. Don Zimmerman, "Feeling Different About My Difference," *Accent on Living,* Fall 1991, pp. 33–34.

5. "What Do Others Call Us? And What Do We Call Ourselves?" *Deaf Life,* May 1993, pp. 23–24.

6. "TIPS You Can Use When Communicating With Deaf People," National Technical Institute for the Deaf, Rochester, NY, no date, p. 3.

7. Ibid., p. 2.

8. "The Blind Pedestrian and the Driver," National Federation of the Blind, Baltimore, MD, no date.

9. Michael L. Hardman et al., p. 421.

10. Bradford McKee, "The Disabilities Labyrinth," *Nation's Business,* April 1993, p. 19.

11. Helynn Hoffa and Gary Morgan, *Yes You Can: A Helpbook for the Physically Disabled,* Pharos Books, A Scripps Howard Company, New York, 1990.

12. Leo F. Buscaglia, *The Disabled and Their Parents, A Counseling Challenge,* Charles B. Slack, Inc., Thorofare, NJ, 1975, p. 19.

13. R. L. Schalock, K. D. Keith, K. Hoffman, and O. C. Karan, *Mental Retardation,* 27 (1989), p. 27.

14. Helynn Hoffa and Gary Morgan, p. 9.

11 Life-Span Development

Learning Objectives

After completing this chapter, you will be able to do the following:

1. Indicate at least two characteristics of a person's development during each stage of life-span development.
2. Explain why the development of trust is the foundation for later stages of positive psychosocial development.
3. Classify examples of behavior as characteristic of different types of maturity.
4. Identify two trials and two triumphs an adolescent might experience during this stage of life.
5. Define stages of moral development, according to Kohlberg, and give examples of Stage 1 and Stage 4 behavior in reaction to a particular situation.
6. Indicate whether you consider the behavior of individuals mature, immature, or understandable in given situations and explain your decisions.
7. Describe what you consider mature and immature reactions to a number of problem situations.
8. Explain how you think you might become more socially mature.

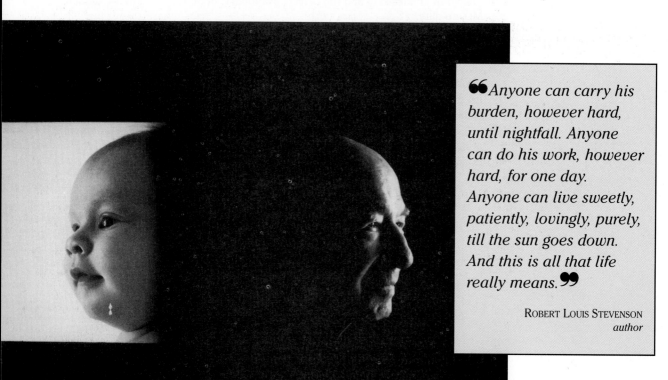

66Anyone can carry his burden, however hard, until nightfall. Anyone can do his work, however hard, for one day. Anyone can live sweetly, patiently, lovingly, purely, till the sun goes down. And this is all that life really means.99

ROBERT LOUIS STEVENSON
author

How many birthdays can you remember? How many birthdays have you had? The answers to these questions are only a small part of the more obvious ways in which you have developed, learned, grown, or matured since the day you were born. A number of types of development will be discussed in this chapter.

If we think of **development** as a type of growth, we have to acknowledge that not all types of growth are desirable. Although we are concerned when an infant or child does not gain weight in a normal way, we also know that it is possible to gain too much weight. Further, we know that other types of growth or learning can be unfavorable, as in the learning of bad habits. Another type of growth that is threatening is cancer.

For the most part, however, this chapter is concerned with types of development and maturity that are desirable. Some of these are natural or automatic. For example, physical growth takes care of itself under favorable conditions. Other types of development, such as cognitive or mental development, occur quite naturally under favorable conditions. Still other types of desired development require effort throughout life.

The main types of life-span development considered in this unit are physical, mental, moral, and what Erikson calls psychosocial. Emotional, social, intellectual, and vocational maturity will also be discussed, primarily as they relate to adults. You should be able to apply each of these to yourself in terms of past, present, and future development. You may note that all the terms—development, growth, maturity, learning—are ways of describing types of life-span development. For that reason there will be references to both earlier and later chapters. **Life-span development** is not only continuous but it also involves every aspect of a person's being and functioning.

YOUR LIFETIME AND LIFE SPAN

A family photograph album may contain pictures of you engaged in activities at different times of your life. You probably have also heard your parents or other relatives talk about their lives before you were born. You may have read history books about events that occurred hundreds, or even thousands, of years before your life began. In spite of all this knowledge, however, it is difficult to think of yourself as not existing, isn't it?

You probably also know some elderly people and have noticed that they are somewhat bent over and walk slowly. It may be difficult for you to visualize yourself as being old—but if you live long enough, you will be! Some of you reading this will live to be one hundred years old or more. Many of you will live to be in your eighties and nineties. It isn't likely that you are giving much thought to this at this time of your life, of course. You are no doubt busy with the present and making plans for your more immediate future: This is the way it should be. It does make sense, however, to have long-range goals and to have an understanding of the totality of life-span development. It also helps us to understand others, younger and older, in our personal lives and in society.

It is difficult to discuss types of life-span development separately because a number of different types of development are going on in your life at any particular time. We will therefore discuss various types of development taking place in a person's life at certain times, such as early childhood and adolescence; and we will discuss types of development such as moral development and psychosocial development across the life span in order to see how various stages relate to one another. Any repetition you notice should help you to understand the interrelatedness of types of life-span development.

LIFE-SPAN STAGES

One's life-span development can be studied in a number of different ways. Before we look at the stages of life-span development discussed in this chapter, several other approaches to understanding this subject should be recognized.

Dan Levinson, a noted psychologist in this subject area, divides the adult life span into eleven stages according to age ranges and what he calls "life structures"—or the dominant tasks and transitions associated with a particular decade of one's life. Levinson calls the first stage Early Adult Transition covering the years from 17 to 22. The fourth stage, covering years 33 to 40 is designated as Settling Down. A number of the stages are identified as transition stages, for example, Age 30, Transition, which he describes as, "Change in life structure. Either a moderate change, or, more often, a severe and stressful crisis."[1] All of the stages, for those interested, would be available in Levinson's book, *The Seasons of a Man's Life,* or in Berger's, *The Developing Person Through The Life Span.*

Another approach to understanding the stages of adult development is what Robert Havighurst calls "developmental tasks." He states:

> A developmental task is a task which arises at or about a certain period in the life of the individual, successful achievement of which leads to his happiness and to success with later tasks, while failure leads to unhappiness in the individual, disapproval by the society, and difficulty with later tasks.

He identifies what he considers developmental tasks for six different periods in a person's life ranging from infancy to old age. Developmental tasks for Young Adulthood, for example, include such tasks as selecting a mate, learning to live with a partner, becoming a parent, beginning a career, assuming appropriate civic responsibilities, and establishing a social network.[2] Havighurst's further explanation of the life span can be found in his book, *Developmental Tasks and Education* or in Guy Lefrancois's book, *The Lifespan.*

Times and events in an individual's life can also be described in terms of one's biological clock, psychological clock, and social clock. David G. Meyers, in *Exploring Psychology,* defines social clock as "the culturally preferred timing of social events such as marriage, childbearing, and retirement."[3]

This chapter will discuss the following stages of life-span development: prenatal development, early childhood, childhood, adolescence, young adulthood, middle adulthood, and later adulthood.

PRENATAL DEVELOPMENT

When does human life begin? This is a controversial issue in today's society, and both pro-life and pro-choice advocates have firm beliefs in answer to the question. We do know that prenatal development has its beginning when the ovum of a female is fertilized by the sperm from a male, resulting in a single cell called a *zygote.* The first two weeks of prenatal development are called the *germimal period.* The next two to eight weeks, during which cells divide and begin to form specific body organs and features, are called the *embryonic period.* The remainder of prenatal development, until birth, is known as the *fetal period.* The term for the newborn baby is *neonate.* Of course, some parent refer to "our baby" as soon as they are aware of a pregnancy.

There is increasing concern today about the development of the unborn. Evidence shows that the health of an expectant mother as well as her habits can affect the development of her unborn child. Therefore, expectant mothers are advised not to smoke, drink alcohol, or take any drugs not prescribed by their doctors. It is also recommended that they limit their drinking of coffee, tea, and soft drinks that contain caffeine. Some fathers-to-be also avoid these things in order to give their partners moral support.

Although there is much more that could be said about prenatal development, this is adequate for our consideration here and now. If and when you want additional information, it is readily available from clinics and a number of other sources.

EARLY CHILDHOOD

The life of newborn infants might be considered relatively simple. Some of their behavior is unlearned and automatic. They suck, cry, and react to discomfort. They have startled reactions to loud noises and to sensations of falling.

The senses of newborn infants function quite well. Babies can see light, dark, and color. They follow a moving object with their eyes even when they are only a few days old. Visual sharpness and ability to focus the eyes develop in the early weeks of life. Normal infants can also hear well at birth, and they have a good sense of touch and taste.

The initial physical contact of a newborn with its mother is called **bonding.** In recent years it has been common for the neonate to be laid on the mother's body immediately after delivery to initiate this bonding experience. Although some specialists in this area now say that immediate bonding is not as important as once assumed, it is still important that close human contact and responses begin as soon as possible.

It is important for parents and others involved with infants to recognize that human beings need tender physical handling and love. From birth on, children need to feel secure and have their physical needs satisfied. Psychologist Erik Erikson claims that in the first year of life a baby develops a sense of either trust or mistrust toward others, which will affect later development. Erikson has also identified other stages in development, and we will consider those later in this chapter.

Babies begin to smile at about six weeks of age. They may make responsive sounds in the early months, but they do not usually say words until after a year or so. The use of short, simple sentences is normal around the age of two years. Experts in the study of language development discourage the use of baby talk in communicating with children. Children learn to talk primarily by imitation; therefore, adults should use good speech for children to imitate.

Maturation refers to development of the nervous system and physical development of the body. The development of physical abilities is particularly apparent in infants and young children.

There are average ages at which children develop physical abilities. For example, most children crawl at about eight months and walk at about one year.

FRANK & ERNEST reprinted by permission of NEA, Inc.

However, children usually crawl or walk when they are ready, and attempts by eager parents to get them to do so earlier do not make much difference. There seem to be family patterns both in language development and in the rate of physical development in children.

The abilities of children develop rapidly during the first few years of life. This can be a very exciting time for both the children and their parents. Two-year-olds can walk, run, and climb. They recognize a number of people, animals, and things, and they learn new words every day. Between the ages of two and three, children quickly absorb the countless new experiences in their lives.

Young children also develop in other ways during the first two years of life. They learn that people and things do not cease to exist just because they are out of sight. They also develop ways of reacting to others. Infants do not react to strangers in the same way, for example. Some of them are fearful of strangers; others are not. Some youngsters are content to play with toys by themselves for long periods of time; others cry when they cannot see a familiar person. This is the beginning of social development, or individual ways of interacting with others. This early social development contributes to the formation of what we called personality in Chapter 2.

The arrival of a new little brother or sister may have varying effects, especially on the first child. A child who is included in the waiting and preparation for the new baby will feel a part of the event and is not likely to feel threatened. On the other hand, children who have been the focus of the parents' attention may suddenly feel that the new baby is taking their place. It is natural that children would resent this and would consider the newcomer a rival. Young children in this frustrating position may return to earlier forms of behavior such as thumb sucking or wetting their clothing. If children are given some exclusive attention and are allowed to enter into what is happening, such behavior is usually short-lived. The children make an adjustment, as discussed in Chapter 8, "Coping with Stress." Good adjustments in these situations help children make better adjustments later.

What do you RECALL?   To what extent can you recall your own early childhood years? Can you think of any particular person or event that affected your development?

CHILDHOOD

It is not necessary for us to follow all of the types of development from year to year. However, some childhood developmental experiences are discussed here. In addition to continued physical growth, children become better coordinated in physical activities. They develop better control over the use of their bodies. It is also desirable that preschool children learn to control their behavior to some extent.

They must learn to do some things for themselves and to share things and experiences with others. Language development should continue. Some children have problems in learning to talk properly, and it is also common for preschoolers to have difficulty with certain sounds. Some young children may lisp or stutter. Undue alarm of parents can make the problem worse. Many such early language difficulties are outgrown. Obvious abnormalities, of course, will probably be noticed and should get attention. Children with serious language difficulties may also have a hearing problem, for example.

Intellectual development was discussed in Chapter 7, "Thinking and Problem Solving." You will recall, or can review in that chapter, the stages of cognitive, or mental, development identified by Piaget. This is a very important aspect of life-span development, including the beginning of ability to reason, around seven years of age. Cognitive development is involved in our education and in career choice and success.

ADOLESCENCE

Adolescence is a time of transformation from child to young adult. It is a period of physical and psychological growth or transformation during which a person achieves a new degree of independence and competence as an individual. Another term for adolescent is teenager. The teen years, particularly those from 13 to 17, are generally considered the period of adolescence.

A group of teenagers enjoy a sports event and don't seem to mind the cold.

Transition: Child to Adult

Sexual development, making the young person capable of reproduction, is known as **puberty.** Production of the hormone estrogen in females and the hormone testosterone in males stimulates the development of sexual characteristics.

Physical growth for both sexes during the years of puberty may be erratic. One part of the body may grow faster than another. It is not unusual for a teenager to have feet that are temporarily too big for the rest of the body. Adolescents develop a new consciousness of their bodies and physical appearance. The 15-year-old who disliked cleaning up may now spend hours on personal hygiene and hair care, for example.

Girls tend to mature earlier than boys in terms of physical development. This is noticeable in any group of first-year high school students. Girls experience a spurt of physical growth and development, on the average, between the ages of 11 and 13. Boys, on the other hand, experience this spurt several years later. This difference in the rate of growth can be awkward for both sexes. The girls, for example, are generally taller than the boys for a few years. By the end of the senior year, most of the boys will be taller than the girls, as is characteristic of adults.

Interest in the Opposite Sex

Adolescence usually marks the beginning of dating and other male-female social experiences. The fact that young people are interested in members of the opposite sex shows that they have one characteristic of social maturity. This type of maturity will be discussed further later in this chapter.

The fact that young people mature physically and are capable of reproduction, or becoming parents, before they become economically independent can also cause problems. Too many young people who are not mature enough for the responsibilities of adulthood start a family before they realize all that is involved.

Influence of Peers

Social customs, particularly what others one's own age, or **peers,** are doing, are important factors in teenage relationships. Adolescents are influenced to a great extent by what others of their peer group think of them and by what they think the others think of them. Some of their apprehensions are imaginary.

Adolescents are at an age when they are developing into socially mature, independent people and are psychologically in need of approval from other young people with whom they identify. Adolescents express their admiration of leaders in their school, class, or other groups, for example, by imitating their behavior. Whatever a recognized leader is doing, some others have a tendency to do also. In more recent times, however, there has been a turn toward independent thinking and saying "No" to drugs, sex, or whatever a teenager believes is wrong for him or her. This is related to moral development, which will be discussed later in this chapter.

Influence of Parents

Childhood and adolescence are special times in an individual's life. This is emphasized by David Elkind, the child psychologist in his book *The Hurried Child.* He says:

> No matter what philosophy of life we espouse, it is important to see childhood as a stage of life, not just as the anteroom to life. Hurrying children into adulthood violates the sanctity of life by giving one period priority over another. But if we really value human life, we will value each period equally and give unto each stage of life what is appropriate to that stage.
>
> Valuing childhood does not mean seeing it as a happy innocent period, but rather, as an important period of life to which children are entitled. It is children's right to be children, to enjoy the pleasures, and to suffer the pains of a childhood that is infringed by hurrying. In the end, a childhood is the most basic human right of children.[4]

Accelerated growing up is sometimes encouraged indirectly by parents. These parents may be seeking a sense of security or social status for themselves by having achieving, popular offspring. Or they may want their children to have things they couldn't have or to do the things they couldn't do, which may prove to be too much too soon. Dr. Bruce A. Baldwin, a practicing psychologist, refers to the dangers of giving one's children too much in "Positive Parenting: How to Avoid Raising Cornucopia Kids," He defines them as young people who are self-centered, avoid responsibilities, and only want to have a good time. Even after they leave home, according to Baldwin, they expect someone else to foot the bills. In his article, Baldwin says:

> Cornucopia Kids simply don't deal well with the "real world" because they have never been exposed to it. They are children who learn through years of direct experience in the home that the good life will always be available for the asking, without personal accountability or achievement motivation. These indulged children have lived their lives in an artificial environment created by naive and compliant parents. Life is always easy. They've never had to struggle; nor are they expected to give back in return for what they've been given. The real world, when at last they confront it, finds them unprepared and overwhelmed.[5]

Trials and Triumphs

Adolescents experience many ups and downs, trials and triumphs. Many think there has been too much emphasis of negative aspects of adolescence. There is always more emphasis on problems in any subject area, because problems are obvious and disturbing. But many young people, and others who admire them, have objected to the publicity given to juvenile delinquency and other problems that involve a small percentage of their age group.

Young people during these years are more apt to take risks, often defying the possibility that they could be seriously harmed. Some psychologists have referred to this attitude as the "personal fable." Such attitudes include, "I can handle this drug," "I won't have an automobile or motorcycle accident," "I won't get pregnant," or "I can take care of myself," whatever the particular risk happens to be.

Adolescence offers the developing individual new opportunities but also requires more decisions. Young people during these years may become confused about their ambitions and may feel pressured by parents, instructors in school, and others in the fast-moving, demanding world. Some become troubled enough so that they need professional help; they have problems that they will not simply outgrow.

Adolescence is a time of mixed feelings and reactions for young people. Their lives are a combination of situations calling for both childhood dependence and adult independence, a subject that will be discussed later in this chapter. There can be no denial that adolescence is a turning point in life and can be trying to young people who are not certain which way they should, or even want to, go. Although, as indicated earlier, adolescence is usually associated with the teen years, some psychologists include early years of the twenties as part of adolescent experience.

In spite of the perplexities and contradictions of this time of life, adolescence can be exciting and rewarding for both young people, their parents, and others who are part of their lives. Life at this time is promising and challenging in ways it has never been before, and it is also filled with potential triumphs, or good experiences.

What would you SAY? How would you respond to someone who says, "I can't understand why teenagers can't just be kids until they get to be adults."?

YOUNG ADULTHOOD

Age can be confusing in studying stages of development. What a person can do and is doing is more important than age. Look around you. You see young adults acting in differing ways don't you? That is why deciding whether legal age for various types of activities and responsibilities has created some problems. Some young people are mature enough for new responsibilities. Others are not. Some are adult in a number of ways even before they are 18. For the most part, we should be thinking of the young adult, during this discussion, as ranging from 18 through the early thirties. There is considerable difference between the maturity and perceptions of those at the beginning and end of this age range, but they nevertheless have a great deal in common.

Young adulthood involves a number of important challenges and decisions. Most people during this time of their lives complete the major phase of their formal education, decide on an initial career, and decide whether they want to marry or be single. There may be some conflict between giving up some independence in order to establish meaningful interdependence in marriage or other relationships.

This time of one's life also involves new relationships with one's parents and any brothers and sisters. There can be a sharing of oneself and ideas and experiences that is not possible at a younger or less mature level.

The author of an article in *Psychology Today* has this to say about adult sibling relationships:

Rivalry forged in childhood and carried into early and middle adulthood becomes less and less important with time. What matters more is that as constants in our lives, siblings provide a reference against which to judge and measure ourselves. They know us in a unique way during childhood and share a history that can bring understanding and a sense of perspective to adulthood. Friends and neighbors move away, former co-workers are forgotten, marriages break up, parents die, but our brothers and sisters remain our brothers and sisters. As we age and begin to sense our own mortality, many siblings rediscover the values and strengths of family.[6]

Have you found this to be true in your life?

Raising a Family

Young adults have many more options, and decisions, related to family responsibilities than their parents or grandparents had. Some married couples decide not to have children. Others choose to have smaller families. Some adopt children; others experience parenthood roles by caring for foster children. Still others become stepparents. It is apparent that "the children" may live in a number of parent-child relationships. Relationships in all of these types of families can be equally close and rewarding. And, unfortunately, with every type of family there can also be conflict and even abuse.

The total parent-child relationship in a family has the utmost significance in the lives of all family members. Again, such relationships have changed greatly in recent times. For example, fathers are more involved now in caring for young children than in previous times. Children themselves notice less difference in the roles of their mothers and fathers.

Part of the role of parents is to guide and sometimes correct the behavior of their children. Children need discipline that is neither too strict nor too permissive. They need the assurance that their parents love them enough to care what they do and don't do. They need discipline that is relatively consistent but that is reasonable in view of circumstances.

A parent should ask, What result do I want? Do I want my children to suffer in some way? Do I want to release my own frustrations by using my children as whipping posts? Do I want my children to learn and to improve their behavior? Consideration of these questions will help the parent to react more rationally and to use methods of discipline that have favorable results. A parent should keep in mind the purposes of discipline: to teach children respect for others and the rights of others, to prevent harm to the children themselves, and to teach children self-control or discipline, which they will use throughout life. Lack of discipline in childhood is blamed for some of the insecurity in the lives of young people today.

Responsible adults—whether raising their natural children or adopted children or temporarily caring for foster children—are concerned with their present and future behavior. Rules and guidelines are necessary and even give the children a sense of security, but the ultimate goal should be self-discipline.

DEPENDENCE OR INTER-DEPENDENCE?

Before we continue to look at later stages of life-span development, consideration of the life-span dependence/interdependence curve can give us some insight into our own past and future development. Although we started our lives almost totally dependent on others, there is a natural striving for independence that becomes evident very early in life.

Life-Span Dependence/Interdependence Curve

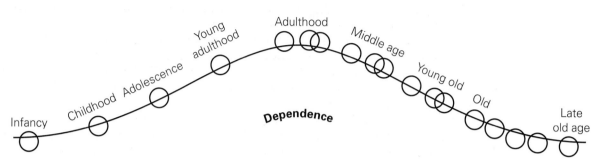

The goal of a young adult is usually to be "on my own," or as independent as possible. This is understandable and is encouraged by society. Total independence is seldom achieved, or even desired, in today's society, however. We live in a complex, specialized world where a degree of dependence upon one another is a part of normal living. We may derive satisfaction from doing things for ourselves, but in most life-styles we are more **interdependent,** or dependent upon one another, than we realize.

Besides the increase in daily dependence on one another to satisfy our physical needs, there is voluntary interdependence, which can enrich living. This type of dependence is different from earlier dependence on one's parents or others. It is only possible as long as persons involved are able to be independent in some respects. Interdependence of this type is related to emotional and other psychological needs, as well as to physical needs. In voluntary interdependence a person must be able and willing both to give and to receive love and support of various kinds. It involves risks in allowing ourselves to be dependent on others when it is not necessary to do so. However, the most rewarding of human relationships cannot be achieved without such voluntary interdependence and risks. A successful marriage is an example of voluntary interdependence.

The above figure illustrates the extent to which a person can be dependent, independent, or voluntarily interdependent at various times during his or her life span. The Life-Span Dependence/Interdependence Curve combines life-span development with variations in dependence, independence, or interdependence. It also shows how these might apply to different life-styles during one's adult life. The curve itself represents the life span from infancy to possible late old age. The area below the curve represents dependence; the area above the curve represents independence. The interlocking of circles represents voluntary interdependence. Persons who share a degree of voluntary interdependence still maintain a large measure of independence in their lives. Positions of the circles above or below the line show the degree to which a person is (or may be) dependent or independent at various times of life. Note that at adolescence, for example, the circle is halfway above and halfway below the line. Also note that human beings are almost totally dependent at birth and some may become so again if they live to be very old and become feeble and unable to care for themselves. Although this will not happen to most of us, it is realistic to recognize there are many aged adults in nursing homes today who are almost totally dependent on others. Although it is not represented on the curve, we also know that, at any time during the life span, persons can become dependent because of accidents or illness.

The life span is represented as a curve to show that during young adulthood, adulthood, and middle-age years, persons have greater choice in their life-styles. They are also more likely to have an interdependent relationship or life-style, which is more complicated in many ways than independence. But, it may be more desirable.

Most human beings in today's society move from the dependency of infancy, through the blend of dependence/independence of adolescence, to the independence of young adulthood. From there to the possible dependency of old age, there can be a variety of independent or voluntarily interdependent life-styles.

It could be of value to sketch one's own dependence/interdependence curve up to one's present life-style and to project one's anticipated life-styles in the future. Although we cannot always foresee what we might do in the future, the changing of our life-styles and relationships with other people should not be haphazard. The better we understand ourselves, our goals, and our relationships with other people, the more satisfying and rewarding our lives will be.

MIDDLE ADULTHOOD

As with other life-span development stages, there are a number of different ways of describing middle age. For many, it is the first personal awareness of "getting old." Many persons just entering this stage actually feel older, for this reason, than they may feel ten years later in their life span. Others react with a new sense of freedom and challenge. Many see this as a "now or never" turning point in their lives when they decide whether to further their education, change careers, or make some other significant change in their lives. Others may come to the realization that they are on the "right track" in their lives in terms of self-understanding, work, family relationships, and progress toward fulfillment of goals.

Many middle-aged adults are involved in activities for which there might not have been time in earlier years. This time of life has been referred to as "the empty nest," with reference to the fact that one's children have been raised and have left home to be on their own. Another expression, "overcrowded nest," however, has been coined to refer to a relatively common experience today, in which adult sons and daughters return home to live with parents, at least temporarily. This may be due to illness, loss of job, or relocation that involves housing delays. A definition of family and home that would apply here: "Home is where, when you have no place to go, they take you in." Although that may not always be the case, it has worked out for many on a short-term basis.

Roger Gould, who has done extensive research on adult development, believes that individuals typically give up a number of false assumptions or myths as they go through the stages of adult development. According to Gould, these "false childhood assumptions that we must lose" are:

We'll always live with our parents and be their children.
Our parents will always be there to help us out.
Our parents' version of reality is correct.
There is no real death or evil.[7]

In terms of how these myths have applied to you, it should be pointed out that there is a difference between "knowing" something intellectually and understanding it and accepting it in terms of your own experience. It is very possible, for example, to know something "in your head" such as "people die" and yet not apply the truth or reality of it to yourself and those you love until you are confronted with the experience or repeated evidence that affects your life. When we have learned to cope with such realities, we have become adults in the full sense of the word. This can be at any age of adulthood, or it may never happen at all. Frequently, it happens during middle adulthood.

LATER ADULTHOOD

Exactly what the term later adulthood means could depend on the entire life-span of the individual. There is an obvious effort in today's society to avoid referring to people who have lived a long time as "old." Instead they are called "seniors," "senior citizens," or "the elderly." They may also be spoken of as in their "golden years" or "harvest years."

There is a definite physical decline in a number of respects in one's later years. Sight and hearing usually weaken, and older people may have difficulty walking or using their hands. Part of this may result from arthritis, a common ailment in later adulthood.

The life span of humans has lengthened in recent years. A wellness lifestyle may also keep a person feeling and looking younger for more years. But physical maturity continues on its course. The growth process turns to aging and physical deterioration in later years.

There is no doubt that many abilities continue to decline with age. Some people experience memory problems and may remember what they did long ago better than they can recall what happened recently. However, the common belief in intellectual decline in old age is largely a myth. In actual practice, society provides older citizens with relatively few opportunities to remain active. Since intellectual activity is affected by boredom and lack of motivation, in addition to other causes, we might question whether the decline in mental alertness results partly from the absence of challenge and stimulation. There are many examples of old people who live full, productive lives characterized by energy and alertness.

To some extent, age represents an attitude rather than the number of years a person has lived. Many older persons continue to learn, to be socially active, and to have a variety of new experiences. You probably know older people who continue to work toward new goals and lead meaningful lives. It is interesting to note that it is common for men and women to change some personality characteristics as they get older. Men, for example, have a tendency to become less aggressive and more interested in human relationships, and women have a tendency to become more independent and assertive. This doesn't necessarily mean that that's the way it will be in the future, however. As roles of males and females change during their lifetimes, this may change, also.

So far we have dealt with a number of types of development taking place at various times from prenatal development to later adulthood. "Psychosocial" pertains to the development of feelings about oneself and attitudes towards others. According to Erik Erikson, there are eight stages of psychosocial development, with the type of development taking place at each stage having some influence on development at later stages. These eight stages and the approximate time in life they normally occur are shown in the figure below.[8]

During infancy, or the first year of life, an individual develops a sense of either trust or distrust toward others. Since in most cases infants spend most of their time with their parents or some other primary caretaker, the type of care they receive largely determines whether they develop trust or mistrust. This doesn't mean that children lie in a crib or sit in a playpen and think, "If he doesn't come with some food pretty soon, I won't trust him." Obviously, infants are not capable of this type of thinking. But if they receive care and loving attention, trust is likely to develop. If they are neglected and live in an environment full of discord and tension, distrust is likely to develop. In the first year of life, therefore, the basis for either favorable or unfavorable psychosocial development is formed.

Erikson's Eight Stages of Psychosocial Development

1	2	3	4	5	6	7	8	
							Ego integrity vs. despair	Later Adult
					Genera-tivity vs. stagnation			Middle Adult
				Intimacy vs. isolation				Young Adult
			Identity vs. role confusion					Adolescent
		Industry vs. inferiority						Elementary School Child
	Initiative vs. guilt							Preschool Child
Autonomy vs. shame, doubt								Toddler
Basic trust vs. mistrust								Infancy

Adapted from *Childhood and Society*, Second Edition, Revised, by Erik H. Erikson, with the permission of W. W. Norton & Company, Inc. Copyright 1950, © 1963 by W. W. Norton & Company, Inc.

As you look at the figure shown on page 263, you will notice that the first term of each one of the stages could be considered positive, or desirable, and the term following *vs.* could be considered negative, or undesirable. It would be generally agreed, for example, that it would be better to develop a sense of trust toward others than a feeling of mistrust. This doesn't mean that a person should develop trust toward others without exception or limitations. The basic idea is that trust is the foundation of other meaningful relationships with others.

What do you THINK?   If a person does not develop trust during his or her first year of life, does that mean that the rest of that person's psychosocial development will be negative? Think about this as you read about psychosocial development.

When children are two or three years old, or toddlers, they develop either autonomy or shame and doubt. If they have developed trust during infancy, it is more likely that they will develop autonomy during these years. The term **autonomy** refers to a sense of independence or competence. Now, obviously a toddler cannot be very independent. But if you know any two- or three-year-olds, you are aware that they like to do things for themselves. They want to pour their own juice or dress themselves, even if a few things get on backward. If Mandy is not allowed to "help" or do some things for herself, she is not likely to develop a sense of autonomy. If she is constantly scolded for doing things wrong, making a mess, or getting in the way, she is likely to develop a sense of shame or doubt.

The next two childhood stages of psychosocial development follow along essentially the same lines. **Initiative** at age 4 or 5 primarily refers to interest in trying new things, in going ahead with responsibilities and activities of interest. At this age, responsibilities may be as simple as putting clothes or possessions away. This leads to a sense of worth and achievement, however, that is important to the child and leads to further positive development. On the other hand, if William's behavior receives negative response, he is likely to develop a sense of guilt. The guilt of a preschool child is likely to lead to a sense of inferiority in the elementary school child, and a feeling of inferiority is not likely to lead to activity that is challenging and constructive in the child's development.

If you were to visit any of the grade schools in your area, and observe the children's behavior, you would see some who would seemingly be hesitant to go ahead with assignments and activities or be timid about asking the teacher for help or reciting in class. This reflects both children's feelings about themselves, or self-concept, and their attitudes toward others. They are not willing to become involved if they feel unsure of themselves, are afraid to make mistakes, and do not trust others.

You could correctly conclude that such children are going to have still further problems at the next stage or adolescence. This is the stage where they begin to develop identity as an individual or experience role confusion. **Identity** refers to understanding yourself as an individual with personal values and goals. **Role confusion,** on the other hand, refers to values and behavior that frequently change, often being influenced by one's companions at the time. If Sarah doesn't feel good about herself, she will have difficulty making independent decisions and determining some goals for her future. She is more subject to peer influence, relying on identity with others or with a group, rather than establishing her own identity as an individual. She is experiencing role confusion.

Before we consider the last three stages of psychosocial development, let's consider the question asked in "What do you THINK?" earlier: "If a person does not develop trust during his or her first year of life, does that mean that the rest of that person's psychosocial development will be negative?" The answer is, "Not necessarily so, although it is more likely to be negative than positive." It will take some special influence or particular effort by the individual to counteract an unfavorable psychosocial beginning. Fortunately for the child, and for society, this is possible. When children start going to school and become involved in other activities, they have contact with a number of different people and environments. Often a scout leader, a coach, an older brother or sister, a teacher, or some other person with whom the child feels comfortable can have a positive effect on the child's development. The child may begin to feel better about himself or herself, develop more self-confidence, and be willing to try more things. Essentially he or she has to develop a sense of trust and then progress through the positive aspects of other stages of psychosocial development. This takes time but it can and does happen.

If you are a young adult, you should be able to recognize yourself as having some degree of intimacy or isolation. It is important to keep in mind that there are degrees of psychosocial characteristics as well as different stages. **Intimacy** refers to the ability to establish a close, sharing relationship with at least one other person. This could be a boyfriend or girlfriend, a spouse, a best friend, or some other special person or persons. You are not likely to share your feelings, your dreams and disappointments, or the person you really are with someone you do not trust. Trust in this sense, quite obviously, does not refer to our money or possessions. We are more likely to risk those than we are to risk being ridiculed and rejected.

A person can be married and still not experience intimacy in this sense. It is also possible to have a great deal of interaction with other people and yet have a personal sense of **isolation,** or aloneness. These ideas will be discussed in Chapter 12, "Interpersonal Relationships." The person who is afraid to become psychologically close to others probably has had unfavorable psychosocial development. It is not realistic for us as adults to blame someone else for the person we are today, however. We can learn to understand ourselves and to make changes in ourselves and in our lives. It helps to have support, and we can give support to others, but psychosocial disadvantages can be overcome with self-understanding, determination, and time.

The middle adult stage in this type of development pertains to what happens to a person after some of life's major challenges have been met (or avoided). **Generativity** means reaching out and becoming involved in what is happening outside one's immediate sphere of life. After their own family has been raised, many middle-aged people become interested and involved in other activities that benefit youth or the community and keep themselves active and stimulated in the process. Others experience *stagnation,* or a lack of meaningful activity and sense of purpose. For many of these people life was always more frustrating than challenging and stimulating, and it is easier to fall back into a passive existence.

By the time a person reaches later adulthood, or what we commonly think of as old age, he or she has developed either *ego integrity* or *despair*. If persons at that stage in life feel good about themselves, are satisfied with what they have done with their life, and have rewarding relationships with others, they have acquired ego integrity. On the other hand, if they feel dissatisfied with themselves, and their accomplishments (or the lack of them) and are disgruntled with their family and others with whom they have contact, they are experiencing despair. If you have contact with some older persons you can probably recognize the difference. Persons experiencing despair are telling us that they have had frustrating, relatively meaningless lives.

This discussion of psychosocial development should have been helpful in understanding yourself and others. Remember that as adults we can change ourselves and our situations. We can also be supportive to others who seem to lack trust or other positive characteristics of this type of development. Having had some psychosocial disadvantages is no reason to miss out on present and future stimulating experiences and challenges.

MORAL DEVELOPMENT

We were not born with a sense of right and wrong. Yet all of us today believe that some types of behavior are "right" and others are "wrong." It is unlikely, however, that all of us would agree on what kinds of behavior belong in each category.

What do we mean by moral development and how is it acquired? Moral development essentially means acquiring a standard of what we believe to be right and wrong. Since this type of development is learned, a natural question to ask would be, How is moral development learned? To begin with, what we *must* do or *can't* do was learned from those with whom we lived or from those with whom we spent considerable time in the early years of our lives. In today's society that would most likely be parents, or personnel in day-care centers. As one moves along in life, moral development is influenced by many others and becomes more complicated. Eventually we become responsible for our own moral standard.

One of the best known theories of moral development is that of Lawrence Kohlberg.[9] He describes moral development in terms of six stages that motivate one's behavior. The following is a simplified explanation of why people act the way they do at each stage, according to Kohlberg's theory.

The Six Moral Stages

Reasons for Doing "Right"

Stage 1	Fear of punishment.
Stage 2	Concern with meeting one's own needs; expects others to do the same.
Stage 3	Belief in the golden rule; it is important to treat others right; they will then also treat you right.
Stage 4	Belief that society and other groups need rules to function properly; therefore, I must obey the rules; respect for authority.
Stage 5	Belief in democratic approach; since everyone does not want the same things, what is best for the majority is right.
Stage 6	Belief in universal moral principles and one's personal commitment to them.

Notice that the first stage is related to fear of punishment and the last stage is based on a personal commitment to what one believes is right or wrong. Although stages in moral development seem to follow the order outlined by Kohlberg, individuals may function at different stages for different reasons. A person may not speed when driving, for example, for fear of paying a fine. That same person would not steal a car because he or she believes it is wrong to take the possessions of other people. Also, there are some people in society who may never function at the higher stages of moral development. In fact, some individuals may never progress much beyond Stage 1. That would mean that there isn't anything that they wouldn't do if they thought they wouldn't be punished or suffer undesired consequences. If this were common, we would not have a civilized society.

In fact it is questioned whether Stage 6 should be included as few people, if any, reach that stage in their moral development. According to Laura E. Berk in *Infants, Children, and Adolescents,*

> A striking finding is that moral development is very slow and gradual. Stages 1 and 2 decrease in adolescence, while Stage 3 increases through midadolescence and then declines. Stage 4 rises over the teenage years until, by early adulthood, is the typical response. Few people move beyond it to stage 5. In fact, postconventional morality (Stages 5 and 6) is so rare that there is no clear evidence that Kohlberg's Stage 6 actually follows Stage 5. The highest stage of moral development is still a matter of speculation.

Berk defines the postconventional level as the level "in which individuals define morality in terms of abstract principles and values that apply to all situations and societies."[10] The two levels preceding the postconventional level (Stages 5 and 6) are identified by Kohlberg as the preconventional level (Stages 1 and 2) and the conventional level (Stages 3 and 4.) We must remember that many factors, such as culture, learning, influence of others, and personal choices, influence moral development, so that it is difficult to predict how an individual will react in a particular situation. We can conclude from reviewing the stages, however, that moral development begins with fear of punishment, before a child is capable of making rational choices. From there it can move to the recognition that society needs rules and laws and a respect for what is best for the majority.

What would you SAY? How would you respond to someone who says, "Laws are to be broken, as long as you don't get caught"?

In the determination of rightness and wrongness, many people maintain that the situation must be considered. Those who believe in **situational ethics** consider the total situation rather than just the behavior itself in determining whether an act is right or wrong. Judd may believe it is wrong to steal, for example, but he may believe it would be acceptable for a person to steal food for her starving family. Problems arise in legal matters in this respect, as situations can be interpreted and evaluated differently. This is related to one's right to self-defense, for example.

So far we have dealt with a number of types of development throughout the life span. We must keep in mind that not all types of maturity occur as stages in a process. Some require conscious effort by the individual. In addition to moral development, such types of maturity include emotional, social, intellectual, and vocational development. All these aspects of maturity deserve the attention of young adults.

James W. Vander Zanden in *Human Development* gives us the following definition of maturity:

> "Maturity is the capacity of individuals to undergo continual change in order to adapt successfully and cope flexibly with the demands and responsibilities of life. Maturity is not some sort of plateau or final state but a lifetime process of becoming. It is a never-ending search for a meaningful and comfortable fit between ourselves and the world—a struggle to "get it all together."[11]

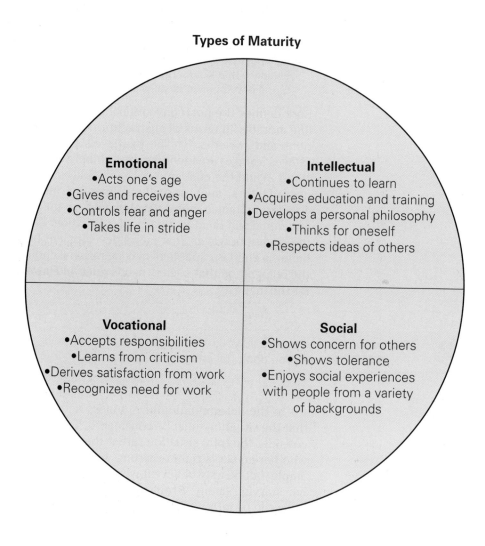

Types of Maturity

Emotional
- Acts one's age
- Gives and receives love
- Controls fear and anger
- Takes life in stride

Intellectual
- Continues to learn
- Acquires education and training
- Develops a personal philosophy
- Thinks for oneself
- Respects ideas of others

Vocational
- Accepts responsibilities
- Learns from criticism
- Derives satisfaction from work
- Recognizes need for work

Social
- Shows concern for others
- Shows tolerance
- Enjoys social experiences with people from a variety of backgrounds

EMOTIONAL MATURITY

Reference to mature behavior usually means what is here identified as emotional maturity. Probably the reason for this is that emotional immaturity can be conspicuous and troublesome. Emotionally mature people have learned to control and use their emotions sensibly and for the greater enjoyment of life.

Paul J. Gelinas in his book entitled *Coping With Your Emotions* shares his ideas on emotional maturity in saying,

> If you are realistic, you'll face the truth even when it hurts your feelings. Many disturbing situations affect your life and those of your loved ones, and this fact must be anticipated if you are to achieve emotional strength. As the years go by you will encounter severe disappointments, sorrows, and shocks. You may develop a stoic philosophy, becoming hardened to possible disasters, shutting off your emotions in resignation. However, such an outlook on life not only saves you from being hurt, but it also robs you of love and many other emotions that make life worthwhile. Accordingly, you should accept difficulties as challenges to be used as a means of further emotional growth. Courage will be your helpmate, preparing you to fight firmly when hardship strikes. Either you must struggle to avert tragedy or seek to change defeat into success.[12]

Emotions can create difficulties and cause pain or can make life more satisfying and exciting.

Mature people experience love, fear, anger, and other emotions, but they do not let their responses become harmful to themselves or to others. Mature people may even occasionally act in an irrational, or emotional, way. They may not have perfect emotional control at times or always act with complete emotional stability, but they usually make better responses than others under an existing set of circumstances. Mature people also are able to recognize immature behavior.

Act Your Age

What might be acceptable behavior at one age may not be acceptable at another. If at 10 years of age you had a disagreement with your teammates during a game and walked away and went home, you were acting your age; you had not yet learned that dropping what you are doing and stalking away do not settle differences. However, an 18-year-old would be expected to use more self-control, even though some people that age and even older may act like balky 10-year-olds.

Give and Receive Love

Mature people know that you may love in different ways. A woman does not love her spouse in the same ways as she loves her brother, for example. Mature people have an unselfish interest in and are concerned with the welfare and happiness of other people. This is an essential characteristic of love.

Control Fear and Anger

Even though it is normal to have some fears, mature people do not let these interfere with their normal activities. They recognize that it is sensible to fear things and situations that pose a threat to them. But mature people know what

Anger is directed not only at other people but also at objects and systems that don't "work."

their fears are and know what to do about them. They can maintain emotional control in emergency situations without their fears turning into panic.

Anger is a basic human emotional response. Even very young children show behavior that can be interpreted as anger. But they express such feelings with no attempt at control or consideration for others. Adults who lose their temper at the least provocation are acting like children in an emotional sense. Justifiable anger of mature adults is expressed in a nondestructive way. Many of life's problems would not be solved if people did not become disturbed enough to try to solve them. The question is to determine what is worth fighting for or against. Then you can act in socially acceptable, effective ways.

Take Life in Stride

Mature people respond calmly to most disappointing situations. They understand that some things just aren't worth getting worked up about. Angelina, a graphics student, was not assigned the particular task she preferred on Tuesday morning, but she was able to accept another assignment and did her best work on it. If, because of the time schedule, she cannot take a particular class she needs to complete her program, on the other hand, she has reason to be disturbed. She should still be able to solve the problem in a mature, rational manner, however. It is better for all concerned to approach most of life with a calm interest and rational concern and to save emotional involvement for issues that really matter.

Mature people recognize the relative importance of what happens to them and what they do. They have learned to laugh at themselves, at their human limitations, which sometimes get them into predicaments. They can be amused by their occasional stupidity and the harmless but ridiculous consequences of some of the things they do. On the other hand, they should not react with a laugh-it-off response to all mistakes and problems. Mature people can distinguish between the harmless boner and the serious error. A sense of humor includes recognizing such differences.

SOCIAL MATURITY

Social maturity can be defined as having mutually satisfying experiences with both sexes, people of different ages, and individuals from a variety of backgrounds. Socially mature people relate well to people of different races, religions, and occupations. They do not live in their own little world. They share experiences with friends and with many others, at home and at work. They are also dependable in obligations and promises. Some of the characteristics of this type of maturity are discussed in the following sections.

Show Concern for Others

Concern for other people is a characteristic of social maturity that must be learned and often takes effort and self-denial. Human beings by nature, and therefore from birth, are self-centered. The satisfaction that people get from doing things for others, however, can be greater than the pleasure they get from thinking only of themselves. It is an ironic, or unexpected, twist in life that the more people give of themselves to others, the more content they themselves will be.

Everyone is familiar with the golden rule, "Do unto others as you would have them do unto you." An interpretation of this rule, "Do unto others as they would have you do unto them," is based on the principle that each human being is different. Perhaps other people don't want to be treated the same way you would like to have them treat you. You should try to understand other people, to use empathy, and to act accordingly. The golden rule can also be interpreted to mean "Do not do unto others as you would not have them do unto you." In other words, some types of behavior should be avoided—for example, insult, distrust, neglect, or deliberate harm.

In an old legend, Jupiter, ruler of gods and mortals in Roman mythology, is persuaded by Juno, his wife, to help out a man in his problems with other human beings. Jupiter teaches the man to take advantage of the principle of reciprocal behavior. The point is to treat others with consideration and respect so that they will react the same way toward you and make your life easier and happier.

Mature people are interested in others for their own sake rather than for personal benefit. One finds that when mature people treat others with consideration, they benefit too. Whether people are concerned with others from a selfish or unselfish motive, they find themselves better off. A comparison of two young home appliance demonstrators in their sales work is an example. Larry is attentive and helpful in explaining and demonstrating appliances to customers because he knows that it will help him sell more appliances and increase his commission. This is a selfish motive, but it is effective in sales nevertheless. Karen also shows interest in customers and is helpful, but primarily because she is interested in people and gains satisfaction from helping them make the wisest selection and use of appliances. Both people have similar sales records, but it is apparent that Karen is more socially mature and, therefore, experiences more complete satisfaction in her work.

Show Tolerance

Another characteristic of social maturity is tolerance. Tolerance is readily accepted as desirable but can be extremely difficult to practice. The familiar saying, "It is easier said than done," applies to tolerance as well as to many other characteristics of maturity. Tolerance includes allowing others to be what they are as long as they are not interfering with the rights of others. It is the recognition and acceptance of different backgrounds with different values and customs. It also includes being open-minded about differences in personal appearance and lifestyle within one's own culture. Mature people strive to see such differences from other points of view. Tolerance does not mean understanding or agreeing, however. Even when we "can't imagine why . . . ," we can at least be tolerant of others when we and others are not adversely affected.

Enjoy Social Experiences

The definition of social maturity includes the idea of having mutually satisfying experiences with people with a variety of characteristics. If Mark goes to a family reunion, for example, he talks to the old people, aunts and uncles, and even children. He may spend most of his time with relatives his own age, it is true, but it can be a good experience for both him and others to move about and become more actively involved. In another type of situation, if Carole goes to a reception and knows only one person there, she still introduces herself to others. She does not confine herself to being with just that one guest. A socially mature person can adapt to a large variety of situations and make them enjoyable experiences.

INTELLECTUAL MATURITY

Learning, thinking, and interpreting are classified as *intellectual* behavior and development. Human beings begin to learn at birth, and they have new experiences throughout life. The ability to understand various concepts, for example language and mathematics, is largely developmental. Children have only a vague notion of the length of a week, or a month, or a year, partly because they have had less experience in living. You may recall, or can review, Piaget's stages of cognitive development discussed in Chapter 7. When a person has reached the Formal Operations Stage (usually around 12 years of age or during the teen years) he or she is capable of abstract thinking. The individual can evaluate ideas and can think more critically. This is one of the reasons adolescents often challenge thinking and values of their parents. They are using intellectual ability they haven't had before, even though they are characteristically overconfident about being right.

Continue to Learn

Mature people know how to make learning more efficient, interesting, and lasting. They recognize that learning is a lifelong process, which can continue to make life stimulating and challenging. In addition to taking classes, some of the ways people continue to learn are by reading, by general observation, by association, and by experience. Mature people seek new experiences and exposure to different ideas. They change and continue to expand their interests as they grow in years and experience.

Acquire Education and Training

People not only must develop their learning abilities but must take advantage of educational and training opportunities. Intellectually mature people know that mental and manual competencies are valuable attributes in today's technological world but that they are not acquired easily and quickly.

How adults learn changes somewhat as a person ages, however. Older persons do not respond as quickly as they did when they were younger. It takes them longer to learn. Older people also seem to relate what they are learning to their experiences and ideas more than younger people do. It might be said that a younger person is sharper mentally, whereas an older person is wiser.

Develop a Personal Philosophy

How and what people think is much more than automatic mental development, however. In fact, *how* the mind functions and *what* one thinks are actually two different topics. People in the process of growing up must seek answers to **philosophical questions.** These pertain to the meaning of life and to the significance of one's particular existence.

Intellectually mature people have established a set of beliefs or principles that give direction to their lives. These beliefs and principles are usually written; in fact many people are not aware of them on a day-to-day basis. If you asked some people what their philosophy of life is they might respond: "What are you talking about?" Nevertheless, everyone does have a formal or informal philosophy of life that directs personal behavior.

What one believes and values includes some kind of code of morality and a sense of right and wrong. This may be based on religious belief, social approval, or personal standards. One's behavior and relationships with others are affected by these convictions and values. This type of maturity is thus related to levels of moral development discussed earlier.

Think for Yourself

Intellectual independence is a part of intellectual maturity. People who are maturing are learning to think for themselves and to make their own decisions. They evaluate new ideas objectively for what they are worth, rather than blindly accepting or rejecting them. They develop thoughtful self-discipline and assume responsibility for their own behavior. To do what individuals themselves think they should do, whether they are required by others to do it or not, is considered by many to be an essential feature of mature character. Their behavior is neither completely imitative nor purely automatic. They are conformists in many aspects of living, but they know what they are doing and why.

Respect Ideas of Others

Mature people are willing to listen to and consider the ideas and advice of others. They are also pleased when someone else asks them for their opinion or advice. But they are not offended if the person decides not to follow their suggestions. Experience in living gives one wisdom, but no one ever reaches the point in life of having all the answers. Mature individuals have respect for authority. Everyone has a supervisor—if not the boss, at least others who require accountability in some way. Most people at some time in their lives also have some degree of authority over others. Mature people do not misuse this authority to bolster their self-esteem or to show they have power. It is well to remember that many people have authority only because it is given to them by others. Mature people recognize the need for rules and regulations in an orderly society and do not expect special privileges. This also involves some aspects of social maturity, just discussed.

VOCATIONAL MATURITY

Even in early years, today, much attention is given to career education. Career is a broader term than job. A person may be preparing for a marketing career, for example. This, in turn, would include a number of different jobs. You are probably now enrolled in some specific program of education, preparing yourself for a particular type of career. Finding the right job will be a task deserving your full attention when you finish. What is right for someone else may not be right for you. At that time it would be to your advantage to consider the approach-avoidance conflicts discussed in Chapter 3.

As important as it is to choose a career, prepare for it, and find a job, these events are only preliminary to vocational maturity. Some of the other characteristics of vocational maturity are discussed next.

Recognize the Need to Work

Most members of a society must be productive. In fact, many people consider themselves fortunate to have a job and to be able to do it. Maturity, in a sense, is doing what you are expected to do, even when you might enjoy doing something else more.

There are very few people who do not need to work—in their homes, for themselves, or for others. Some people are not expected to hold full-time jobs in the world of work, of course. These would include the very young, the very old, and those with severe disabilities. And, of course, there are still people, in our society who are able to work and—if all facts were known—would be expected to be in the work force, but they are not. They are being supported by those who do work. This is not a reference to the unemployed who want work but rather to those who take undue advantage of social programs and entitlements. This situation is becoming less of a problem for everyone because of various assistance programs that require persons to receive some kind of job training and to become financially independent over a period of time. In reality, this is what many people who are receiving temporary assistance want.

A vocationally mature person accepts work as a reality of life and tries to find work that he or she is suited for, rather then resenting the fact that work

A counselor can provide guidance and direction not only in vocational decisions but in other aspects of living as well.

is necessary. There are some persons who face this reality most of their lives, every morning when their alarm goes off, but who have never accepted the fact with a constructive attitude.

A young person who has given careful thought to the choice of a career and is preparing for a career through education and training has a sound beginning in vocational maturity. Since we spend so much of our lives on our jobs, vocational maturity is one of the most important types of maturity we can develop.

Derive Satisfaction from Work

It is common for young people starting out in their careers to experience "reality shock." Young people typically have confidence in themselves and have high expectations of what they can do and what the world of work will offer. Although such qualities can be favorable, they are not always realistic. There are aspects of most jobs that are not enjoyable or particularly satisfying, but which must be accepted and performed as well as one can. Over the years, work becomes a part of one's identity as a person. The answer to "What kind of work do you do?" is a significant factor in how we perceive ourselves.

When people can accept the need to work and the realities of the world of work, they can learn to gain satisfaction from work. This can be done in a number of ways. First, satisfaction comes from doing your best no matter what the job is. Another kind of satisfaction comes from increasing your skill. There are very few things a person can't learn to do better. Some improvement comes with experience, but attention and an effort to learn also make a difference. It is largely through work that most of us achieve esteem and move toward self-actualization as well as satisfy the lower-level needs on Maslow's hierarchy. We can continue to develop our work potential whether we advance on a job, change jobs, or become more skilled at the job we now have.

Some satisfaction can also come when the quality of our work is recognized by others. Additional satisfaction can be measured in material rewards—raises, bonuses, and the like. People who gain satisfaction from their work do not need as much extrinsic motivation as those who work only for a living. Some find their work so satisfying that they would continue it even if they did not need the pay.

 What would you DO? What would you do if you didn't have to work for a living?

Learn from Criticism

Mature people realize they have weaknesses and will always have much to learn, especially in our rapidly changing world. There is always the possibility that we may not be doing our work the best way or that we have made a mistake. Mature persons are willing to accept and attempt to profit from criticism, without holding grudges. Although criticism may not always be given in a constructive manner, we should "keep our cool" think about it, and decide what we can learn from it. This subject will be discussed further in Chapter 13, "Human Relations at Work."

Accept Responsibilities

Any type of maturity requires responsibility. This might be thought of as fulfilling reasonable expectations without undue supervision. Vocationally mature people follow through with what is expected of them on the job. They are on time, take care of equipment, use sick leave wisely, help out as needed, follow company policies, and, of course, do the expected work. They are also reasonable in what they expect from their employer in terms of wages, fringe benefits, and other job conditions. They realize employers must make a profit to be able to continue in business.

Even people who are self-employed have responsibilities. They are a link in the total chain of the work force. If they are weak or broken links, other parts of the work force are affected. They are also responsible to their customers if their work involves a product or service.

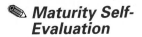

Maturity Self-Evaluation

The purpose of this exercise is to give you a better understanding of yourself and some direction for self-improvement rather than to provide an accurate analysis of your behavior. Check your response to each question. Possible answers are listed on page 279.

Behavior	Yes	Somewhat	No
a. Do I catch myself acting silly or juvenile when I feel awkward or lack confidence in a situation?	____	____	____
b. Do I admit mistakes that I make and accept the consequences of what I do or don't do?	____	____	____
c. When I don't get my own way with another person or in a group, do I try to cooperate and to make the experience worthwhile anyway?	____	____	____
d. Can I accept disappointment and frustration without becoming depressed or difficult to get along with?	____	____	____
e. Do I show consideration for others by following ordinary rules of courtesy?	____	____	____
f. Am I concerned about problems that others have and do I make some attempt to help them or help eliminate the problems?	____	____	____
g. Am I both a contributor and a receiver as a member of an interdependent society?	____	____	____
h. Do I make up my own mind on issues and decisions after availing myself of information and advice?	____	____	____
i. Am I tolerant of others even though I may not like them personally or agree with their ideas?	____	____	____
j. Do I say or do things when I am angry that I regret later?	____	____	____
k. Do I have a sense of responsibility and belongingness toward other members of my family?	____	____	____
l. Are there at least a few people toward whom I feel deep affection and from whom I can accept affection?	____	____	____
m. Do I recognize unfounded fears and try to overcome them?	____	____	____
n. Am I unsure of my goals in life and of what my real values are?	____	____	____
o. Am I interested in becoming better educated and in keeping well informed on current events?	____	____	____
p. Do I gain satisfaction from work?	____	____	____
Totals	____	____	____

All members of a group in a democratic society are expected to carry their share. This is true within a family or within society as a whole. It pertains to people who work but do not necessarily receive wages. Anyone can give fuller meaning and satisfaction to his or her life through work. Most people spend a large share of their lives on their jobs. They may change jobs a number of times in life, as many people do. But work constantly offers people a chance for meaningful activity, a sense of achievement and self-development that cannot be found in any other way.

In the preceding pages, a few characteristics have been described for a number of different types of maturity. It is no doubt evident that some of the characteristics pertain to more than one type of maturity. Accepting responsibility applies to our relations with others in our personal lives as well as on the job. We can learn to react calmly and constructively to criticism in many different situations. We cannot entirely separate types of maturity.

SIGNS OF IMMATURITY

It is easier to recognize signs of immaturity than of maturity. These are always more obvious, just as a dirty shirt is more obvious than a clean one. Common examples of immature behavior are blaming others, making excuses, breaking appointments and promises, and satisfying only immediate wants. Others are continual tardiness, panic in a crisis, unfinished business, abuse of others, and revenge.

It is easier to recognize immature behavior in others than in ourselves. You may recall from Chapter 8 that both neurotic behavior and use of coping mechanisms are basically immature. Although immature behavior in others may be disturbing to us, it is more important to recognize such behavior in ourselves.

SUMMARY

There are a number of ways of determining stages of life-span development. Levinson refers to different times and related tasks in a person's adult life as life structures. Havighurst uses the term developmental tasks in referring to life-span stages. Times and experiences can also be measured by "clocks": biological, psychological, and social.

The approach in this chapter was to consider developmental characteristics and experiences at the following times in an individual's life span: prenatal development, early childhood, childhood, adolescence, young adulthood, middle adulthood, and later adulthood.

Human development, which begins before birth, can continue, at least in some respects, until death. The first years of a child's life involve great physical growth and also the beginnings of emotional, mental, and social development. How children learn to feel about themselves and others also begins at an early age.

Adolescence is a time of great physical and psychological change. Young people are struggling to become independent but are still dependent in several ways. They may experience a number of trials and triumphs during these years. They may be influenced more by their peers than by their parents or other adults, but they are also on their way to becoming more independent in their thinking and in making decisions.

A person reaches a peak of both physical and mental development in the early twenties. Ability to learn continues into late adulthood, but older persons usually respond more slowly in a learning situation. Sight, hearing, and other physical abilities also decline in later years.

One's development and options throughout life can be understood in another respect—through the Dependence/Interdependence Curve. There are times during the life span when a person can make choices about relationships with others in this respect.

Erikson has identified eight stages of psychosocial development that begin in the first year of life and continue into later adulthood. Each stage develops in either a positive or negative way in relation to stages preceding it.

The theory of moral development by Kohlberg has become widely accepted, with some reservations. Kohlberg's original six stages of moral development have been modified to eliminate the last stage, because of the conclusion that few if any people ever reached that stage of development.

Young adults, especially, should be concerned about the development of four basic types of maturity: emotional, social, intellectual, and vocational. The development of these types of maturity is not automatic. We can evaluate our present state of maturity in each of these respects and work at acquiring related characteristics.

It is relatively easy to become familiar with what maturity is in its various forms, and even to recognize immaturity in others. However, it seems more difficult to recognize immaturity in ourselves—and even more difficult to overcome problems of immaturity. Growing as a person requires conscious, constant effort.

The maturity of individuals also affects interpersonal relationships, the subject of the next chapter.

Answers to "Maturity Self-Evaluation"
The answers to questions *a, j,* and *n* should be "No." The remaining questions are best answered "Yes." A "Somewhat" answer is not the best response to any of the questions, even though you are likely to have several such answers. Although there is no precise measure of maturity, mature young adults should respond as indicated to twelve or more of the questions. Fewer than eight such answers signal a degree of immaturity that might cause a person serious problems.

 Psychology In Practice

1. Observe a child less than six years old for at least half an hour. Write a description of the child's behavior and development as you interpret it. Observe as many types of development as you can.

2. Describe and demonstrate both mature and immature responses to various situations you are either involved in or observe during a week's time. With two other students, present a brief oral report to the class.

3. Ask two people you know well and respect how they believe moral standards develop. Also ask their opinions on situational rightness or wrongness. Tell each person you do not necessarily expect a discussion of personal moral standards.

Learning Activities

Turn to page 423 to complete the Learning Activities and Enrichment Activities for this chapter.

Notes

1. D. J. Levinson, *The Seasons of a Man's Life,* Alfred A. Knopf, New York, 1978. Reference from Kathleen S. Berger, *The Developing Person Through the Life Span,* 2nd ed., Worth Publishers, Inc., New York, 1988, p. 432.

2. Robert Havighurst, *Developmental Tasks and Education,* 3rd ed., David McKay, New York, 1972. Reference from Guy Lefrancois, *The Lifespan,* 4th ed., Wadsworth Publishing Company, Belmont, CA, 1993, pp. 48 and 49.

3. David G. Meyers, *Exploring Psychology,* Worth Publishers, Inc., New York, 1990, p. 488.

4. David Elkind, *The Hurried Child,* rev. ed., Addison-Wesley Publishing Company, Inc., Reading, MA, 1988, p. 202.

5. Bruce A. Baldwin, "Positive Parenting: How to Avoid Raising Cornucopia Kids," *PACE Magazine,* November 1988, p. 16.

6. Jane M. Lbder, "Adult Sibling Rivalry," *Psychology Today,* January/February 1993, p. 93.

7. Roger Gould, *Transformations: Growth and Change in Adult Life,* Simon & Schuster, New York, 1978, p. 39.

8. Erik H. Erikson, *Childhood and Society,* 2nd ed., W. W. Norton & Company, Inc., New York, 1963, p. 273.

9. Lawrence Kohlberg, "Moral Stages and Moralization: The Cognitive-Developmental Approach," In T. Lickona (ed.), *Moral Development and Behavior: Theory, Research, and Social Issues,* Holt, Rinehart and Winston, New York, 1976, pp. 34 and 35.

10. Laura E. Berk, *Infants, Children, and Adolescents,* Allyn & Bacon, Boston, 1993, p. 582.

11. James W. Vander Zanden, *Human Development,* 4th ed., Alfred A. Knopf, New York, 1989, p. 493.

12. Paul J. Gelinas, *Coping With Your Emotions,* The Rosen Publishing Group, Inc., New York, 1989, p. 10.

12 Interpersonal Relationships

Learning Objectives

After completing this chapter, you will be able to do the following:

1. Describe an example of how an interpersonal relationship might develop from Stage 1 to Stage 4, according to Bradley and Baird.
2. Suggest ways in which two different people might deal with their shyness in particular situations.
3. Contrast assertiveness and aggressiveness by describing both types of reactions in a problem situation.
4. Describe the encouragement you could give a close friend who is feeling "down" about leaving friends for a job in another state.
5. Identify two ways a person might enlarge the open area of his or her Johari Window and explain why this could be desirable.
6. Compare a real home you consider reasonably happy with the characteristics of a happy home given in the chapter, and state your conclusion about the comparison.
7. Identify a group to which you might like to belong in the future and explain how you might use past experience or what you might do now to prepare yourself to become an active member of that group in the future.

> 66*Before I built a wall I'd ask to know*
> *What I was walling in or walling out,*
> *And to whom I was like to give offense.*
> *Something there is that doesn't love a wall,*
> *That wants it down.*99
>
> ROBERT FROST
> *poet*

Each of us comes into contact with many people every day. We make choices about the quantity and quality of relationships we develop, and the depth of each relationship differs from person to person.

Satisfying relationships with other human beings are important to the purposes and happiness in the lives of most people. Nearly every individual's life is interwoven with the lives of others. Some of our best human activities have become a network of shared experiences. Many contacts with others are casual. Some of your contacts with others are continued associations, whereby people get to know things *about* each other but do not get to know the inner person. A few are close, special interpersonal relationships.

WE HAVE A SOCIAL NATURE

The need for human interaction begins at birth. Newborns start their lives with the need for human contact and support. They need warm human attention in addition to satisfaction of their physical needs.

An infant's attachment to his or her primary caregiver results in his or her first personal relationship. A **relationship** can be defined as human interaction that is more lasting than mere contact with another person. It involves feelings between two people, although these are not always positive or easy to deal with.

HOW DO INTERPERSONAL RELATIONSHIPS DEVELOP?

It would not be difficult for you to think of at least three different people with whom you have different types of relationships. How did these relationships develop? Bradley and Baird, authors of works in the area of communications, explain this development in terms of six stages through which various types of relationships develop.[1] These are shown on page 283.

According to these authors, "It is important to note that relatively few relationships occur at the most intimate levels." Moreover, a relationship can cease to exist at any stage. That is, although we have many relationships at the first stage, we have considerably fewer at the second level. Only one or two may reach intimacy. This means that first there must be *perceived perception* or awareness of one another. (He's looking at me!) This first contact may result in either a friendly smile or an embarrassed gesture of turning your attention in another direction. On the first day of a class, for example, you are naturally curious about who else is taking the course. So you look around and perceive who else is present. (Remember that perception can involve any of the senses, but at this point you are primarily using your sense of sight.) There may be some people in the group who don't interest you at first sight; others look like people you might like to get to know better. With some of the people, the relationship may stay at the perceived perception stage. With others, during the coming weeks of the class, you will move on to other stages.

Before the class has met for very many sessions, you may be *greeting* some class members—and perhaps the teacher. You may say "Hi" to the person who sits next to you, for example. This may be just to be friendly or you may be interested in getting to know the person better, or moving on to Stage 3. "How are you today?" or "It's a nice day, isn't it?" are examples of *clichés* or social expressions without much intended meaning.

After the class has met for a few weeks, members of the group are getting to know one another better, and you are probably saying "Hello" to more peo-

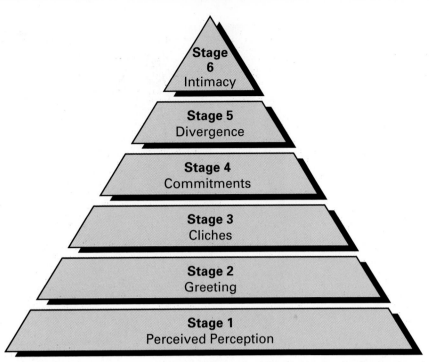

From Patricia Hayes Bradley and John E. Baird, Jr., *Communication for Business and the Professions,* 2d ed., Copyright © 1983 W. C. Brown Communications, Inc. , Dubuque, Iowa. All rights reserved. Reprinted by permission.

ple and carrying on small talk with various members of the group. Interrelationship at this stage is friendly but rather impersonal. It involves greetings and clichés but does not involve sharing of how we feel, which is a characteristic of Stage 4.

It is generally considered desirable to be able to open and carry on casual conversation with people we don't know very well. You may be seated next to them at a club meeting or attend the same social function. Everyone is more comfortable when people can talk to each other.

Stage 4, however, involves closer relationships. When we make *commitments* we are in a sense telling others that we care about them and that they can depend on us, at least to a degree. If we set up a car pool with Mark and Anna, for example, we are making a commitment. So are they. We can also make more personal commitments that do not involve written or verbal agreements but that are understood. Even quite regularly eating lunch with the same people is an understood commitment. If you didn't show up at lunch for a few days, these people would become concerned. They care about you and hope that you aren't ill or that you don't have some other serious problem.

Stage 5, or the *divergence* stage, may be defined as a crossroads or possible turning point of the relationship. Bradley and Baird describe this stage by saying:

> This stage really represents a crossroads for the relationship, determining whether it will proceed to the next stage or recede to Stage 4. As the participants become more secure in their relationship, they also become more willing to express their true feelings. Disagreements, arguments, frank

The beginning of friendship includes the discovery of mutual interests and feelings.

discussions, and expressions of strong feelings typically occur as a consequence, and the relationship undergoes examination and may be threatened. How each person reacts to these expressions determines whether involvement will increase to Stage 6 or revert to Stage 4.[2]

The divergence stage, then, does not seem to be a lasting stage. At this stage Maria and Richardo, who have been dating, might decide to break up. Or a new family in the neighborhood, who had become friendly with their next door neighbors, may decide that they would not like to become close friends with them. They may, therefore, become more casual in their greetings and look for others with whom they would be more compatible as a family.

It is likely by this time that you have noticed some similarity between this human relationship pyramid and Maslow's hierarchy of motives, discussed in Chapter 3. You may recall that not everyone reaches self-actualization in Maslow's hierarchy. So, too, not everyone establishes relationships that can be called intimate, according to Bradley and Baird. An explanation of why this is difficult for some persons was discussed in Chapter 11, in what was called psychosocial development. *Intimacy* involves a very close, sharing, revealing relationship. We allow certain people to know us as we are and are confident they will accept us for what we are. For this to happen we must be psychologically capable of forming such close sharing relationships and we must want to develop such relationships with people who are special to us. They may be persons of the opposite sex, best friends, or members of one's family. Some sisters, for example, have a "best friend" relationship; others share a family relationship but do not have intimacy. Bradley and Baird's explanation of this stage is:

At this level the participants express true feelings without fear while accepting and respecting the other's feelings. They confide in one another, support each other, contribute to each other's growth—indeed, they love each other. At this point, then, the maximum of attraction and involvement has been achieved.[3]

SOLITUDE OR LONELINESS

We all know what it is to be alone. Some of us like to be alone more than others. Well-adjusted people appreciate and enjoy a degree of aloneness. But nobody wants to be lonely. Solitude means to be alone, which may be either desirable or undesirable. Loneliness is unwanted, unpleasant aloneness or a sense of lacking in interpersonal relationships. We might say aloneness is physical, whereas loneliness is psychological. A young adult might move to a large city after graduating from a community college in a much smaller locality, for example. She might be aware of many people in her environment, but she may feel lonely as she has not had the time or opportunity as yet to develop any close interpersonal relationships.

The young graduate might also feel lonesome, a keen sense of missing members of her family and friends back home. This is an emotion that most people experience at some time in their lives, but it can be adjusted to with time and the effort to meet people and make new friends. The graduate is experiencing what R. Evans and L. Hubbs-Tait, in their book, *Applying Psychology in Today's World,* call situational loneliness.[4] Her situation is temporary and can be expected to improve as time goes on.

Evans and Hubbs-Tait also identify chronic loneliness. This could be described as a continuing sense of being isolated from other caring human beings. Individuals may experience chronic loneliness because they never established meaningful relationships or perhaps as the result of a drastic, but relatively permanent, change in their life-style. They may be widows or widowers, persons in nursing homes, or others who live alone in their own homes with very little social contact. Refugees may also experience extreme loneliness for relatives and friends left behind. Moreover, they may greatly miss their homeland and former way of life.

Many other people, however, are lonely unnecessarily. They may expect others to make the total effort for human interaction. People who say "Nobody calls me" or "They never come to see me" ignore the fact that they can call other people or invite other people to visit. If they are able, they can make more of an effort to visit others. Some of this type of loneliness is caused by lack of effort, and some of it is caused by lack of confidence in oneself as a likable person.

Self-understanding and self-acceptance are **intrapersonal** factors, or experiences *within* ourselves. Our relationships with others are **interpersonal.** They are closely related, however. People who have difficulty accepting themselves are likely to have difficulty relating to others as well. If you like yourself, you are more likely to like other people and feel comfortable with them.

SHYNESS

You may know from your own experience what it is to be shy, because nearly eighty per cent of the people in a survey by P.G. Zimbardo, a noted psychologist and an authority on the subject of shyness, reported being shy at some time in their lives. Different people experience shyness in different ways and to different degrees. But what is shyness generally? According to V. Walker and L. Brokaw, shyness involves feelings, physical reactions, and thoughts. They explain each of these as follows:

- Feelings: Feelings associated with shyness include anxiety, insecurity, stress, loneliness, mistrust, embarrassment, tension, fear, confusion, and so on.
- Physical reactions: Physical reactions associated with shyness include nausea, butterflies in the stomach, shaking, perspiring, pounding heart, feeling faint, blushing, and so on.
- Thoughts: Thoughts associated with shyness include: I'm not an interesting person," "I'm not as good as they are," "They won't like me," "I lack self-confidence," "I don't have the social skills," and so on.[5]

Shyness is excessive self-consciousness. Shy persons give too much attention to themselves and to their concerns about how other people will react to them. Essentially, shyness refers to a lack of self-confidence that results in being afraid to become involved with others.

It may take time for some people to overcome shyness, however. It can also be painful to be shy. It can be difficult for some people, for example, just to say "Good Morning." Being shy is not the same as being an introvert, as dis-

ZIGGY Copyright ZIGGY AND FRIENDS, INC. Dist. by UNIVERSAL PRESS SYNDICATE. Reprinted with permission. All rights reserved.

cussed in Chapter 2, "Self-Concept and Personality." You may recall that an introvert *likes* to do things alone; an introvert enjoys more solitude than an extrovert. Both an introvert and a shy person may go about their work with little contact with other people. The basic difference is in how they feel about themselves and what they would like to be doing. Shy persons are lonely, as discussed earlier in this unit. They may eat by themselves rather than approach someone to have lunch together. These people on the exterior may seem snobbish, or the type of people who think they are better than others. In actuality they may feel inferior.

People who are shy experience the most difficulty in (1) associations with strangers, (2) unfamiliar situations in which they feel inadequate, and (3) associations with the opposite sex. If you consider yourself shy, you can overcome it. In fact, it could be the best thing you do for yourself, as it will affect many different types of relationships the rest of your life. Following are a few suggestions for overcoming shyness and gaining confidence in yourself.

- Get your mind off yourself; pay more attention to others. Ask about their interests or, if you don't know them well, about the current situation or events.
- Pay enough attention to your appearance to look acceptable and "fit in," and then don't worry about it. Don't call negative attention to your appearance or your clothes. Accept compliments with a thank-you or some other appreciative statement.
- Remember that nobody's perfect. You don't notice minor flaws and imperfections in others, and they, for the most part, aren't paying attention to yours. We should be aware of them and learn from them, but we should realize it is human to make some mistakes. We should try to avoid mistakes, and correct those we make as best we can, but we should recognize that everyone makes mistakes.
- Cultivate the belief that every human being has intrinsic worth—you are important just because you exist. The behavior of some people is more acceptable on the job and in society than that of others, but the person has value.
- Make an effort to meet new people, even if it isn't easy at first. Don't avoid going to social events, such as parties or weddings, because "I won't know anybody." If one person seems unfriendly, approach someone else. Be friendly.
- Consider taking an assertiveness class. Assertiveness will be discussed in the next section of this chapter. It will help you to have more confidence in yourself and improve your relationships with others.

There are many other ideas for overcoming shyness. You can do it; you owe it to yourself. Let the world get to know who you really are. If you do not consider yourself shy, be open and responsive to those who are. You may be glad you did. The following section will help you understand yourself better in this respect.

 What would you SAY? If someone said to you, "How you act toward others reveals more about how you feel about yourself than about how you feel about them."

YOUR JOHARI WINDOW

There are some things that you know about yourself that other people don't know, aren't there? Could there also be some things that others know about you that you don't know about yourself? You are even more complicated than that. This idea of "who knows what about you?" can be better understood through the Johari Window, designed by Joseph Luft and Harrington Ingham. The word "Johari" was formed from their two first names. The four areas of the window, as shown below, represent four areas of who you are in terms of what is known or unknown about you.[6]

If you follow both the vertical and horizontal identifications of the areas of the window it can be interpreted as the following:

Open area	Known to self; Known to others
Blind area	Not known to self; Known to others
Hidden area	Known to self; Not known to others
Unknown area	Not known to self; Not known to others

The following example will give us further understanding of these areas. Brad wanted the promotion to sales manager very badly. The promotion, however, was given to Karen, who had two years fewer experience with the company than Brad. Karen and a number of others knew that Brad wanted the job (open area). It was also commonly known that Brad probably wouldn't get the promotion because he talked too freely about confidential company business matters. Brad, however, was not aware that this was a problem that was standing in his way (blind area). Brad had hoped that Karen would leave the company and join a competitor before this promotion came up, although she never mentioned this to anyone (hidden area).

Brad is actually jealous of Karen, but he is unaware of this. Brad has repressed his feelings of jealousy because it is unacceptable to him to be jealous of another person's success (unknown area). At the department meeting, in

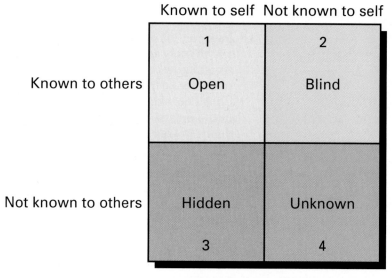

The Johari Window

fact, Brad congratulated Karen on the promotion and pledged his cooperation (open area again). One's unknown area could also refer to potential that one has that neither the individual nor others are aware of.

The Johari Window can be used as a means of increasing self-awareness and improving relationships with others by sharing who we are. This is often referred to as self-disclosure. J. C. Pearson and P. E. Nelson, in *Understanding and Sharing,* have the following to say: "Self-disclosure includes statements a person makes about himself or herself that another person would be unlikely to know or discover." They go on to say, "Self-disclosure is important for two reasons. First, it allows us to establish more meaningful relationships with others. Second, self-disclosure allows us to establish more positive attitudes toward ourselves and others."[7] Self-disclosure would be involved in the intimacy level of the relationship pyramid discussed earlier. Disclosing information about ourselves will usually allow others to be more comfortable in doing the same, and relationships will grow.

The degree to which we share ourselves with others differs with respect not only to those with whom we are sharing but also to who we are as individuals. The more self-confidence we acquire, personally and in our careers, the more open we will be willing to be with others. We will have less need to be self-protective and defensive. Naturally, as mentioned earlier, we don't need or want the same degree of openness with everyone. As we enlarge one area of the window, other areas become smaller. The large window (square) is representative of who we are as a person.

 What would you SAY? What would you say to a person who asks you a question, the answer to which you do not care to share with that person?

ASSERTIVENESS

Ideas about assertiveness vary. Some people consider it a threat. Others consider it a challenge. It is most accurately thought of in terms of rights. **Assertiveness** refers to protecting your own rights in a situation without intending to harm others or to abuse their rights. Some people confuse assertiveness with aggressiveness. There is an important difference, however. **Aggressiveness** refers to taking advantage of other people, thus abusing their rights. (Being aggressive can also mean being ambitious and a "go-getter" in a competitive sense, but that is not the meaning intended here). Assertiveness is related to aggressiveness in the sense that assertive people do not allow themselves to be victimized by the aggression of others. John M. Reardon, of Phoenix Process Consultants, gives us the following comparisons of how people tend to act out conflict:

Passively	Assertively	Aggressively
Fear: "I won't get what I want."	"I deserve what I want."	Fear: "I won't get what I want."
"So I'll stop now before I get disappointed	"So, I'll say or ask for what I want."	"So, I'll take what I want before the others do."
Leads to: Depression	Leads to: Negotiation	Leads to: Hostility[8]

Becoming an Assertive Person

If you sincerely believe that others take advantage of you, what can you do about it? It isn't easy to protect yourself without sometimes taking advantage of or hurting others in some way. But you are entitled to protect yourself as much as possible from being hurt by others, intentionally or unintentionally. A maxim worth applying is "Try not to hurt anybody, including yourself." Everybody has rights that should be respected. Nobody likes to get hurt. Some guidelines for being assertive without being aggressive follow.

Know Yourself   As we discussed in Chapter 2, "Self-Concept and Personality," self-knowledge and self-understanding go beyond the mere facts of who you are. Self-knowledge is essential to meaningful living and rewarding relationships with others.

Accept Yourself   You are unique. You should not only recognize this but also appreciate it. This does not mean you cannot grow in a number of respects or that you cannot improve yourself in a number of ways. But you should not be dissatisfied with yourself to the point where you feel inferior or worthless. If you have trouble accepting yourself, you can hardly expect others to accept you. If you learn to be comfortable with yourself, you will have more satisfying relationships with others. Being comfortable is not, however, a matter of being smug or conceited. Equality among human beings must extend in both directions.

Express Yourself   The inability to express what you think and feel can lead to a kind of victimization. You can learn to say what you like or don't like—what you want to do or don't want to do—without antagonizing others. Others may not be happy when you don't give in to their ways, but that's their problem. People who have become accustomed to being aggressive do not like it when their victims become assertive. You should be considerate and tactful. But you cannot always avoid disappointing others. You can learn to say no without feeling guilty. This is discussed by Herbert Fensterheim and Jean Baer in *Don't Say Yes When You Want to Say No.* You may also want to read Manuel J. Smith's book *When I Say No, I Feel Guilty.*

PEANUTS reprinted by permission of UFS, Inc.

"GOOD MORNING STUDENTS. I AM GOING TO BE YOUR TEACHER FOR THIS ASSERTIVENESS TRAINING COURSE... THAT IS... I MEAN... IF YOU DON'T MIND."

Expressing yourself does not mean that you must constantly give explanations or make up excuses. Neither does it mean that you must never say yes or offer explanations. **Discretion,** or good judgment depending on those involved and the situation, is always important in relationships.

Have you ever wanted to ask a question of your instructor or your supervisor but didn't because you thought it might be a dumb question? If you don't know something in such a situation, you have a right to ask and to receive an answer without ridicule. Anyone who belittles another person for asking a question is probably being defensive, as discussed in Chapter 8, "Coping with Stress." We cannot control the way other people respond to us, but we can control the way we feel about it and about ourselves. Nobody can make you feel inferior unless you allow him or her to.

The ability to accept and give compliments is related to the ability to accept yourself. But you also must accept others. Some people "put themselves down" in reacting to a compliment. If Ross tells Wendy that he thinks she sings beautifully, she should say, "Thank you, I enjoy singing," rather than "Oh, I'm not really that good." Some find it difficult to give compliments to others. If they feel inferior to begin with, it makes them feel even more inferior to build someone else up. A person who recognizes equality and the individual worth of all people can easily and sincerely both express and receive compliments.

Expect Respect   There is truth to the idea that people react to you largely according to what you expect. You should show that you care about yourself.

You should indicate through the way you dress and walk and act toward others that you expect consideration as another human being. It should not be that you consider yourself superior, of course.

Respect Others   If we are going to treat others as we would like to be treated, we show them respect. In reality, we can act respectfully without feeling respect, which is an attitude. But if we consider others as worthy and care about them and their concerns, we will treat them with the type of consideration we want for ourselves.

"Respect," in this discussion refers to accepting others as equals rather than relying on position or status. It would be foolish, however, not to recognize that some others actually have positions of authority over you. But you can still expect to be treated with the respect that every human being deserves and you can respect others in the same way.

Suggest Reasonable Solutions or Alternatives   We should let people know that we are interested in improving total situations rather than merely interested in defending our own rights. When workloads are inequitable, for example, the department is not functioning as efficiently as it might. Be tactful, however, in how you make suggestions. Instead of saying, "I know what would correct this problem in a hurry," one might say, "Have you considered the possibility of . . . ?" or "It might work better if we tried . . ." Remember that others are likely to become defensive if they feel they are attacked. We want to be assertive without becoming aggressive, as explained previously.

What would you SUGGEST?   If the department manager of a retail store offers you considerably less than you think you should get for a returned item, for which you do not have a sales receipt, what would you suggest?

THE BOND OF FRIENDSHIP

A person you know and recognize is an acquaintance, whereas a person with whom you have a continuing relationship is an associate. A person you know well, with whom you have a bond of mutual understanding, sharing, and affection, is a friend. An associate—a person with whom you work, for example—may also be a friend, but you do not form a bond of friendship with everyone you know.

A relationship that can be called a friendship must be voluntary. You cannot select your relatives; you may decide at least to tolerate certain neighbors; you may feel an obligation to work with someone you don't particularly like; but you can choose your friends.

Friendship develops over a period of time. You may meet someone at a party whom you immediately like. Your personalities seem to be compatible, and you discover that you have similar interests. You may remark, "We hit it off from the beginning." As you get to know the person better, you both will reveal additional personality characteristics, including both strengths and weaknesses, which are accepted as a part of that person. This sharing of ourselves helps strengthen the relationship. A bond of admiration, respect, and loyalty that is defined as friendship develops. In your intangible values, friendship may rate very high.

Who Are Your Friends?

You probably did not decide ahead of time that you and Lucia and José were going to become friends. Many friendships develop from continued contact with other persons. Co-workers, neighbors, and classmates, for example, often become close friends. However, you will not become close friends with all your co-workers, neighbors, or classmates. For one thing, relationships require time. You can be casual "friends" with many people, but generally people have a small number of close friends.

You may be aware that there are some differences in how males and females relate to friends of their own sex. Females are more apt to share personal problems and use more self-disclosure than do most males. Males, on the other hand, talk about shared interests and are more interested in doing things together. Let's not stereotype by assuming that all men are alike or all women are alike, but these general tendencies in relating to friends have been verified by research. Both males and females are supportive to their same-sex friends, however. Their ways of relating, to some degree, are just different.

Factors that lead to friendships are similar personality characteristics, common goals, similar backgrounds, interests, and values, and even similar difficulties or sorrows. Friends may include relatives, neighbors, and co-workers, but friendships are voluntary.

In addition to being voluntary, the following characteristics of friendship are common.

Friendship Is Understanding

To be understood is important to all of us. It would be unrealistic to expect everyone who knows us to understand us, however. And it isn't necessary that everyone understand us. But there is a bond that develops between people who know and appreciate each other's motives and values and who understand one another.

More human relations problems than we might realize are based on misunderstandings. Understanding one another involves much more than understanding the meaning of words. Some of the related causes and what we might do about them are discussed in the communication section later in this chapter. Friends have an understanding of one another that goes beyond ordinary means of communication, however. In fact, friends often have a good idea of how we feel without our telling them. **Empathy**—or understanding, to the best of our ability, what another person is experiencing—is easier with friends. Indications by others that they are at least attempting to understand what we are undergoing can support us in many aspects of life. It's also valued by friends to know that others support them even when they are unable to understand a particular experience. In other words, friends are there for us when we need them.

Friendship Is Accepting

A friend knows you well—in some ways better than you know yourself. Since everyone has strengths and weaknesses, good habits and bad ones, a friend may have to tolerate you when you are not at your best. Others may avoid you or ridicule you, but for the most part a friend accepts you as you are. Even good friends may disagree or have difficulties with their relationship, however. This is characteristic of all human contact, but a friendship can weather such moments. In fact, friendships can be strengthened by conflicts that might divide or permanently separate people who are not friends.

It is never advisable to be hypocritical, or to pretend to be something you are not. But there is a relaxation of self as well as a mutual acceptance in friendship that no other human relationship outside of one's family can claim.

Friends are also forgiving. As humans we can be selfish, thoughtless, even unintentionally hurtful at times. To forgive, and if possible to also forget, is a very difficult human experience. It is probably based on the need to protect one's positive self-concept and pride, but we must remember that a positive self-concept should also be realistic. It can be expected that we as humans, and our friends as humans, are not perfect. We should also be willing to apologize and seek the forgiveness of others if we have hurt them in some way.

In *How to Say Hard Things the Easy Way,* Richard Walters has this to say about apology:

> Apologizing is the corrective for an offense against another person. It is an act of strength. It is evidence of the maturity you already have, and it helps build greater personal maturity. It has great benefits, but unless you're different than the rest of us, you'll hate to do it. The greatest barrier to apologizing is embarrassment, or to use a word that is even uglier because it is more accurate, pride. We may mistakenly think apologizing is for the benefit of another person. To some extent it is, but when you apologize you are the one who gets the greatest rewards: release from guilt and shame, and from fear that you will be found out to be less than perfect or that the other person will retaliate against you. Apologizing is the best defense against retaliation.[9]

Apology and forgiveness should be sincere, of course. Empty words, to please others or to create some effect, are usually apparent and add insult to injury. This is no way to treat any other human being, and certainly not someone we call a friend.

There is a relaxation of self and a mutual acceptance in friendship that no other human relationship outside of one's family can claim.

Friendship Is Caring

There are different kinds and different degrees of caring. We can care in a sense about all other human beings. We can care to a degree about anyone we know. If you read in the local newspaper than an acquaintance has had an accident, you may think, "That's too bad" and hope that the person isn't seriously hurt. If a friend has an accident, you probably immediately inquire about your friend's condition and whether you can be of any help. You may go to see your friend and communicate your caring.

We may care about friends in different ways, depending on differences in age or sex. Caring can be experienced and expressed as different kinds of love. You may consider the old man across the street your friend and may have deep affection for him. You probably have a friend of your own age and sex for whom you care deeply. You can openly tell this person and others how much you care about him or her without being embarrassed. Friendships with persons of the opposite sex also can be platonic, or close but nonsexual in nature. Perhaps only the people involved in such a relationship can really understand it, but that is friendship, nonetheless.

Whatever the degree or type of mutual affection between you and others, there can be no substitute for friendship.

What do you THINK?

Does it ever really matter whether other people understand how you feel about a particular person? Why or why not?

Friendship Is Sharing

We may give our chosen friends gifts on their birthdays or other special occasions. They, in turn, may give us gifts. The monetary value of such gifts is not really important, however, for we also appreciate the things they do or make just for us. We also treasure gifts that have been selected to suit a special interest, which only a friend would know about. It wouldn't matter to us if the items were obtained at a flea market or rummage sale. The important thing is that a friend saw the item and thought of us.

We may be very good friends with others, however, and not exchange any gifts at all. Friendship itself is a gift. We can share ourselves and our time. There is a sense of trust in a friendship that allows others to know our needs and makes it possible to respond to one another's needs. This makes many types of sharing possible.

Old Friends and New

Most people do not remain within a small circle of acquaintances and friends throughout their lives. Modern men and women will doubtless move about in their lifetimes, often to change employment or go on vacations. Everyone thus makes new acquaintances and has the opportunity to develop new friendships.

You may have qualms about leaving behind old friends and meeting new ones as you change job locations or depart for further education or training. After several such experiences, however, most people conclude that they have gained rather than lost. You do not have to drop previous friendships to establish new ones. You may see old friends less, but bonds of friendship are durable; they can be maintained across thousands of miles and over decades of time.

Making new acquaintances and developing friendships can be a lifelong adventure. The better you understand yourself and others, the easier it will be for you to relate to others in social experiences. You will never know two people in exactly the same way, but you will discover that people have much in common the world over. Possibilities for mutually satisfying friendships are everywhere.

GROUP ACTIVITY

The geographic size of the United States and the global community, and the complexity of modern living have caused many people to feel insignificant and alone. They lack a sense of importance and belonging that is important to one's sense of psychological security. One of the reasons people join groups is to offset this sense of emptiness and satisfy emotional needs. There are numerous other reasons why people form or join groups, of course.

People working together can accomplish objectives that they cannot accomplish individually. "The whole is more than the sum of its parts" is true of a group. A **group** can be defined as a number of people with common backgrounds, interests, or concerns who interact with one another on a regular basis for a common purpose. We probably belong to more groups than we realize.

Types of Groups

Groups can pertain to family, ethnic background, religion, volunteer activities, politics, careers, recreation, and other responsibilities and special interests. There has also been a recent growth of groups for support of emotional needs and personal problems. Divorced people, single parents, parents of children with specific problems, people with terminal illnesses, alcoholics, and family members of alcoholics are examples of those who benefit from such support groups. They meet with others who have had similar experiences or undergone crises in order to learn to deal with their feelings, to receive emotional support, or to find resources for outside help. These groups also allow individuals to vent frustrations, to learn that they are not alone in their experiences, and to gain insight into improving the quality of their lives.

There are also numerous groups seeking to bring about social change. Among the reasons for interest in the future, as we observed in Chapter 1, was a commitment to help bring about desired change or to attempt to avoid undesirable change. The interests of one group don't always agree with the interests of another, but at least people are working for or against what they believe to be or not to be in their best interests—and usually the interests of the society as a whole. Without those who are willing to work for such causes as peace, efficiency and equity in government, the environment, better educational systems, and safer communities and cities, the world in which we live "could and would be worse." The term "silent majority" was coined to represent those in society who may have good ideas and intentions but who allow a minority of those who are vocal and active to determine actual outcomes.

Family: Characteristics of Happy Homes Your family may not be the first group you would identify as one to which you belong, but it does come under the definition of group, doesn't it? And it can be the most valued group membership we have. Changes in the family were discussed in Chapter 1, and references to family are included in additional chapters in this book. In fact, we can hardly discuss interpersonal relationships without including our relationships with members of our families.

When we think of family, most of us think of home. The word itself can bring forth a wide range of memories and emotional reactions. Some of us may have come from unhappy homes for whatever reason, but each of us can resolve to do our best to make our own homes and family relationships happy now and in the future. Let's consider then, some characteristics of a happy home.

A traditional Navajo family share a meal.

In a happy home there is a bond of love made up of dedication to common goals, interest in the endeavors of individual members, and respect for one another. There is a sharing of hopes and fears, sorrows and joys. A happy home, regardless of the type of house, is a special place where each member is free to bring friends and feels proud to introduce them to members of the family.

In a happy home there is open communication between husband and wife, between parents and children, and between siblings. This communication may not always be complimentary and agreeable, but each individual appreciates honest self-expression. Each member of a happy family has a sense of responsibility to the others. They share many things in common, and all members do their share. Children develop an increasing amount of independence in the process of growing up, but they also experience the benefits of people doing things for one another. This can be a practical arrangement, but in a family it is the reciprocal behavior of people who care about, as well as for, one another.

Ethnic   The United States today includes many **ethnic** groups whose members identify with one another because of common language, customs, and values. For many years in American history there was a tendency to try to break down or deny ethnic barriers and promote "Americanization." In recent years there has been evidence of renewed sense of pride in the ethnic group to which one belongs. Every large city contains diverse ethnic groups.

Religious   Although religious beliefs about the origin of human life, one's purpose on earth, and one's final destiny vary greatly, active members of all religious denominations can be equally sincere and can respect the beliefs and practices of one another.

Related to religious groups is the question of what a cult is and why people join cults. Those who have studied cults and their questionable hold on people believe that the need to belong and to identify with a common cause leads many lonely persons into a relationship with others that destroys their individuality.

Volunteer   Much of what is accomplished by groups is achieved through the willingness of individuals to join with others to work for a worthy cause. In the past, most volunteer work was done by middle-aged women who were looking for ways to fill their time usefully, after their families were grown. Now many women are working outside their homes and, therefore, have less free time. Men and women increasingly volunteer some of their free time, however, to schools, churches, hospitals, and other community activities and programs. Many students and retired persons also are involved in volunteer services.

Any group that bases its membership on volunteers must have purposes considered worthy by society. Examples of such groups that depend on volunteers are the United States Armed Services, the Peace Corps, the American Cancer Society, Big Brothers and Big Sisters, Meals on Wheels, disaster relief projects, church activities, and political campaigns, among many others.

The benefits of volunteerism, as with other types of group activity, can be many. Objectives of the group are accomplished, and in many cases it is only through volunteers that a group can function at all. There are few volunteers who report having received no benefits themselves. But what may be satisfying for one person may not be so for another. Everyone has something to offer, even if it is only a little time or money. Those who criticize all charitable groups or volunteer workers may only be rationalizing their own selfish refusal to help others.

Political   Citizens in a democracy are responsible for the society in which they live. They are also affected by the whole of the society of which they are part. As citizens, therefore, we have both an obligation and an opportunity to express ourselves and to be involved in civic affairs. It is through political action, which can be the business of everyone, that the most qualified people can function in elective government offices. A major element of politics is the political party. The two major parties in the United States today are the Democratic and Republican parties. Although many Americans still affiliate with a political party, independents are growing in number. This was evident in the 1992 presidential election, when Ross Perot received nearly 19 percent of the popular vote.

Recreational   Increased leisure time has given Americans more opportunity for recreation, and our pleasures seem to be greater when we can share them with others. As a result, the membership lists of sports teams and recreational and travel clubs have grown. In some parts of the country seasonal changes make it possible for club members to water-ski in the summer and to snow ski in the winter.

If a group's activities are intended to provide recreation, people should not join just because everyone else is doing so. And if an activity fails or ceases to provide relaxation and enjoyment, it should be discontinued. Some types of recreation can become so organized that they lose their sense of spontaneous pleasure and fun. Dropping out of any group, however, should be timed properly so that the activities of the whole group are not disrupted. For example, it is unfair for a person to quit a team in the middle of the season, unless it is for a reason acceptable to the rest of the team.

All the major sports have professional teams that are supported by fans, but there also are thousands of amateur teams that play for their own relaxation and recreation. Some people begin an activity such as baseball for recreation and then continue it as a profession. In their opinion, the ability to function with other members of the team is as important as one's own pleasure and ability.

What would you SUGGEST? If a person your age, who was new to your community, expressed interest in joining a group to which he or she could make a contribution, what would you suggest?

Your Group-o-Gram

The illustration shown below is an example of a group-o-gram, which illustrates an individual's past and present group membership and ambitions for

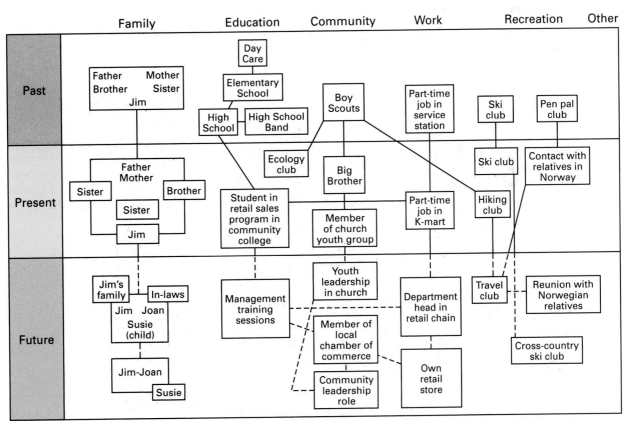

A Group-O-Gram for Jim at Age 20

future group memberships and activities. A group-o-gram is a means of examining the interrelatedness and value of group activities in your life. Group-o-grams vary as greatly as people do; some of them are extremely complex.

Notice in the illustration that types of groups are listed across the top, and there is space for additional types. Note also that lines from one group to another cross over into different types of group. Broken lines are used in the "Future" section of the group-o-gram.

Developing a group-o-gram will help you to check whether the groups you have belonged to in the past are a useful foundation for groups you now belong to or would like to belong to in the future. For example, belonging to the Boy Scouts as a young boy has led Jim into Big Brother activities at present. Both groups will be helpful to him in the future as a youth leader in his church and as a community leader. The group-o-gram also will indicate whether some voluntary groups you belong to now should be dropped in order to give you time and resources to devote to some more important activity. Jim decided to drop out of the local music group in order to give more time to his studies. A group-o-gram also will help you see whether there are groups to which you would like to belong in the future and whether belonging to a particular group now might be helpful toward becoming a member of the other groups. Since Jim would like to operate his own retail business in the future, he is making use of both his past and his present work experience in his studies of retail sales. Both his experience and his education should help him in his goal of becoming a department head in a retail chain after he graduates. In turn, such group experience will be helpful to him in his own business in the future.

Although this illustration may look complex, it is only a sample of what it might be. You might want to develop your own group-o-gram on a large sheet of paper. The value of membership in particular groups is not indicated in the illustration, but you should consider that factor in developing your group-o-gram. After beginning with the "Family" column, there is no particular direction in which you should proceed. Some students like to begin by determining their ambitions for the future and then considering what past and present experiences will help them achieve their goals. Others prefer to begin with the past and then proceed to the present and future. Still others move about randomly in developing a group-o-gram, but it has an organized structure when it is completed. The width of the Past, Present, and Future sections should also be determined by where you are in your life span.

EFFECTIVE COMMUNICATION

The ability to communicate is a highly valued human characteristic. Also, the inability to communicate effectively has often been identified as one of the greatest problems in interpersonal relationships. Misunderstandings lead to feelings of fear, anger, and tension between people. These, in turn, block growth of the relationship or cause it to deteriorate. Although some misunderstandings are to be expected, we can all improve our ability to communicate.

The educational program in which you are now involved very likely includes at least one course in some form of communication. The ability to communicate effectively is highly valued by employers and is often mentioned by former students as an important part of the preparation for their jobs. Employers, as well as counselors, parents, and couples, are becoming more aware of the importance of communication. Companies often hire professionals to come to their workplace to teach all levels of their employees better communication skills. Practical application of communications skills as well as problems related to ineffective communications on the job will be discussed in the next chapter, "Human Relations at Work."

Communication consists of a variety of modes or ways of communicating. Although both written communication and technological communication involving computers and other electronic devices are an essential part of our lives and work, they will not be included in our discussion here. Emphasis will be primarily on oral communication, nonverbal messages, and listening problems and skills.

Oral Communication

Oral communication, or speaking, has a number of advantages over written communication. It is more personal and in most cases it is easier, although direct oral communication is sometimes avoided when there are psychological factors that can be disturbing to those involved. One of the disadvantages of oral communication is that one does not have a record of what has been communicated, assuming recording devices are not used. For this reason, there can be more misunderstanding with speaking than with putting information and instructions in writing. To counteract this somewhat, oral communication has tone of voice, facial expression, and body language that contribute to meaning. These factors, and others, should be taken into consideration in deciding what mode of communication to use in a particular situation.

Each of us has the right and the responsibility to share our thoughts and feelings in a relationship that is important to us. But you may have heard statements such as "You should have told me" and the response, "I was afraid you wouldn't listen" or "I knew you would get angry." Often statements like these cause a defensive reaction in both people and may lead to further statements such as "See, you are angry," or "You never listen when I try to tell you something." Discussions including such statements usually have a very high emotional content and do not help to resolve an issue.

The "I's" have it. We are all responsible for our own thoughts, feelings, and actions. However, we are not responsible for those of others nor are they responsible for ours. Therefore, it is much more productive in a discussion to begin statements with "I."

"I feel angry."

"I thought the game was at 7 P.M."

"I want to go skating after dinner."

"I am disappointed that you're watching TV when I'm talking to you."

"I" statements express your feelings, thoughts, desires, and perceptions. We can only report these things about ourselves and let others do the same. Statements like "You are angry," or "You make me angry," do not allow other persons opportunity to share their feelings and are ways of avoiding responsibility for our feelings. There are times when we have the right to say we are angry. We need to take responsibility for our feelings and express ourselves honestly, but with consideration for others.

Nonverbal Communication

"I didn't say that!"

"You didn't have to. I got your message from the way you looked."

If you haven't been involved in similar exchanges, you can probably still identify with what is going on between these two people. Nonverbal communication includes facial expressions, body postures and movements, and overall physical appearance. Often nonverbal messages contradict what we are saying. If so, our listeners/observers are more likely to believe the nonverbal message. It is true that nonverbal messages can be unintentional and can be misinterpreted, but we should be aware that they are messages, nonetheless. In "Saving Relationships: The Power of the Unpredictable," in *Psychology Today,* the authors state, "What gets lost is that all behavior is communicative. Even silence conveys some message. There is no such thing as *not* communicating."[10] It would be well for us to keep this in mind both as we attempt to understand others and also as others are interpreting our reactions to them.

Barriers to Communication

You may have identified some barriers to communication in preceding discussions, inasmuch as anything that interferes with the intent of communications

ZIGGY copyright ZIGGY AND FRIENDS, INC. Dist. by UNIVERSAL PRESS SYNDICATE. Reprinted with permission. All rights reserved.

can be considered a barrier. There are a number of additional barriers that can be associated with content of earlier chapters. Do you recall factors that affect perception from Chapter 4? Our past experience and perceptual set, related to our immediate needs or wants, for example, affect not only our perception but also how we communicate. Two people may have a problem agreeing on how to solve a problem, each attempting to convince the other, because they are interpreting the situation differently. Attitudes also affect our communications with others. Attitudes, you recall, are composed of what we think and how we feel about people, things, situations, or experiences. If we have a negative attitude toward a person or toward what a person is proposing, it is obvious it is going to affect our communication with that person. Another chapter that deals with creating barriers is Chapter 8, "Coping with Stress." A person under stress, for example, has difficulty communicating objectively and constructively. Another example from that chapter relates to coping mechanisms. A person who is being defensive is likely to take casual comments as personal criticism and is therefore not open to another person's intended message. Although various types of language difficulties can also be barriers, it is the psychological barriers such as those mentioned that cause the most problems.

Barriers to communication are often referred to as "noise." However, this is not the type of noise that interferes with our hearing. It could include such disturbance, but it also includes any conditions, external or internal, that interfere with understanding. And understanding is essential to sending and receiving messages with any degree of accuracy.

One way we can attempt to remove some of the barriers to communication is to ask questions. The more specific the question, the easier it is for the other person to give further information. "How does that make you feel?" "What do you want to do about the leaky faucet?" or "When do you need this done?" Questions starting with who, what, when, and how—relating to specific actions, ideas, feeling and reported information—usually lead to more productive discussion and effective problem solving. We have to be careful about asking too many questions, the answers to which should be obvious, however. Also, "Why?" questions can cause some people to react defensively, as they may be interpreted as criticism. A number of factors—to whom we are speaking, the subject, and the total situation—should be taken into consideration in effective communication.

Are You Listening?

Listening is the receiving end of communication that helps us make sense of our interaction with others. Listening involves paying attention in a number of ways. None of us likes to talk to someone if we think that person isn't listening. There are a number reasons for ineffective listening, which are the foundation for the following suggestions for improving your listening skills.

Suggestions for Better Listening

- Know why you are listening. We listen to learn, to evaluate, to enjoy and relax, or to give others attention.
- Become actively involved in listening. Respond with facial expression and body language. Be careful about interrupting, but ask questions if necessary.

PEANUTS reprinted by permission of UFS, Inc.

- If you are listening to learn or evaluate, try to determine the main idea of the message. Listen for ideas and relate facts to ideas rather than paying attention to facts alone. Separate facts from opinion. Some people would like you to accept their opinions as facts.
- Relate what you are hearing to your past experience. This will make what you are hearing more meaningful. Also relate it to your present and future needs and interests. Determine whether you can use it in any way.
- Do not jump to conclusions about what the person is going to say. Hear him or her out, if time permits, even if you think you are going to disagree. We have a tendency to use the perceptual principle of closure in listening.
- Be flexible. Adjust your manner of listening to your purpose and the situation. Some listening, perhaps to music, should be for pleasure and relaxation. Listening for evaluation, on the other hand, requires critical thinking—comparison of strengths and weaknesses or advantages and disadvantages of action. Listening to give attention to others, on the other hand, is a courtesy. Giving someone our attention at times is the kindest thing we can do for them.

Effective communication does not always lead to getting what you want or satisfying others. However, a clear, well-intended message from a speaker and receptive listening improve most communication efforts and results. It is important to understand each other even when we don't agree. We can live and work together more productively when we understand one another and can tolerate or work out differences in a constructive way.

INTERPERSONAL GROWTH

People have to make some effort to put variety into their social experiences. It is easier to do the same old things with the same people. These may be worthwhile experiences, but they are limiting and do not permit social growth. People who do not know what to do on weekends, for example, can find out about social activities and events in their community or area and perhaps gain new experiences and make some new acquaintances. Such adventures are not always considered rewarding, but the objective is not becoming bored because "there was nothing to do."

Careful listening demands concentration, attention, and commitment.

The apprehensiveness you may feel about meeting people in new situations, at school, on the job, or in a new neighborhood stems from your basic need for acceptance and security. An interest in meeting new people, on the other hand, stems from the need for variety and new experiences. You can have ambivalent, or mixed, feelings, therefore, about meeting new people. It is possible for you to experience both anxiety and pleasant expectation at the same time.

Our daily lives involve a variety of interpersonal relationships. The lives of all of us also include some special occasions, such as birthdays, holidays, or milestones in education or work. We also attend the special-occasion functions of others.

Because "special" means these experiences are not a part of our daily lives we may sometimes wonder how we should dress or what we should do. "When in Rome, do as the Romans do" is an old expression that can be applied to many modern situations. When you are in doubt about how to dress or what to do for a particular special occasion, the best rule is to find out what others are wearing or doing. It is often more comfortable to conform than to be conspicuous by being the only one who is different. In many situations, on the other hand, whatever you feel comfortable wearing or doing is acceptable.

There is an emotional element to most special occasions. We may be experiencing joy or pride or even sorrow. It seems to enhance a pleasant emotional experience and lessen an unpleasant one to have others join us. The characteristics of friendship discussed earlier are observed or sensed at these special times.

There are some occasions to which we may invite others, such as weddings. It can be disappointing if they do not attend or even let us know that they will not be able to do so. There are other occasions that are not invitational, such as funerals. It may be inconvenient and difficult to attend or express sympathy. People sometimes feel that no one will notice whether they are there or not. In most cases people do notice and appreciate your expression of caring.

Showing interest in others and being willing to share their experiences—except when they choose otherwise—are among the finest things you can do for them. Whether the occasion is one of joy or sorrow, you can make a difference. Your presence alone often means more than what you say or do.

A Healthy Balance

Most of us are neither extreme introverts nor extroverts, but ambiverts, as discussed in Chapter 2. There are times when it is easier to meet people, communicate with those we know, or even ask for help. Comfortably asking questions, sharing experiences, or even being alone are just some of the ways we can maintain a healthy balance in our lives and relationships with others.

Not only should we be aware of our own needs but we should also be understanding and considerate of the needs of others. Interpersonal relationships present some of our most difficult and challenging experiences; but they are also rewarding in many ways. Our relationships with others can cause us sorrow and disappointment, but they can also bring us love and joy. Our emotions, as discussed in Chapter 5, are an integral part of our relationships with others.

SUMMARY Nearly every person's life is interwoven with the lives of others. The need for human interaction is evident at birth and continues throughout life. A relationship is human interaction that is more lasting than casual contact.

Bradley and Baird explain the development of relationships by means of a six-stage pyramid beginning with perceived perception and possibly continuing with stages of greeting, clichés, commitments, divergence, and intimacy.

There is a difference between solitude and loneliness. Solitude means to be alone, which may be either desirable or undesirable. Loneliness is unwanted aloneness and a desire for the company and support of others. Well-adjusted people appreciate and enjoy a degree of solitude, but nobody wants to be lonely.

Some loneliness may be due to shyness, which can result from excessive self-consciousness. Suggestions for overcoming shyness include accepting oneself as less than perfect and making an effort to pay attention to the needs and interests of others.

An approach to self-understanding that can improve our interpersonal relationships is the Johari Window. This "window" consists of four areas identified as the open area, blind area, hidden area, and unknown area. The open area represents both what we know about ourselves and what others know about us. Enlarging this area is intended to give us more self-understanding and improve our interpersonal relationships.

Assertiveness should be thought of in terms of rights. It involves direct expression of one's feelings, preferences, needs, or opinions in a manner that is neither threatening nor punishing toward another person. Aggressiveness, on the other hand, is a type of attack on another person or group.

A friend is a person with whom you have a bond of mutual understanding, acceptance, caring, and sharing. Friendship can be maintained across thousands of miles and decades of years.

Group activity is involved in some of our interpersonal relationships. Types of groups include family, ethnic, religious, volunteer, political, and recreational. A group-o-gram is a means of examining the interrelatedness and value of group activities in your life.

Communication is probably the single most important factor in developing successful interpersonal relationships. To improve our communication we should do our best to understand ourselves and others, be aware of nonverbal messages, recognize and try to remove barriers, and improve our listening skills.

We can experience interpersonal growth during most of our lives. We may have mixed feelings about new experiences, but we need new experiences to grow. Our relationships with others can be the source of both pleasant and unpleasant experiences, but are an integral part of our lives. We need a healthy balance between seeking to satisfy our own needs and respecting the needs of others in interpersonal relationships.

Some references to interpersonal relationships in the workplace were included in this chapter, but the various aspects of this subject will be discussed in the next chapter, "Human Relations at Work."

 Psychology In Practice

1. Visit someone who lives alone. Try to determine whether he or she enjoys solitude or is lonely. If the visit results in a mutually satisfying experience, plan to visit the person occasionally.

2. With a classmate, observe a variety of types of interpersonal relations for several days. Include children as well as adults in different situations in your observations. Prepare a brief report that describes six examples of behavior that support the statement, "We have a social nature."

3. Select one of the suggestions for becoming a better listener and put the suggestion into practice in a variety of situations for a week. Evaluate the quality of your listening as a result.

Learning Activities

Turn to page 429 to complete the Learning Activities and Enrichment Activities for this chapter.

Notes

1. Patricia H. Bradley and John E. Baird, Jr., *Communication for Business and the Professions,* 2d ed., William C. Brown, Dubuque, IA, 1983, p. 113. All rights reserved. Reprinted by permission.
2. Ibid., p. 114.

3. Ibid., p. 116.

4. Ronald Evans and Laura Hubbs-Tait, *Applying Psychology in Today's World: Strategies for Personal Growth,* Prentice Hall, Englewood Cliffs, NJ, 1991, p. 201.

5. Velma Walker and Lynn Brokaw, *Becoming Aware: A Look at Human Relations and Personal Adjustment,* Kendall/Hunt Publishing Company, Dubuque, IA, 1992, p. 15.

6. Joseph Luft, *Group Processes: An Introduction to Group Dynamics,* Mayfield, Palo Alto, CA, 1970, pp. 11–12.

7. Judy C. Pearson and Paul E. Nelson, *Understanding and Sharing,* 5th ed., Wm C. Brown Publishers, Dubuque, IA, 1991, p. 192.

8. John M. Reardon, "Creative Conflict Resolution," Phoenix Process Consultants, Edina, MN, p. TF–50.

9. Richard Walters, *How to Say Hard Things the Easy Way,* Word Publishing, Dallas, 1991, pp. 151–152.

10. Barry L. Duncan and Joseph W. Rock, "Saving Relationships: The Power of the Unpredictable," *Psychology Today,* January/February 1993, p. 49.

13 Human Relations at Work

Learning Objectives

After completing this chapter, you will be able to do the following:

1. Distinguish between hygiene factors and motivation factors, according to Herzberg, and give examples of how a factor of each type affects employees.
2. Identify fears that are common among employees of large companies today and suggest how the fears might be reduced.
3. Explain how you would handle a complaint of a customer who is angry because a product she or he purchased didn't work.
4. Compare conflict, competition, and cooperation by describing a work-related experience involving each.
5. Describe advantages of a work team composed of members with a variety of responsibilities within a company or business.
6. Suggest a solution to a possible problem in the functioning of a work team.
7. Explain what is meant by a manager's open-door policy and give an example supporting your attitude toward such a policy.
8. Define sexual harassment and explain why some cases of sexual harassment might not be reported.

> **"**I will pay more for the ability to deal with people than for any other ability under the sun.**"**
>
> JOHN D. ROCKEFELLER
> *businessman and philanthropist*

Are you a different person when you are at work than you are at home or wherever else you may be? Hopefully not. Why, then, a separate chapter, "Human Relations at Work"? We know that psychology is the study of human behavior, which certainly involves attempting to understand one another and our interactions with one another wherever we may be. And the chapter on interpersonal relationships, just completed, is primarily about human relationships.

What we will be doing in this chapter is extending our knowledge and understanding of what we have already studied to improving human relations in the workplace. This can be very valuable to you in the your future career. If you already have work experience, you can personally relate to the content of this chapter. If so, you may be willing to share your experience with the class. John D. Rockefeller, quoted at the opening of the chapter, was one of the most successful and one of the wealthiest men of the United States. He understood the value of human relations in the workplace.

In Chapter 2, you read about roles we assume in different situations. The statement was made: "It is natural and appropriate to act differently in different situations, or to assume the role or type of behavior that is called for in particular circumstances." Since it is fairly obvious that a situation at work is different from one at home, in school, or in a community setting, it is expected that our behavior would be at least somewhat different. We have a boss or supervisor (unless we are self-employed), co-workers, and customers or clients, and there are expectations of us in order to earn our pay and possibly other benefits. Topics that relate to work situations will be discussed in this chapter.

You will be reminded as we go along of the relationship of previous chapters to human relations at work. Although relating chapters to one another has been a feature of this book throughout, there will be even more such references in an attempt to make our work more satisfying and rewarding.

Characteristics of vocational maturity discussed in Chapter 11, "Life-Span Development," for example, can be specifically applied to human relations at work. There are human relations problems in job situations that one can learn how to solve or respond to appropriately. We may also be able to prevent some problems from developing if we improve our ability to apply basic principles of human relations.

Robert A. Baron and Paul B. Paulus, in *Understanding Human Relations: A Practical Guide to People at Work,* state:

> Human Relations is concerned with the factors that help and hinder effective relationships in the work environment. Indeed, one of the most basic assumptions is as follows: In order to have an effective organization, we must provide for effective, satisfying relations between the people in it. Consistent with this point of view, human relations generally concentrates on two major goals: (1) increasing our understanding of interactions between individuals, and (2) developing practical techniques for enhancing such relations.[1]

MOTIVATION TO WORK

Three basic motivational theories—the psychoanalytic, behavioristic, and humanistic—were discussed and compared in Chapter 3. Another theory, more directly related to work, was also explained. This was McGregor's Theory X and Theory Y approach to attempting to understand motivation (or lack of it) in the workplace. You may want to review these.

Hygiene (Maintenance) Factors	Motivation Factors

Work environment	Recognition for work well done
Relationship with supervisor	Opportunity for advancement
Pay/fringe benefits	Enjoyment of work

Numerous other theories can be identified, some of which have developed from perceived weaknesses in theories existing at the time. One additional theory frequently associated with the workplace is Herzberg's two-factor theory.[2] Herzberg identified two sets of outcomes related to job satisfaction as **hygiene** factors and **motivation** factors. Hygiene factors, also referred to as maintenance factors, pertain to avoiding and eliminating conditions that cause workers to be dissatisfied with their jobs. These factors are not directly related to the work itself but might include the work environment, relationships with supervisors, or other outcomes or factors related to extrinsic motivation.

Motivation factors, on the other hand, are positive and are related to outcomes that increase job satisfaction. These factors would include recognition for work well done, opportunities for advancement, and enjoyment of the work itself. These factors are more directly associated with intrinsic motivation.

From THE WALL STREET JOURNAL. Permission, CARTOON FEATURES SYNDICATE.

Lilly M. Berry and John P. Houston, in *Psychology at Work: An Introduction to Industrial and Organizational Psychology,* point out that, even though research hasn't given a great deal of support to Herzberg's theory, it has influenced organizations and managers to redesign jobs "to make work more interesting and challenging, and to increase responsibility and opportunities for achievement."[3] Various interpretations and applications of this theory can be beneficial to both companies and employees in different ways. Becoming aware of conditions that dissatisfy workers and of other conditions that promote satisfaction, if acted upon constructively, can do a great deal to improve human relations in the workplace.

The need for achievement, referred to in textbooks as *nAch,* is also frequently associated with work motivation, but it, of course, would apply to other facets of one's life also. David McClelland is the psychologist primarily associated with this theory, although others have also had input into the theory and its application.[4] According to this theory, individuals have different levels of a need for achievement. Those with a high level of this need set high standards for their own performance, like activities and work that challenges them, and are more persistent in working toward achieving goals. They are self-motivators and are naturally highly valued by employers.

Fear of failure has been contrasted with the need for achievement by J. W. Atkinson, another psychologist who worked with McClelland on development of the "need for achievement" theory. Atkinson pointed out that we must also understand a person's fear of failure.[5] Individuals not only have different levels of need for achievement but also have different degrees of fear of failure. Those who are motivated primarily by a fear of failure often will only study as much as necessary to avoid failing the course or will work only as hard as necessary to avoid losing their jobs. Those with a high level of need for achievement are more concerned with meeting their own high standards of performance than they are about failing.

Maslow's hierarchy, discussed in Chapter 3, is related to all human behavior as we are always attempting, consciously or unconsciously, to satisfy our needs. Every level of the hierarchy, from satisfying survival needs to achieving self-actualization, can be applied to both why people work and satisfactions from work. Those who achieve self-actualization, or development of their potential through their jobs, not only enjoy their work more than the average person, but they enjoy life more, as so much of one's lifetime is spent working. Preparing yourself for a type of work that you expect to find challenging is the first step, but people with a high level of need to achieve, as discussed above, would also be likely to develop a high degree of self-actualization in any number of careers. Liking one's work is related to one's attitude and motivation as well as to the work itself.

Can too much attention be given to satisfying one's need for recognition and esteem according to Maslow or to Skinner's emphasis on positive reinforcement? A warning related to satisfying such needs is expressed by Robert J. Samuelson in a *Newsweek* article, entitled "The Trophy Syndrome." He says,

> Everyone likes praise. At the age of 6, an extra pat on the back is helpful. A few trophies are no big deal. Our problem is that we perpetuate childish customs. Praise given too easily or too lavishly is worse than none. Trophies are worth something only if they are earned, not bestowed.[6]

Samuelson's observation might be applied to recognition given at work as well as to numerous other types of experiences in our lives. On the other hand, some would say recognition is lacking, or too scarce in the work force. It depends on the company or organization and numerous other factors.

 What do you THINK?

Do you think medals, plaques, trophies, and bonuses are given out too freely in today's society? Support your response with an example, if possible.

JOB ENRICHMENT AND SATISFACTION

Business and industry in recent years have responded to better understanding of employee motivation by giving at least some of their employees more freedom in how their jobs are done and more authority in making related decisions. This is known as job enrichment. An explanation of job enrichment is given by R. V. Dawis, R. T. Fruehling, and N. B. Oldham in *Psychology: Human Relations and Work Adjustment*. They say: "Job enrichment is not accomplished by job rotation (moving workers from one boring job to another) or by job enlargement (simply adding more monotonous tasks). Rather, job enrichment requires a radical redesign of the job to make greater use of a person's abilities."[7] Realistically it must be recognized that not all aspects of a job or work can be made more challenging nor can all workers be relied upon to assume more responsibility. But job enrichment has not only increased satisfaction in many instances, it has also improved productivity and employer-employee relations.

EMOTIONS IN THE WORKPLACE

How do emotions fit into workplace relations? However that question might be answered, as long as we have human beings in the workplace, there will also be evidence of emotion. Your understanding of pleasant and unpleasant emotions, physiological effects of emotion, and constructive use of emotions from Chapter 5 should be helpful in understanding the effects of emotions in the workplace.

Caring

Although unpleasant emotions and expressions of them are more evident in the workplace, pleasant emotions should not be overlooked. Caring about what we are doing and about other people we work with or for involves our emotions, even though there are different degrees of caring and it may be expressed in different ways. Our discussion at the beginning of the chapter about situations and circumstances calling for different types of behavior applies not only to caring but also to expressions of other emotions on the job. If you don't care about what you're doing you'll never be good at it. Well-adjusted workers also care about their co-workers, their customers, and their supervisors, managers, and themselves.

Anger

People become angry when they are frustrated—when others aren't acting the way they think they should or things aren't going the way they want them to. We want to keep in mind that becoming disturbed isn't necessarily bad. If you didn't care about yourself, the quality of work you do, or even whether you keep your job or not, you wouldn't experience much frustration. But is that what you want in your work experience?

How can we apply the suggestions given in Chapter 5 for using anger for constructive purposes to workplace situations? One of the suggestions pertained to understanding what causes you to become angry and to becoming a better problem solver. If a co-worker borrows a tool, for example, and does not return it, what should you do about it? You are justified in not wanting to be taken advantage of, but what can you do to solve the problem?

First we should give ourselves time to calm down, if we do feel angry, and to decide how to react to the situation. You can remind the person to return the tool (it is possible that he or she forgot), inform the person that you need it available for yourself in the future, and possibly suggest that the person purchase or requisition his or her own tool. In other words you can use your frustration to solve the problem and to prevent frustration in the future rather than to become angry.

If you do become angry, your anger could be suppressed, which is not healthful, or it could be expressed in a destructive way that would cause a problem with co-worker relations. It could even cost you your job or an opportunity for promotion. You should note that trying to solve the problem and avoid similar instances in the future is an assertive, rather than an aggressive, response to the situation, as discussed in the previous chapter on interpersonal relationships.

If we experience frustration with our supervisor because we did not receive recognition for extra work or are upset because what we thought was a reasonable request was not granted, we have a different type of situation. Naturally our decision on how to react depends on the type of communication and relationship we have with him or her. (Employer/employee relationships will be discussed further later in the chapter.)

If we cannot or don't resolve the problem, we are likely to use the coping mechanism called displacement—taking out our frustrations on someone else not involved in the cause of our frustration. Displacement might also be used as a psychological defense when we are disturbed by an encounter with a patient, customer, or client, depending on the nature of our work.

Fear

How would you associate McGregor's Theory X with fear in the workplace? Do you recall, from Chapter 3, that Theory X was based on the belief that most people don't want to work and will only do so if they feel threatened? Although fear of losing one's job due to this type of threat is not as common as it once was, many in today's world of work have fear of losing their jobs for other reasons.

Many Americans have been losing their jobs due to their companies being acquired and/or "downsizing," going out of business, reducing production, or moving to another location. Uneasiness about job security is worse if communication within the company is poor and employees are confused about what might happen next. This type of uneasiness can interfere not only with the quality of work, but also with all types of human relations within the company.

Such negative feeling can also be reflected in relations with customers and others not directly involved.

Jealousy

The important thing to remember about jealousy is that it springs from a feeling of insecurity. This is true whether it pertains to a relationship with a special person in our personal lives or whether it pertains to a situation at work. People who feel insecure, either in their jobs or in their relationships with co-workers have a tendency to be overly sensitive to being slighted. They may be also discontented with the advancement or achievement of others and are often unrealistic in thinking they were more deserving. Jealousy can cause friction that is disruptive to harmony within a company or organization and can interfere with benefits of job enrichment and job satisfaction. If the situation is such that someone is jealous of you, the best way to react is with confidence in yourself and honesty, without being accusing or argumentative. Otherwise we are allowing the jealous person to interfere with our ability to control ourselves and take advantage of opportunities available to us.

EMPLOYER-EMPLOYEE RELATIONS

An important aspect of employer-employee relations is that both parties understand what is expected in their relationship. Although most people would admit we are all equal as human beings, situations may temporarily put another in a position of authority. Examples are law enforcement officers dealing

A police officer may deal with citizens in a role of authority or as someone providing assistance and support.

with citizens, instructors with students, and employers with employees. In a sense we all have "bosses" who have rights in terms of what to expect of us under mutually understood, and often agreed upon, conditions.

Know Management Structure

Knowing the management structure of the company or the organization for which you work helps to know who has authority over you and what authority you yourself may have. This depends somewhat on the size of the company or organization, but other factors are also involved. It also depends on the philosophy of the company about how authority should be distributed. In a centralized organization, all important decisions are made by those in top management positions, for example. It is the responsibility of department supervisors to see that the decisions are carried out. There is a trend today toward decentralized organization, however, where top management delegates much of the decision making to lower levels.

In many companies, employees have the opportunity for input into decisions. It is recognized today that those doing the actual work can contribute valuable input to company policies and practices. This is one of the reasons for the emphasis on teams in today's world of work. A common term for this kind of organizational structure and functioning is participatory management.

If you know who has what authority, you can make appropriate referrals in difficult problem situations. If you know how much authority you have, you can avoid frustrating others with problems that you should be handling yourself. An essential element of effective employer-employee relationships is to know not only who your boss is but what he or she expects of you.

*"You could take a lesson from that clock . . .
it passes the time by keeping its hands busy."*

Reprinted from *The Saturday Evening Post*.

Loyalty and Trust

Loyalty has always been valued in employer-employee relationships. Loyalty can be defined as standing up for and behind your company and those you work with. You believe in them and you make that evident by how you talk and how you act. Loyalty, however, does not come as easily today as it did when jobs were more secure. It is harder to maintain in a world of work that has numerous economic problems and challenges. Employees have difficulty being loyal to a company who, they fear, may lay them off next week. Middle management people and even those at the top of an organization may feel insecure in their own jobs. As long as we work for a company, however, we should be as loyal as we reasonably can.

Loyalty and trust go hand in hand. They both are essential elements of employer-employer relationships. Trust has to do honesty and reliability between employers and employees. We may hear more about lack of trust than having trust, just as we always hear more about problems than desirable situations. We may also hear more about employers and managers who are not reliable in following through on their commitments, since they have more power than employees. It is essential, however, that employees also be trustworthy in any organization. A great deal of damage can be done by employees who are not honest and reliable in what they say and do.

 What would you SAY? If a co-worker has a habit of speaking negatively about the company, how would you respond?

Labor Unions and Management

Both employers and employees admit to having difficulties with one another related to union negotiations, contracts, and possible grievances. A union is a group of workers who collectively bargain with management on such issues as working conditions, working schedules, seniority rights, wages, fringe benefits, and whatever issues are important to that particular group. Contracts are not only in the interest of workers, however. Contracts are negotiated by representives of management and representatives of employees, and both are attempting to obtain agreements favorable to them and to the organization.

Some employee associations are also unions, but they may have a number of other purposes in addition to the negotiable items mentioned above. They may be interested in safety factors, educational and training opportunities, service to the community, or assistance to members in need, for example. Some labor unions also have similar objectives.

In today's world of work, employers and employees recognize the reality of organized labor and in most cases can work out equitable agreements without damage to their relationship. If this isn't possible, all the effort put into improving employer-employee relations can be lost when it comes time to negotiate a new union contract. Strikes are not as common as they used to be, for a number of reasons—two being that both management and labor unions recognize that strikes are costly for everyone and also that negative feelings develop that may never heal.

Another reason is related to the effects of the media and public opinion on both management and unions today. This is explained by D. Benton and J. Halloran, in *Applied Human Relations: An Organizational Approach.* They say:

> No longer can unions or management count on blind support from their members or employees. So many aspects of labor problems have been brought to public attention, that union employees cannot help but know the effects of their proposed actions even before they are taken. Workers are forced also to take public reaction into account now because the public, through television, may know about the strike or walk-out even before some of the workers do, and public reaction will be instantaneous. In the past, news of strikes wasn't heard until the following day or by word of mouth. Public sympathy for a strike for higher wages or increased fringe benefits cannot be gained by simply making the facts known, no more than management can get the public on its side by claiming low profits and increased costs.[8]

A further reason is that mediation and arbitration are more commonly used to settle management/union differences. Mediation is a process whereby both groups are brought together with a mediator, or unbiased third party, who tries to help the parties settle their differences. Both management and employees must agree to mediation following their impasse, or inability to come to an agreement between themselves.

If an agreement cannot be reached through mediation, the issues of disagreement may go to arbitration. With this procedure, a hearing is held in which both sides present their cases with supporting facts and evidence. The arbitrator then studies what both sides have presented, considers similar agreements and settlements, and, in due time, returns a written decision in favor of either management or the union. Both sides must have agreed to accept this decision before the arbitration process begins. Arbitration is costly and, for all practical purposes, one side loses. Therefore, if an agreement cannot be reached in contract negotiations, agreement is often reached through the mediation process without resorting to arbitration. There are variations in these procedures depending on existing contracts and the laws of the state where the parties reside.

Trust between employers and employees, discussed earlier, must survive contract negotiations if favorable relations are to be maintained between contract negotiations. Both management and employees will admit that this is a difficult challenge. To negotiate in "good faith," with the intention of reaching an equitable agreement, can help to maintain trust and respect for one another. Because of complex economic conditions, some of which were discussed in Chapter 1, "Our Changing World," unions have had to become more conservative in what they are asking for in negotiations. If they want their employers to stay in business and want to keep their jobs they must share their concern in making a profit. Work teams and employee-involvement programs are also accomplishing some of the cooperation formerly sought by unions.

CO-WORKER RELATIONS

When employees have good feelings toward one another, they enjoy their jobs more and morale is usually higher. There is more respect for one another's rights and property, and absenteeism is lower. With good company spirit and a feeling of job togetherness, employees hesitate to miss work except for very good reasons. Individuals realize that if they are not there to do their share of the workload, their co-workers will be inconvenienced and often overworked. They will not want to do this unnecessarily to people they care about. They will come to work more dependably because they feel a bond with their co-workers.

Also, since employees generally enjoy association with their co-workers, they miss their company when they are not there. S. Strasser and J. Sena comment on this in their book, *Work Is Not a Four-Letter Word*. They contend,

> One of the great joys of work has nothing to do with money, power, or prestige; it has to do with people. It is the pleasure derived from meeting people, building relationships, forming friendships, and experiencing companionship; it is the enjoyment and good feeling we get from working with others and sharing with them our thoughts and feelings, our hopes and fears.
>
> For numerous people, however, the joys derived from socialization at work are minimal or nonexistent. Instead of interacting with others, these individuals remain isolated, alienated, and estranged. Instead of building relationships, they build walls that separate themselves from colleagues. Sometimes the isolation is unwittingly self-imposed; sometimes it is imposed upon them. In either case, the enormous personal and professional benefits obtained from connecting with others—the exhilaration of comradeship—is denied, and work becomes a sterile, lonely experience.[9]

Liking the people one works with is known among industrial psychologists as social facilitation. Many employees may have limited opportunity to talk to others while actually doing their work, but they still enjoy being among their co-workers and talking to them before and after work, during their lunch period, and during breaks. It has been found that a ten- to fifteen-minute break twice during the working day does not interfere with the amount of work produced. In fact in many cases, even with less total time spent working, production has increased. This is because people can be refreshed physically and mentally in even a short period of time and return to work with new vigor and increased motivation.

Businesses and industries that recognize the value of social facilitation sponsor bowling teams, arrange for parties, and provide other social events outside working hours. These may be considered fringe benefits, as indeed they are, but management benefits also by establishing bonds among employees and between themselves and their employees. The company benefits in terms of improved attitudes, increased loyalty, and improved productivity.

Further aspects of co-worker relations will be considered in the chapter section on Teams at Work.

CUSTOMER OR CLIENT RELATIONS

We all have had the experience of being customers or clients, and many of us have had experience with serving others in job situations. The most important thing to remember about customers or clients is that they are human beings like us. They do not suddenly turn into another kind of being when they are seeking a product or service.

What Can You Offer?

A customer, or a potential one, appreciates recognition. If a person is a regular customer, it helps to greet him or her by name. Even if you do not know the person's name, you can offer an appropriate greeting such as "Good morning" or "Good afternoon." Some people want immediate attention, others may want to look around, but everyone—except a shoplifter—appreciates recognition.

You can project friendliness in your attitude and total behavior, as well as in what you say. Many people shop at certain stores or do business with particular companies because, in addition to offering good service, the people they deal with are friendly. Friendliness makes a person feel that you are interested in him or her as an individual, not only as a customer or possible source of profit.

In addition to friendliness, helpfulness is important in serving customers. As human beings, customers have normal needs and wants, and you should try to identify an individual's particular need at the moment. If you are attentive and perceptive, there are several ways you can identify the person's need. One good way, obviously, is to ask how you can help. Observe what the person is looking at or seems to be looking for. The overall behavior of customers may indicate whether they are in a hurry and want help or are interested in browsing on their own. The better you understand people in all situations, the better the chance that you can be really helpful to a customer.

People seeking goods or services are also seeking reliability. They want to deal with people they can trust. Most people in business depend heavily on repeat business and steady customers. Customer or client relations, therefore, should be sincere and trustworthy. The product or service and everything connected with them should be what they are claimed to be.

The successful sales associate projects friendliness, helpfulness, reliability, and knowledge of the product.

Handling Complaints

In spite of efforts to offer high-quality products and services, there will always be some dissatisfied customers. The following suggestions should be considered in responding to customer complaints. Remember, however, that customers are individuals and situations vary. There is no absolute best way to respond.

- Listen. Just talking (sometimes yelling?) about his or her dissatisfaction may cause the customer to calm down. You also should be alert to discovering how the customer perceives the product or service and the situation.
- Ask questions. This shows that you are interested in the person and in knowing more about the situation. You can't make a judgment or even explain the complaint to a supervisor unless you have the facts.
- Do not accuse the customer or be too quick to admit fault on your part. If you say, "There must have been some misunderstanding," or "Perhaps there has been some mistake," you are being attentive to the customer, but are still withholding a conclusion on what actually happened.
- Don't lose control of your temper. No matter how angry the customer is or how abusive his or her language may be, you are expected to be rational and courteous. Your calmness may have a quieting effect on the customer.
- Assure the customer that you will do whatever you can to correct the situation or satisfy the customer. And follow through on your word.

"I'M A GOOD MECHANIC, BUT I HAPPEN TO BE A LOUSY ESTIMATOR."

Reprinted by permission of Bob Schochet.

- Refer the customer to the manager (unless you are the owner of the business) if that is the store or company policy. But give the customer attention first, so he or she does not feel like a victim of a runaround.
- Expect some complaints. Remember that dealing with dissatisfied customers is part of your job. Most customers with complaints will continue to do business with you or the company you work for if they feel they have been treated fairly. Also, keep in mind that customers are more likely to tell others about their bad experiences than about their good experiences. In the long run, your reputation and future business for the company are at stake.
- Be courteous. Everyone likes to be shown courtesy and appreciation. "I appreciate your bringing this to my attention," or "I'm sorry for your inconvenience," can make a significant difference in customer relations and in handling complaints.

ETHICAL STANDARDS AND RELATIONS

The discussion of moral development and moral behavior in Chapter 11 pertained to what we call ethics, or standards of right and wrong. Ethics pertains to more than just what the public will tolerate. Ethics is based on fundamental beliefs about what individuals and organizations stand for and what they will do and not do.

Many professional groups have their own ethical standards, in writing at least. The medical and legal professions, government, education, and many businesses have ethical codes, for example. If individuals are known to seriously violate these codes, members may be expelled from professional membership or lose their jobs. Unethical practices by some members of these groups are a major societal concern today. An association with a code or even taking an oath does not guarantee honest, ethical behavior.

Small businesses and individuals also have ethical standards. What is right or wrong is not determined by the size of the group to which one belongs. For those who not concerned about honesty and fair treatment of others, however, unethical practices are sometimes easier to disguise or hide in large organizations or governmental bodies. Some individuals also rationalize, or make excuses, for their unethical behavior. They convince themselves, for example, that everyone "is doing it."

What is considered ethical is not confined to what is legal. It is relatively easy to find out what is legal and what the consequences are. We, or others, may not always know whether something illegal is involved in a particular transaction, however. We may not know, for example, that a co-worker is stealing company tools. Then let's suppose he offers to give you some of them, which you could use. Do you accept them? Do you question your co-worker about where he got them? Do you report him to management? These are ethical decisions.

Some people make a distinction between what they consider ethical behavior in their personal lives and in their work. They would not cheat a friend, for example, but they might overcharge a customer. Over time, an individual's reputation and the reputation of a business are developed by the perception of their practices related to ethics. But with most individuals, how they feel about themselves and their relationships with others is of greater importance. They still must realize that others may have different standards, however.

Our daily lives are affected by ethics whether we realize it or not. We would be foolish to believe everything anyone tells us about a product, service, or treatment. We would be equally foolish, however, not to believe anything others tell us. So we have to make judgments. And others make judgments about our integrity, or basic honesty, in their relations with us.

What do you THINK? What do you think is the primary cause of unethical practices in the world of work today?

CONFLICT, COMPETITION, OR COOPERATION

How do conflict, competition, and cooperation fit a discussion of human relations at work? Some say they want to avoid conflict, they expect competition, and they seek cooperation. Each of these can be productive, however. Let's briefly consider each of these types of human interation and their effects on our work.

Conflict

Conflict is a clash of opposing ideas, interests, or activities. Although it is realistic to expect some conflict in our work, people generally want to avoid conflict or hope to resolve it without harm to feelings or productivity. It is not so much the conflicts themselves that cause problems or promote progress but the means by which they are resolved.

Those who work with conflicts describe three types of conflict resolutions. These are:

Lose-Lose In this type of conflict resolution neither party is satisfied with the results, and negative feelings become stronger. The conflict isn't really resolved. It becomes similar to smoldering ashes that readily flare up if given a little fuel.

Conflict can be a cause of anxiety that interferes with our well-being and performance on the job. Aggressiveness, as discussed in Chapter 12, can be associated with conflicts. When people are working against each other in a cutthroat way, both individuals and organizations suffer.

Win-Lose Someone gets his or her way in this type of conflict, as the name suggests. However, in many cases the loser becomes defensive and looks for the opportunity to win the next round. In a work situation the win-lose approach to conflict resolution is similar to "I'm the boss, so do it my way or look for a job somewhere else." Most bosses and managers today know that causing fear of losing one's job is not the best way to motivate employees.

Win-Win Can both sides in a conflict win? The idea with this approach is to resolve the conflict so that both sides benefit as much as possible and there is mutual understanding of why whatever solution is agreed upon is best. This type of conflict resolution requires cooperation and effective communication, but results warrant the effort.

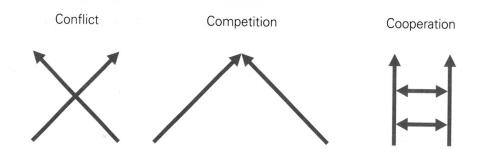

Conflict   Competition   Cooperation

Competition

Competition is trying to gain something that another person or persons are also trying to gain. There is rivalry in competition, but it can spur motivation and productivity rather than being a negative force. Most of us grow up with a sense of competition in many areas of our lives—winning the game, getting better grades, getting the job, getting the promotion.

Businesses are in competition with one another. This can be healthy for them as well as for the economy and individuals. Competition can bring out the best in both individuals and organizations.

Cooperation

Cooperation is working together to achieve a common goal or common purpose. Our society needs competition, but we also need cooperation to get our tasks completed and to reach our goals.

When we recognize our own strengths and weaknesses, along with those of others, we can determine the best ways to cooperate, or work together to achieve what one person cannot do alone. In a group situation, success is a result of each person's depending on the others to use their abilities well.

Cooperation is important in our personal lives also. A cooperative attitude, an acceptance of ourselves, as well as others, helps us to work together as teams. All those involved in cooperative efforts should feel comfortable expressing their needs, ideas, and values so that they will not be lost in the interest of others or in a group effort.

TEAMS AT WORK If and when you are anticipating a job interview, be prepared for such questions as: What experience have you had working as a member of a team? How would you describe yourself as a team player? What do you see as the purposes and advantages of teams in the workplace?

If you don't have a ready answer to the last question now, keep the question in mind as team functioning in the workplace is discussed. You should also note how important understanding others, communications skills, and application of human relations guidelines are to productive team functioning.

Those who have not studied psychology often think human relations is simply being friendly and considerate, but there is much more to it than that. In fact it can be one of the most complicated subjects you'll ever study as it involves not only the behavior of others, but also your own behavior. And both of these are somewhat unpredictable. We cannot improve our ability to understand human relations in teams unless we first know something about human behavior, about team structures, purposes, and functions, and how we might function as a member of a team.

The idea of people cooperating at work to accomplish objectives and solve problems is not new. There has been a new emphasis in recent years on the team approach in the workplace, however. Companies and organizations are involved in quality-improvement teams, decision-making teams, and teams or groups of different types to increase employee input and satisfaction and to accomplish common goals.

Team functioning in the workplace is often associated with the quality circle that originated in Japan and was described in Chapter 7. Variations of the quality circle are still being widely used in business and industry. The idea of a circle has advantages in team functioning because everyone has an equal position. There is no head of the table, so to speak. This is important when it comes to individual team members feeling comfortable in expressing their ideas or even constructively criticizing the ideas of others. Of course a circle isn't always practical when it comes to a team project. Some teams function in the actual work situation, which presents its own setting. In any situation or setting, however, team members should be able to communicate effectively with one another.

How common are teams in the workplace today? A special report, based on a survey, entitled "Work Teams: How Far Have They Come?" in *Training: The Human Side of Business,* states: "We found that eight out of ten U. S. organizations with 100 or more employees have assigned at least some people to some working group identified as a team. In the largest organizations, those with 10,000 or more people, the figure is closer to 90 percent."

Most of the respondents to the survey "aren't talking about an isolated work unit here and there, but about significant numbers of people. In the average organization that has any 'teams' at all, more than half of all employees (53 percent) are members of one."[10] Teams can be found in smaller businesses and organizations also. Interaction between teams can also be valuable for specific purposes.

Team Types and Structure

It is recommended that team membership be relatively small so that everyone can, and likely will, play an active part. Much of the time team membership is voluntary, but even then some employees sense some pressure to "volunteer." Employees who are interested in their work and in contributing to common goals will usually want to be part of a team, but they still appreciate a choice of teams to which they might belong. Teams can be relatively permanent, similar to what is called a standing committee in some organizations. Their purpose is ongoing, such as to explore and arrange for training opportunities for employees and other company personnel. Other teams may be for a specific immediate need, similar to an ad hoc committee. An example of this would be to suggest ways to implement a new "no smoking" policy within the organization.

In cases such as these it is best if membership is voluntary so members have a real interest in the purpose of the team. It is also advisable to have a mix in background of team members. If all members of the team have the same experience and same idea, much of the value of team consideration is lost.

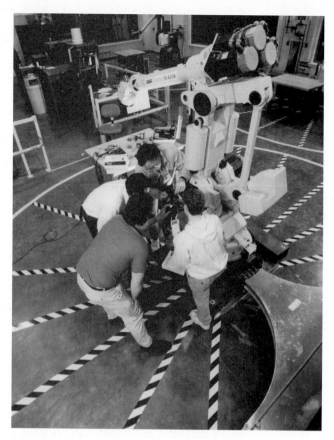

In a Saturn plant, the approach to teamwork is the empowerment of employees, whereby each group manages its own budget, inventory control, and hiring.

Team Purposes

Team purposes were referred to in the discussion of types and structure. Although it may seem obvious that a group or team have a purpose, it frequently happens that a member of the team cannot explain what it is. They may get in the habit of attending meetings or participating in team projects halfheartedly and may not be sure what the team is trying to accomplish. It is primarily the responsibility of the person who has organized the team to make the purpose clear and to explain why it is a worthwhile purpose. Some of the purposes of teams relate to work schedules, and customer, client, or patient service. (There is a trend today toward calling anyone who receives service a customer, but there are objections to this.) Other purposes may be related to performance evaluation, quality control, or budgets. The nature of the company or organization will determine other purposes.

Advantages of Teams

Not only may teams accomplish their specific purposes but teams can also promote personnel getting to know one another better. There can be numer-

Possible Problems of Team Functioning	Advantages of Team Functioning

Team Interaction

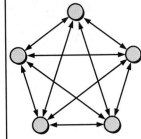

Problems
- Wasted or poorly used time
- Ineffective leadership
- Retribution from management
- Suggestions not considered or implemented
- Conflicts and jealousies
- Groupthink leads to illogical decisions

Team Interaction

Advantages
- Contributes to cooperation belongingness, and loyalty
- Contributes to tolerance and helpfulness
- Generates more workable ideas
- Participants motivate one another
- Fosters sense of achievement

ous advantages to this, but one is that it contributes to a sense of belongingness and loyalty to one another and to the organization.

Members of a team can learn how to work together more effectively, not only in team situations, but on the job where they have individual responsibilities. A spirit of cooperation can develop that contributes to tolerance and helpfulness when needed or appropriate.

If all members of a team are participating, more workable ideas are generated. Ideas that are presented spontaneously can be evaluated from different perspectives. Creative thinking can be stimulated by a number of people communicating freely with one another. If a number of different problem-solving strategies or models are familiar to the group, better decisions can be made.

A sense of team achievement, of getting things done, can also be an advantage. Teams can accomplish things that individuals cannot. Members of the team also motivate one another so that team members want to be part of the action and a member of the group that solved the problem or achieved the purpose of the team. All of these possible advantages improve morale, which is the prevailing attitude within the company or organization. When morale is high, employees feel good about both their jobs and their relationships with others within the organizations, and are motivated to do their best work.

Possible Problems

There are teams that function as described under Advantages of Teams, but realistically teams can also have problems. These are not because of what a team is or should be, but are the result of how the team functions. Let's consider some of these possible problems.

Team meetings can be time wasters. This is often the result of individuals not really wanting to be a member of the team. They are wasting their time and it reflects on the efficiency of the whole team. Another reason may be lack of understanding the purpose of the team or the agenda for a particular day's activity. As indicated earlier, this is primarily the responsibility of the team's leader or facilitator. The leader of the team can be an employee, but whoever it is, the person should have some leadership skills.

Some team members seldom participate for whatever reason. One of the values of smaller membership is to make it easier for everyone to have input of one kind or another. It is also the responsibility of the leader to encourage reluctant members to participate by asking them for their ideas or suggestions.

When the team consists of a cross-section of personnel, such as managers and employees from a number of different departments, individuals may not feel free to express themselves openly. Even though managers and supervisors may say, "While we are functioning as a team, everyone has equal status and everyone is free to express his or her opinion," some employee do not feel comfortable criticizing their boss's ideas. They are afraid about possible retribution. And they may be right.

Some team members often complain that their suggestions and solutions are not considered or implemented. They therefore do not feel valued as team members or as individuals and lose interest in spending more time and energy making further suggestions. They say they hear a lot of talk about team input, participatory management, and empowerment of employees, but they don't see it in practice.

There can be conflicts and jealousies among team members, or even between different teams, just as there can be between individuals. An individual may feel that another team member is getting credit for his or her idea, for example. Or a member may feel that he or she is being slighted by the leader. If such were true, this would be unfortunate because it should be a function of the leader to prevent or resolve conflicts and negative feelings among members rather than to add to them.

A further possible problem with a team or group has been called group-think. This happens when there is pressure within the group to conform or when a group is isolated from outside input or evaluation. They fail to use their own ability to think critically or to consult others and therefore make decisions that are not logical or rational.

Become a Team Player

It is very likely that you will be expected to function as a member of a team in your future work experience. You may even be asked to organize or lead team activity. Following are some suggestions that could be helpful.

Increase your ability to understand and work with people. Even though you may not be aware of any particular problem you have in this respect, we can all improve this ability. As has been discussed earlier in a number of chapters, the workplace will be much more diversified in the future than it has been in the past. Tolerance, acceptance, understanding, and respect are keys to effective human relations on the job today and in the future. These qualities will be especially important in working in teams, where interaction is continuous and more involved, but they are also valuable in all human relations experiences.

Improve your communication skills. All of the suggestions in Chapter 12, "Interpersonal Relationships," pertaining to communications skills are applicable in team situations. Understand yourself and your present communications skills and habits, in order to avoid two extremes: the person who talks too much and the person who sits or stands back and doesn't contribute. It is especially important to improve listening skills—which we all can do. Members of a team cannot build on the contributions of one another if they are not listening to one another. Communication at Work is the next section in this chapter.

Develop or improve critical thinking skills. This involves a number of other abilities. In order to think critically about an issue, for example, we need some knowledge about the subject. We also have to be an effective listener (or reader, depending on the situation). Once we know and understand what is being said, then we can examine it critically. This means examining the content for validity, or workableness. In this respect, it is important to be able to distinguish between what is fact, and can be verified, and what is a person's opinion. Often these are closely interwoven, intentionally or unintentionally, so that it is difficult to tell the difference. However, a good listener and a critical thinker does not hesitate to ask a person for some factual verification on what he or she is saying. This can be overdone and can become a distraction to the whole team, but used with discretion, it is essential to making the best decisions. Examining the practicality or workability of ideas is also an important aspect of critical thinking.

Know the team's purpose, your particular role as a member of the team, and how the team functions. This was referred to earlier but it is essential for each member of the team who desires to make a contribution. In addition to the overall purpose of the team, there should be a specific agenda that is known by all team members for each meeting or activity. Although it is the responsibility of the team leader to make this known, team members should take the initiative to find out, if it isn't apparent. Also, keep in mind that you may become a team leader yourself at some time.

Be willing to work or contribute without personal recognition. If you are a team player, it is the ultimate success of the team's objective that is important. This doesn't mean that individuals don't often receive recognition for outstanding contributions within the team, but we should be able to identify with the team's achievement, rather than seeking individual recognition or compensation. If you are a team player, this becomes known eventually throughout the company or organization.

Support other members of the team. This doesn't mean that you should agree with everything they say or propose. As mentioned earlier, this would lessen the effect of the team itself or lead to groupthink. But we should be able to recognize that other members of the team have their particular strengths and contributions and support them when we do agree or think they are proposing what is best for the team or organization. Those who are insecure and defensive about their own position in the group have the most difficulty supporting others.

 What would you DO? If you were a member of a work team that you believed wasn't accomplishing its purpose, what would you do?

Effective communication is important at work because the wrong instructions or misunderstood instructions can result in injuries, damage to equipment and materials, dissatisfied customers, stress, and negative feeling among co-workers or between employees and supervisors. The guidelines discussed in the previous chapter on communication apply to situations at work also. It is important to ask questions, for example, when you aren't sure whether you understand a procedure. This is particularly advisable until you gain experience on the job and until you know how your supervisor wants a task done. After you have some experience, you may have the opportunity to make suggestions on how a procedure could be improved, but it is wise to refrain from making too many suggestions until you have established some credibility as a member of the organization.

Sharing Experience and Knowledge

Ideally, in today's companies and organizations, everyone has an opportunity for input through teams, as discussed earlier. Everyone can make a unique contribution, even though you may have the same job title and receive the same pay as someone else. It can be especially valuable for older workers—who have a great deal of experience—and younger workers—who usually have the advantage of recent education and training—to pay attention to one another. Everyone can learn from others if he or she is receptive to learning. Nobody knows everything on the job or anywhere else. Asking experienced persons for their opinion or reasonable assistance not only is helpful to a new employee, but it also can contribute to establishing a relationship that can be beneficial to everyone.

Open-Door Policy

What is known as the open-door policy in organizations and companies isn't always reality in practice. An open-door policy means that employees are welcome to go into a supervisor's or manager's office at any time to discuss a problem or concern or to make a suggestion. Some employees say, "Sure you can go into her office, but she doesn't listen or seem to care." Others may say, "He has an open door, but you're lucky if you can find him in." Whatever the intentions or related problems, the open door does give employees communications opportunities that were not ordinarily available years ago. Just knowing there is an open-door policy, if one believes that it is a reality, makes one feel more comfortable. Naturally, taking the time of a person with many responsibilities should be used with discretion. On the other hand, supervisors or managers who are interested in their employees and their concerns do not wait for the employees to come to them. They are part of team efforts and are visible and available in a number of other ways.

The Grapevine and Rumors

A. J. DuBrin, in *Human Relations: A Job Oriented Approach,* describes the grapevine as follows: "The grapevine is the major informal communication channel in an organization. The term refers to tangled wires or branches that can distort information. For example, valid news about a pending company merger often passes along the grapevine before it is officially announced."[11] The grapevine is not necessarily an undesirable form of communication. It is a way for employees to know what is going on within an organization without continuous formal notification. Managers sometimes purposely use the grapevine to allow employees to react to the idea of a change in policy, for example, before it actually takes place. If there is too much negative feedback, the policy may be modified or even not adopted. The grapevine should not be the primary means of management/employee communication, however. There should be open, face-to-face communication on a regular basis—especially when there are issues of major importance or concern.

Rumor, as compared with the grapevine, often has less basis in fact. Very frequently, rumors are negative in nature and cause worries and anxieties among employees. It is difficult to know how rumors get started, but considering all the possibilities for misunderstanding in communication, it is not surprising that rumors develop. During a work break, for example, someone may comment, "I suppose the next thing they will be doing is . . ." Someone may interpret that to mean that it is in the planning stage and repeat it to others as a foregone conclusion. And the rumor spreads.

Ideally, communication should be accurate and responsive to feedback. Communication will never be without error, however. We can all do our part to make it as effective and as error free as possible.

SEXUAL HARASSMENT AT WORK

What is sexual harassment? How serious is it? What can be done about it? Can it be prevented? Everyone should know the answers to these questions. Those who have been sexually harassed should know what to do about it. Others should be aware of how to react if they are accused of sexual harassment. It is a subject that must be taken seriously in society today, not only in the work environment but also in schools and other settings.

Although sexual harassment has been going on in the workplace ever since males and females have been working in the same environment, it has received widespread attention in recent years. The Civil Rights Act of 1964 prohibited sexual harassment in the workplace, but as with other civil rights, it has taken a long time for attitudes and behavior to change. It wasn't until 1986 that the Supreme Court ruled that sexual harassment violated human rights, giving those so abused legal access to protection.

M. Dalton, D. Hoyle, and M. Watts in *Human Relations* describe sexual harassment as follows:

> Sexual harassment includes any unwelcome sexual advances, requests for sexual favors, or verbal or physical conduct of a sexual nature. Examples are telling sexually oriented jokes, standing too close, touching and making physical contact, displaying sexually oriented material, or making sexual comments about a person's body if these actions are unwelcome.

Either sex can commit sexual harassment. Men can harass women, and women can harass men. Additionally, men can harass men, and women can harass women. Harassment can be from a co-worker, supervisor, an agent of the employer, or a nonemployee such as a repair person who comes on the company premises to perform work. Organizations are responsible for stopping the harassment from a co-worker, nonemployee, or agent of an employer as soon as a management official becomes aware of the harassment. Furthermore, they are responsible for the harassment from a supervisor whether other management officials are aware of the harassment or not."[12]

It is the responsibility of the person being harassed to let the offender clearly know that his or her behavior is unwelcome and that it should be stopped. If that does not take care of the problem, it should be reported to the appropriate authorities in the company, school, or other organization.

There are more cases of males harassing females than the other way around, but women do harass males. Males file one tenth as many complaints with the Equal Employment Opportunity Commission each year as do the females. The number of complaints does not give us a true picture, of course. Do all people who are sexually harassed file a complaint? Are females or males more likely to file a complaint?

What would you DO?   If you were being sexually harassed at work by your supervisor, what would you do?

FRIENDSHIPS AT WORK

Many people have become overly cautious about what could be considered harassment. Can co-workers give one another a hug on a special occasion? Can you compliment someone on their appearance? Can a pat on the back still be used to show appreciation for a job well done? There are no absolute answers to these questions, but what we should keep in mind is that sexual harassment is unwelcome because "harassment" is part of the definition.

Fear of being accused of sexual harassment should not interfere with sincere friendliness or friendships at work. Just as individuals have different attitudes toward their jobs, they have different attitudes about human relationships at work. Some people want to go to work, earn their pay, and be left alone. They may be very good employees, but they are the exception when it comes to human relations at work.

Enjoying association with one's co-workers was discussed earlier in the co-worker relations section of this chapter. When we consider the amount of time we spend at work during our lifetimes compared with time spent in personal relationships, we can appreciate the value of mutually satisfying human relations in the workplace. Even though we aren't likely to be working in the same place and with the same people throughout our working years, those who like people will make new friends easily when change affects their work.

What is the difference between friendly and being a friend? Being friendly is functioning on the lower levels of Bradley and Baird's pyramid, discussed in the previous chapter. Although a co-worker who is friendly would probably help you out if you needed help, there is not the commitment that we find in friendship. The primary characteristics of friendship, also discussed in the last chapter, are understanding, accepting, caring, and sharing. These create a bond that contribute to making one's work a rewarding part of one's life.

Can managers and supervisors have friendships with those they supervise? This is a controversial subject, and the answer ultimately would depend on the individuals involved. Some employees might attempt to take advantage of a friendship with a supervisor. "She gets all the favors," according to co-workers. In other cases a supervisor may feel uncomfortable evaluating or correcting an employee who is also a personal friend. This has more to do with the personality characteristics of the individuals involved than with their working relationship, however. On any level of an organizational structure, persons who feel they cannot be friends with some others at work probably feel relatively insecure in their positions.

No one, of course, has the time or desire to be friends with a great number of people at work or in other areas of one's life. If we are friendly, friendship will develop quite naturally in time without much special effort.

It is a common experience to have friendships at work with persons we see only in that particular environment or at social activities sponsored by the company. In other cases, a friendship developed at work can carry over into sharing vacation experiences or other types of leisure-time activities. None of us want someone else to give us rules to follow in forming friendships. Our friends are ours to choose.

SUMMARY

Our human relations at work can make a difference in how well we do our work and in how much we enjoy our work. These relations involve supervisors and managers, co-workers, and customers or clients. How we interact with others depends not only on our particular relationship with them, but also on the situation.

In addition to motivational theories discussed in Chapter 3—psychoanalytic, behavioristic, humanistic, and McGregor's X and Y theory—two additional theories related to work motivation are Herzberg's two-factor theory and the "need for achievement" theory. Job enrichment is also used to increase worker satisfaction and provide employers with the benefits of fuller use of employee capabilities.

Evidence of emotions can be found in the workplace and is not necessarily undesirable. Caring is important to a sense of achievement, to the quality of work we do, and to mutually satisfying relationships with others. Unpleasant emotions such as anger can cause problems, but, if understood, can be controlled or used constructively. Fear and jealousy, if not checked, can also cause problems with work itself and with relationships with others.

There are a number of variations in employer-employee relationships today. It is important, therefore, to know the management structure of the company for which you work. Loyalty and trust are also important in employer-employee relationships. Labor unions and management must work together to accomplish objectives and still maintain favorable relationships.

Co-worker relations are more relaxed than those between employers and employees. Liking the people one works with is known as social facilitation. Customer or client relations require courteous attention, satisfaction of needs, and if necessary, handling complaints. Ethical standards and practices are a concern to business, organizations, and individuals today. We should be aware of the ethical standards of those we work for and have contact with, and we should live up to our own ethical standards.

Conflict, competition, and cooperation are a part of the world of work, and each can contribute constructively to people working together or in the same line of work. Teams in today's workplace are used to improve human relations, solve problems, and accomplish objectives not readily possible for individuals. There are advantages to team functioning, but there are also potential problems. One should be prepared to be an effective team player as he or she enters, or reenters, the workplace today.

Communication at work should apply suggestions for effective communication discussed in Chapter 12. There should also be willingness to share knowledge and experience. An open-door policy by management can contribute to the resolution of problems and concerns of employees. The grapevine and rumors should also be recognized as means of communication at work, even though they are not always accurate.

Sexual harassment has received increased attention in recent years. Everyone should know what it is and how to protect oneself from unwanted sexually related attention. Friendships at work can interfere with some working relationships, but they also can contribute greatly to job satisfaction and enjoyment.

Chapter 14, "Goal Achievement," completes the book. Establishing and achieving goals can draw on much that you have learned thus far, but it also requires special consideration.

 Psychology In Practice

1. Read an article about one of the human relations subjects discussed in this chapter. Identify the main idea of the article and explain how it could be applied to a situation you have been involved in or know about.

2. Working with a classmate, ask four owners of small businesses or department managers of larger businesses what they consider the most common human relations problem they encounter in their work. Ask them how they handle it. Prepare a group report and present it to the class.

3. Describe an ethical situation (real or hypothetical) pertaining to the career you are preparing to enter. Identify those factors you believe should be considered in making ethical decisions.

Learning Activities

Turn to page 433 to complete the Learning Activities and Enrichment Activities for this chapter.

Notes

1. R. A. Baron and P. B. Paulus, *Understanding Human Relations: A Practical Guide to People at Work,* Allyn and Bacon, Boston, 1991, p. 2.

2. F. Herzberg, *Work and the Nature of Man,* World Publishing Company, Cleveland, OH, 1966; reference in L. M. Berry and J. P. Houston, *Psychology at Work, An Introduction to Industrial and Organizational Psychology,* Brown & Benchmark, Madison, WI, 1993, pp. 85–86.

3. L. M. Berry and J. P. Houston, *Psychology at Work, An Introduction to Industrial and Organizational Psychology,* Brown & Benchmark, Madison, WI, 1993, p. 85.

4. D. C. McClelland, *Human Motivation,* Scott, Foresman and Company, Glenview, IL, 1985.

5. J. W. Atkinson, An *Introduction to Motivation,* Van Nostrand Reinhold, Princeton, NJ, 1964; reference in Rod Plotnik, *Introduction to Psychology,* 3rd. ed., Brooks/Cole Publishing Company, Pacific Grove, CA, 1993, p. 332.

6. R. J. Samuelson, "The Trophy Syndrome," *Newsweek,* December 21, 1992, p. 45.

7. R. V. Dawis, R. T. Fruehling, and N. B. Oldham, *Psychology: Human Relations and Work Adjustment,* McGraw-Hill Book Company, New York, 1989, p. 297.

8. D. Benton and J. Halloran, *Applied Human Relations: An Organizational Approach,* Prentice Hall, Englewood Cliffs, NJ, 1991, p. 386.

9. S. Strasser and J. Sena, *Work Is Not a Four-Letter Word,* Business One Irwin, Homewood, IL, 1992, p. 147.

10. J. Gordon, "Work Teams: How Far Have They Come?" *Training: The Human Side of Business,* a periodical, October 1992, p. 60.

11. A. J. DuBrin, *Human Relations: A Job Oriented Approach,* Prentice Hall, Englewood Cliffs, NJ, 1988, p. 250.

12. M. Dalton, D. Hoyle, and M. Watts, *Human Relations,* South-Western Publishing Company, Cincinnati, OH, 1992, p. 274.

14 Goal Achievement

Learning Objectives

After completing this chapter, you will be able to do the following:

1. Develop your own definition of success, compare it with a definition from another source, and explain how and why your definition is different.
2. Determine what you consider to be the relative importance of a number of concepts related to goal achievement.
3. Identify factors that you believe have contributed to a young person's progress toward achieving her career goal.
4. Define and give examples of three types of mistakes. Also describe a mistake you have made, identify the type you believe it to be, and explain what you did about it.
5. Determine causes of failure that are likely to interfere with your achieving your goals and suggest how each might be minimized or eliminated.
6. Identify a company you might like to work for and develop answers to interview questions the prospective employer might ask.
7. Describe three types of learning by which you can continue to add to your career competency after you begin working full-time, and indicate where you could continue each type of learning.
8. Identify three reasons for procrastination and suggest how each might be counteracted with constructive behavior.
9. Describe a person you believe to be an effective leader, identify the leadership characteristics you believe he or she has, and indicate what you consider this person's style of leadership to be.

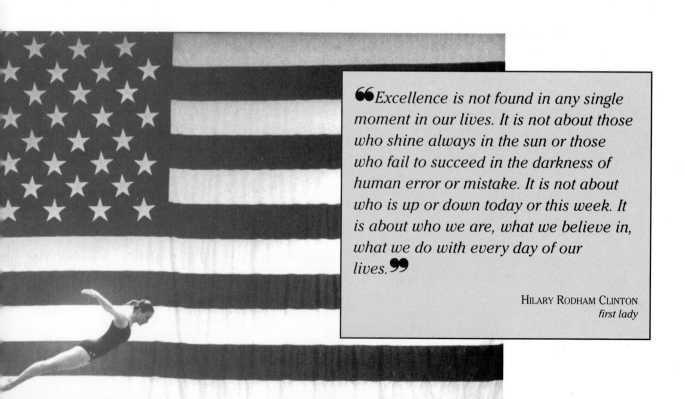

66 *Excellence is not found in any single moment in our lives. It is not about those who shine always in the sun or those who fail to succeed in the darkness of human error or mistake. It is not about who is up or down today or this week. It is about who we are, what we believe in, what we do with every day of our lives.* 99

HILARY RODHAM CLINTON
first lady

Everybody wants to be successful. But what does being successful mean? Certainly there are many variations to the answer. Is it possible that some of those who want to be successful really do not know what it would take for them to feel that way? If so, it is possible that they do not have goals. And unless we know what our destination is, on a trip or in life, it isn't very likely that we will reach where we might have wanted to be.

In order for our lives to be meaningful, we need to have goals. We also need to have some idea of how we are going to attain them. Our goals should be specific and should be stated in positive terms. In other words, think about what you want rather than what you don't want. It also helps to write goals down so you can review them periodically.

Stating your goals doesn't mean that you should never modify them or even develop new ones. But it does mean that at any particular time in your life you should have a clear idea of your personal and career objectives and how you might be successful in achieving them.

Some persons who consider themselves successful often state that their efforts and experiences in working toward their goals were as stimulating and satisfying as the achievement of the goals themselves. You probably recognize this as intrinsic motivation, which was discussed in Chapter 3. Persons who enjoy the process of working toward a goal lead happier lives.

CONSIDERATION FOR OTHERS

Each of us has his or her own life to live, but our lives are interwoven with the lives of others. For the most part we can determine our own values in life, but we must keep in mind that how we attempt to live according to those values affects the lives of others. If you have a family, for example, what you want to do with time and money, and other resources, also affects other individuals. You will recall that values were discussed in Chapter 3, "Motivation and Values." In reality, our values affect everything that we do.

Another way your goals could affect another person is if you are married and your spouse also has a career. Ideally, both partners in the marriage establish some mutual goals and take into consideration how their individual goals would affect the other person.

Keep consideration for others in mind as we give our attention to individual goals and goal achievement in the remainder of this chapter.

WHAT ARE YOUR GOALS?

It is unlikely that a person would say, "I have one goal in life and that is to . . ." Even if a person would make such a statement, it would probably be based more on lack of self-understanding than on a clear determination of that one goal.

Goal setting begins with self-understanding. Remember that there is no other human being exactly like you. You have the right to determine what is important to you and what you want out of life and your working career. The better you understand yourself as an individual the easier it will be to determine goals. Some of the questions each of us should think about are: What do I enjoy? What subjects have I liked best in school? Who is the person I most admire and what do I admire about that person? Do I consider myself an introvert, extrovert, or ambivert? Am I a "morning lark" or a "night owl" in terms of

A fabric importer examines sample swatches in preparation for placing an order.

what time of day I am at my best? How important have my relationships with others been in the past? What kind of relationships would I like with others in the future? How do I best like to spend my free time? How important are material possessions to me?

Let's consider some of the major factors that should be taken into consideration in determining our goals.

What Is Your Primary Purpose?

It is desirable not only to determine the purpose of life in a universal sense but also to work out the primary purpose of your individual life. It is not necessary that you interpret the meaning of life in the same way as someone else, but it is important that your life have meaning and purpose. Determination of your life's primary purpose will affect all of your other goals. Often a person's primary purpose is closely related to one's religious beliefs or a basic belief in the origin of life.

Money—What Does It Mean?

Most of us have to work for a living, and perhaps none of us will ever have to worry about being "too rich." There can be a wide range of differences, however, as to what extent money relates to our goals. The following are some examples.

- I'll do whatever pays the best.
- It has no value in itself. It's simply a means of exchange.

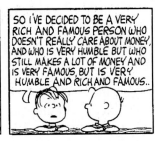

PEANUTS reprinted by permission of UFS, Inc.

- Money may not buy happiness, but it can sure buy comfort.
- There is too much emphasis on money in today's society.
- Who doesn't want to be rich? Isn't it everyone's dream?
- There are probably as many happy poor people as happy rich people.
- I need it so I work to get it; if I didn't need it, I wouldn't work.
- The best things in life are free; that makes us all rich.
- I want all I can get. It's easier to spend or give it away than it is to get it.

 What would you SAY? How would you respond to a person who asks, "How important is making a lot of money to you?" (Assume the person is in a position to have the right to ask.)

How Important Is Work?

Have you determined a goal pertaining to the career you are preparing to enter? Even though your first thought may be "to get a job and make some money," it is important that you think about the kind of job you want, and what you would like to be doing five, ten, or even twenty years from now. A prospective employer might ask what your long-range goals are. If so, it wouldn't be advisable to say, "I don't have any. I just want to get a job and make some money."
Occupational Outlook Quarterly/Fall 1992 states:

> Choosing a career is one of the hardest jobs you will ever have. You should devote extensive time, energy, and thought to make a decision with which you will be happy. Even though undertaking this task means hard work, view a career as an opportunity to do something you enjoy, not simply as a necessity or as a means of earning a living. Taking the time to thoroughly explore career opportunities can mean the difference between finding a stimulating and fulfilling career or hopping from one job to the next in search of the right job. Finding the best occupation for you also is important because work influences many aspects of your life—from your choice of friends and recreational activities to where you live.[1]

You no doubt have given consideration to the kind of work you will find satisfying if you are enrolled in a particular educational or training program. You may also know of people who have changed programs or jobs because they didn't think the work was appropriate for them. You may have done this yourself. Some say persons who do this don't know what they want: In reality, they may be giving more thought to what they want than persons who stay in jobs they find boring and unrewarding.

It might be well to be aware here that dissatisfaction is not always due to the job; it may be a person's attitude toward work itself. Some people think of work solely as a means of making money to satisfy other needs. A few think of it merely as something to do. Others recognize these purposes but view their work as an opportunity to lead a challenging, productive life. They are involved in developing their potential, in becoming more self-actualized. With almost everyone, work enters into the concept of success. This is true even for people who say, "If I were rich, I wouldn't work." For most of us, then, it is practical to consider how work-related goals fit into our broader goals in life.

Special training and education don't always guarantee that you will make more money. But they usually allow a person to find work that is satisfying and rewarding in a number of ways.

Where Do Others Come In?

Probably all of us have personal goals that involve our relationships with others. For some of us, establishing and maintaining mutually satisfying human relationships may be considered the most important goal in our lives. It seems common, however—even for people who highly value their relationships—to

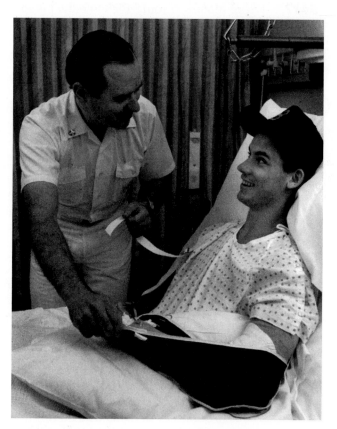

Nursing is one of the more widely recognized service-oriented careers.

take them for granted much of the time. It is not wise for our total happiness to be dependent on a relationship with another person, but it can be a prime factor in what is important to us.

Another type of involvement with others is not so personal but can be an integral part of what we want to do with our lives. This involves service to others. For many people, service to others is a primary goal. It can be related to one's career, as many careers are service-related, or it can be voluntary service outside one's work. Dr. Albert Schweitzer, the multitalented humanitarian and physician, spent much of his life treating those in need at a hospital he established in Africa. He is an excellent example of those who consider serving others a primary goal in life. There are many more examples.

How Important Is Freedom?

You may not have thought of freedom as a goal you would like to achieve. If you haven't, it could very well be because at this time you already have all the freedom you want. Freedom is an intangible value that many of us take for granted. This value is evident in the problems of adjustment that arise when one loses a degree of freedom.

Real or perceived restrictions in our life and work can also affect our sense of freedom. A number of individuals can be in the same basic situation and evaluate their circumstances differently, for example. Do you remember our comparison of influence and control in Chapter 3, "Motives and Values"? Some individuals experience and enjoy almost complete freedom in their lives. Others in similar situations believe they have little freedom and often feel restricted and frustrated. For them, a goal may be to have greater freedom; however, they may already have more than they recognize or appreciate. One's sense of freedom is not always determined by the situation itself, but rather in how he or she interprets the situation.

A sense of freedom is considered by many to be a deciding factor in determining both personal and career-related goals. Of course, voluntarily giving up some freedom for an interdependent relationship or in a particular type of work situation is more acceptable than being denied freedom by outside forces.

FACTORS THAT CONTRIBUTE TO GOAL ACHIEVEMENT

Individuals who have achieved goals or have already experienced considerable progress toward achievement of their goals frequently refer to the following contributing factors: unified purpose, money management, time management, flexibility, recognition of opportunity, self-confidence, perseverance, and constructive reaction to criticism. Each of these factors will be discussed in further detail on the following pages.

Unified Purpose

Individuals have numerous wants and may even have conflicting motives, but to be successful they must establish priorities and make choices. Successful people know what they want as well as what they want to be and do, and they

are willing to pay the price in time and effort. Whatever the guidelines, the successful person has both short- and long-range goals. One's primary purpose in life can be thought of as one's personal philosophy, as discussed in Chapter 11. Life lived on a daily basis and over the years consists of numerous ambitions and goals, however. We may have long-range goals, for example, related to savings or material possessions, career achievements, interpersonal relationships, or service to others. Each long-range goal can be broken down into short-range goals. These are what we work at on a day-to-day basis. We find, then, that achieving a series of subgoals helps us to reach a long-range goal.

It is important that all of these goals be related, in a sense that achieving one goal makes it easier to achieve others. Those who do not determine goals might develop one habit or activity that is in conflict with something else they want. Although we can expect to have conflicts, we should learn to recognize and resolve them in a way that does not defeat our own purposes.

People with clear goals live one day at a time, but they know what they are trying to accomplish and why. They have a primary purpose and related goals and subgoals. Each day, therefore, has meaning and purpose.

Money Management

It is important not only to earn an adequate amount of money but also to manage it to your advantage. This is especially true in a society that has established liberal credit practices.

Many people rationalize their not having a budget. Either they "don't have enough money to budget" or they "have enough money so that I don't need a budget." But many money problems and financial crises can be avoided by setting at least some general guidelines about how much money is coming in and where it is going. People can also acquire possessions related to long-range goals by using foresight and saving for those goals.

The way one's income is spent depends on short-term and long-term goals as well as one's underlying concept of success. Some people want more costly vacations; others will value travel; still others may be more interested in security. Some spend less money on food or clothing in order to spend more on education and other types of self-improvement.

In setting up a budget you must consider both fixed expenses and variable expenses. Fixed expenses may include such items as house payments or rent, real estate taxes, insurance, church support, and installment payments. The word "fixed" does not necessarily mean that the costs of these expenses do not change. For example, your rent or your real estate taxes may go up. Rather, fixed expenses are fairly stable from month to month in a year's budget plan. In contrast, variable expenses include such items as clothing, utility bills, medical care, recreation, and gifts. These expenses are usually not the same from month to month, and an estimated percentage of one's income is set aside for them.

Many successful people report that they always save a percentage of their income regardless of variable expenses, unexpected situations, or immediate wants. Although this may not be easy, one young adult reports that voluntarily deducting savings from her paycheck had become as automatic as payroll deductions for income tax or health insurance. Even a small amount adds up as time passes. Once the habit of saving has been established and some long-range goals have been set, you can pay more attention to your immediate

"SO I FIGURED, FOR $39, WHY BREAK MY NECK?"

Reprinted by permission of the artist, Leo Cullom.

concerns and short-range goals. You also gain satisfaction from seeing regular progress toward long-range goals.

Time Management

"You can't save it and use it later.
You can't elect not to spend it.
You can't borrow it.
You can't leave it. Nor can you retrieve it.
You can't take it with you either."[2]

You can't find more time but you can learn to use the time you have more effectively. This is one of the key reasons some people accomplish more than others. They do not have more time. Some people do live more years, but we among the living all have the same number of hours in a day. Of course, you know that; but occasionally it helps to be reminded of things we know, so that we do not overlook or neglect the obvious.

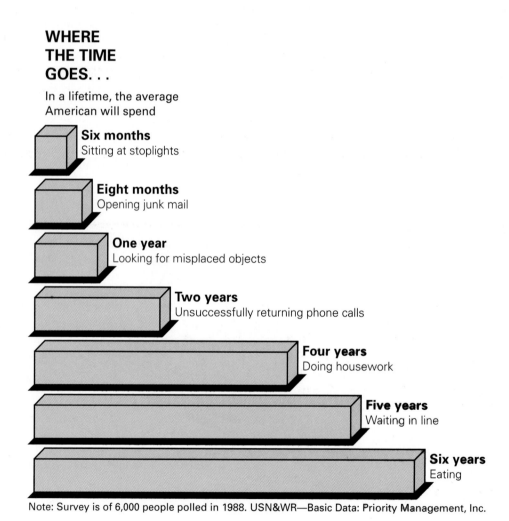

WHERE THE TIME GOES...

In a lifetime, the average American will spend

Six months
Sitting at stoplights

Eight months
Opening junk mail

One year
Looking for misplaced objects

Two years
Unsuccessfully returning phone calls

Four years
Doing housework

Five years
Waiting in line

Six years
Eating

Note: Survey is of 6,000 people polled in 1988. USN&WR—Basic Data: Priority Management, Inc.

Once we make certain decisions we do not have control over all of our time. We agree to take a job where we are expected to work so many hours a day. If we drive an automobile, we spend time sitting at red lights. If we decide to see a doctor about our swollen glands, we spend some time in the waiting room. And you also spend time waiting in various lines, don't you? We cannot easily eliminate these experiences from our lives, but we can learn to use time in waiting rooms and standing in line to do some creative thinking, work on a small project we carry with us, or even to relax, instead of getting frustrated and wasting time.

During the time you can call your own—that during which you can plan what you are going to do—setting priorities should be your first step. That doesn't mean that the top priority should be related to accomplishment of a task; one's top priority may be exercising, or talking to one's spouse, or playing with one's children. It means deciding what is most important to you. A top priority doesn't necessary have to be the first thing that you do. It only means that it is more important than other things that you decide to do and therefore you plan time for it in your day's activities.

In order to make use of our time, we should identify time wasters in our lives. Out of habit, we do many things that are relatively unimportant to us. Do you watch TV programs that you really aren't interested in? Do you wander around aimlessly before you decide what you are going to do? Do you take a nap even when you don't need the sleep? We all should be able to identify some time wasters or things we do that have such low priority for us that we really should not use our time for them. When we do, we are neglecting something that has higher priority, because we only have so much time. Knowing your priorities and your time-wasting habits is essential to using time more effectively in order to accomplish our short-range goals and to progress toward long-range goals.

 What would you DO? Is there something you would like to do that you don't seem to have time for? What can you do to use your time more efficiently in order to include this activity?

Flexibility

To change your behavior with purpose is to have flexibility. It takes continual evaluation and decision making, and often courage, to be flexible, but it is a common factor in goal achievement. It is easier to react according to habit or established rules, and many do, especially those who wonder why they are not more successful. Achievers are movers, but they constantly take related factors into consideration in charting or changing their course of action toward their destinations. They are not afraid to say they were wrong and to try something new. They may have many failures, or setbacks, but they also have more successes than those unwilling to modify their goals or take new risks.

Recognition of Opportunity

Factors often associated with timely recognition of opportunity are insight, intuition, pull, or luck. But the better you as an individual understand yourself, your priorities, your strengths, and your limitations, the more readily you will recognize and react to opportunities for goal achievement that others may miss. Those who achieve their goals seldom make it completely on their own, but they recognize the who, what, where, and when of opportunity. A strategy for goal achievement that is used increasingly today is called networking. A person who networks is using all possible human contacts to find ways to achieve a goal. Networking is often related to finding a job but it can also be helpful in accomplishing other purposes. Individuals with the need or purpose inquire of co-workers, neighbors, relatives, and everyone they have contact with for leads on achieving their goal. Those who do not know what you need or want may have valuable information that you will never know about. Networking is not intended to take advantage of anyone or to ask for unreasonable favors. It is not luck or pull, but an accepted strategy today for getting results.

Self-Confidence

Self-confidence results from a positive, realistic self-concept as discussed in Chapter 2, "Personality and Self-Concept." It is bolstered by knowing what you want and recognizing your capabilities. It can be the determining factor in what you achieve. Henry Ford, the pioneer automaker, once said, "Whether a person believes he can do a thing or not, he is right."

Those who have overcome problems of inadequate self-confidence frequently state that the key was getting their minds off themselves. If people are concerned with others and what they want to accomplish, they don't have time to dwell on inadequacies, which are often imaginary or exaggerated. This suggestion has also been given for overcoming shyness, which often is related to lack of self-confidence.

People gain more self-confidence as they establish realistic goals and begin to see that they are making some progress toward attaining those goals. If they see that they are lacking a skill, they can do something about it, such as taking a class to learn the skill. As they overcome their deficiency, they begin to see themselves as more competent individuals, and justifiably gain more self-confidence.

Perseverance

"Stick-to-itiveness" is another term used for **perseverance.** It's also been called stubbornness, as an undesirable trait. One person expressed the difference this way: When I don't give up, it's perseverance; when you don't give up, it's stubbornness.

Many successful people could tell you about the importance of working long and hard, of not giving up when you believe in yourself and what you're doing. The path to success is often uphill, progress is not always assured, the next milestone is not always in sight, and it is natural to slacken in motivation and become discouraged. Persevering people work toward their goals when encouraged and work harder when discouraged.

A characteristic closely related to perseverance is self-discipline. Success lies in the ability to follow through with whatever is needed to achieve one's goal. Many people say they want something, but they don't want it badly enough to make the required effort.

Constructive Reaction to Criticism

Another characteristic of many successful people is the ability to accept criticism and profit from it. This isn't easy, because it is more natural to resent criticism, to defend yourself from an attack on your self-esteem. You must give yourself a chance to calm down, therefore, before evaluating criticism. Then you should examine the qualifications of critics to determine whether they know what they are talking about and have valid reasons for criticism. Secondhand criticisms should be treated lightly, as they are likely to be inaccurate.

A person who pays attention to criticism should remember that it is impossible to please everybody. No matter what you do or how you do it, you are a target for a certain amount of criticism. If you expect occasional criticism, it will lessen the blow to your pride and be easier to cope with. Probably the best approach is to develop habits of self-evaluation and criticism. Constructive self-criticism can be an important step toward self-improvement.

WHEN YOU FAIL

"When You Fail" is the heading of this section rather than *"If* you Fail." Each of us can think of examples of when we have fallen short of what we have attempted. There is a big difference, however, between the verb *fail* and the noun

Factors That Contribute to Goal Achievement

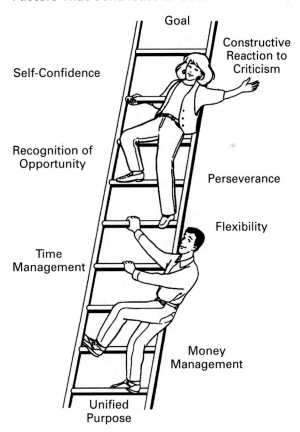

Goal

Self-Confidence

Constructive Reaction to Criticism

Recognition of Opportunity

Perseverance

Flexibility

Time Management

Money Management

Unified Purpose

failure. It has been said, "No one need think of himself as a failure unless he gives up on a goal he would still like to achieve." Even then there can be reasons why one should not be considered a failure. If one fails to achieve a particular goal, he or she can set a new goal and likely experience success. Ordinarily, people do not deliberately fail. All people want to be successful when they begin working toward a goal they have set for themselves.

It has been found that there are common characteristics of people who frequently fail just as there are common characteristics of people who reach most of their goals. And since success and failure are opposites, some of these characteristics are opposites. Common characteristics of failure are discussed in the following section.

Trying to Get Something for Nothing

Somebody is paying for everything that is "free." Most of the time you are paying for it yourself, but the costs are hidden. Very seldom is the person or the company offering free items or services covering the actual cost. Sooner or later most people learn that achieving goals is seldom easy and that rewards must be earned one way or another. Those who expect to achieve goals by following the path of least resistance often wonder why they are not happy or successful.

Poor Money Management

"What a waste of money" can be heard almost any day. You may even think or say to yourself, "I certainly wasted that money." When we come to the conclusion that we have wasted money ourselves we often lay it to lack of knowledge or poor judgment. When someone evaluates the use of money by others (even when it's none of his or her business) the main issue is one of different values.

Some of our conclusions about waste might also be due to conflicts. We may decide to spend a month's earnings on a two-day vacation, but when it's over we may decide it was a waste of money. We wanted the vacation, but we evidently didn't want to pay the price. Some ways in which we may be wasting money or at least spending it unwisely are discussed next. Keep in mind that what is wasteful for one person may not be so for another. Also notice that some of the ways we waste money are the opposite of how we manage money, discussed earlier.

Impulse Buying   Many people buy things they don't need and don't even really want. Remember, advertisers and merchants want to profit from your impulses. *You* should be the judge of how you want to spend your money.

Fad Buying   "Because everyone has one" is sometimes the reason for making a purchase. Fad purchases seldom are useful and soon lose their appeal.

Wasteful Living   Wasting food, power, fuel, and other supplies is like throwing money away.

Overpaying   Try to avoid paying more for products than you need to pay. Shop around for major purchases. Watch for sales.

Excessive Risk-Taking Be aware of risks. Know the extent of risk and whether you can afford to take it. This pertains to various types of gambling, but it also refers to making major purchases without carefully checking their condition and value.

Buying Carelessly Take your time and shop around for important purchases. For example, people sometimes buy the wrong kind of insurance for their situation. The type of insurance one needs is highly individualized. It should not be purchased hastily or carelessly.

Overbuying on Installments This may pertain to credit card purchases as well as to payments on a home. It is often the total amount of installment payments that causes financial problems. If your home payments put a strain on your budget, avoid buying other items on an installment plan.

Outdated Ideas and Useless Habits

Modern men and women live in a rapidly changing world, as we discussed in Chapter 1. Unless they can accept new ideas and change old habits, they will be left behind and will not experience personal progress, or success. If they reject examination and evaluation of the new, they may be setting themselves up to fail. The world of success is a world of change. Those who fail may not have developed the important trait of regularly examining habits of thinking and behavior.

Developing constructive habits, on the other hand, can free your attention from the numerous details of daily living. With freedom to concentrate on more interesting, challenging activities, you will be more productive and will have time to pursue your personal goals.

Habits pertaining to well-being and personal care can help you look better and feel better with little effort. They can be major factors in goal achievement.

Unfavorable Personality Characteristics

A single dominant negative personality characteristic can cause failure. Or a number of minor irritating personality weaknesses can do the same. Unfavorable personality characteristics cause more failures than any other factor. People who are intolerant, inconsiderate, or hard to get along with, for example, lose jobs, friends, and chances for success in life. They are their own worst enemies and, therefore, cannot escape failure.

Fear

Ironically, fear of failure can be the very cause of failure. "The only thing we have to fear is fear itself," Franklin Delano Roosevelt told the nation in his first inaugural address in March 1933, during the Great Depression. Fear has been a major cause of failure before and since. It can cripple or smother initiative and potential success. It may cause a person to take the wrong course of action or may prevent her or him from doing anything at all—which can be worse than trying and failing.

Without realizing it, some people are even afraid of success itself. They experience a conflict between the advantages of attaining their goals and the responsibilities or risks involved with their success. Such fear may relate to possible rejection by family and friends if one's situation changes as a result of achievement. This need not happen. Reaching our goals should not make us different as persons, and success need not change our relationships with others.

Success and efforts toward success often involve risk-taking, however. It's excessive risk-taking that should be avoided. We must be willing to assume the further challenges that go with attaining our goals. Successful persons know what risk is and know what they will do if they lose in a particular risk. They also know what they are not willing to risk. They are not overcome, therefore, by the fear of failure.

Not Profiting from Setbacks

Every area of success includes winners who, at some time in their struggle toward their goals, experienced disappointment and temporary setbacks. The important word in this statement is *temporary*. For some people a setback means failure and giving up. For them it *is* failure, but only because they allow it to be. A disappointment or setback only means a person has failed *this* time or in a particular way.

Thomas Edison conducted thousands of unsuccessful experiments before he succeeded with his electric light bulb. Those who do not profit from setbacks have difficulty experiencing success. On the other hand, repeated setbacks do not guarantee success. A person must be able to accept a temporary hindrance or setback but must also be able to use it as a stepping-stone to success.

A temporary setback can even be a learning experience. The following realizations can help you see such disappointments as positive experiences:

- People are not perfect. You are human, and no human being is perfect.
- People learn from mistakes. Disappointment or failure can help you to reassess your abilities and opportunities.
- It builds personal character to experience occasional setbacks.
- You can try again, or you can try something different.
- Family and friends accept you for yourself, not for what you accomplish or don't accomplish.
- Setbacks can release tensions and give you a temporary rest and a chance to rebuild your strength, resources, and spirit for another try.

Making Too Many Mistakes

There are different kinds of mistakes that might be classified as careless, reasonable, and innocent. Let's consider how some of these types of mistakes are made and how some of them might be avoided.

We make *careless* mistakes when we are not paying enough attention to what we are doing or are in too much of a hurry. A person in a hurry, for example, may neglect to turn off a machine or lock a door. Careless mistakes can also occur when one is doing repetitious work that does not require much thought. We can avoid careless mistakes by having a routine that includes essential tasks or by paying more attention to activities when we know that mistakes could be costly.

A *reasonable* mistake might be misplacing correspondence in the file of a person by the same name. In this type of error, a person can explain to those inconvenienced and make every effort to see that there is no delay in satisfying the customer or otherwise correcting the problem.

Innocent mistakes are made by inexperienced employees who haven't as yet learned exactly how something should be done. An effective training program or job orientation will reduce the number of such mistakes. Nevertheless, they do happen. Although we can learn by all mistakes, this is the "experience is a good teacher" type of mistake. Someone appropriately remarked, "Considering what it can cost, experience should be the best teacher."

If you make too many mistakes, your employer may justifiably decide that giving you a job is too costly. Let's remember that we are not perfect, but we can avoid many mistakes, we can correct most of those we make, and we can learn from all of them.

What do you THINK?   Why do you think so many people have difficulty admitting they have made a mistake?

PROCRASTINATION

"I'll do it tomorrow." If you have ever said that, does that make you a procrastinator? Hardly. But a person who has said that might be a procrastinator. Merely putting something off to another time might be a logical thing to do. If you're painting a house and the weather is bad, it would be logical to put off completing the job until another time. **Procrastination,** on the other hand, is a habit of putting things off without having a logical, sensible reason for doing so. Oh, we use the coping mechanism of rationalization to convince ourselves that we have a good reason, but it would not hold up under close objective examination.

Characteristics of Procrastination

In addition to procrastination's becoming a habit, it has other characteristics that interfere with goal achievement. It puts us behind schedule. If we put off a job today, we probably are already in the habit of doing so. That means we started out the day with things put off from yesterday. Tomorrow we start out with the carryover from today.

We not only get behind, but we get discouraged, and lessen our motivation and enthusiasm for each day's activities. Short-term goals give us direction and a sense of achievement as we move toward long-term goals. Procrastinators are functioning with a feeling of futility much of the time.

Putting off tasks also upsets priorities. It is usually the unpleasant chores that are put off and lessen our motivation for getting started "tomorrow." The answer provided by some individuals is to do unpleasant tasks first in each day's schedule. That can be a good idea, but only if the tasks are necessary, do not take too much time, and it doesn't make any difference when they are done. Otherwise, we may be neglecting tasks that should have higher priority. It is possible that we put off doing some things that don't need doing in the first place. In that case, we are only burdening ourselves with an empty carton. Although our priorities for a day, as well as for life, should be flexible, in order to accommodate unforeseen complications and interruptions, we should always know what our priorities are and why.

Procrastination can produce feelings of anxiety about having too much to do tomorrow and a feeling of guilt for not doing what we at least unconsciously know should have been done today. Although it was recognized earlier that procrastinators rationalize, we are not always that good at kidding ourselves. These unpleasant emotions can reduce our energy and self-confidence.

Why Do We Procrastinate?

We know from our study of human behavior thus far that individuals do similar things for different reasons. Let's consider some of the common reasons for procrastination. Perhaps you will identify reasons why you procrastinate among them.

Procrastination becomes a personality characteristic. If we get in the habit of responding to situations in a certain way, we continue that type of behavior without giving it much thought. If you ever ask someone to write a job recommendation for you, you wouldn't want that person to say you were a procrastinator, would you? Now is the time, not to procrastinate about when you are going to break the habit, but to do something constructive about it.

Another reason for procrastination is lack of clear goals. An individual is unsure of the value of the activity in itself or of how it relates to long-range goal achievement. If we don't know the purpose of what we are doing, we often aren't motivated to get it completed. Although we have been talking primarily about work-related tasks, we don't want to lose sight of recreational or leisure activities as worthwhile activities. But we aren't as likely to put those off, are we?

Individuals also procrastinate because their goals may be unrealistic and they are unsure of their ability to do or complete a particular task. None of us want to be embarrassed, to feel incompetent, or to fail. Lack of self-confidence, therefore, can cause us to procrastinate.

Difficulty of the task is a further common reason for putting a task off. This can be related to being unsure of oneself, but it can also be for other reasons. If a task is very demanding of both our mental and physical abilities, even though we can do it, we may avoid the related stress by putting it off.

There are additional reasons for procrastination. Maybe you could add a few yourself.

 What would you DO? If you became aware that you have a habit of procrastinating, what would you do to break the habit?

In spite of economic conditions, there will always be openings in the job market. There might not be enough jobs at any particular time for everyone who wants a job, however. Unemployment has been a serious problem in the country and for many individuals in recent years. It is more important than ever not only to be qualified for the type of job you would like, but also to know how to go about seeking and getting a job.

Getting the Job

Many persons receive jobs with a particular business or company as a result of a referral from a current employee. It's important to keep in mind that ongoing businesses and companies are continually hiring new employees to replace those who retire, move, are fired, or leave for other reasons. In spite of numerous downsizings, or cutting down on the scope of business and number of employees, some companies are expanding. Companies want the best employees they can get just as job-seekers want the best jobs they can get. It takes strategies and alertness on the part of both for good companies and potential good employees to make a match.

Other ways to get a job are through help-wanted ads, employment agencies, college placement offices, referrals by friends or relatives, and other networking. Sometimes walk-ins, without knowing whether a business or company is even hiring, lead to jobs, but the chances are much slimmer.

Have a Resume   Some owners or managers of businesses do not require a resume. They may go entirely by a job application, a brief interview, and references. However, even if you think you may not need a resume, it's recommended that you prepare one and have it available. It gives you a picture of your objectives, your educational background, your work experience, and related achievements that you might overlook unless you seriously think about them and put them in writing. If you are taking a written communications course as part of your education, you may be required to prepare a resume. If so, be thankful for the requirement. A resume might be difficult to prepare, but it's easier to do under the guidance of an instructor than to do on your own. Of course, it is important over time to keep your resume up to date. If it can be prepared on a computer, you have the advantage of easily being able to add experience.

Help-wanted ads and other sources of information about available jobs say "Send Resume." This is the first impression a prospective employer has of you, and if he or she doesn't like your resume, you will not be contacted for a personal interview. It's worth your time and effort, therefore, to prepare an accurate, complete, and good-looking resume. Be sure that it is accurate. If you have held a number of jobs in the last several years, it is recommended that you include all of them. There is more tolerance toward job-hopping than there used to be.

If you have not prepared a resume in a class, library references are likely available. Other more work-experienced persons can offer helpful suggestions or review your resume after you have the first draft prepared. When you have completed it, do not run multiple copies on a copy machine. It is relatively inexpensive to have professional-looking copies made at quick-print businesses, and it could make a difference in whether you get a job. If the person doing the hiring has dozens or even hundreds of resumes to review, those that make a poor first impression are quickly discarded.

Prepare for Your Interview   When you are contacted for a job interview, properly prepare yourself for this next critical step in getting a job. The job interview is often the determining factor in whether a person is hired. An individual must have the required training qualifications, but beyond that which is expected, the prospective employer tries to determine what kind of person you are. Employers evaluate your qualifications, recommendations, appearance, and ability to communicate to determine whether you will be reliable and trustworthy and whether you will be able to get along with fellow employees. More than 80 percent of workers who are fired from their jobs are released for personality traits rather than inability to do the work. Interviewers must therefore try to determine whether prospective employees will be an asset to their company. Here are some suggestions for this door-opener to success at work.

Know Your Qualifications   Your qualifications include education, training, and experience. You should be able to recall and discuss your qualifications easily, even though the employer has the factual information in writing.

Also, be prepared to answer questions, and consider ahead of time what they might be. Interviewers often ask, "What do you consider your greatest weakness?" An employer may want to know not only how you evaluate yourself but also how you intend to compensate for your weakest job-related characteristic. You should be honest, but an example might be, "I don't like paperwork, but I know it's important so I do it as soon as possible." Or, "I've had difficulty with reading, but I took a remedial course in college, which really helped. I intend to continue to practice the skills I learned and may take another course in the future." In other words, indicating what you have done or are doing about a weakness can be considered a strength.

Know Your Potential Employer   This doesn't mean you need to know your employer or interviewer personally, but if possible know his or her name and how to pronounce it correctly. Use Mr., Mrs., Ms., Dr., or whatever is appropriate before the person's last name. Do not call a person by his or her first name in an interview situation unless the interviewer requests that you do.

Also learn as much as you can about the company or business. The size of the business determines to some extent how much information is available, but there are many ways to obtain information. Employees, former employees, the library, local job service agencies, and a chamber of commerce are some possibilities. Impress the interviewer with the idea that you not only want a job but that you want to work for that company or business. You may even be asked, "Why do you want to work for us?" If you don't know anything about the company, you aren't going to have a good answer.

Be Alert   Listen attentively to what the interviewer tells you. Ask a few questions to indicate your interest in the company and what it does. Also ask questions about what you believe you have a right to know about a company before agreeing to work for it. Your questions should be concerned with more than wages and fringe benefits, however.

Look Good   You should be well groomed and appropriately dressed. This may be thought of as "it goes without saying" advice, yet many employers can point to stacks of applications that have been rejected because the applicants' appearance made a poor impression in the interview. If you appear as if you don't care much about yourself, you are not likely to convince an interviewer that you will care about your job.

Be Appreciative   If the interview is successful and you get the job, the company may be as pleased to have you as a new employee as you are to have the job. But never hesitate to thank someone for his or her time and interest regardless of the results. The positive last impression you make may be the deciding factor in whether you are offered the job.

Some of the common reasons stated by employers for rejecting job applicants are the following:

- Poor personal appearance
- "Know-it-all attitude"; claims to be able to do anything
- Lack of confidence
- No goals; just wants a job
- Wants too much too soon
- Lack of knowledge about the company
- Critical of others, especially past employers and teachers
- No outside interests or activities
- Has no questions about the job or company
- Lacks common courtesy and appreciation

Notice that none of these reasons pertains to one's lack of ability to do the work. One is expected to know how to do the actual work involved in a job, but employers are looking for additional qualifications in people who will become part of their company.

Keeping Your Job

You may not want to keep your first job until you are ready to retire, as was often the case in past generations. You may recall reading in Chapter 1, "Psychology in Our Changing World," that some people will change jobs six or seven times during their lifetime. Others may change to a completely different career. But you would like to keep your job until you decide that you want a different one, wouldn't you?

There is less job security today than a decade ago because of economic conditions, already discussed. Some people are still relatively secure because of seniority rights and contracts, but it isn't likely you'll have much seniority in the near future. Besides, it is much more satisfying to keep your job because you are needed and considered a valued employee than because you are protected in some way. A few suggestions for keeping your job on your own merits follow. You will notice they relate to vocational maturity and employer/employee relations, discussed in previous chapters.

Be Dependable   There are certain requirements of the job pertaining to hours, work standards, and company policies. The company values the employee who is reliable in doing what he or she is expected to do and has agreed to do.

Produce   There are some people who rationalize that they are working if they somehow keep themselves occupied during working hours. Piecework in a factory is one of the easiest ways of measuring production, but there are many others. In fact, it doesn't take too long on a job before both management and other employees know who does the work and who slacks off. Producers work harder, but they enjoy their work more. They also contribute more to the success of the company or organization because they like their job. Management, as can be expected, values such employees.

Harmonize   An ability to harmonize has many applications. It is related primarily to human relations, or getting along with fellow workers, supervisors, and all others who are part of the same organization. Requests can be made reasonably, dissatisfactions can be expressed with emotional restraint, and cooperation can be given on all levels. Harmonizers are successful at problem solving and adjusting. Their interests go beyond their immediate tasks and minor frustrations.

Be Loyal   When you take a job with a company, you immediately become a part of that organization. Loyalty does not mean being weak or dishonest in public relations. But it does mean emphasizing the positive rather than negative aspects of an organization. It means giving your best efforts to support and improve the company.

Advancing at Work

What does it mean to advance at work? This question must be answered in terms of an individual's definition of success and in terms of his or her goals. Some people think of advancement in terms of more money; others think of it as related to status or a sense of esteem; others may think of more responsibility. It can be any one or even all of these things. It can also involve the opportunity for self-actualization, which usually includes at least some of the other rewards. A few suggestions for the highly motivated individual interested in advancing at work follow.

Seminars and training courses, offered by many companies, are excellent ways to further one's knowledge as well as to reflect enthusiasm and commitment.

Continue to Learn   Continuing to learn is characteristic of the intellectually mature person, as discussed in Chapter 11, "Life-Span Development." People who increase their knowledge and broaden their learning are likely to advance in their jobs. One-time training is an impossibility in the rapidly changing workplace of today and tomorrow.

Fortunately, continuing to learn is a principal factor in maintaining interest in work. Those training for jobs today don't have to be concerned about doing "the same old thing" for the rest of their working lives. Those who not only accept change but are active in their vocational fields, determining what some of the inevitable changes will be, are the ones who will advance in the future.

There are many ways to learn. We can take classes, go to seminars, study on our own, learn from others, or learn from experience on the job. The importance of learning in the job is expressed as follows in the book, *When Smart People Fail:*

> I don't divide the world into the weak and the strong, or the successes and the failures, those who make it and those who don't. I divide the world into learners and unlearners.
>
> There are people who learn, who are open to what happens around them, who listen, who hear the lessons. When they do something stupid, they don't do it again. And when they do something that works a little bit, they do it even better and harder the next time. The question is not whether you are a success or failure, but whether you are a learner or a nonlearner.[3]

Know Your Company   It was suggested earlier that you show knowledge of and interest in a company when applying for a job. This step is only the beginning, however. The more you know about the company and how it functions and what all its products and services are, the more valuable you will be to that company. People who want to advance in an organization ensure that someone else knows how to do their job and that they become familiar with the work of those above them on the work hierarchy. In this way, they can quite easily be replaced and can make a relatively easy transition to a job at a higher level. Aside from this, people who are eager to give their best to their work can be assured that the organization will be interested in receiving the best contribution they have to make.

Know Your Competition   Knowing the competition is especially important for those in management and decision-making positions, but it is also useful for the employee interested in advancement. Successful businesses can be assured of competition, and unless a company can meet competition, it is in jeopardy. Ambitious people are interested not only in their jobs and the company for which they work but also in the entire career field of their employment. They may even decide at some point in their careers that they would rather work for a competitor than for the company of their original employment. This keeps people focused on their place in the total occupational scene and is advantageous to a free-enterprise economy.

Be Receptive to Change   Many people do not advance in their company or line of work simply because they are satisfied with where they are and what they are doing. It cannot be denied that these people are successful if they have accomplished their goal and are not motivated by what others call further vocational advancement. Those who seek advancement, on the other hand, must be willing to accept changes in responsibilities, human relationships, and environment.

Do a Little Extra   Most of what we do at work is "our job." We are expected to do a certain number of tasks with an acceptable degree of competence. We may also have some responsibilities in our work situation. What we do beyond these expectations may be a small percentage of our total effort and may take only a few extra minutes. But it shows that we care about the company, have pride in our work, and take personal satisfaction in our performance.

There are always some who criticize such efforts and others who actually heckle an ambitious, dedicated employee—a form of defensive behavior that is a cover-up for their own inadequacy. You can learn not to let this type of behavior bother you. A positive attitude can apply to a total outlook on life, including one's work. Decide what you want to do and how you want to do it. Then, don't let negative reactions of others prevent you from pursuing your goal. Extra effort is usually recognized in some way. Measure the rewards—including personal satisfaction and inner peace— against the immature reactions of a few people whose effort is poor.

WHO BECOMES A LEADER?

Every company and organization needs people in leadership positions. Who will be these leaders? Why do some people become leaders? One response to the latter question is that some people want to be leaders and others do not. Or an individual may be a leader in one group but not in another.

If you were to make a study of effective leaders in different types of groups or even various groups of the same type, one of the conclusions you would soon draw is that not all leaders are alike. Individuals have distinctive personalities, and there are different leadership styles. Three of the most common leadership styles are authoritarian, democratic, and laissez-faire. The **authoritarian** leader uses a great deal of control. He or she makes many of the decisions and delegates the work. A group of this type, if they accept their leader, may complete a large quantity of work. Leaders who follow the **democratic** style involve members of the group in discussing alternatives and making choices. The leader gives direction but is not as dominant as the authoritarian leader. Quality and originality have been found to be characteristics of this type of group's activities. The **laissez-faire** style is to let others do their work without interference. Some groups seem to have this type of leadership when they have an inexperienced leader with no particular leadership approach. There are other leaders who use the laissez-faire style because they believe it is the best approach to have individuals work together to achieve a common goal. As you might expect, a group with this type of leadership often has the lowest productivity. Perhaps too much time is spent deciding what is going to be done and who is going to do what.

Effective leaders, regardless of their particular style, usually have a number of the characteristics described next.

Personal Effectiveness

To be an effective leader of others, a person must be effective as an individual. You must have control over yourself before you can expect to influence others. This ability to handle yourself and your own affairs promotes a sense of self-confidence that inspires support from others. You deserve and receive admiration and trust.

Organization

Leaders use a variety of available resources, including time and money, as well as opportunities to use special equipment and to consult others. What may appear to others to be luck—such as being in the right place at the right time—is often the result of careful planning with an element of risk-taking.

Organization requires setting priorities. Progress toward some goals requires a definite order of effort and activity. There is a step-by-step pathway to achieving many goals. In other situations, the main factors may be total time and effort.

Ability to Communicate

You cannot get very much accomplished by your club, team, or other type of organization unless you can make yourself understood. The messages you deliver must be honest and straightforward, yet be received without offense. This ability requires a diplomacy that is developed from an understanding of human nature and an interest in individuals.

Energy and Enthusiasm

Leaders know how to organize and develop a plan of action, but they are also enthusiastic workers. They motivate and inspire others by their own eagerness to get a job done well and their willingness to work at least as hard as anyone else. They make members of a group feel they are working with them rather than for them.

Courage and Integrity

Courage involves taking risks. We may ordinarily think of courage as risking one's life in some heroic way, but there are other ways to act courageously. For example, it requires courage to take a stand in support of a subject that is unpopular.

Integrity is related to courage in the sense that one's beliefs and behavior are consistent even though other actions might be easier. Integrity includes basic honesty and responsibility. Leaders with integrity can be trusted.

Members of a group respect leaders who don't back down when problems arise or when opposition becomes a threat. Effective leaders believe in themselves and the purpose of the group. They encourage active participation by members, but they also are willing to carry their own responsibilities.

Fairness

If a leader expects others to work together in a constructive manner, they must feel that their leader is not playing favorites. This can be a problem in some situations because individuals do not always perceive what is happening accurately. Nevertheless, a person in a leadership position must try to be impartial and fair.

Appreciation

"Good job, Andrew." "Nice work, June." Words can have tremendous power, especially when we know that they express honest appreciation. A leader must organize, assign responsibilities, and communicate what is to be done, but he or she is also aware of what has been done and who has contributed to the achievement. Effective leaders observe, listen, and express appreciation. They also acknowledge efforts and achievements to the entire group, when appropriate. They are more concerned with achieving goals than with looking good personally or with receiving credit. But, of course, when their group does well, they do look good.

Interest in Company Goals

We all have our own goals and we also are aware that others in our personal lives affect these goals—as we affect theirs. Persons who are interested in advancing at work should also be aware and concerned about the goals of the company or organization they work for. R. L. Williams and James D. Long, in *Manage Your Life,* explain this as follows:

As you work toward your professional goals (e.g., seeking more responsibility, taking on a major project), ask yourself how your supervisor, your division, and your organization are likely to benefit from your pursuit of those goals. Whose reputation will be enhanced and who will gain materially from what you are doing? We're not suggesting that you must set aside your own preferences, but rather you should consider how others' professional prosperity will be affected. For example, if you are working as a sales representative, you might prefer to focus your efforts on products that already have a good market. On the other hand, management might want to develop new markets. Because the bottom line for any company is the profit margin, adjustments you make over the short run to benefit the company will likely benefit you in the long run.[4]

PUTTING THE PIECES TOGETHER

Looking back at each of the chapters, learning objectives, learning activities, and associated materials, you should be able to see numerous interrelationships that could contribute toward achieving your goals.

Learning about psychology, the scientific study of human behavior, will help you to describe, understand, predict, and control or influence your own behavior and the behavior of others. Recognizing that we live in a rapidly changing world will help us to prepare for the future, to control or influence to some degree what is happening to us and our environment, to prevent what is undesirable from happening, and to promote desired changes or to make things happen.

Self-concept and personality were discussed in Chapter 2, but they are also related to numerous other subjects. How we perceive ourselves is probably the most important factor in what we do and what we are willing to attempt to do. Our personality characteristics affect our relations with others and many facets of our work.

Becoming a well-adjusted, integrated person must be a lifelong process. It is sometimes referred to as "getting it together." But we must be motivated to work at "keeping it together," or we will miss out on much of what life can offer.

To a certain extent each of us lives in his or her own world. Although we may have similar experiences through our senses, it is our interpretation of these experiences that makes a difference. Understanding factors that affect perception will help us understand our own world and to some extent the worlds of others.

Your emotions make you human, but your emotions can either help you or hinder you, and you are free to make the choice. Uncontrolled emotions can cause endless difficulty and unhappiness, but you can learn to be the master of your feelings and behavior in ways that will contribute excitement and joy to your life.

Your attitudes, or how you think and how you feel, affect your behavior. We may be prejudiced toward people or groups; that prejudice in turn can lead to discrimination. Positive, constructive attitudes lead to behavior that is also positive and constructive. It can be beneficial to all of us, therefore, to examine our attitudes periodically. If we can become better problem solvers our lives will be less stressful and we are more likely to achieve our goals. There are a number of approaches to problem solving, including various methods of creative thinking. We often think of problems as disturbing, which they can be, but problems can also be stimulating and challenging.

When we cannot achieve the results we would prefer from problem solving we must learn to adjust or accept what we cannot change. Failure to do so in a logical, rational way is one of the reasons for our use of coping mechanisms, which often block the path of our development as mature, fully functioning human beings.

Our total wellness affects all areas of our lives. There are physical, emotional, mental, and other aspects of total wellness. We have a tendency to take our wellness for granted, but maintaining it requires care and effort.

Exceptional persons make up an important part of today's society. The many ways they can be independent and lead meaningful lives are being recognized. You may be an exceptional person yourself, or you may have an exceptional person in your family, or you may become an exceptional person in the future. Understanding and relating effectively to persons who are exceptional can be to everyone's benefit. We are all entitled to have goals and opportunities to achieve them.

Life-span development includes a number of different types of development, including emotional, social, intellectual, and vocational maturity. To mature is to grow, and that is what we must do to achieve our long-range goals in our personal lives and in our careers.

Interpersonal relationships are important in the lives of most people. These may pertain to members of our families, members of the community, friends, and people at work. Voluntary interdependence entails some risks but can also lead to high levels of satisfaction in human relationships.

Human relations at work are also interpersonal but they have some other characteristics as well. Some distinctions must be made in our relations with co-workers, customers or clients, and management, for example. The person who not only has job-related skills but has effective human relations skills has a combination that will contribute greatly to career-related goals.

Only a few of the key points of Chapters 1 through 13 have been reviewed here to show their interrelatedness in meaningful living and in achieving our work-related and personal goals. Reviewing the summaries of each chapter would give you a gestalt overview. The summary of Chapter 14, which follows, also incorporates references to earlier chapters. It all fits together.

SUMMARY

A person who wants a meaningful life has long-term goals and short-term goals. In most cases, the determination of these goals involves consideration for others who are part of our personal lives.

In deciding upon goals in life one should consider the following questions: What is my primary purpose? How important is money to me? How important is work? What kind of relationships do I want with others? How important is freedom? It is also vital that one determine priorities since one doesn't have the time, energy, or other resources for everything.

Factors that contribute to goal achievement are unified purpose, money management, time management, flexibility, recognition of opportunity, self-confidence, perseverance, and constructive reaction to criticism. The effects of these factors must be continuously considered in our efforts to attain our goals. Although it's important to keep our focus on our goals, the experience of working toward goals should also give us satisfaction.

Common causes of setbacks are trying to get something for nothing, poor money management, outdated ideas and useless habits, unfavorable personality characteristics, not profiting from setbacks, and making too many mistakes. Some setbacks should be expected in life. Instead of thinking of them as failures, however, they can be opportunities to evaluate our priorities and to learn from mistakes.

Procrastination is a habit that not only can lessen what we achieve but also can interfere with an ongoing sense of achievement. When we are always trying to catch up or are faced with yesterday's unpleasant tasks, we are depriving ourselves of some of the daily joy of life and achievement.

Many of our goals are work related, since work is so much a part of our lives. It is to our advantage, then, that we give attention to getting a job that is appropriate for us in the first place and that we also give attention to keeping the job, at least as long as we want it. There are also ways to advance at work for those who are motivated to do so.

Who becomes a leader? It has been found that leaders have characteristics such as personal effectiveness, organization, ability to communicate, energy and enthusiasm, courage and integrity, fairness, appreciation, and interest in company goals. These are admirable characteristics for anyone, but they are especially valuable to those who aspire to be leaders.

Not every leader has the same style of working with others. Three of the most common leadership styles are authoritarian, democratic, and laissez-faire.

As you become an established part of the world of work and develop new relationships with others, you will become more aware of how all of the elements of human behavior interact. Better understanding of yourself and others will enrich your life and help you to achieve your personal and career goals.

Psychology In Practice

1. Ask three persons employed in different types of jobs, "How important is your work in your life?" Also ask at least one retired person, "How important has your work been in your life?" Compare their answers and relate them to your own ideas about the importance of work in a person's life.

2. Plan a mock interview with another student, who will act as the employer. You might want to conduct the interview in both the right and wrong ways. Videotape the activity, if possible, in order to evaluate your performances.

3. Make a list of things you plan to do on a particular day on which you expect to be very busy. List the items in order of priority and check them off as they are completed. Determine whether the list helped you to be more organized and get things done.

Learning Activities

Turn to page 437 to complete the Learning Activities and Enrichment Activities for this chapter.

Notes

1. *Occupational Outlook Quarterly,* Fall 1992, p. 3.
2. Alec McKenzie and Kay Waldo, *About Time,* 1981; reference in Velma Walker and Lynn Brokow, *Becoming Aware: A Look at Human Relations and Personal Adjustment,* 5th ed., Kendall/Hunt Publishing Company, Dubuque, IA, 1992, p. 199.
3. Carol Hyatt and Linda Gottlieb, *When Smart People Fail,* Simon and Schuster, New York, 1987, p. 232.
4. Robert L. Williams and James D. Long, *Manage Your Life,* 4th ed., Houghton Mifflin Company, Boston, 1991, p. 184.

Glossary

A

abstraction Quality apart from the physical object or person having that quality.

aerobics Physical fitness program or exercises to stimulate functioning of heart and lungs.

affirmative action Action following guidelines pertaining to the hiring, or attempts to hire, representative numbers of minorities and women.

aggression Behavior that is intended to hurt someone or to violate the rights of others for one's own advantage.

aggressiveness Behavior that is intended to hurt someone or to violate the rights of others for one's own advantage.

alcoholism Compulsion to consume alcohol caused by physiological, psychological, and social factors.

ambivert Person having both introvert and extrovert characteristics.

amnesia Loss of memory and identity, usually brought on by stress.

anorexia nervosa Disease, most common among young females, in which people believe they must continue to lose weight even after becoming dangerously thin.

apathy Attitude of lacking interest; unconcern about events and circumstances.

articulation Production of speech sounds.

artificial intelligence The actual and potential problem-solving abilities of computers.

assertion Expression of one's feelings, preferences, needs, or opinions to protect one's rights without infringing upon the rights of others.

association Awareness of the relatedness of one thing or experience to another.

astrology Study of believed influences of the positions of the stars and planets on personality behavior and events.

attitude Disposition, or readiness to act, involving both thinking and emotions.

auditory Attribute pertaining to the sense of hearing and sound.

authoritarian leader Leadership style whereby a leader uses a great deal of control; the leader is "boss."

autonomy Independence; control of oneself and one's behavior.

B

behavior Characteristic pertaining to what a human being does.

behavioristic theory Belief in the motivation theory that emphasizes the influence of environment and learning on behavior.

behavior modification Approach to improving behavior through a system of rewards or withholding of rewards.

biochemical therapy Use of prescription drugs to treat psychological disorders.

biofeedback Awareness of and response to one's internal body functioning such as blood pressure, heart rate, and other indicators of stress.

bonding Close emotional tie such as that formed between a mother and her baby shortly after birth.

brainstorming Group creative thinking involving a period of wild, uncritical generation of ideas.

brainwashing Attempt to change a person's thinking and feelings completely, causing him or her to reject former loyalties and adopt new beliefs.

bulimia Eating disorder whereby persons gorge themselves with food and then try to rid themselves of the effects, usually by inducing vomiting.

burnout Sense of exhaustion and ineffectiveness in one's work or other major activity.

C

calorie Unit of energy or fuel value of food.

clairvoyance Type of extrasensory perception whereby one is aware of the location of objects without the normal use of the senses.

cognitive Characteristic related to mental development.

cognitive dissonance Conflict or inconsistency between one's attitudes and/or behavior.

color coding Use of specific colors to convey messages or warnings.

common sense Approach to problem solving involving reason and use of what has been learned in the past to solve new, similar problems.

compensation Coping mechanism in which a person who is prevented from doing something by a disability or circumstance substitutes some other activity.

compulsion Irresistible impulse to engage in a certain activity.

concrete operations stage Cognitive development stage involving ability to retrace thoughts, to consider various characteristics of objects, and to recognize an unchanging quantity.

conditioning (1) Process of becoming accustomed to repeated stimuli so that one reacts automatically; (2) association of a secondary stimulus with a primary stimulus so that one eventually reacts to the secondary stimulus alone.

conflict Opposing ideas or goals.

conscious Quality of being aware; characteristic of mental alertness to experiences and the environment.

coping Effectively problem solving, adjusting, or accepting what one cannot change.

coping mechanisms Unconscious behavior pattern used to maintain self-concept.

covert behavior Activity of an individual, usually mental or emotional, that is not observable to others; hidden.

cutaneous Characteristic pertaining to the sense of touch.

D

daydreaming Coping mechanism in which the mind wanders freely as a momentary means of escape from reality.

democratic style Leadership style whereby the leader involves others in discussing alternatives and making decisions.

denial of reality A coping mechanism in which one refuses to believe a hurtful or threatening event or circumstance.

discretion Good judgment in human relationships.

discrimination Behavior, usually unfair and harmful, toward an individual because he or she belongs to a particular group.

displacement Coping mechanism in which a person transfers frustration from another source to an innocent third party.

drive Urge resulting from physiological imbalance that causes a person to seek satisfaction of a specific need.

E

ego state Term used in transactional analysis to refer to the Parent, Adult, and Child positions or roles in each person.

electroconvulsive therapy Electric shock used in treatment of psychological disorders.

emotion Complex feeling that begins with some type of mental experience, which, in turn, leads to physiological changes and possible changes in behavior.

empathy Sharing of feelings; understanding of what another person is experiencing.

emulation Attempt to develop characteristics similar to those of an admired person.

envy Desire to have what someone else has or to be what someone else is.

ethics Standards of right and wrong related to both one's personal life and work.

ethnic Characteristic pertaining to one's cultural background, such as race, nationality, and customs.

eustress Stress or tension that contributes to satisfaction and achievement.

exceptional Characterization of people who are different with respect to degrees of abilities, including the gifted and talented as well as those with impairments and disabilities.

extinction Elimination of behavior that is not positively reinforced.

extrasensory perception (ESP) Awareness that does not arise from the ordinary use of the exterior senses.

extrinsic motivation Motivation related to external reward.

extrovert Person who enjoys being with other people, is interested in the material world, and likes to be involved.

F

fixation Coping mechanism in which a person develops psychologically to a certain point and then arrests or "fixes" the personality development there.

flextime Somewhat flexible work schedule developed to fit the needs of employees.

formal operations stage Stage in cognitive development, beginning around 12 years of age, during which an individual can reason logically and think about abstractions.

G

general adaptation syndrome According to Hans Selye, three stages of response to threats: alarm reaction, resistance, and exhaustion.

generativity   An interest in others, including those outside of one's family, associated with middle adulthood.

graphology   Study and analysis of handwriting.

grief   An emotion involving a keen sense of loss, usually associated with the death of a loved one.

group   Collection of people with common backgrounds, interests, or concerns who interact with one another on a regular basis for a common purpose.

group therapy   Interaction with others in a group situation, under the guidance of a professional, as treatment for psychological disorders.

groupthink   Failure of a group to effectively problem-solve due to a desire to conform or lack of external input.

gustatory   Attribute pertaining to the sense of taste.

H

habit   Pattern of behavior that has been repeated and has become automatic.

heredity   Genetic transfer of characteristics from parents to their offspring.

heterosexual   Quality of being attracted to persons of the opposite sex.

hierarchy   Grouping of persons or things by order of importance.

homosexual   Quality of being attracted to persons of one's own sex.

humanistic theory   Belief in the motivational theory that recognizes some environmental and unconscious influence, but emphasizes personal control and responsibility.

hypochondria   Type of neurosis characterized by imaginary physical ailments.

I

id   According to Freud, a person's most basic urges.

identification   Coping mechanism in which a person's own identity is associated with that of an admired person.

illusion   Misinterpretation of stimuli received by the senses.

imitation   Process of acting like another; mockery.

insight   Deep understanding of a situation, often referred to as wisdom.

instinct   Inborn, unlearned behavior.

intangible   Attribute of having no material or perceivable characteristics.

intelligence   Different kinds of mental ability a person possesses.

interdependence   Dependence of people on one another.

interpersonal   Relationships with others.

intimacy   Very close, sharing human relationship.

intrapersonal   Experiences within oneself.

intrinsic motivator   Motivation from within; quality that is inherent.

introvert   Quiet person who enjoys solitary activity, often an imaginative person and one interested in art and nature.

intuition   Immediate understanding without conscious attention or reasoning.

J

jealousy   Fear of losing the love of another person based on a feeling of psychological insecurity.

job enrichment   Increased freedom in how one's job is done and more authority in making decisions.

job sharing   Working part-time by sharing a job with another person.

L

laissez-faire leader   Leadership style whereby the leader interferes as little as possible.

lateral thinking   Taking different viewpoints and approaches to problem solving.

life-span development   Growth and change throughout one's life, from conception to death.

M

McGregor's Theory X   Workplace motivational theory based on fear and negative expectations.

McGregor's Theory Y   Workplace motivational theory based on belief that workers are interested in doing their best work.

mainstreaming   Placing persons with exceptional characteristics in a normal classroom situation except for periodic special help.

manic-depressive disorder   Type of psychological disorder in which person goes from periods of mania (extreme activity and excitement) to depression (extreme sadness and gloom).

memory   Retention of knowledge or understanding.

mnemonic device   Attribute pertaining to a memory aid.

morale   Mental state or attitude of an individual or group.

motivation   Combination of forces or needs and wants causing a person to act in a particular way.

N

negative reinforcement   Action that causes an undesirable experience to stop.

network families Families that actively support one another in meeting each others' needs.

neurosis Maladjustment and excessive anxiety in one or more respects without serious mental illness.

normal Quality of being similar in behavior or qualities to most other people or to what is typical of an individual; the opposite of what is commonly considered abnormal.

O

obsession Persistent, compelling idea or exaggerated feeling about some imagined threat.

olfactory Attribute pertaining to the sense of smell.

olfactory fatigue Adaptation to an odor so that one is less aware of it.

optimist Person who habitually displays positive attitudes toward life in general and to particular events.

overt behavior Activity of an individual that is observable to others.

P

parapsychology The psychological term for extrasensory perception.

peer Member of one's own age group, with similar characteristics.

perception Awareness through the senses and one's personal interpretation.

perseverance Continuing effort; determination to succeed.

personality Person's total habitual social behavior or social self; personal identity as perceived by others.

pessimist Person who habitually displays negative attitudes toward life in general and toward specific events.

philosophical questions Considerations pertaining to the meaning of life.

phobia Abnormal, illogical fear, out of proportion to any threat involved.

phrenology Pseudoscience that studies bumps on a person's head to understand individual traits.

positive reinforcement Favorable response to behavior; reward.

precognition Type of extrasensory perception that involves the ability to know in advance that something is going to happen.

preconscious Things that you know but that you are not thinking about or aware of at the moment.

prejudice Prejudgment made without adequate information or reason.

preoperational stage Stage in cognitive development during which a child learns to anticipate future events and recognize characteristics of an object, usually between 2 and 7 years of age.

problem Situation that offers a choice of actions and requires a decision.

procrastination Action of putting things off; postponement for insufficient reason.

pseudoscience System of theories, assumptions, and methods erroneously regarded as scientific.

psychoanalytic theory Belief in the motivational theory that emphasizes unconscious influence on behavior.

psychokinesis Type of extrasensory perception that pertains to mind over matter.

psychological Attribute pertaining to behavior resulting from human needs and wants.

psychological disorder Difficulty or inability to adapt to the realities of life.

psychosomatic illness Characteristic of a physical organic disorder caused or aggravated by stress and unpleasant emotions.

physiological Characteristic pertaining to the functioning of the body.

puberty Physical development during adolescence, making the individual capable of reproduction.

Q

qualitative approach Consideration of differences in kind rather than in amount or degree.

quality circle Small group of employees and their supervisor from the same work area who meet to discuss problems.

quantitative approach Consideration of differences in amount or degree rather than kind.

R

rational Quality of being logical or reasonable.

rationalization Coping mechanism in which a person makes excuses for otherwise unacceptable behavior.

recall Act of remembering without a specific clue or external stimulus.

recognition Perception of something as familiar or known as result of a clue or external stimulus.

regression Coping mechanism in which a person temporarily returns to an earlier form of behavior.

relationship Human interaction that is more lasting than mere contact.

repression Coping mechanism in which a person pushes back or buries in the unconscious that which is unacceptable.

response Reaction; behavior that results from a specific stimulus.

reverse discrimination Unfair treatment of white males in an effort to give employment opportunities to minorities and women.

role Activity of a person in a particular situation, involving personality characteristics that may not be dominant in another situation.

role model A person one admires and uses as an example in developing his or her own potential.

S

self-actualization Development of one's abilities and potentialities.

sensorimotor stage Stage in cognitive development between birth and 2 years involving development of self-awareness and recognition of objects.

sensory gating Our mind's allowing certain things to come to our attention, while ignoring others.

set Predisposition to react in a particular way.

sexuality State or sense of being male or female.

situational ethics A system of ethics by which acts are judged within their contexts instead of by categorical principles.

social facilitation Enjoying association with those one works with.

sound Sensation perceived through the hearing mechanism caused by vibrations in the air.

stage Recognizable type of behavior that is characteristic during a fixed period in a process of development.

status quo The way things are at present or were at a particular time.

stereotype Set pattern; use of predetermined ideas.

stimulus Cause producing a reaction or response.

superego According to Freud, judicial force within a person that prevents the id from ruling behavior.

suppression Conscious control of one's behavior in order to be acceptable.

T

tangible That which is real, material, or perceptible.

technological Attribute related to machines, devices, and processes used to produce goods and provide services in modern society.

telepathy Type of extrasensory perception in which ideas are transmitted from one person to another without ordinary means of communication.

temperament Predetermined ways of reacting to environment.

threshold of audibility Frequency at which one hears sound.

tolerance Acceptance of others without frustration or prejudice.

trait Personality characteristic.

U

unconscious Characteristic of being unaware of motivation or behavior.

unisex Characteristic of pertaining to either or both sexes.

V

value Worth of a thing to an individual or a group.

values clarification Attempt to understand one's values and their relative importance to oneself.

vertical thinking Logical thinking that proceeds from step to step in a given situation.

visual Attribute pertaining to the sense of sight.

W

willpower Determination to establish and observe priorities in situations involving motivational conflicts.

work personality Personality characteristics that are apparent within a work situation.

Index

1 Psychology in Our Changing World

Learning Activities

IDENTIFY

1 Prediction is one of the purposes of psychology. Although no one knows what will happen in the future, explain how you believe the ability to predict future events or behavior of others might be useful to you in your future work.

ESSAY   Attitudes. Emotions.

2 Reasons for interest in or concern about the future are contained in the following incomplete statements. Complete the statements by expressing your particular interest in or concern about the future. Make your statements as specific as possible.

a. I am curious about

b. I would like to prepare for

c. I am interested in controlling or influencing

d. Something I would like to have part in preventing is

e. A possible change that I would like to promote is

3 It is becoming more common for individuals to choose careers that are considered nontraditional for their sex. The definition of nontraditional, as well as examples of a male nurse and a female law enforcement officer, were given in the chapter. Explain what you believe to be the effects of nontraditional careers on individuals or on society as a whole.

What I believe to be the effects on individuals (which could be the person choosing the nontraditional career):

What I believe to be the effects of nontraditional careers on society as a whole:

4 Locate a recent newspaper article or column pertaining to a human behavioral problem such as crime, drug abuse, alcoholism, divorce, or suicide. State the name of the newspaper, date, and subject of the article, and write a brief summary of it. On the basis of your summary, explain why, in your opinion, society has such problems.

5 There is an increase in the number of people working in their own homes, either as self-employed workers or as contractors for other businesses. List what you believe to be both advantages and disadvantages of using one's home as a workplace.

a. Advantages:

b. Disadvantages:

6 Greater use of robots both at work and in our personal lives has been predicted for the future. Suggest possible effects on humans in regard to satisfaction from work, use of time, and human relationships.

7 Cultural diversity has become increasingly evident in today's world. Suggest two ways in which this can be beneficial.

a.

b.

Enrichment Activities

1 Talk to an older member of your family, such as a grandparent or great-grandparent, and compare life-styles between when he or she was young and today.

2 Set up a bulletin board or make a collage, with articles and pictures showing recent changes in the world.

3 Your little brother has just asked you, "Why do we have wars?" What will you tell him? Role-play the incident, with another member of the class taking the role of your little brother.

4 Interview a person who is employed in the area of work for which you are preparing. Ask him or her how the type of work has changed and how it might be expected to change in the future.

5 Talk to your major instructor about how he or she keeps up with the changing world of work for which he or she is preparing students. Ask for advice on how you might keep abreast of such changes after you finish your present education.

2 Self-Concept And Personality

Learning Activities

- -

 Compare "self-concept and personality" in respect to both similarity and difference.

- -

 After reading the following descriptions of Scott and Amy, determine whether you believe each is an introvert, extrovert, or ambivert. Circle the appropriate term and underline the key words in the description that influenced your decision.

a. Scott enjoys his part-time delivery job for a dry-cleaning company. On Friday evenings he often referees basketball games, and he is active in intramural sports at the college he attends. He has a grade-point average of 3.4, and his instructors say he contributes a great deal to class discussions.

Scott could be classified as an:

     introvert   extrovert   ambivert

b. Amy works four nights a week taking care of children while their mother works. She is saving her money for tuition at an art institute. She has enjoyed sketching and painting ever since she attended a youth camp when she was 12 years old. Her art instructor has encouraged her to develop her talent further, and she would like to become an art teacher if she can afford the tuition. She has also considered becoming a graphic artist for a newspaper in a large city.

Amy could be classified as an:

     introvert   extrovert   ambivert

● ●

3 Astrology is the study of the influence of the positions of the stars and planets on personality, behavior, and events. Explain why it is classified as a pseudoscience. Name another pseudoscience and describe the belief associated with it.

Explanation:

Another pseudoscience:

● ●

4 Define the terms "nature" and "nurture" and explain what you believe to be the influence of each in personality development.

a. Definition of nature:

Influence in personality development:

b. Definition of nurture:

Influence in personality development:

● ●

5 According to Sigmund Freud, there are three main forces influencing each person's behavior: id, ego, and superego. Compare the relationship between the id and the superego and explain the effect they have on the ego or the person you *are*.

6 According to transactional analysis, each person has three ego states: Parent, Adult, and Child. Write the ego state that matches each type of behavior in the blanks and give a specific example of behavior arising from each ego state.

Behavior	Ego State	Specific Example
Joy and laughter	_____	_____
Criticism and correction	_____	_____
Problem solving	_____	_____

7 The following self-portrait can give you insight into who you are. It is designed to give you a more objective understanding of self-identity characteristics, personality strengths and weaknesses, abilities, habits, ideas, and ambitions.

For each of the following categories, describe yourself as completely and accurately as possible. If change is possible, describe the changes you would like to make. This self-portrait is for your use and is not to be handed in.

Category	Change Desired	Category	Change Desired
Marital status		Habits	
Health		Relaxation	
Present occupation		Sleeping	
Political affiliation		Eating	
Religion		Physical exercise	
Financial status		Personal hygiene	
Income		Studying	
Savings		Worst habit	
Debts		Best habit	
Experience		Driving record	
Work		Honors and awards	
Travel		Failures or setbacks	
Education		Dependency	
Group activity		Responsibilities	
Emotional stability		Ideas about	
Love		Dating	
Control of temper		Marriage	
Jealousy		Population	
Fears		control	
Anxieties		Nuclear power	
Phobias		Natural	
Frustrations		resources	
		Religion	

Category	Change Desired	Category	Change Desired
National defense		Entertainment	
Abortion			
Freedom		Social relationships	
Politics		Family	
Purpose of life		Friends	
Education		Neighbors	
Morality		Co-workers	
Outlook on life		Ambitions	
Optimistic or		Career	
pessimistic		Marriage and	
Conformist or		family	
individualist		Continued	
		education	
Most valued		Talent	
possession		development	
		Vacations	
Hobbies		Travel	
		Cultural	
Sports		experiences	
		Retirement	

Enrichment Activities

1 Inquire of several adults whether they have ever taken a personality test. Prepare four questions to ask them—pertaining to when the test was taken, the type of test, its purpose, and its effect on the person taking it. Report to the class without using actual names.

2 Find out what personality characteristics Adolf Hitler of Nazi Germany had. Explain to the class why you think you would or would not have obeyed him if you had been a German youth during World War II.

3 Think about ten different people you know well. Select people who are different in age, background, and occupation. Label them 1 through 10. List at least six personality characteristics of each. Discuss similarities and differences.

4 Describe someone whom you know personally and admire very much. What combination of hereditary and environmental factors do you think was responsible for what he or she is? What factors does the person feel were influential in this way?

Motives and Values

Learning Activities

1 Identify the type of motivational conflict involved in each of the following situations as approach-approach, approach-avoidance, double approach-avoidance, or avoidance-avoidance.

a. Francesca wants to begin a marketing career in the local branch of a national chain. But she does not want to begin a training session in the month of July.

b. Megan and Barry are planning to buy a house and have been looking at houses in their price range in the part of town where they would like to live. After looking at houses for several months they have found two that they like equally well and are having difficulty making a decision.

c. Rick has been informed that because of a special order at the shop where he works, everyone will have to work late three nights next week or work all day on Saturday. He doesn't like working overtime during the week, and he has already made other plans for Saturday. Yet he is supposed to inform his supervisor by 4 p.m. today when he will do his share of the extra work.

d. Tricia has an opportunity to live with three other women in an apartment. This idea appeals to her, but the apartment is unfurnished, and she has no furniture to contribute and no money she can spare toward purchasing furniture. She also has a chance to rent a room close to school. The room has a kitchenette area, but she doesn't like the idea of living alone. The other women in the apartment want to know her decision as soon as possible so they can consider someone else if she decides not to live with them. She is considering all factors in both situations but still hasn't made up her mind.

2 The psychoanalytic, behavioristic, and humanistic are three of the major motivational theories. Briefly describe each theory.

Psychoanalytic theory:

Behavioristic theory:

Humanistic theory:

3 Characteristics common to self-actualizers are listed below. Evaluate yourself as a self-actualizer with respect to these characteristics.

They are realistic.
They are aware of their strengths and weaknesses.
They are concerned with problems outside themselves.
They recognize and use opportunities.
They enjoy a certain amount of privacy.
They appreciate the ordinary things of life.

Evaluation of myself:

4 A challenging problem in business and industry is the motivation of employees to do their best work. Indicate the type of job you will be prepared for immediately upon completing your present education. Suggest three ways in which you might be motivated to do your best work.

a.

b.

c.

5 Self-motivation involves an understanding of one's needs and wants and a desire to make use of available means of satisfying them. Sandra is graduating from a merchandising course in two months. She knows she should be checking into available jobs, but somehow she just has not gotten around to it. What suggestions might you give Sandra in order to help her motivate herself toward seeking a job?

6 Some parents, teachers, political leaders, clergy, and law enforcement personnel claim to have control over the behavior of others. Determine whether you believe control or influence is being used in each of the following situations, and then write a brief justification for each of your decisions.

a. A father tells his teenage daughter to vacuum the living room after school. When the father comes home in the evening, he sees that the room has been vacuumed.

b. An instructor tells a student he must have his report turned in by the end of the week. On Thursday, the student turns in his report.

c. A member of the clergy informs the congregation that every adult member must contribute to the debt-reduction campaign. The following week, Brad Barrot, who had not contributed until then, contributed $400.

d. A person charged with causing an accident while under the influence of alcohol was ordered to attend a group dynamics class on the effects of alcohol. The following Tuesday this person was present for the first session of the class.

7 Terms from the chapter are listed below. Definitions of some of them are found in the glossary. Use a dictionary, if necessary, for the others. Select four of the terms and write the sentence or clause from the text in which the term is used. Rewrite it, substituting a synonym or synonymous phrase for the term. Underline the term in the first sentence and the synonym or synonymous phrase in the second sentence. An example is given after the list of terms.

Conflict	Illogical	Principles	Response
Drive	Intrinsic	Priority	Stimulus
Extrinsic	Overt	Physiological	Theory

Example: Strictly speaking, a person has <u>physiological</u> needs for survival as well as psychological wants for comfort and happiness.

Rewritten: Strictly speaking, a person has <u>bodily</u> needs for survival as well as psychological wants for comfort and happiness.

. . . .

8 Analyze the nature of the following values and determine whether each is primarily tangible or intangible. Circle *T* if the value is primarily tangible and *I* if the value is primarily intangible. Add two tangible and two intangible values of your own.

a. Motorcycle	**a.** T I
b. Friendship	**b.** T I
c. Set of books	**c.** T I
d. Ring	**d.** T I
e. Compact disc player	**e.** T I
f. Photographs	**f.** T I
g. Safety plaque	**g.** T I
h. Television	**h.** T I
i. Uniform	**i.** T I
j. _____	**j.** T I
k. _____	**k.** T I
l. _____	**l.** T I
m. _____	**m.** T I

Enrichment Activities

1 Find out more about behavior modification and ways it is being applied today. Talk to two parents about their use of rewards and punishment as a means of changing their children's behavior. Then form your own evaluation of behavior modification.

2 Make a list of your own needs and wants. Compare your list with those of at least two people. (This could be two other students carrying out the same activity.) Try to determine reasons why the lists differ.

3 Describe or illustrate a situation in which a person would have conflicting motives. Indicate what considerations affect decision making in the various types of conflict situations: approach-approach, approach-avoidance, double approach-avoidance, avoidance-avoidance.

4 Give an oral report on a book that deals with motivation. It could be a biography of a person who achieved his or her goal because of determination and other motivational qualities.

5 Make a list of ten things that you value. Then number them in the order of their importance to you. Observe your activities for several weeks and evaluate whether you are giving adequate attention to what you have listed high on your values list.

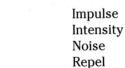

4 Senses and Perception

Learning Activities

1 Terms from the chapter are listed in the following. Use a dictionary, if necessary, for the terms not defined in the chapter or found in the glossary. Write a short paragraph pertaining to perception, using any six of the terms correctly. Underline those terms in your paragraph.

Acoustics	Deviation	Impulse	Sensation
Amplified	Distorted	Intensity	Set
Activated	Flexibility	Noise	Sound
Chronic	Hazards	Repel	Vibrations

2 Select a television commercial and a magazine advertisement to use as examples of how such commercials and advertisements are designed to appeal to the senses. Describe or give the script of the television commercial, and describe or attach a copy of the magazine advertisement. Indicate the sense or senses to which each advertisement appeals.

3 The following colors have the designated functional effects. Consider the functional effect and suggest an appropriate use for each color.

Color	Functional Effect	Use
a. Blue-green	Relieves glare	
b. Gray	Is nonstimulating	
c. Bright orange	Attracts attention	
d. Pale green	Relaxes	

4 We are constantly exposed to loud sounds and noise. Referring to the following situations, suggest two ways the individuals involved might protect themselves from the hazards of sound.

a. A music enthusiast has a stereo at home and plays records of favorite groups several times a day. This person also frequently attends concerts on weekends.

b. A young married couple have an apartment close to the downtown area in a city of 200,000. They live on one of the busiest streets leading into the downtown business district. There are continual commuter train and construction noises during the day and sirens blowing throughout the night.

5 Some of the factors that affect perception are listed next. Give an example of how each factor has affected *your* perception.

a. Physical ability or limitation:

b. Environmental condition:

c. Past experience:

d. Set—needs and wants:

e. Attention factors:

• •

Identify the principle of perception involved in each of the following experiences. Write the name of the principle in the space below each incident.

Principles of Perception

Constancy	Totality, or gestalt	Closure
Figure-ground	Camouflage	Conditioning

a. Sherry recently purchased new tinted designer eyeglasses. She could hardly wait for her friend Pam to see them. Yet Pam didn't even notice them until Sherry brought them to her attention.

b. Lance grew up in a quiet small town. His first job after graduation took him to a city with a population of 150,000. The first week of living there he woke up several times a night because of sirens and other night sounds of large cities. After the first week, however, he slept soundly and didn't seem to notice them.

c. Beth and Jon went shopping for a cart for their microwave. They saw just what they wanted on display in a department store. They discovered that it came unassembled and they would have to put it together. Since it came with a shelf, a sliding door, and a drawer, the box contained a number of pieces. After carefully studying the enclosed instructions and diagram, they figured out how to put it together.

d. Dennis saw a police squad car stop across the street and the officer get out and approach the house. He immediately assumed that the woman who lived there was the driver of a hit-and-run accident. He remembered seeing some damage to the front of her car last week.

e. Mark, who lives in a northern state, where snowbanks often reach six feet high in winter, was in the market for a new car. "I definitely do not want a white one," he commented to a dealer, "because it would be too difficult to see against the snow."

Enrichment Activities

1 Find two additional examples of illusions. Prepare a sketch or demonstration to show to the class. Give an explanation for the illusions.

2 Play excerpts from classical, folk, jazz, and rock music from records, tapes, or CDs. Ask students to identify which they like best and ask them whether they know why they prefer one kind of music to the other. Give your own explanation of how likes and dislikes are acquired. Be sure to plan the activity within the time limit allowed by the instructor.

3 Spend a leisurely half-hour in a park, a shopping center, a library, or any other place of your choice. Notice sounds, colors, shapes, odors, and other stimuli that you ordinarily miss. Describe this experience in a small group including others who have also carried out this activity. You may also want to share your experience with the class.

5 Emotions

Learning Activities

 1 Emotions can be classified as pleasant or unpleasant. Identify what you believe to be three pleasant emotions and three unpleasant emotions. Then suggest how a person might have more experiences involving pleasant emotions and fewer experiences involving unpleasant emotions.

Pleasant Emotions

a.

b.

c.

Unpleasant Emotions

a.

b.

c.

Describe how a person might have more experiences involving pleasant emotions and fewer experiences involving unpleasant emotions:

 2 The description of the physiological effects of fear experienced by Pam in the following incident is partially erroneous. To the right of each effect, circle *C* when the effect is *typical* of a fear response and *I* when the effect is *incorrect*. Next to each incorrect description, restate the effect to make it typical of a fear response.

> Pam had arrived earlier in the day in a large city to begin her first full-time job after her graduation from a community college. Since this was her first night in her apartment, she was a little uneasy. At four o'clock in the morning she heard what she thought was someone trying to open her door. She became frightened and didn't know what to do about it.

a. Her heart beat faster.	**a.** C I
b. Her mouth felt dry.	**b.** C I
c. She felt extremely hungry.	**c.** C I
d. Her hands perspired.	**d.** C I
e. Her muscles became limp.	**e.** C I
f. Her breathing became very slow.	**f.** C I

3 Propose one method by which each of the people in the following case studies might lessen or overcome his or her fear.

a. A 12-year-old boy is afraid to ride in a car after dark. Six months earlier, he was riding in a car with his brother when they ran out of gas on a lightly traveled stretch of road late at night. The youngster sat in the car alone for two hours while his brother went for help. Since that experience, the 12-year-old will stay at home rather than go somewhere in a car after dark.

b. A mature woman is afraid of thunder and lightning. She remembers that as a child she would sit in a hallway until a thunderstorm passed. Although too old for that type of escape now, she will sit terrified in a dark room during a storm.

4 List the characteristics of fear and anxiety under each of these terms. Give an example of each and explain why fear can be more useful than anxiety.

Fear

Characteristics:

Anxiety

Characteristics:

Example:

Example:

Fear is more useful than anxiety because:

5 Following is a description of a situation involving justifiable anger and a constructive reaction to it. Give another example from your own experience or observation that involved justifiable or reasonable anger and explain what you believe would be a constructive reaction to the incident.

Marilyn has worked for the You-Name-It Packaging Company for four years. She has taken two night classes in management and sales and has had the impression that she would be made a department manager in the near future. Last Friday during a coffee break the personnel manager of the company introduced a person no one had ever seen before as the head of the sales department. Marilyn's first reactions were shock and disappointment. As she thought about it during the day, she became angry that she had not been offered the job. She believed herself to be better qualified and to be deserving of recognition for her record with the company in the past four years. She made an appointment with the personnel manager to discuss the situation and the possibility of her advancement in the future.

Example from your own experience or observation:

Constructive reaction or result:

 6 Jealousy is an emotion that can cause problems for both the person who is jealous and the person of whom one is jealous. Briefly describe a situation in which Roxanne is jealous of Tim. Explain what you believe to be the cause of Roxanne's jealousy and suggest how she might deal with or overcome her jealousy.

Situation in which Roxanne is jealous of Tim:

Possible cause of Roxanne's jealousy:

Suggestion to help Roxanne deal with or overcome her jealousy:

· ·

7 According to Erich Fromm in his book *The Art of Loving,* there are five different kinds of love: brotherly love, motherly love, erotic love, self-love, and love of God. A definition of erotic love is given. Write your own definitions of the other four types of love in the spaces provided. Explain why you agree, or disagree, with Fromm's classifications of five kinds of love.

Erotic love: romantic love involving sexual desire.

Brotherly love:

Motherly love:

Self-love:

Love of God:

Why I agree, or disagree, with Fromm's classifications of five kinds of love:

Enrichment Activities

1 Make a bulletin board, collage, or other display showing different types of emotions being expressed. Be as original as possible in the way you do this.

2 Get together with a group of friends and talk about your fears. Compare common fears and discuss how some childhood fears have been overcome. Report (in writing or orally) whether this experience was of value to you.

3 Select several poems on the subject of love and read them to the class. (A collection of poetry from a library would probably have many from which to choose.) Ask the class for their comments.

6 Attitudes

Learning Activities

1 Match the following numbered definitions with the terms given. Place the letter of the term in the answer blank to the right of the definition. More terms than definitions are given.

a. Apathy   **e.** Discrimination   **i.** Revengeful
b. Belligerent   **f.** Humane   **j.** Stereotype
c. Contradiction   **g.** Peer   **k.** Tolerance
d. Pessimist   **h.** Prejudice   **l.** Unrealistic

1. A person belonging to one's age group   1. _____

2. Behavior that is the opposite to previous behavior   2. _____

3. Readiness to argue and fight   3. _____

4. Lack of interest in events and circumstances   4. _____

5. Not seeing things as they really are   5. _____

6. A person who habitually holds negative attitudes   6. _____

7. Acceptance of others as they are, without ill feeling   7. _____

8. Prejudgment without adequate information or reason   8. _____

9. To assume that all members of a particular group have the same characteristic   9. _____

10. Trying to get even with another person   10. _____

2 The development of attitudes is influenced by your family, your peers, role models, your experience, and your culture. Identify two attitudes you have and state what you believe to have been the main influence in the development of each.

a. Attitude:

Main influence:

b. Attitude:

Main influence:

3 Attitudes may change with time as one has new experiences and changes some values. Describe a possible difference in attitude, between a teenager and a parent, pertaining to the use of money.

Attitude of Teenager   Attitude of Parent

4 An example of reasonable prejudgment is given next. Explain how this type of prejudgment differs from prejudice. Trish ordered a sweater from a catalog, as it came in the style and color she has been looking for. When she received the sweater, she found that it was defective and returned it. She was sent a new sweater but found that this one was poorly made also. She mentioned this to her friend Andrea, who said she had also bought a sweater of that brand and was dissatisfied with the quality. Soon after, another friend mentioned to Trish that a local store had this particular brand of sweater on sale and wanted to know whether she was interested in going along to look at them. Trish told her, "No, I will not spend my money on that brand of sweater."

Explanation:

5 Causes of prejudice were identified in the chapter. Describe an incident of behavior resulting from prejudice and list possible causes of the prejudice.

Description of behavior resulting from prejudice:

Possible causes of the prejudice:

· ·

Using the example of the Reliable Construction Company described under "Discrimination" in the chapter, compare the definitions of prejudice and discrimination. Then compare the effects of prejudice and discrimination.

Comparison of prejudice and discrimination:

Comparison of *effects* of prejudice and discrimination on individuals:

· ·

Work-related attitudes from the chapter are listed below. Name an additional attitude and explain why you consider it important.

a. Loyalty to the company

b. Willingness to work

c. Willingness to learn

d. Willingness to work with others

e. Respect for supervisors, co-workers, customers, and clients.

f. Positive attitudes toward change

g. _____

I consider this work-related attitude important because:

• •

8 Unless your attitudes and behavior are in harmony, you become uncomfortable. Give an example of such disharmony other than the examples in the chapter. Explain whether you think the attitude or the behavior should be changed, and why.

Example of attitude or behavior disharmony:

Which should be changed and why?

Enrichment Activities

1 Keep track of your reactions resulting in negative or positive attitudes within a two-week period. Then try to determine how you developed each of these attitudes. Also, decide whether you should make an effort to change either the attitudes or the related behavior or both.

2 Visit an employment office and ask an appropriate person there for information about discrimination and affirmative action. Determine your own ideas about affirmative action and reverse discrimination. Check with two other students to see to what extent their ideas agree with or differ from yours.

3 Ask several employers you know what work-related attitudes they consider important in people they hire. Also ask them whether they have any way of detecting these attitudes in interviews with employment applicants.

7 Thinking and Problem Solving

Learning Activities

· ·

1 The following incidents involve the use of either recognition or recall. Determine the type of memory involved in each incident, and write either *recognition* or *recall* in the space provided.

a. A student knows that another student belongs to the Student Governing Board by the emblem on the jacket he is wearing.   _____

b. Allyson knows the answer to the question, "What is the meaning of overlearning?"   _____

c. Bart lost his list of supplies to buy at the bookstore, but he remembered them anyway.   _____

d. Lainie forgot the house number of a classmate she agreed to pick up but drove down the street and knew the house when she saw it.   _____

· ·

2 In the blank above each age range given on the left, write the appropriate stage of cognitive development, according to Piaget. In parentheses before each stage, write the letter of the mental ability characteristic of each stage.

Cognitive Stage	**Characteristic**
( ) _____ Birth to 2 years	a. Can look forward to his birthday
( ) _____ 2 to 7 years	b. Knows that soda in a tall, slender glass is the same amount when poured into a short, wide glass
( ) _____ 7 to 11 years	c. Knows that when a ball rolls under the sofa, it still exists
( ) _____ 12 years and up	d. Can think about the idea of heaviness without relating it to a certain heavy object

3 Identify a skill related to your major area of study (such as information processing if you are a business student). Write this skill in the blank. Then, describe how each of listed factors that contribute to learning and memory could be applied to learning this skill.

Skill: _____

a. Motivation

b. Meaningfulness of material

c. Concentration

d. Association

e. Repetition

4 Describe a problem or situation that requires immediate action and explain how the given components of common-sense problem solving could be considered or used to handle it.

Problem or Situation

a. Identify possible danger to life

b. Identify possible hazards to equipment

c. Consider probabilities in cause and effect

d. Engage available human resources

e. Make appropriate use of available tools and materials—improvising, if necessary

· ·

5 Define an actual or hypothetical problem, and explain how each of the following problem-solving guidelines might be used in solving it.

a. Definition of the problem

b. The total situation

c. Problems within the major problem

d. Possible causes

e. Possible solutions

© by Glencoe.

f. Plus and minus factors of two of the solutions

Solution	Plus Factors	Minus Factors
(1)		
(2)		

g. Possible sources of advice and assistance

h. Solution decided upon

i. First action step to be taken

j. How effectiveness of solution will be evaluated

....

6 Getting from one place to another presents problems of different magnitude depending upon the situation or time in a person's life. The following are hypothetical transportation problems for you to analyze. In the space provided after each problem, suggest two possible sources of advice or assistance.

a. *Past problem:* When you were 12 years old, you wanted to go to a circus 15 miles away but had no means of transportation.

b. *Present problem:* You need a daily ride to school, which is 8 miles from where you live; you don't have a car, and there is no public transportation.

c. *Future problem:* You would like to take a 1,000-mile trip, but you aren't sure about the best route or means of transportation.

· ·

7 Problems faced by Tony and Margo Lombardo, a young married couple, are described below. Suggest two possible solutions for the problems, and circle the number of the solution you believe to be the better one. Give a reason or reasons for your choice.

Tony's working hours have been cut back from forty to thirty hours a week. Tony and Margo are making house and car payments and are living on a tight budget. They can foresee a problem in making the payments with Tony's smaller paycheck.

(1)

(2)

Reason or reasons:

Enrichment Activities

1 Make a poster or collage, using newspaper headlines, magazine articles and pictures, and material from other sources, that gives evidence of a modern social problem that has not as yet been solved. On the basis of what you have learned in this course in previous chapters, explain the poster or collage in writing or orally to the class. Explain why problems involving people are often more difficult to solve than problems involving equipment or materials.

2 If you have a pet or are interested in animals, give an account of how animals learn, what you may have taught your pet to do, and how animal "thinking" differs from human thinking.

3 Reviewing and overlearning can be interesting and rewarding if done in teams or small groups, with an exchange of questions and answers. Try overlearning material you now know in order to retain it for later use. Also review material and procedures for a test in another class with someone else taking the same class. Report on the results.

8 Coping With Stress

Learning Activities

1 Some of life's experiences require major adjustments. Give a specific example of how a person might adjust in adolescence, independent living, marriage, illness or disability, grief, or retirement. Relate your example to an experience you have had or know about.

2 Cheryl is beginning a new job as a salesperson in the electronics department of a large chain department store. Suggest five types of information or orientation experience that would be helpful to her in becoming competent in her new job.

3 A number of job-related situations are given. Listed below them are aspects of life affected by job situations. Determine which aspects of life are affected by each job situation. Write the numbers of the situations in the answer blank space. Use numbers more than once, or use more than one number for an aspect of life if more than one applies.

Job-Related Situations

1. First full-time job

2. Rotating shifts

3. Getting new department supervisor

4. Promotion within company

5. Transfer to branch plant

6. Employment layoff

Aspects of Life

a. Family schedules   a. _____

b. Work procedures   b. _____

c. Residence   c. _____

d. Finances   d. _____

e. Social Relationships   e. _____

 An apparel manufacturing company decided to cut back on its line of clothing, causing a reduction in the number of employees. Jack had been working for the company, which is in his home town, for 14 years when he received his layoff notice. Jack has a family, with a son and daughter in high school; his wife, Marie, works part-time at the post office. Jack's elderly father and Marie's elderly parents live in their own homes, but Jack and Marie are available to assist them when needed. Add one additional factor to their situation. Explain how the family might cope with this change in their total situation.

a. Additional factor:

b. How the family might cope with their total situation:

 The five stages of coping with the approach of one's own death, according to Dr. Kübler-Ross, are (1) denial, (2) anger, (3) bargaining, (4) depression, and (5) acceptance. Explain why you believe or don't believe a person experiences these stages in this particular order.

●●

6 Common coping mechanisms are listed below. Identify the coping mechanism being used in each of the incidents described and write the name of the coping mechanism in the blank space following the description.

Coping Mechanisms

Daydreaming	Displacement	Repression
Rationalization	Projection	Compensation
Regression	Denial of reality	Fixation

a. A bookstore employee has difficulty paying attention to her work. She frequently stands around and imagines she is a fashion designer and has visions of models parading before her in her creations. _____

b. A 34-year-old man had a hard day at his auto supplies sales and service store. His assistant was on sick leave, so his work was constantly interrupted by having to answer the phone and having to talk to customers. One of the customers had complained, "I specifically told you . . . and now why isn't it done?" although no one had any record or recollection of his requests. He worked 45 minutes overtime and had a headache by 5:45. When he got home, he blew his top at his kids for having the television too loud and at his wife because his coffee wasn't hot enough.

He was obviously using _____.

c. A mechanical-drafting student is supposed to graduate from college in two weeks but has fallen far behind in his drawings. He just never seems to get around to them—for various reasons. One day he feels as if he might be coming down with a cold and decides he really should get some rest so he can accomplish more the next day. On Thursday afternoon, "everybody else" (two of his classmates who are caught up with their work) goes home early, so he decides he wouldn't get much done anyway and puts his unfinished work away and follows. He doesn't have his work done, but he has very good excuses, at least excuses that are acceptable to him at the time.

This student is using _____.

d. A woman wanted to be a model, but an evaluation of career opportunities determined that she wasn't tall enough to qualify for the type of assignments that would interest her. So she decided she would rather become a clothes designer and is specializing in clothes that make short girls appear taller.

The coping mechanism used is _____.

e. A 22-year-old man has had an excellent record as an automobile salesman. He really gets a thrill out of selling someone a new car and works hard at making a sale. Those who work with him, however, say he regularly throws a tantrum if he thinks he has a deal just about closed and it doesn't go through. He has even been known to dent a car with his fist in his furious disappointment. The coping mechanism used is _____.

f. After three years of marriage and the birth of two children, Harry finds it difficult to give up his independence and nights out with his friends. Each week he gives his wife what he considers adequate money to run the house and pay for the children's needs and keeps the rest of his check for his "expenses." Harry's wife barely manages on her allotment, yet he constantly accuses her of spending money foolishly. Actually he is unconsciously using the coping mechanism known as _____.

....

7 Rebecca has enrolled in an information processing course at a community college 70 miles from her parents' home. She has saved $600 toward her living expenses and also intends to get a part-time job. She rented an unfurnished apartment within walking distance of the school. This is the first time she has been on her own. Give two suggestions that she might use in learning to live independently.

Enrichment Activities

1 Visit a rehabilitation center if there is one in your vicinity and ask for information on ways to help the disabled in their rehabilitation.

2 What adjustments would a person who worked for a company ten or twelve years and was transferred to another state have to make? Compare hypothetical old and new situations.

3 Visit several retired people you know. They will probably welcome the company. Ask them about their adjustments to retirement. Listen carefully. Ask them whether the transition to their retirement could have been made easier in any way.

9 • **Wellness**

Learning Activities

● ●

1 Plan a day's menu for yourself including recommended amounts from each of the six categories of the Food Guide Pyramid. Plan three meals, but include any combination of foods you prefer in each meal as long as they add up to the recommendations for a day. You need not include items from each of the categories for breakfast, for example.

   Then evaluate how close your eating for a typical day is to the day's menu you planned.

Breakfast:

Lunch:

Supper or Dinner:

Comparison of my eating in a typical day to the menu (circle the appropriate response):

   Right on   Very close   ⎡Not bad⎤   Way off

● ●

2 Describe a way in which you are not as physically fit as you might be. Indicate two types of activity that would be realistic ways for you to improve that condition. Then explain why you intend (or do not intend) to follow through with the activity to become more physically fit. If you are as physically fit as you might be, explain in the following spaces how you achieved that state of fitness.

I believe I would be more physically fit if I _Do situps & Jogg_____

_____

Activities that would be realistic for me to improve the condition:

a. S.t ups ~~Jogg~~

b. Jogg

Why I intend, or do not intend, to follow through to become more physically fit (circle either *intend* or *do not intend* and complete the statement):

I ntend to Exercse more often and To stop cooking heavy food.

• •

3 Explain the difference between drug abuse and drug addiction and give an example of each.

Explanation of difference:

Example of drug abuse:

Example of drug addiction:

• •

4 Explain the difference between an obsession and compulsion as components of obsessive-compulsive disorder and give what you believe to be an example of each (other than the examples given in the chapter).

Difference between an obsession and compulsion:

Obsession is doing something conccisly
Compulsion: is doing something without thing

What I believe to be an example of an obsession:

What I believe to be an example of a compulsion:

. . . .

5 Identify a habit you would consider desirable for your wellness. Then devise a plan for forming this new habit. State whether you expect to follow this plan and be successful in acquiring this habit, and give reasons for your decision.

Habit:

Plan for forming the habit:

Expectation for following the plan:

. . . .

6 Identify a habit you have now that you consider detrimental to your wellness and set up a plan for breaking this habit. State whether you expect to follow this plan and be successful in breaking this undesirable habit, and give reasons for your decision.

Habit:

Plan for breaking the habit:

Expectation for following the plan:

Enrichment Activities

1 There have been many superstitions and "old wives' tales" about health. Find out about some of these from older people or from other sources. Explain how you think they developed and why they are no longer practiced.

2 Check on the training practices of professional athletes. Give a report on a particular athlete you admire.

3 Arrange (after discussing it with your instructor) for an authority on alcoholism to talk or present a program to the class. Most communities have people qualified and willing to do this. Take the responsibility of program chairperson and introduce the speaker to the class.

4 Make a collage showing characteristics of good mental health. You may want to contact your local mental health organization for some materials.

10 Exceptional Persons

Learning Activities

 1 A young man who is physically disabled said in a job interview, "I realize I have a disability, but I do not consider it a handicap." Explain the difference in the meaning of these two terms.

A disability is:

A handicap is:

 2 It was explained in the chapter that exceptional persons have quantitative differences rather than qualitative ones. Compare these two terms by defining each and give an example of a quantitative difference as it pertains to any disability.

a. Definition of quantitative difference:

b. Definition of qualitative difference:

c. Example of a quantitative difference:

3 You are planning to visit your cousin Christa in another city for the holidays. You know that she has a 14-year-old mentally retarded brother, Tom. You want to be sure that you don't hurt Tom's feelings or offend the family either by ignoring him or by treating him inappropriately.

Describe an incident involving you, your cousin Christa, and your retarded cousin Tom, and explain how you would act or what you would say in that situation.

Incident:

How I would act or what I would say:

4 Assume you want to communicate with a deaf person. (If you are deaf yourself, assume someone wants to communicate with you.) You know this person can speech read quite well. Identify three suggestions from the National Institute for the Deaf you should follow.

a.

b.

c.

5 Some blind persons use white canes; some use guidedogs. Explain one thing according to the National Federation of the Blind that you should *not* do when meeting a person using each.

a. When meeting a blind person using a cane I should not:

b. When meeting a blind person with a guide dog I should not:

Darlene, the six-year-old daughter of Curtis and Jan, was struck in a hit-and-run accident on her way home from school. She is paralyzed from the waist down. The family lives 20 miles from the nearest town. They also have two children younger than Darlene and two older. Indicate four factors Curtis and Jan should consider in caring for Darlene and the rest of the family.

a.

b.

c.

d.

 Many people with disabilities still feel that behavior of others toward them—resulting from biases and prejudice—interferes with their opportunities for full participation in activities. Give two suggestions for how such behavior might be modified.

Suggestions for modifying behavior—resulting from biases and prejudice—toward disabled persons:

a.

b.

 Andrea is a 12-year-old girl in a poverty section of a large city. She misses school frequently to help care for her younger brothers and sisters. Her parents do not speak English well and cannot read or write. Identify two disadvantages Andrea has and suggest a way they might be overcome.

a. Disadvantages:

(1)

(2)

b. How they might be overcome:

9 One of your classmates must use a wheelchair because of a spinal injury in an automobile accident. You would like to be friends with her but want to be realistic about what to expect in your relationship. Suggest how you can follow three of Buscaglia's guidelines in relating to her.

a.

b.

c.

Enrichment Activities

1 Find out about sources of help for exceptional persons in your community. Investigate types of assistance available from one of these sources.

2 Find out how the school that you attend or have attended provides for the education of exceptional persons. If possible, talk to the special education teacher for that school about his or her work.

3 Read a biography or autobiography of an exceptional person. Report to the class about the person, identifying what you believe to be important factors in his or her adjustment and success.

11 Life-Span Development

Learning Activities

 Six stages in life-span development are listed. In the spaces provided, indicate at least two characteristics of a person's development during each stage. Characteristics may pertain to any types of life-span development.

a. Early childhood:

b. Childhood:

c. Adolescence:

d. Young adulthood:

e. Middle adulthood:

f. Later adulthood:

2 Trust vs. Mistrust is the first stage of psychosocial development, according to Erik Erikson. Explain why the development of trust is the foundation for later stages of positive psychosocial development.

3 Four types of maturity discussed in this chapter are listed. Write in the blank to the right of each lettered example the number of the type of maturity. You may identify more than one type of maturity in any example if appropriate. When you do, be able to provide brief oral explanations of your choices.

1. Vocational   **3.** Social
2. Emotional   **4.** Intellectual

a. Reacts calmly to disappointment   a. _____

b. Associates with people of both sexes   b. _____

c. Is responsible to others   c. _____

d. Can make independent judgments   d. _____

e. Associates with people of differing ages, religions, and occupations e. _____

f. Gains satisfaction from work   f. _____

g. Is tolerant   g. _____

h. Show justifiable anger   h. _____

i. Seeks meaning to life   i. _____

j. Can say "I was wrong"   j. _____

k. Can endure injustice without seeking revenge   k. _____

l. Is dependable in obligations and promises   l. _____

4 Troy's father died when he was 12 years old, leaving him the oldest of five children. His father owned a small business, which his mother has been managing. Troy is now a junior in high school, hasn't been an honor student, but hopes to receive a scholarship to a vocational-technical college in his state.

   You may assume any additional information about his situation that you wish. Identify what you would consider two trials and two triumphs in his life during his adolescent years.

© by Glencoe

Trials

a.

b.

Triumphs

a.

b.

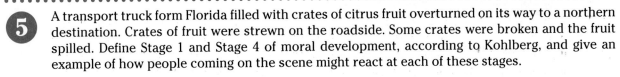

5 A transport truck form Florida filled with crates of citrus fruit overturned on its way to a northern destination. Crates of fruit were strewn on the roadside. Some crates were broken and the fruit spilled. Define Stage 1 and Stage 4 of moral development, according to Kohlberg, and give an example of how people coming on the scene might react at each of these stages.

a. Definition of Stage 1:

Reactions of people coming on the scene:

b. Definition of Stage 4:

Reactions of people coming on the scene:

Following are descriptions of behavior of three people. Determine whether you would consider their behavior mature, immature, or understandable. Understandable should be interpreted as not mature, but to be expected for the person's age and probable experience. Circle your choice and explain your decision.

a. Carla, age six, pushes her friend off the playground swing because it is "my turn."

mature   immature   understandable

Reason for decision:

b. Andrew, age 15, turns off the television program that his sister wanted to watch because he has to do homework. Her homework is finished.

mature   immature   understandable

Reason for decision:

c. Bruce turns down two free tickets to a sports event because he promised to take his daughter skating.

mature   immature   understandable

Reason for decision:

 Describe what you would consider a mature and an immature reaction to the situations described. There can be a number of both mature and immature ways of reacting to a situation, of course.

a. Brenda and Myles have been married for six months. After their marriage, Myles wanted to rent a furnished apartment until they could save some money for the kind of furniture they wanted. Brenda, however, was firm in her belief that they should get all their furniture immediately and make monthly payments, and they did. Now, after six months, Myles is working fewer hours, so their income is lower; their car needs repair; their insurance payments are due; and they can't see how they can make their furniture payments for the next few months.

BRENDA

Mature reaction:

Immature reaction:

MYLES

Mature reaction:

Immature reaction:

b. Hank's supervisor informs him that he will have to keep his work area clean and will have to return all tools to their proper place before he leaves every day.

HANK

Mature reaction:

Immature reaction:

c. Sully was assigned a person of a different (objectionable, in his opinion) race as a work partner. The person assigned as Sully's partner acted friendly and seemed eager that they work together as a team.

SULLY

Mature reaction:

Immature reaction:

8 Select one of the characteristics of social maturity from the chapter. Explain how you think you could become more socially mature in this respect. Give a specific example.

Characteristic of social maturity: *Tolerance*

How I could become more mature in this respect: *Learning more about a different culture*

Enrichment Activities

1 A 17-year-old boy feels that his parents consider him immature. He would like to become more mature, if they are correct. How might he go about this? Role-play the situation with another person.

2 Make a list of all the characteristics of maturity mentioned in the chapter. Give an example of each. Are there any characteristics that you would add to the list?

3 Visit a grade school classroom with the teacher's permission. Observe examples of mental (cognitive, according to Piaget) and psychosocial development and any other type of maturity discussed in the chapter. You may want to check your conclusions with the teacher of the observed class. Report your experience to your class or instructor.

12 Interpersonal Relationships

Learning Activities

1 Describe how an interpersonal relationship might develop from Stage 1 through Stage 4 of Bradley and Baird's pyramid. Describe both how a person might act and what he or she might say at each stage. You may use a real or hypothetical example involving the same person through all four stages.

a. Stage 1: Percieued Perception:

b. Stage 2: Greeting

c. Stage 3: Cliches

d. Stage 4: Committments

2 For each of the following experiences, suggest a way the person might deal with his or her hesitancy due to shyness.

a. A high school junior would like to ask Gretchen, a classmate, to go to the spring dance but he's hesitant to ask her for fear she will turn him down.

b. Polly has an interview for a part-time job as a word processor in an insurance office. She is very nervous and unsure of how she will do in the interview even though she knows her skills are above average.

Contrast assertive behavior with aggressive behavior by describing how a person could react to the following situation in each way:

Al and Ted live in the same neighborhood and work for the same company, 20 miles away. They decided to ride together starting in June and to alternate driving each week. The arrangement worked well for two months. Then, frequently, when it was Ted's week to drive he had a reason why he couldn't. Several reasons have been "I seem to be having a little trouble with the brakes" and "Mary needs our car this week to take the kids to school." Ted has not made any type of offer to change the driving arrangement with Al. He seems to expect Al to drive when he has a problem.

Assertive reaction by Al:

Aggressive reaction by Al:

A close friend of yours is moving to another state to start a job that offers a challenging future. In spite of interest in the job, your friend is feeling "down" about leaving old friends. What encouragement can you give this person regarding interpersonal relations and friendships?

The open area of the Johari Window represents what is known to both oneself and others. Identify two ways a person might enlarge the open area and explain why this could be desirable.

a. Ways to enlarge open area:

(1)

(2)

b. Why enlarging the open area could be desirable:

6 The chapter discusses the following characteristics of a happy home. Compare these with the characteristics of a real home which you consider to be happy. State your conclusion regarding this comparison.

A bond of love
Dedication to common goals
Interest in the endeavors of individual
  members
Respect for one another
Sharing of hopes and fears, sorrows and joys

Freedom to bring friends home
Pride in family members
Open communication and honest self-
  expression
Sense of responsibility toward others
Children developing independence

a. Description of a home I consider to be happy:

b. Conclusion following comparison:

7 Identify a group to which you might like to belong in the future. It can be any of the types shown in the text group-o-gram: family, education, community, work, or recreation. Explain the purpose of the group (as you understand it) and what you think you might gain from membership. Also explain how you could use past group experience or possible present group experience to help you become an active member of this group in the future.

a. Group to which I might like to belong in the future:

b. Purpose of the group:

c. What I might gain from membership:

d. How I could use past group experience or possible present group experience to help me become an active member of this group in the future:

Enrichment Activities

  With a small group of classmates, brainstorm how to overcome shyness. Review brainstorming procedure in Chapter 7. Share the results with the class.

Ask three people you know quite well to give you three or four characteristics of a "good friend." Compare these characteristics with your idea of a good friend and with the characteristics of friendship discussed in the text. Make a list of all the characteristics mentioned. Evaluate yourself in terms of these characteristics.

Develop your own group-o-gram. Use the same basic structure and major divisions given in the text but change the groups and group membership to pertain to you. On the bottom of the group-o-gram explain how this has given you a better understanding of how you might reach your goals identified in the Future section.

13 Human Relations at Work

Learning Activities

 Distinguish between hygiene factors and motivation factors, according to Herzberg. Identify a company that makes a certain product or sells a certain service and give an example of how you believe a factor of each type affects its employees.

Explanation of hygiene factor:

Explanation of motivation factor:

Company (real or hypothetical):

How I believe a hygiene factor affects employees:

How I believe a motivation factor affects employees:

 Identify two fears that are common among employees of large companies today. Suggest how these fears might be reduced:

a. A common fear among employees of a large company:

How this fear might be reduced:

b. Another common fear among employees of a large company:

How this fear might be reduced:

● ●

3 Explain how you would respond to a customer who is angry because a product he or she purchased from you didn't work. Give specific application of at least three suggestions for handling customer complaints.

Product that customer says didn't work:

Application of suggestions for handling the customer's complaint:

a.

b.

c.

● ●

4 Interpersonal relations can involve conflict, competition, or cooperation. Compare these by describing a work-related experience involving each. The experience you describe should be a work situation related to your major but may be real or hypothetical.

Work experiences involving:

a. Conflict

b. Competition

c. Cooperation

5 Describe two advantages of a work team that would include the following types of members: (1) president of the company or owner, (2) production or service manager, (3) secretary to service department, (4) production or service employee, and (5) maintenance employee.

Advantages of team composed of members described above:

a.

b.

6 Select one of the possible problems of team functioning and suggest a possible solution to the problem.

Possible problem of team functioning:

Possible solution to the problem:

7 Explain what is meant by an open-door policy within an organization. Explain your attitude toward such a policy and give an example supporting your attitude:

Explanation of open-door policy:

My attitude toward an open-door policy:

Example (real or hypothetical) supporting my attitude:

8 Define sexual harassment in your own words. Explain why, in your opinion, some cases of sexual harassment might not be reported.

My definition of sexual harassment:

Why, in my opinion, some cases of sexual harassment might not be reported:

Enrichment Activities

1 Look up information on the charges of sexual harassment by Anita Hill against Clarence Thomas in 1991. Draw your conclusion about the charges and give an explanation for your conclusion.

2 Develop a dialogue involving a misunderstanding between two people, in any type of work relationship, and explain how communications problems and human relations problems are interrelated.

3 Find out from an instructor in your major area of study how you might expect to be involved in team functioning in your future work. Ask this instructor about his or her opinion of teams in the workplace and about his or her related experience.

14 Goal Achievement

Learning Activities

• •

1 The chapter begins with a discussion of success. First write your own definition of success (without the use of a dictionary). Then obtain a definition of success from another source. This can be another person's definition or one from a reference. Compare the definitions and explain how and why yours differs.

a. My definition of success:

b. Definition from another source:

c. Source of second definition:

d. How and why my definition differs:

Name _____ Date _____

Questions related to goal achievement are listed in the following. Indicate the importance of each of these concepts to you by circling the appropriate number on the right. Write a brief explanation of why you consider any one of them "very important." Use the following rating scale:

1 = very important; 2 = important; 3 = not important

a. Money—what does it mean?   1 2 3

b. How important is work?   1 2 3

c. Where do others come in?   1 2 3

d. How important is freedom?   1 2 3

Why I consider _____ very important.

In the following description of Melanie and her career goal, identify four factors that you believe have contributed to her progress thus far:

It was Melanie's ambition to "have my own furniture store." She frequently made remarks to her family and friends such as "When I have my furniture store. . . . " While she was attending the local community college, she took numerous courses in both business and marketing, and she took an additional course in word processing in the evening. She also worked as a salesperson in a furniture store on weekends and two evenings a week. She had hoped to get an internship as an assistant buyer in the store, but it was determined that the buyer could not supervise an internship at that time. She was disappointed, but after she contacted several other furniture stores, a manager told her to check back in about two months. When that time came, she went to see the manager again and was assigned an internship. She continued to work at this store after she graduated, as she wanted a greater variety of experience. She was also able to work more hours so that she could add to her savings.

Melanie plans to get a few more years of experience, take some additional evening classes, and then either open her own independent store or seek a franchise for a nationally known furniture line. She is more enthusiastic than ever about "having my own store" and is planning to use part of her next vacation visiting a furniture merchandise mart.

Factors that I believe have contributed to Melanie's progress thus far toward achieving her career goal:

a.

b.

c.

d.

· ·

4 Three types of mistakes were identified in the chapter. Briefly define each type and give what you believe to be an example of each. Also describe a mistake you have made, identify the type you believe it to be, and explain what you did about it.

Type of Mistake	Definition	Example
Careless		
Reasonable		
Innocent		

A mistake I made:

Type of mistake it was:

What I did about it:

· ·

 5 Common causes of failure are listed below. Determine the two causes most likely to interfere with your achieving your goals. Suggest how each might be minimized or eliminated.

Trying to get something for nothing:

Poor money management:

Outdated ideas and useless habits:

Unfavorable personality characteristics:

Fear:

Not profiting from setbacks:

· ·

6 Identify a company for which you might like to work. Develop answers to the following questions the prospective employer might ask during an interview:

a. What do you consider your greatest weakness?

b. What do you consider your greatest strength?

c. Why do you want to work for our company?

7 Describe three types of learning by which you can continue to add to your career competency after you complete your education and begin working full-time. Indicate where you could continue each type of learning.

	Type of Learning	**Where**
a.		
b.		
c.		

8 Identify three reasons for procrastination and suggest how each of these reasons might be counteracted with constructive behavior:

a. Reason for procrastination:

Constructive behavior to counteract it:

b. Reason for procrastination:

Constructive behavior to counteract it:

c. Reason for procrastination:

Constructive behavior to counteract it:

 9 Studies of leaders reveal common characteristics, as listed on the following page. Describe a person whom you consider an effective leader and identify the leadership characteristics you believe he or she has. If the person has additional leadership characteristics, mention them. Indicate what you consider this person's leadership style to be by circling one of the descriptive terms.

Personal effectiveness

Organization

Ability to communicate

Energy and enthusiasm

Courage and integrity

Fairness

Appreciation

Interest in Company Goals

Additional Characteristics

I believe this person's leadership style to be:

authoritarian   democratic   laissez-faire

Enrichment Activities

1 Collect at least six different quotations relating to goal achievement. You may obtain these from posters, books of quotations, persons, or any other source. Indicate which quotation you like the best and explain why.

2 Talk to two different people who, in your opinion, seem to have been successful in achieving goals. Ask them for their explanation of how they determined what they wanted and why they have been successful. Note any similarities between the two. Be able to give an explanation of any differences.

3 Read an article or biography of a person you consider successful. Identify characteristics you believe helped that person achieve his or her goal. Also note experiences that the person considered disappointments or setbacks. How did the person overcome or learn from the setbacks?